D0077013

REVOLUTION IN BAVARIA

REVOLUTION
IN BAVARIA
1918-1919

The Eisner Regime
and the Soviet Republic

BY ALLAN MITCHELL

PRINCETON UNIVERSITY PRESS
PRINCETON, NEW JERSEY
1965

Publication of this book has been aided by
the Ford Foundation program to support publication, through university presses, of works
in the humanities and social sciences.

Printed in the United States of America
by Princeton University Press, Princeton, New Jersey

For my parents
George and Jane Mitchell

PREFACE

IN WRITING this book my first concern has naturally been to keep my story straight. Necessity as well as convenience place at the center of it the man whom Arthur Rosenberg once called "the only creative statesman" to emerge in Germany during the revolutionary period. Although Kurt Eisner does not deserve that accolade, in my opinion, his personal fortunes did reflect both the possibilities and the limitations of the revolutionary situation in Bavaria. Yet this is not exclusively a political biography of Eisner. I have also attempted to examine the constitutional development of the Bavarian state, the role of the political parties, the appearance of the revolutionary councils, the condition of the economy, and even the weather. At the same time I have felt and tried to fulfill an obligation to relate the course of events in Bavaria to circumstances in the rest of Germany and in Europe as a whole.

Thorough research of the revolution in Bavaria has not been possible until recently. After May of 1919 the documentation of the preceding six months was placed in archives closed to all but a few men engaged in the hundreds of legal suits prosecuted during the next decade. Between 1933 and 1945 these archives were completely inaccessible to independent scholars. Not until the creation of the Bonn Republic, therefore, has the documentation become available. A great many documents have unfortunately been scattered or lost, but a notion of the collections which remain and which are now open to researchers may be gained from a perusal of the bibliography. I am indebted to the Director of the Bavarian State Archives, Professor Dr. Puchner, for his cooperation in making my investigation possible. Permission to use the Kautsky Archive was granted by Professor A.J.C. Rüter, Director of the International Institute for Social History in Amsterdam. Of the many librarians and archivists who have given me their personal encouragement and professional help during the past few years, I want especially to acknowledge Dr. Ludwig Hollweck of the Münchener Stadtbibliothek and Dr. Bernhard Zittel of the Bayerisches Hauptstaatsarchiv.

Insofar as this study is an act of imagination as well as research, I owe a particular debt to the man who witnessed its inception—Professor Alfred Grosser of the Fondation Nationale des Sciences Politiques in Paris—and to the man who saw it through to completion as a doctoral thesis—Professor H. Stuart Hughes of Harvard University. In the course of revision several colleagues and friends have read individual chapters and enabled me to profit from their excellent suggestions: Klemens von Klemperer, Klaus Epstein, Guenter Lewy, Reginald Phelps, Istvan Deak, and Beate Ruhm von Oppen. I am grateful to all of them, but they will understand that the major share of gratitude belongs to my wife Ingrid who managed, sometimes literally, to type with one hand and hold off the children with the other.

Northampton, Massachusetts
June 1964

CONTENTS

CONTENTS

ILLUSTRATIONS

REVOLUTION IN BAVARIA

LIST OF ABBREVIATIONS

I. Archives

BGS	Bayerisches Geheimes Staatsarchiv, Munich
BHS	Bayerisches Hauptstaatsarchiv, Munich
IISG	Internationaal Instituut voor Sociale Geschiedenis, Amsterdam
LC	Library of Congress, Washington, D.C.
NA	National Archives, Washington, D.C.

II. Newspapers

RF	*Rote Fahne* (Berlin)
MRF	*Münchener Rote Fahne*
NZ	*Neue Zeitung*
MP	*Münchener Post*
MZ	*Münchener Zeitung*
MNN	*Münchener Neueste Nachrichten*
MAA	*Münchener-Augsburger Abendzeitung*
BK	*Bayerischer Kurier*
BV	*Das Bayerische Vaterland*
BSZ	*Bayerische Staatszeitung*
MGZ:B	*Münchener Gemeindezeitung: Bekanntmachungen*
MGZ:S	*Münchener Gemeindezeitung: Sitzungen*

III. Political Parties

KPD	Kommunistische Partei Deutschlands (German Communist Party)
VRI	Vereinigung Revolutionärer Internationalisten Bayerns (Union of Revolutionary Internationalists of Bavaria)
BBB	Bayerischer Bauernbund (Bavarian Peasants' League)
USP	Unabhängige Sozialdemokratische Partei (Independent Social Democratic Party)
SPD	Sozialdemokratische Partei Deutschlands (German Social Democratic Party)
DDP	Deutsche Demokratische Partei (German Democratic Party)
NLB	Nationalliberale Landespartei in Bayern (Bavarian National Liberal State Party)
BMP	Bayerische Mittelpartei (Bavarian Middle Party)
BVP	Bayerische Volkspartei (Bavarian People's Party)

IV. Council Bodies

MAR	Münchener Arbeiterrat (Munich Workers' Council)
MSR	Münchener Soldatenrat (Munich Soldiers' Council)
RAR	Revolutionärer Arbeiterrat (Revolutionary Workers' Council)

CHAPTER I

The Origins of Revolution

IT HAS usually been said of the 1918 revolution in Bavaria, as of the German revolution in general, that it was the result of a collapse rather than a seizure of power. There is no reason to resist this view except that it may provide an excuse to avoid the difficulties of locating the sources of revolution. Bavaria was no doubt suffering in November of 1918 from a temporary political insanity. But anarchy in itself does not explain the revolution unless one knows how a hiatus of public authority occurred, who was prepared to take advantage of it, and by what means a new order was imposed. By surveying the background of the revolution, it should be possible both to put the actual coup d'état in perspective and to determine more precisely its origins.

Bavarian history in the nineteenth century began with the foundation of the monarchy and ended with its dissolution. This is to fix the chronology of the century before 1918, not its main theme. The revolution did terminate the monarchy, but more importantly it continued social and political developments already well advanced. For most of the century —excepting the three decades before 1848—the Bavarian monarchs were dominated by a ministerial and bureaucratic oligarchy. After 1890 a transition began toward the establishment of parliamentarianism. This was achieved in all but constitutional law by 1912. The revolution was to change the law and to secure a parliamentary system based on political parties. In this sense, far from being an aberration from tradition, the revolution came as a concluding episode in the accomplishment of reform.

If one can find a certain logic in this, the Bavarian revolution was still not without its incongruities. Measured by the usual standards of the nineteenth century, industrialization and urbanization, the state had experienced a remarkably

BAVARIA IN 1918

LOWER FRANCONIA

UPPER FRANCONIA

UPPER PALATINATE

LOWER BAVARIA

UPPER BAVARIA

MIDDLE FRANCONIA

SWABIA

RHENISH PALATINATE

Hof

Bamberg

Würzburg

Fürth

Nuremberg

Regensburg

Ingolstadt

Passau

Danube

Dachau

Munich

Rosenheim

Augsburg

Garmisch

Lindau

Ludwigshafen

Kaiserslautern

Speyer

50

0

KM

lethargic development. Rural, parochial, and predominantly Roman Catholic, Bavaria seemed to offer an unlikely setting for political insurrection. Moreover, Social Democracy in Bavaria was the most moderate, the most outspokenly reformist representative of Socialism in all of Germany. It is virtually impossible, in fact, to locate anything which might properly be considered a radical movement in Bavaria before 1918. Yet Bavaria was the first of the German states to become a republic and the last to be released from the grip of radicalism. This is a curious and, in many respects, a tragic story. The handbooks and textbooks of Bavarian history invariably lament the passing of the monarchy rather than celebrate the founding of the republic. The purpose here is to do neither, but to reconstruct the story and to evaluate the consequences.

Before the War

By some reckoning Bavaria is the eldest of the German states and one of the most venerable of all European political formations. At the beginning of the nineteenth century the House of Wittelsbach could already look back to more than eight hundred years as the leading family of what is now called *Altbayern*. But the elevation of the Bavarian Elector Maximilian Joseph to the title of King of Bavaria in 1806 was not so much the culmination of some evolutionary process as the direct result of Napoleonic diplomacy. It was the personal discretion of the French Emperor which placed an ally rather than a relative on the throne and then determined that Bavaria should balance Jerome Bonaparte's Kingdom of Westphalia at the southeastern extremity of the Confederation of the Rhine. By the terms of this arrangement Bavaria was nearly doubled in size through the acquisition of adjacent lands in Franconia and Swabia. And King Max was not ungrateful: he remained loyal to France until October of 1813, when he concluded the Treaty of Ried with the Allies. The results of this agreement, which guaranteed the territorial integrity of his kingdom, were then ratified two years later in

5

the Vienna peace settlement. If the new form of the Bavarian state had initially been a convenience of French hegemony, it was one which Napoleon's opponents were willing to perpetuate. With the formal addition of the Rhenish Palatinate in 1816 Bavaria was even granted a stake, along with Prussia farther down the Rhine, in the containment of France. Despite Max's long devotion to his benefactor, therefore, he emerged from the Congress of Vienna with *Neubayern* intact and securely established among the sovereign states of Central Europe.[1]

This is to exaggerate the actual importance of the monarch. As everyone knew, Max reigned while his first minister governed. It was the Count Montgelas who had instigated the financial, judicial, and administrative reforms necessary to convert a family holding into a modern bureaucratic state. The "constitution" which he drafted and released with the royal seal in 1808 carefully stipulated that "several ministries can be united in a single person." In the execution of the affairs of the monarchy, Montgelas was literally a one-man majority, holding three of the five ministerial positions himself. Bavaria's age of enlightened despotism thus came late and abruptly, the work of a single minister within a single decade.[2] For all his ability, however, Montgelas had a number of counts against the longevity of his ministry. Precisely because of his previous achievements, he was too closely associated with the Napoleonic order; sharing the sentiments of liberal anti-clericalism, he was less than ideally suited to be the servant of a Catholic monarchy; and having bent every

---

[1] The authoritative study of Bavarian history to the end of the nineteenth century is that of Michael Doeberl, *Entwicklungsgeschichte Bayerns* (3 vols.; Munich, 1908-1931). The best recent examination of the period before the Congress of Vienna is by Enno E. Kraehe, *Metternich's German Policy: The Contest with Napoleon 1799-1814* (Princeton, 1963).

[2] Walter Schärl, *Die Zusammensetzung der bayerischen Beamtenschaft von 1806 bis 1918* (Munich, 1955), 5.

effort toward a centralized state, he was increasingly opposed by those who valued class privilege or local autonomy more than administrative efficiency.

In 1817 Montgelas resigned. Within a year most of the characteristic features of his policy were reversed. A concordat with Rome restored harmonious relations with the Church; the new and (so it would still seem a century later) permanent constitution of 1818 specified that "each of the five state ministries will be occupied by a single minister"; and the promulgation that same year of a *Gemeinde-Edikt* provided the municipalities with a legal check to administrative centralization. But the constitution formally retained one essential plank of the Montgelas construction: "the highest executive position is constituted by the combined ministers of state." Apart from the apparent intention to prevent the dominance of a single cabinet member, this clause was ambiguous. When Ludwig I succeeded Max in 1825, however, he immediately let it be known how the constitution was to be interpreted: the role of the ministers, he announced, was "definitely only advisory."[3] Whereas Montgelas had observed the letter of the constitution and violated the spirit of the monarchy, Ludwig was a monarch to the letter and violated the spirit of the constitution. As the King said: "In Bavaria it is not the minister who rules, but the monarch; and I take exact account, as is well known to every one of my subordinates, of whatever occurs."[4]

For more than twenty years Ludwig both reigned and governed. To do so he labored compulsively over the slightest details of policy and administration. He frankly regarded the preceding era as "anti-monarchist," and he consciously attempted to rectify his father's dependence in foreign and domestic affairs. Bavaria's poverty of natural resources and minority of Protestants reinforced Ludwig's personal inclination to preserve the rural and Catholic character of his state. It

[3] *Ibid.*, 6-7.
[4] Doeberl, *Entwicklungsgeschichte*, III, 126.

was to remain for most of the century a society of peasants and artisans, an economy based on small acreage farming and handicraft enterprise. The King's deliberate policy of retarding industrial development was all the more evident after the unsettling events of 1830. He was successful insofar as he may be credited with the fact that Bavaria had scarcely any social element by 1848 which could be described as a proletariat. Ludwig likewise succeeded in dominating his ministers throughout this time, having the good fortune to find in Karl von Abel a civil servant both decisive and reliable in enforcing royal prerogatives. By virtually any standards, and certainly by those of the Montgelas years, Ludwig's reign was a period of undisguised reaction.[5]

As a monarch Ludwig I had few weaknesses; as a man he allowed himself one indulgence which brought him—and with him the monarchy—to grief. It would be correct to say that Ludwig was compromised by the Countess Landsfeld rather than by the actress Lola Montez. It was one thing to have a none too private affair with an exotic dancer, another to create a public scandal by rewarding her with a title. Even Karl von Abel was moved to suggest that the King had overstepped the bounds of propriety. Ludwig promptly dismissed him, indignant at the notion that a minister should presume to reprimand the monarch. But he was soon forced to admit the serious nature of his indiscretion and to realize that the revocation of Lola's new estate was insufficient amends: "I have ceased to rule in any case, whether I retain or relinquish the Crown." Injured feelings rather than popular agitation caused Ludwig to abdicate in favor of his son on March 20, 1848. "I am proud to call myself a constitutional monarch," said Maximilian II later that day, perhaps unwittingly emphasizing that his father's pride had been in accomplishments other than constitutionality. Of the several reforms which were adopted in the succeeding hundred days, the most significant was the explicit provision that all of the King's de-

[5] *Ibid.*, 91-97, 127.

crees would henceforward require the countersignature of a responsible minister. From this blow the monarchy never quite recovered. For the next half-century Bavaria was to be governed by the cabinet of ministers.[6]

It is conceivable that the authority of the monarchy might have been retrieved had it not been for the monarchs. Max II was hampered from the outset by recurrent headaches and an excessive admiration for the brilliance of his ministerial advisers. The ministers regulated the affairs of state, and the headaches were probably symptomatic of the insanity which subsequently enveloped Max's two successors. It mattered very little, practically speaking, when Ludwig II assumed the monarchy in 1866. "The King sees no one now," wrote Chlodwig von Hohenlohe as Prussia and Austria were mobilizing for the conflict which would decide Bavaria's political future; "he lives on the Roseninsel and has fireworks displayed."[7] At the same time neither Hohenlohe nor his predecessor, Ludwig von der Pfordten, would have been a likely match for Bismarck's diplomatic skill even had they been determined to resist it. The idea that Bavaria should organize a southern union as a third force in a confederated Germany never became a concerted policy or a serious alternative to Bismarckian unification. In 1870 the ministers gave first thought to political realities and only secondary consideration to the grandeur of the Wittelsbach dynasty. Some historians still consider this to have been "a decision for Prussia, against Germany, against Bavaria!"[8] That may be, but it was above

[6] *Ibid.*, 137-146, 173-178. Veit Valentin, *Geschichte der Deutschen Revolution von 1848-1849* (2 vols.; Berlin, 1930), I, 115-140. Contrast with the sensationalized account of E. Amort (Erhard Auer), *Ein Stück bayerische Geschichte* (Augsburg, 1921), 61-67. Also see Max Spindler, "Die politische Wendung von 1847/48 in Bayern," in the recent anthology edited by Otto Schlottenloher, *Bayern: Staat und Kirche, Land und Reich* (Munich, n.d.), 326-340.

[7] Doeberl, *Entwicklungsgeschichte*, III, 556.

[8] Ernst Deuerlein, *Bayern und die Deutsche Einheit von der Paulskirche 1848 bis 1948* (Altötting, 1948), 277.

all a victory for the ministerial oligarchy. The autonomy of diplomacy, of the army, and most conspicuously of the monarchy was curtailed in the bargain, but not so the authority of the ministers in state affairs. The federal character of the Bismarckian settlement was something of a fiction—except for the maintenance of the state bureaucracy, whose function and personnel were scarcely affected by national unification. The special concessions granted to Bavaria, notably the state administration of beer and brandy taxes, assured the continuation of ministerial control in state policies. The Crown, but not the bureaucracy, could have been financed by other independent means. By 1870 Bavaria may have reached "the terminus of its history" as an autonomous state,[9] but within its borders the conduct of government remained as before in the hands of "the combined ministers of state."

During the next two decades the chairman of the cabinet came to be acknowledged and addressed as the Prime Minister (*Ministerpräsident*). In 1880 Johan von Lutz formally assumed this position, although he had in reality been the leading political figure in the state throughout the difficult period of adjustment in the 1870's.[10] While Ludwig II squandered Bavaria's gold at his fancy, Lutz attempted to maintain the state's economic and political equilibrium. Under his direction Bavaria avoided the excesses of the *Kulturkampf* and began to experience the first effects of urbanization and nascent industrialization. Without comparable resources of capital or coal Bavaria could not hope to compete industrially with neighboring Saxony, not to mention the Ruhr or Silesia. By the turn of the century there would still be less than a million "workers" in all of Bavaria, of which no more than a

[9] Karl Schwend, *Bayern zwischen Monarchie und Diktatur* (Munich, 1954), 24-29.

[10] See the monograph by Fritz von Rummel, *Das Ministerium Lutz und seine Gegner 1871-1882* (Munich, 1935).

third could be called "industrial."[11] Yet, if the immediate results were less than startling, it would be fair to regard Lutz as a patron of modernization and to note the conscious change of policy since the reign of Ludwig I.

By the 1890's the political scene was beginning to change as well, a fact which had very little to do in a positive way with the fortunes of the monarchy. The strange death of Ludwig II in 1886 meant the accession of his even more completely demented brother Otto. The appointment of a regent was necessary and the selection of Luitpold, the third son of Ludwig I, was in every respect appropriate. Correct and colorless, the Prince Regent was perfectly suited to the strictly ceremonial functions now assigned to the Crown. Luitpold has been referred to as "the first true constitutional ruler of Bavaria,"[12] but he was, of course, not the ruler at all. The reality was a ministerial regency which outlived Johan von Lutz and which was still in effect when the Regent died at the age of eighty-one in 1912. By then the eclipse of the monarchy had been a fact of Bavarian political life for well over half a century. That the end of the ministerial oligarchy can be dated in the same year is largely coincidental, a matter which must now be treated in some detail.

The new phase in Bavaria's history after 1890 was a consequence of the onset of mass politics. Since 1818 Bavaria had formally had a bicameral legislature, a Chamber of Deputies and a Chamber of *Reichsräte*, but it would be improper to speak of even a rudimentary party system in Bavaria before the 1860's. The first noteworthy parliamentary grouping was the Middle Party (*Mittelpartei*), formed in support of liberal

[11] *Statistisches Jahrbuch für den Freistaat Bayern 1919* (Munich, 1919), 134-135. See Otmar Emminger, *Die bayerische Industrie* (Munich, 1947), 21-25.

[12] Doeberl, *Entwicklungsgeschichte*, III, 575. But see Schwend, *Bayern zwischen Monarchie und Diktatur*, 40.

11

ministerialism. This faction was rivaled in the Landtag after 1863 by the Progressive Party (*Fortschrittspartei*). Both shared the fundamental objectives of the National Liberal movement prior to 1870, such as constitutional government, freedom of press and assembly, and national unification. Although the differences between the two factions in Bavaria were more personal than programmatic, the Progressives were known to be more avidly *kleindeutsch* in respect to the national problem. This was reflected in the change of ministries in 1866 when Pfordten was replaced by Hohenlohe and the initiative of Liberal leadership thereby passed briefly from the Middle to the Progressive Party. When Hohenlohe formally endorsed the formation of a confederation of southern German states, he did so only to help clear what he regarded as the inevitable path to unification under Bismarck. By the time he resigned in February of 1870, this course had been prepared.[13]

Hohenlohe's fall was due in part to the sudden electoral reversal of 1869. For the first time the Patriots Party (*Patriotenpartei*) gained an absolute majority in the Chamber of Deputies. This grouping represented the interests of Catholic conservatism: against the Liberals, in favor of a "free" monarchy, and for the maintenance of extensive states' rights in a loose federal system of national government. But the Patriots were immediately split between those who were willing to accept Prussian leadership and those adamant to retain traditional bonds with Austria. Even the *Kulturkampf* was not pursued with enough vigor in Bavaria to afford the common political martyrdom which might have restored party unity. The Patriots were consequently forced to endure another twenty years without being able to exploit their majority effectively, at a time when Bavaria was still far from having a genuine parliamentary system and when the state was capably administered under Johan von Lutz.[14]

[13] Doeberl, *Entwicklungsgeschichte*, III, 462-483.

[14] *Ibid.*, 489-490. See Leonhard Lenk, "Katholizismus und Liber-

By 1890 the Patriots Party had officially merged with the national Center Party (*Zentrum*). In that year a congress of the Catholic laity was scheduled for Munich. But on May 15, at the instigation of the Prime Minister, Luitpold dutifully advised that the *Katholikentag* be cancelled. The transfer of the congress to Koblenz, outside of Bavarian territory, marked the last notable demonstration, if only a symbolic one, of the dominating influence of the ministerial oligarchy. Two weeks after the Prince Regent's compliance with his request, Lutz resigned, already gravely ill; by September he was dead. His successor, the Franconian Protestant von Crailsheim, continued in the ministerial tradition without, however, so tenaciously denying concessions to the Catholic majority. In 1895 the next major Church congress was convened in Munich.[15]

Whereas the process of formulating official policy had remained basically unchanged within Bavaria since 1848, the sociological composition of those subject to ministerial control was being transformed. During the twenty-six years of Luitpold's regency, beginning in 1886, the population of Munich more than doubled, while that of Nuremberg trebled. This spurt of urbanization was accompanied by the more obvious signs of technological development: a doubling of Bavaria's railway network and the introduction of telephones, trolley lines, and automobiles in the larger cities. Indicatively, the percentage of male voters rose from 31.2 to 81.9 in the five state elections from 1893 to 1912.[16] In this social and political evolution the Liberals could not keep pace. Their

---

alismus. Zur Auseinandersetzung mit dem Zeitgeist in München 1848-1918," *Der Mönch im Wappen* (Munich, 1960), 375-408.

[15] Karl Bachem, *Vorgeschichte, Geschichte und Politik der deutschen Zentrumspartei* (9 vols.; Cologne, 1927-1932), VIII, 13-17.

[16] *Statistisches Jahrbuch 1919*, 10. Reinhard Jansen, *Georg von Vollmar. Eine politische Biographie* (Düsseldorf, 1958), 63-74. See Wolfgang Zorn, "Probleme und Quellen der bayerischen Sozialgeschichte im 19. Jahrhundert," *Bayern: Staat und Kirche, Land und Reich*, 347-358.

influence had been based on elites: the ministers and bureau-crats, wealthy merchants, successful artisans, and a portion of the comfortable landholders. The Liberal factions lacked the local contacts available to the Center Party through the Church—and the Bavarian population was nearly seventy-five per cent Catholic. The politicians of the Center were there-fore better equipped to meet the challenge of a mass elector-ate and demonstrated their willingness to do so by the forma-tion of the Christian Trade Unions and the Bavarian Peas-ants' Association (*Bauernverein*). As the popular returns of the Liberals began to drop sharply in successive elections after 1890, it became apparent that the rule of the minis-terial oligarchy did not reflect the will of the Bavarian citi-zenry. It was the resulting erosion of the ministerial system which finally cleared the way by 1912 for the establishment of a parliamentary regime.

Two new political factors appeared during the elections to the Bavarian Chamber of Deputies in 1893: the Social Dem-ocratic Party (SPD) and the Bavarian Peasants' League (*Bauernbund,* or BBB). They represented a threat to the majority of the Center Party in urban and rural electoral precincts respectively. At the same time they were in accord with the Center in wishing to end the system of government-by-cabinet and to introduce parliamentarianism. Mention should also be made here of the Conservative Party (*Kon-servative Partei*), composed for the most part of Protestant landholders in the northern part of the state who were affili-ated with the national *Bund der Landwirte*. To ascertain the effects of this activation and multiplication of political parties, it is sufficient to compare the composition of the Chamber of Deputies at the close of the century with that of two dec-ades earlier:

Year	*SPD*	*BBB*	*Lib-eral*	*Center*	*Conserv-ative*	*Other*	*Total*
1881	—	—	70	86	3	—	159
1899	11	8	44	84	10	2	159

The intrusion of Social Democracy into Bavarian politics had been much less abrupt than these figures might suggest. A few workingmen's associations had been formed in 1848, only to collapse again by the end of the next year. Attempts to organize groups of workers were initiated once more in the 1860's by both Lassalleans and Marxists. In the first Reichstag elections in 1871 Socialist candidates polled a total of 812 votes in Munich, 362 in Augsburg, 340 in Nuremberg, and 144 in Hof. Before 1890 only two individuals—Karl Grillenberger in Nuremberg and Georg von Vollmar in Munich—were able to gain popular election on the Social Democratic ticket.[17] The lapse of the anti-Socialist laws then permitted the convocation of a party congress in Regensburg in 1892. This event marked the real inception of a statewide organization, which in the next year elected five deputies to the Lower House. Grillenberger's death in 1897 left Georg von Vollmar without a peer in the party leadership, and the character of Bavarian Socialism thereafter reflected his remarkable personality.[18] Despite a reputation for radicalism gained in his younger days, Vollmar was anything but an irresponsible demagogue. As a Roman Catholic, a crippled war veteran, and a talented orator in rich Bavarian dialect, he could appear convincingly as a folk-leader rather than an emissary of class struggle. Both in public—as in his widely publicized *"Eldoradoreden"* of 1891—and in private, Vollmar expressed confidence in the inexorable and peaceful advance of the Socialist cause. "In Bavaria considerably smaller differences of income exist than elsewhere, less luxury and less poverty," he explained in 1894 to Marx's biographer, Franz Mehring; "as a consequence of this and as a consequence of the pronounced democratic feeling, there is less class hatred. . . ."[19] The program of the Bavarian SPD there-

---

[17] See Franz Schade, *Kurt Eisner und die bayerische Sozialdemokratie* (Hannover, 1961), 13-19.

[18] Jansen, *Georg von Vollmar*, 7 and passim.

[19] *Ibid.*, 48-49.

15

fore disavowed revolutionary ambitions and advocated a parliamentary system, based on direct and universal suffrage, in which the cabinet of ministers would be responsible solely to the Landtag. A unique feature of the Social Democratic program, however, was the demand for abolition of all aristocratic titles and privileges—and, as a necessary result of this, the abrogation of the Upper House. It was this question of unicameralism, as will shortly be clear, which eventually became the principal issue of reform.

Despite the objections of conservative Catholics and radical Socialists, mostly from northern Germany, the Bavarian Center Party and Vollmar's SPD joined in an electoral alliance during the political campaign of 1899. It was a successful venture for both. The Center added ten seats to its delegation in the Chamber of Deputies and the Socialists six; whereas the Liberals lost nearly a third of their number, an uncomfortable statistic for the ministerial oligarchy. In 1903 Crailsheim was replaced by "the first non-Liberal Prime Minister since 1870," Count Podewils.[20] But to change the premier was not quite to alter the ministerial system. In order to obtain a major reform of the electoral system (still based on an 1848 law and the 1875 census) which would move Bavaria in the direction of a genuinely representative parliamentarianism, a majority of two-thirds was required in the Lower House. Through a renewal of their electoral alliance and by dint of the most vigorous political campaigning witnessed in Bavaria to that date, the Center Party and the SPD gained the necessary seats in 1905. A system of direct suffrage was enacted into law the following year. In this partnership, however, it was the Socialists who had drawn the shorter straw: while the Center Party was increasing its deputation in 1905 by eighteen, the SPD managed to add only one more seat. Catholic leaders were understandably eager to continue

[20] Bachem, *Zentrumspartei*, VIII, 40-42. Excepting the brief tenure of the Count von Bray at the time of national unification, this holds true since 1848.

this arrangement—they began their 1907 campaign under the slogan: "With the SPD against the Liberals!"—but the Social Democrats chose to set a new course of cooperation with the Liberals.[21] Together they were able to diminish but not to displace the Center Party's parliamentary majority:

Year	SPD	BBB	Liberal	Center	Conservative	Other	Total
1905	12	4	23	102	16	—	157
1907	20	3	25	98	16	1	163
1912	30	5	33	87	7	1	163

On the eve of the 1912 elections, the Podewils ministry stepped down, to be replaced a week later, on February 11, by the cabinet of Georg von Hertling.[22] A former professor of philosophy, Hertling was the chief of the more conservative wing of the Center Party which had prevailed since the termination of the electoral alliance with the SPD. He claimed to be no more than the agent of the monarchy—but in that claim Hertling was unduly modest and scarcely correct. It was the Prime Minister, not the King, who was the chief political figure of the state. And it was the support of his party, not the frayed tradition of royal prerogative, which really mattered. The debut of Hertling's administration meant, in fact, that a parliamentary regime had replaced the Liberal ministerial oligarchy as the governing authority in Bavaria. What Catholic political interests had lost through the monarchy in 1848 they regained through the party system in 1912. Yet as the war approached, the Bavarian constitution still lagged behind the political reality.

It is necessary now to examine more closely the various movements for constitutional reform. The objective of reform, it may be said at the outset, had never been the abrogation

[21] *Ibid.*

[22] Hertling records his career until 1902 in *Erinnerungen aus meinem Leben* (2 vols.; Kempton and Munich, 1919-1920). See Bachem, *Zentrumspartei,* VIII, 48.

of the monarchy. Several commentators have made special note of the absence of any concerted anti-monarchical agitation in Bavaria between 1848 and 1918. Yet this is hardly surprising in view of the fact that the monarchy had ceased to be the dominant political factor and no longer presented an impediment to reform. The impetus for reform was directed, rather, primarily against the bureaucracy and the aristocracy. Both the ministerial system and the Upper House of the Landtag were subjected to repeated criticism in the nineteenth century, though before 1890 seldom from the same source. The reforms executed immediately after the abdication of Ludwig I had left the ministers in control and the Chamber of *Reichsräte* intact, while setting in motion an opposition to each.[23] Reform proposals current in the 1860's were tabled because of the more pressing issues of national unification. Another reason for delay before 1890 was that those interested in reform were at cross-purposes. The Liberals wished to curb aristocratic privileges but were wary of tampering with the suffrage lest the Chamber of Deputies become a challenge to ministerial authority; the Patriots were committed to preserve the position of the Upper House (its membership being, of course, overwhelmingly Catholic) while favoring a new electoral procedure which would benefit a parliamentary majority at the expense of the cabinet system. It was the appearance of the Social Democratic Party which broke the impasse and determined the course of reform. As they favored both reform measures, the Socialist politicians first allied with the Center Party to gain the electoral reform of 1906 and then joined with the Liberals in the agitation against the Upper House.

The specific terms of the Social Democratic program for electoral reform were outlined on three separate occasions in the 1890's by Karl Grillenberger: direct and proportional suffrage, woman suffrage, and the redistribution of electoral

[23] Doeberl, *Entwicklungsgeschichte*, III, 176.

precincts. Grillenberger refrained from moving the outright abolition of the Upper House, a proposal which would have been certain to alienate Catholic interests. Yet nothing was concretely achieved by the time of his death in 1897.[24] In 1899 another motion was presented by Grillenberger's successor as a Socialist delegate from Nuremberg, Martin Segitz. This time the reform bill was sent to legislative committees, where it remained for nearly four years. When the Segitz motion reappeared in 1903 it was defeated in both houses of the Landtag. By then it was clear that no reform was possible without the undivided support of the Center Party and a major electoral setback of the Liberals. Both were forthcoming in 1905. After the Liberals had been routed by the Center-Socialist coalition, a reform motion sponsored by the Center Party was quickly passed into law on April 9, 1906—fourteen years after Grillenberger's first proposal. The reform bill brought Bavaria's electoral laws into conformity with those of the German Reich. Its principal feature was direct suffrage which was, however, neither proportional nor universal nor based on electoral reapportionment. The reform fell far short, in other words, of fulfilling the Socialist program.[25]

The reform movement thereupon entered a new phase. With nothing more to expect in the foreseeable future from the Center Party, the Socialists disengaged themselves from that political alliance and aligned with the Liberals. A Liberal motion to reform the Upper House was first introduced in 1907. Similar proposals were repeated by Liberal deputies on several occasions between 1909 and 1914—each time with the support of the SPD and each time blocked by the Center Party. Again the Social Democrats favored the proposed reform measure only as a minimum, maintaining that the ultimate result should be a unicameral system with universal and proportional suffrage. Accordingly, the electoral campaign of

---

[24] Schade, *Kurt Eisner*, 21-22.
[25] Doeberl, *Entwicklungsgeschichte*, III, 575-576.

1912 was fought by a Liberal-Socialist coalition, joined by the BBB, against the Catholic Center. Despite its "isolation" the Center Party emerged with a reduced but comfortable majority in the Lower House, a reciprocal bond of political and confessional interests with the Upper House, uncontested control over the cabinet of ministers, and the assistance of a compliant monarchy. Here matters stood in the final two years before the war.[26]

In the entire development of the Bavarian state between 1848 and 1914 the advice and influence of the Crown had counted for very little either in the passage from the cabinet system to a *de facto* parliamentary regime or in the progress of constitutional reform. As he reached his eightieth birthday in 1911 the Prince Regent was respected and honored, but not obeyed. Luitpold's death in the following year left the Hertling administration with a delicate problem since, astoundingly, the legal monarch Otto had managed to survive a regency which had endured for more than a quarter of a century. The question was now whether the regency should be perpetuated or the insane king removed. Good sense if not good politics dictated the latter choice, and on November 5, 1913, Luitpold's son received the royal title as Ludwig III.[27] Since he himself had a son of mature age, the Crown Prince Rupprecht, Ludwig's coronation seemed to assure the succession of the dynasty and perhaps even the restoration of its prestige. Yet both tradition and circumstance were against any significant rehabilitation of monarchical authority for the time being. Already in his late sixties, Ludwig was the first mentally competent Wittelsbach to hold the royal title since Max II; and he owed his accession to a special constitutional change which had to be passed through both houses of the Bavarian Landtag. Thereafter he was King by right but also, as everyone knew, by the grace of the Center Party. If the monarchy was

[26] *Ibid.*, 576-577.
[27] Benno Hubensteiner, *Bayerische Geschichte* (2nd ed.; Munich, n.d.), 391-393.

at last to resume more than a ceremonial function in the affairs of state, it was unlikely to do so in the reign of Ludwig III. Meanwhile, the issues created by political and social evolution remained unresolved. But in the summer of 1914 the movement for reform was suddenly interrupted by the exigency of military preparation.

The War Years

For Bavaria, as for the rest of Europe, the onset of the First World War came as an exhilarating shock. Within weeks the Bavarian Army had several hundred thousand troops under arms; and those on the western front, the Crown Prince wrote in his diary, were "burning to fight."[28] Assigned to the German southern flank, the Bavarian forces were to assist in a diversionary operation while the right flank swung through Belgium and cut into France from the north. It was in Lorraine in the autumn of 1914, for the first and last time since national unification, that the Bavarian Army fought under its own generalship. Despite a creditable performance and despite their unquestioned loyalty, the Bavarian contingents were thereafter more closely integrated with other military units under the direct command of the German General Staff. During the bitter stalemate of the next three years Bavaria sent a million men into service and, by the beginning of 1918, lost nearly 130,000 of them in action.[29]

What was most drastically apparent in the field—the personal sacrifice and the loss of state autonomy—was also evident on the home front. Bavaria's domestic contribution to the war effort was, of course, primarily agricultural. Four days after the declaration of war the Landtag enacted a law granting state administrators the power to fix price ceilings on all sales of Bavarian grain and dairy products. In November of 1914 the War Grain Association (*Kriegsgetreidegesell-*

[28] Kronprinz Rupprecht von Bayern, *Mein Kriegstagebuch* (3 vols.; Berlin, 1929), I, 5.

[29] *Statistisches Jahrbuch 1919*, 61.

schaft) was founded with the goal of storing two to three million tons of foodstuffs in order to meet any future emergency. These and similar measures ordered from Munich soon proved to be ineffective and incomplete. Accordingly, on February 1, 1915, a National Grain Office (*Reichsgetreidestelle*) was invested by the Berlin government with authority to establish a maximum quota for local consumption in the state, and to arrange for the confiscation of surplus. The policy of agricultural quotas and prices was henceforth formulated in Berlin and enforced in Bavaria under the supervision of federal officials. A poor harvest throughout Germany later that year led to the introduction in the nation's capital of a Central Economic Planning Board (*Zentrale Planwirtschaft*). Further encroachments on state administration followed. Separate agencies were empowered by Berlin to regulate the disposition of meats, fats, fish, potatoes, fruit and vegetables, and other commodities (*Reichsfleischstelle, Reichsfettstelle*, etc.). By the middle of 1917 Bavarian agriculture, no less than the Bavarian Army, had been placed under centralized authority and integrated into the national war effort.[30]

At the beginning of the war, apart from a few machine and textile factories in Munich, Augsburg, and Nuremberg, Bavaria had very little heavy industry. In the initial allotment of war contracts Bavaria was consequently neglected in favor of areas already more heavily industrialized, those with an available labor force and more accessible raw materials. Complaints from the Hertling regime, as well as from King Ludwig directly to the Kaiser himself, motivated the Berlin government to plan the location of some wartime industry in Bavaria. The Krupp firm, although reluctant, was prevailed upon to cooperate in this effort and to begin in June of 1916 the construction of a new plant in Munich-Neufreimann, on the northern edge of the capital city. The Bavarian munitions and small arms industry was meanwhile being expanded, and

[30] Alois Schlögl, *Bayerische Agrargeschichte* (Munich, 1954), 540-545.

firms such as the Bavarian Aircraft Plant and the Rapp Motor Works were awarded contracts and converted to war production.[31]

One result of this soon became visible on the sidewalks of the Bavarian cities, especially in Munich which had formerly been known as a "court and residential town." Since the royal house played only a modest ceremonial role and since there were so few great industries or industrialists (other than the brewmasters, whose wealth no one begrudged anyway), Munich had been remarkable in the previous century as "almost a classless city."[32] The war changed that by sharply accelerating the trend toward urbanization. By 1917 there were 52,000 military personnel stationed in Munich alone; in Nuremberg there were more than 20,000; and in Augsburg, Würzburg, and Ingolstadt from 10,000 to 15,000. To this was now added the new recruitment of industrial workers: the number of laborers engaged in war production in factories employing over 200 rose to nearly 200,000 by the end of that year.[33] Translation of these bare statistics into the personal discomforts and administrative problems of housing and provisioning affords some impression of the impact of the war years.

The economic and social changes briefly indicated here might have been without serious political consequences were it not for the unsatisfactory progress of the war itself. The adjustments and privations had been initially accepted in the

[31] Treutler (Royal Prussian Minister to Bavaria) to Chancellor von Bethmann-Hollweg, 27 June 1916. Taken from microfilms of the German Foreign Office on deposit in the National Archives, Washington, D.C. (hereafter cited as NA Washington): file Bayern 51, vol. XXII, serial and frame nos. ACP 156/711-712. See Karl Bosl and H. Schreibmüller, *Geschichte Bayerns* (2 vols.; Munich, 1955), II, 94-95. A survey of Bavarian industry prior to the First World War is provided by Wolfgang Zorn, *Kleine Wirtschafts- und Sozialgeschichte Bayerns 1806-1933* (Munich-Pasing, 1962), 48-55.

[32] See the sketch of Munich on the eve of the war by Moritz Julius Bonn, *So macht man Geschichte* (Munich, 1953), 142-160.

[33] *Statistisches Jahrbuch 1919*, 20, 167.

confident expectation of military victory. The longer that expectation was disappointed, the more audible became the protests from all sides. As early as February of 1916 the leader of the Bavarian Peasants' Association, Dr. Georg Heim, reported to the Munich government that "the attitude of the rural population is becoming more unfavorable day by day, [and] is in part embittered." According to Heim, the growing dissatisfaction among peasants and landholders alike was directly traceable to the "immoral price ceiling policy" established in Berlin. "The worst that can happen has occurred. The rural population is saying that the bureaucratic officials have lied to them [with the result that] confidence has been undermined, the credibility of the officials shaken."[34] Heim's report was corroborated by others, and the matter was presented to the Berlin regime that summer. In July Chancellor von Bethmann-Hollweg found it necessary to alert his colleagues to the "not unmenacing intensification of Bavarian particularism."[35] Since Berlin had assumed control of the war economy, Berlin could be made responsible for every inconvenience. There had not been so much grumbling about the *"Saupreussen"* in Bavaria since 1866. Well founded or not, this recurrence of anti-Prussian sentiment was something which could not be ignored in Berlin and which might be exploited in Munich.

The resentment became more severe and more widespread as the war continued. In the middle of 1917 Bavarian Minister of War von Hellingrath attempted to summarize in a formal report the accumulating evidence of disaffection. "The enthusiasm prevalent at the beginning of the war has been dissipated for some time," he wrote, "it has been replaced to a great extent by a far-reaching pessimism, the danger of

[34] Dr. Georg Heim to the Bavarian Ministry of War, 17 Feb. 1916. Reprinted in *Der Dolchstossprozess in München. Eine Ehrenrettung des deutschen Volkes* (Munich, 1925), 145-146.

[35] Bethmann-Hollweg to Jagow, 22 July 1916, NA Washington, Bayern 50, XV, UM 73/756.

which cannot be underestimated." Hellingrath noted that this feeling had pervaded the cities as well as the countryside, although he considered the organized workers to be the most reliable element of society because of their rising wages and the disciplinary influence of the trade unions and the Social Democratic Party. Infiltrated by "radical circles" (not further specified), the unorganized workers presented a much greater threat to security. Yet the most serious problem in Hellingrath's view was not the workers at all, but the lower middle class:

> They stand to a great extent before the collapse of their existence [since they] have sunk down to an economic proletariat. . . . That the displacement from an economically carefree existence into bitter necessity could lead to spontaneous outbursts of dissatisfaction scarcely needs further explanation.[36]

Hellingrath's evaluation was shared by the Prussian minister in Bavaria, von Treutler, who also reported to Berlin the "widespread dissatisfaction" apparent in Munich and warned that "a combination of scanty provisions with . . . insufficient coal reserves might lead to a catastrophe here in the winter."[37]

In spite of the near unanimity of these and similar reports by other official observers, there is little to suggest that they were considered seriously. Whatever their complaints, the Bavarian people were outwardly docile. It seemed inconceivable, in fact, that the attitude of the civilian population could count for much so long as absolute discipline was maintained in the field—as it was well into 1918. There was some official concern over a number of incidents involving soldiers on furlough who had to be reprimanded for bearing grievances from the

[36] "Erlass des Bayerischen Kriegsministeriums über die Stimmung in der Heimat vom 11. August 1917," *Der Dolchstossprozess*, 147-149.

[37] Treutler to Michaelis, 19 July 1917, NA Washington, Bayern 50, XV, UM 73/757-759.

front and back again.[38] But such measures as were recommended to arrest public criticism were not indicative of any deep apprehension that it might become intolerable. Bethmann-Hollweg's suggestion, for instance, was that the exploits of Bavarian soldiers be given more prominence in the daily reports of the General Staff, that the Kaiser pay a special visit to Bavarian military units, and that more publicity be afforded to the contributions of Bavaria in the national war effort.[39] To publish a flattering telegram from the Kaiser to King Ludwig, however, was hardly to demonstrate that the fundamental problems created by the war had been either assessed or alleviated.

Whereas the declaration of war seemed to set everything else in motion, it had brought the reform movement to a halt. The *Burgfrieden* requested by the national government entailed a moratorium on party activity and, as a consequence, on reform agitation. The delegates who had been elected in 1912 continued to sit in the Chamber of Deputies for the duration of the war. The political balance in Bavaria therefore remained steeply tilted in the direction of the Catholic Center. The several ministerial changes after 1914 had no marked effect on the policy of the regime. Even the departure of Count Hertling for Berlin late in 1917, when he succeeded Michaelis and became the third German Chancellor of the war, did not alter the situation in Bavaria or make a reform of the state constitution any more likely.

By the time Hertling was replaced in Munich by Prime Minister von Dandl the question of reform had at least been reopened. Although there had been no opportunity to establish the fact in state-wide elections, the population changes in the war years had evidently benefited the Social Democratic

---

[38] A breakdown of discipline among Bavarian troops began in the summer of 1918. Rupprecht, *Mein Kriegstagebuch*, II, 402-415.

[39] Bethmann-Hollweg to Jagow, 22 July 1916, NA Washington, Bayern 50, XV, UM 73/756.

Party. The perceptible movement from the countryside into the cities, the importation of labor for wartime production, and the increasing concentration of workers and soldiers in the urban centers had all tended to strengthen the Socialist ranks. The leadership of the SPD in Bavaria was meanwhile changing hands. As physical handicaps increasingly restricted his movements, Georg von Vollmar had been forced to curtail all but the most urgent contact with national politics after 1907; by 1914 he had withdrawn entirely from parliamentary activity, even though he still held seats in both Landtag and Reichstag and was everywhere acknowledged as the leader of Social Democracy in Bavaria. Yet, inevitably, Vollmar soon "lost contact with reality." While treated with deference, not to say reverence, by his party colleagues, his actual position as the party leader became nominal.[40] After his wife suffered a stroke in the summer of 1917, he lived completely withdrawn at his home south of Munich. Vollmar's responsibility was assumed by a younger generation—men like Erhard Auer, Johannes Hoffmann, and Albert Rosshaupter, who had come of political age after the Landtag elections of 1907. Although these leaders were no less committed to national unity than Vollmar, they were more impatient to secure a basic constitutional reform and less inclined to observe the *Burgfrieden* in silence. With the military deadlock seemingly interminable in the field, they resolved to attempt a break in the parliamentary stalemate on the home front. After an opening barrage in the newspapers, a motion for reform was introduced into the Finance Committee of the Bavarian Chamber of Deputies in September of 1917. This paralleled and was encouraged by similar action taken elsewhere in Germany following the "peace resolution" crisis in the Reichstag during July.

Taken as a whole, the so-called Auer-Süssheim Bill represented a proposal to complete and codify the transition to a

---

[40] Jansen, *Georg von Vollmar*, 113.

parliamentary system. And, considered separately, its eleven provisions specified the maximum demands of the Social Democratic Party in Bavaria as the war was about to enter its final year:

1. Elimination of the Upper House and adoption of a unicameral system.
2. Direct and universal suffrage with proportional representation.
3. Legislative initiative of the Landtag.
4. Abolition of the royal veto power.
5. Nomination of ministers by the Landtag.
6. Self-determination of convocation and adjournment by the Landtag.
7. Annual budget.
8. Abrogation of aristocratic titles and privileges.
9. Prohibition of tax-free hereditary holdings (*Fideikommisse*).
10. Elimination of royal exemptions from taxation and judication.
11. Separation of Church and State.[41]

When this measure was brought to the floor of the Chamber of Deputies on December 19, 1917, the formal explanation of the reform program was entrusted by the SPD to its constitutional expert, Dr. Max Süssheim. According to Süssheim, the objective of the proposal was to assure that "what is now already political practice would be secured in the constitution." So far as it went, this evaluation was accurate enough. But even a rapid glance down the list of specific provisions revealed that the Social Democrats in fact wished to legislate much more than the current "political practice," since that practice (as Süssheim charged himself) was obviously "to the advantage of one party." The real basis of the Auer-Süssheim Bill,

---

[41] "Antrag Auer-Süssheim auf eine Verfassungsänderung Bayerns" (18 Sept. 1917), reprinted by Doeberl, *Sozialismus, Soziale Revolution, Sozialer Volksstaat* (Munich, 1920), 113-114.

from the first point to the last, was the insinuation that the Catholic Center had exploited its majority position and the circumstances of the war to convert Bavaria into a one-party state. The issue of reform was not whether Bavaria should have a parliamentary system—in reality that had already been settled by 1912—but whether the Center Party would be forced to rely on its electoral advantage alone to dominate that system. "What the Social Democrats demand," Süssheim conceded, "is . . . the alteration of the entire system."[42] To accomplish this the SPD aimed to remove every impediment to a parliamentary regime based exclusively on party representation. The ultimate purpose of Socialist reform was therefore a curtailment of the political influence of the monarchy, the aristocracy, and the Church—except as these might be represented through the Center Party in the Bavarian Landtag.

The realization of reform depended entirely on the response of those least likely to approve of it. As long as the war continued and parliamentary elections were deferred, the Center Party was assured of an absolute majority in the Lower House. But the longer this circumstance obtained, the less certain the Center leaders could be that their majority would be secure once the war was ended and the normal electoral process resumed. Because of this increasing uncertainty, it became all the more in the interests of the Center Party to protect the other, non-elective bases of Catholic political power: the aristocratic Upper House and the impaired but still potentially useful offices of the monarchy. The objection of his party to the Auer-Süssheim proposal was stated by Heinrich Held: "The motion intends . . . a fundamental restriction of the royal prerogatives and will lead ultimately to the actual elimination of the constitutional monarchy, to the introduction of a parliamentary form of government, and finally to the

---

[42] *Verhandlungen der Kammer der Abgeordneten des Bayerischen Landtags, Stenographische Berichte*, XVII (11 Dec. 1917-22 Feb. 1918), No. 412, 142-155.

republicanization of our state." When representatives of the
Liberals and the Bavarian Peasants' League also stated their
opposition to the reform bill as a whole, the SPD agreed to
send the second and ninth provisions back to separate legislative committees and to vote on the other measures individually. This strategy proved of no avail, however, as a head
count defeated the provisions one by one. The December 19
session of the Lower Chamber was then adjourned immediately after an announcement from the chair that "the entire
motion is rejected."[43]

By the beginning of 1918, therefore, the reform movement
appeared to be effectively blocked for the duration of the war.
Even had the Social Democrats been able to gain the enthusiastic and undivided support of every other faction for their
program, they were incapable of breaching the solid opposition of the Center Party. When Bavaria observed in May of
1918 the centennial of its constitution, that document was,
except for the introduction of direct suffrage in 1906, still
basically unaltered. When a change was finally effected, it
was to be a result of military circumstance rather than parliamentary maneuver.

In 1918 the issue of the war was no longer whether it
would be concluded by a definitive military triumph or
through negotiation, but whether Germany would negotiate
from strength or from weakness. The prospects were mixed.
The winter of 1917-1918 was unusually severe, yet the domestic catastrophe which some had predicted did not occur.
The war in the East was apparently won, but the outcome in
the West was more problematical than ever after the entrance
of the United States as a belligerent power. And although most
German citizens showed themselves willing to carry on the
war to a successful conclusion, there was among the population an unmistakable and universal desire for peace. In view
of all this two decisions had to be reached. Should negotia-

[43] *Ibid.*, 156-162.

tions with the Entente be opened immediately, or not until after another costly but perhaps advantageous offensive in the spring? Should annexationist ambitions be disavowed in order to indicate conciliation, or should they be flaunted to exhibit determination? The decisions, of course, were made by the German General Staff. In all parts of the nation—the 1917 peace resolution of the Reichstag notwithstanding—the majority concurred in silence; a minority protested.

On the last week-end in January a few thousand workers demonstrated in the streets of Munich and Nuremberg for an immediate peace without annexation. The police intervened, several arrests were made, and the workers went back to their jobs the following Monday.[44] This was the only act of organized political insubordination in Bavaria during the initial four years of the war, and the first of any consequence since 1848. Just what the significance of the January strike would be (it was later called a "general rehearsal" for the November revolution) no one could say at the time. Few Bavarians even learned the identity of the imprisoned leader of the strike, Kurt Eisner, and none of them could then guess that his name would ever become synonymous with an insurrection. The prompt action of the regime in quashing the strike attempt seemed to assure both the public security and the continuation of the war effort.

The January strike affords a convenient chronological point at which to conclude this survey of the historical background of the revolution. Thereafter, until the late autumn of 1918, there was not a single noteworthy instance of radical agitation in Bavaria. Nothing more serious was to be reported during the spring and summer months than the continuation of outspoken criticism against the monarchy. Everything else seemed to be held in suspension, pending the outcome of the

[44] General strikes were attempted at the same time in Berlin, Kiel, Leipzig, Braunschweig, Cologne, Breslau, Mannheim, Magdeburg, and Halle. For a more detailed account of the activity in Munich, see Chapter II.

war. Not until that was clear did radicalism suddenly and concretely appear in the form of a revolutionary movement. The origin of this movement and the immediate circumstances of the revolution form, respectively, the subjects of the succeeding two chapters.

Before altering the focus, however, two questions of unequal difficulty require an explicit answer. First, was the revolution to be an outburst of strong republican sentiment? Here the reply is almost certainly negative.[45] The irritation with the King may have some psychological explanation, but it had very little historical justification. The constitutional objections to Ludwig's succession five years earlier were nearly forgotten. He had already become a familiar figure in Munich, a respectable and amiable citizen-king, but in no sense of the word a commanding personality. Ludwig could be facetiously blamed for the thin beer of the war years or accused of profiting personally by the sale of dairy products from his model farm at Leutstetten (a rumor pointedly denied by government spokesmen), but he was scarcely responsible for the economic hardships of the entire state. He was also criticized for selling out Bavarian interests to Prussia and for toadying to the Kaiser, even though this had less to do with Ludwig and more with the Central Economic Planning Board and the Bismarckian constitution. And he was charged with being an annexationist—he was known to favor the permanent acquisition of the Lowlands in order to assure an outlet to the sea for his favorite project, the Rhine-Danube waterway, and he had less well publicized ambitions to obtain territory in France—yet no one suggested that Ludwig exercised the slightest influence on the actual formulation of German policy.[46] In each case it is evident that more general reasons for discontent could be focused by blaming

[45] See Schwend, *Bayern zwischen Monarchie und Diktatur*, 43.

[46] See the recent study of Bavarian war aims in the volume by Karl-Heinz Janssen, *Macht und Verblendung, Kriegszielpolitik der deutschen Bundesstaaten 1914-1918* (Göttingen, 1963).

the monarch. The expression of feeling against Ludwig suggested personal carping rather than anti-monarchist agitation. If many Bavarians did not highly esteem their King in 1918, they had no good reason to despise him or to wish the Crown abolished.

This raises the second and more difficult question. Was the revolution, then, "necessary"? Certainly it was not necessary in the sense of some theory of historical determinism. The absence of a lengthy prelude of revolutionary activity suggests that it was not even the product of an established radical tradition.[47] But one should be careful not to exaggerate its extemporaneous nature. It is true that the revolution was to be largely unprepared and, even for most of those who participated in it, unexpected. The shock and disbelief of defeat, in fact, undoubtedly contributed more than anything else to the accomplishment of a coup d'état. And yet the revolution represented more than the flight of the monarch and the proclamation of a republic. It was also a release for the deeper sources of tension which this chapter has attempted to describe: the incompleted transition to a parliamentary system, the repeated frustration of constitutional reform, the friction of changing social conditions, the popular antipathy in Bavaria to the economic and military hegemony of Prussia, and above all the increasingly urgent demand for peace. The revolution may not have been necessary, but neither was it fortuitous.

[47] See Doeberl, *Sozialismus*, 41.

CHAPTER II

Kurt Eisner

After the collapse of the strike in January, everything was contingent on the success or failure of the German armies on the western front. If American intervention had placed total victory out of sight, it was still conceivable that one great military stroke might break the resistance of French and British troops and establish German supremacy on the continent for the foreseeable future. This was the calculation of General Ludendorff, at least, and had he succeeded there is no reason to suppose that his authority could have been successfully challenged within Germany. The circumstances of revolution were therefore not given until a military reverse became unavoidable and apparent to nearly everyone—that is, not before October of 1918.

This applied to Bavaria as to the rest of Germany. The military outcome did not necessitate the revolution, but it was unquestionably the condition *sine qua non*. In this respect it is self-evident that the revolution in Bavaria can be understood only as a consequence of the national experience. In another sense, however, the Bavarian development was a determining factor in that experience since it was the first direct assault on the tradition of monarchy and, as such, removed the final restraint to revolution in Berlin. Until the abrupt termination of the Wittelsbach dynasty in Bavaria, there was still a chance that open revolution might be averted by the negotiation between Max von Baden and Woodrow Wilson. The only requirement implied by Wilson which was not in the power of the new Chancellor to fulfill was the abdication of the Kaiser. For his part, William understandably regarded himself as the victim of English propaganda in America and was reluctant to accede. Perhaps the strongest argument against his abdication was the incongruity and predictable upset which it would create in the traditionally mon-

34

archical states of southern Germany. The precipitation of events in Munich was thus to reverse the argument and to give impetus to pro-republican forces in the North.

The timing of the revolution in Bavaria also determined its peculiar character. Had it occurred *after* the declaration of the German Republic in Berlin (assuming that the Kaiser would have ultimately been forced to abdicate in any case), the likelihood is that it would have followed the common pattern of the German revolution: initial domination by the Social Democratic Party and resolute opposition to radicalism. But, as it happened, the revolution in Bavaria was to be implemented and at first guided by the Independent Socialist faction. Starting on a different foot, Bavaria never quite fell into cadence with the rest of Germany. Since this was due primarily to a single man and a small coterie of his supporters, a full explanation of the unique course of the Bavarian revolution requires an examination of the life and political experience of Kurt Eisner.

Eisner in Berlin

By his own account, Kurt Eisner was born May 14, 1867, and grew up "in the center of the asphalt culture" of urban Berlin. He was raised and always remained a creature of the city. His boyhood was spent "between the chestnut grove and the *Opernplatz*" as the son of a modestly affluent Jewish shopkeeper, Emanuel Eisner.[1] The father's business, fashion-

---

[1] There is no complete biography of Eisner and the available sources do not always agree in particulars. Most of these facts are taken from Eisner's own notes, usually appended in 1918, to his *Gesammelte Schriften* (2 vols.; Berlin, 1919). See the authoritative sketch by Josef von Grassmann, "Kurt Eisner," *Deutsches Biographisches Jahrbuch* (Berlin and Leipzig, 1928), 368-378. Informative but uncritical are two brief accounts by men who served Eisner as private secretaries: Benno Merkle, in the foreword to Eisner's *Die Neue Zeit* (2 vols.; Munich, 1919), and Felix Fechenbach, *Der Revolutionär Kurt Eisner aus persönlichen Erlebnissen* (Berlin, 1929). The

ably located Unter den Linden, was an official dealership "by appointment" in military accessories and decorations, and was later to be a source of embarrassment and rebellion to the younger Eisner. Reared in the afterglow of Bismarckian unification, he was taught as a boy to accept its values. Accordingly, he was sent to Berlin's exclusive Askanisches Gymnasium where he shared the benches with sons of officers and wealthy businessmen before gaining his diploma at Easter, 1886.[2] Eisner thereupon enrolled at the nearby Friedrich Wilhelm University and spent the following eight semesters there as a student of philosophy and *Germanistik*, projecting research for a doctoral thesis on Achim von Arnim. Near the end of the year 1889, at the age of twenty-two, he suddenly withdrew from university life to begin work in a Berlin news agency.[3]

Journalism was Kurt Eisner's livelihood for nearly thirty years. His published writings, though scarcely known today, still comprise one of the wittiest and best informed commentaries on the public and political life of Wilhelmian Germany. Eisner's wit ranged from light satire to virtually unleavened irony; his information was selective rather than systematic, characteristically marshaled in order to refute or ridicule a spokesman of the imperial establishment. From the beginning of his professional career to the end, Eisner was a

---

frequently repeated assertion that Eisner was born with the name Kosmanowsky is disproved by Schade, *Kurt Eisner*, 104.

[2] Eisner later recalled that, as a boy of eleven in 1878, he "enthusiastically" placed candles in the window for William I when the Kaiser entered Berlin after the second attempt on his life; Eisner then regarded the Social Democrats as "a band of wild criminals." *Wilhelm Liebknecht. Sein Leben und Wirken* (Berlin, 1900), 51.

[3] Eisner's first employment was with the Korrespondenzbüro Herold. The testimony of one of Eisner's daughters (Frau Pfarrer Börner) indicates that his motivation was primarily financial; he chose to make his own way rather than enter his father's declining business. Schade, *Kurt Eisner*, 27.

parti pris in opposition to the Prussian aristocracy and in support of "the people."[4] His debut as a reporter coincided with Bismarck's dismissal from office, and he was one of the few men to witness the actual "dropping of the pilot" on a chilly March day in 1890. He was allowed to accompany the retired Chancellor on the first kilometers of his departure from Berlin. After climbing from the train at Spandau, Eisner was watching it disappear when he was jostled by a crowd of workmen pushing their way onto the next coach for Berlin. The patent symbolism of that moment did not escape him then or later.[5]

In 1892 Eisner married Elisabeth Hendrich and settled briefly in a Berlin suburb. After accepting a position at the night desk of the *Frankfurter Zeitung*, he began to take leave not only of his own home but of the values which prevailed there. He was attracted to the recently rehabilitated Social Democratic Party and began to write in support of it. It was during his brief stay in Frankfurt that he also completed his first book, a study of the work and influence of Friedrich Nietzsche. Eisner's critique requires some attention both because it was one of the first to be published on Nietzsche in Germany and because it disclosed at least as much about the author as about his subject. This was, as Eisner wrote, "a scene out of the drama of my own spiritual emancipation and evolution."[6]

Eisner regarded his book as the testament of his "struggle against Nietzsche," written to help liberate others from the "awful oppression" of Nietzsche's philosophy. He praised

---

[4] "Volkstheater—eine soziale Ehrenpflicht Berlins" (1889), *Taggeist* (Berlin, 1901), 243-258. This volume contains Eisner's earliest professional essays, excepting his first political brochure: *Eine Junkerrevolte. Drei Wochen preussischer Politik* (Berlin, 1889).

[5] "Rein menschlich!" (1893), *Taggeist*, 30-35.

[6] *Psychopathia Spiritualis. Friedrich Nietzsche und die Apostel der Zukunft* (Leipzig, n.d.), 99. Unfortunately the available sources do not allow one to define more precisely the stages by which Eisner became a Socialist.

Nietzsche's style and the playfulness of his "sublime spirit." Above all, Eisner was sympathetic to Nietzsche's repudiation of the cultural mediocrity of the new German Reich, and to his rejection of the institutions whose primary function seemed to be the perpetuation of privilege: the parliaments, the press, the schools, and especially the universities—"these penitentiaries for bureaucrats are too confining for greatness." But in Eisner's view Nietzsche was a better poet than prophet: "Everywhere he detects the weaknesses, the diseased places, with an uncanny perspicacity, but he errs in the discovery of causes, and he loses himself in magic witch-doctoring in his attempts to heal."

The congenital flaw of Nietzsche's philosophy, Eisner thought, was his "unreal vision of a master morality." Nietzsche was an egotist. His moral universe was all too neatly divided into two spheres: above, the select and superior few; below, the many, the masses, the "human worms." In this respect he shared something with Goethe, though Goethe's "healthy universality" contrasted with Nietzsche's chronic "illness of creative excitement." In Eisner's opinion (from which he was not deterred in spite of its apparent banality) *Zarathustra* deserved to be ranked in German literature along with *Faust*: both were great works of art, neither was a guide to the future. It was characteristic of Eisner's writings, as of most Socialist literary criticism, that the latter criterion generally took precedence over the former. An author was required to meet a certain standard of societal pragmatism before his literary talent could be endorsed. From Eisner Nietzsche received no such accreditation. "Nietzsche not only poisons life . . . life also poisons him."[7]

As an example of Nietzsche's perverse influence Eisner pointed out the anonymous best-seller of the 1890's, *Rembrandt as Educator*. Here was a book which pandered to the

[7] *Ibid.*, 6-11, 95-97; and Eisner's review of Book IV of *Also sprach Zarathustra*, "Aus dem Nachlass eines Lebenden" (1892), *Taggeist*, 259-279.

public taste for romantic fantasy but which, in the treatment of practical politics, exposed itself as "sheer nonsense." The author (later identified as Julius Langbehn) obviously shared Nietzsche's cultural despair, but he combined this with feelings of nationalistic superiority and aspiration completely alien to Nietzsche. Eisner found the book full of "ridiculous scarecrows," and described it as "an obstacle . . . for the social war of liberation."[8] Purposely or not, Eisner observed, Nietzsche had emerged as a central figure in the cult of European decadence. His name was becoming a rallying-cry for an assortment of megalomaniacs, imperialists, free-traders, Social Darwinians, East-Elbian Junkers—for all those who claimed the right of the stronger. Eisner denied that Darwinian theories of biological evolution could be literally transposed to the field of public morality, and he accused Nietzsche of having given his name, perhaps unwittingly, to the apologists of social injustice. "The 'struggle for existence' is no justification for the oppression of the sick and the weak, nor is it a way to the superman."[9]

For all Nietzsche's poetic idealism and his skill as a satirist (and Eisner did not conceal his admiration for these) he was a confirmed misanthrope who had squandered his talents in mocking human infirmity and illness. Eisner charged, moreover, that Nietzsche lacked a fundamental "drive for truth"; he was "too witty to be true." His philosophizing necessarily trailed off into caprice or romantic chaos whenever it attempted to escape from its habitual and debilitating negativism. It was always clear what Nietzsche was against, but never

[8] *Psychopathia Spiritualis*, 22-24. See the excellent chapter by Fritz Stern, "Langbehn and the Crisis of the 1890's," *The Politics of Cultural Despair. A Study in the Rise of the Germanic Ideology* (Berkeley and Los Angeles, 1961), 153-180.

[9] *Psychopathia Spiritualis*, 70-73. Eisner seems to qualify as one of the "scholarly oxen" who overlooked Nietzsche's own attack on the Social Darwinians. See Walter Kaufmann, *Nietzsche. Philosopher, Psychologist, Antichrist* (Princeton, 1950), 270-274.

certain what he was for. Eisner cited the fact that Nietzsche was an outspoken misogynist, a quirk which was probably "to be explained medically." He also regarded Nietzsche as an anti-Semite, contaminated with "racial fanaticism" by his sister and her husband.[10] This, in turn, had led Nietzsche to oppose Socialism as "the consequence of the Semitic slave morality." Eisner regretted that Nietzsche hated Social Democracy without knowing anything of its positive goals and ideals. His own attitude and his case against Nietzsche were best summarized by a single phrase, when he called Nietzsche "the most dangerous and most seductive opponent of Social Democracy."[11]

Like nearly everything else he was ever to write, the young Eisner's polemic against Nietzsche was actually an *apologia pro vita sua*. It was a good example of his talent as a journalist, and of his lack of aptitude as a scholar. In theme, style, and even jargon his later writings were an embellishment rather than a revision of the early ones. He always wrote to make a point, and the point remained the same: "In Socialism I see a clear, attainable objective."[12] He tended to define Socialism simply as social justice, and to accept the notion common to most Socialists of his day that political reform would necessarily precede social realignment. He consciously eschewed both anarchism and dogmatic systemization, and gave no inkling that he regarded his own role as more than that of a social critic. He was not born a revolutionary, and it would require nearly three decades before he became one

---

[10] *Psychopathia Spiritualis*, 9, 26, 34-35, 52. Eisner's misreading of Nietzsche's relationship to Elisabeth Förster-Nietzsche and of his attitude toward the Jews was subsequently shared by a number of prominent Nietzsche scholars, but it has lately been corrected. See Kaufmann, *Nietzsche*, 15-28, and the summary of the issue by Michael Hamburger, "A Craving for Hell. Nietzsche and the Nietzscheans," *Encounter*, XIX (1962), No. 4, 32-40.

[11] *Psychopathia Spiritualis*, 82-88.

[12] *Ibid.*, 86.

in surroundings and circumstances which he could not have imagined in the early 1890's.

In the summer of 1893 Kurt Eisner moved to Marburg to become a political editor with the *Hessische Landeszeitung*. The succeeding five years were the only extended period of his life spent away from a metropolitan center, and even then his interests remained primarily attached to the big city and the *Grosse Politik*. The security and slower pace of the countryside gave him a new perspective and the time to develop his proficiency as a journalist: in rapid succession he composed a series of political and literary essays, often as "provincial letters," for various Berlin journals. At the same time he was able to share in the social and intellectual life of the university in Marburg and, in particular, to cultivate an acquaintance there with Professor Hermann Cohen. Since the 1870's Cohen had been noted as one of the leading neo-Kantian scholars in Germany and as a proponent of the view that the essential nature of Kant's philosophy was political. Specifically, he had suggested the lines of compatibility between the ethics of Kant and the objectives of Socialism.[13] By the time he arrived in Marburg, with a personal commitment to the Social Democratic Party already in his baggage, Eisner was both receptive to Cohen's teachings and prepared to go beyond them. It was by resuming his own study of Kant (first undertaken as a university student) and in consultation with Cohen that Eisner began to define more precisely his notion of Socialism. "The question now was not whether a university teacher might profess socialist ideas in his off-hours, but whether active Social-Democrats could adhere simultaneously to Marx and to Kant."[14]

[13] Hermann Cohen, *Kants Begründung der Ethik* (Berlin, 1877).
[14] George Lichtheim, *Marxism: An Historical and Critical Study* (London, 1961), 292. For the whole problem see Karl Vorländer, *Kant und Marx. Ein Beitrag zur Philosophie des Sozialismus* (Tübingen, 1911), 117-130, 152-154.

The starting-point of Eisner's thinking was the conviction
that the triumph of Socialism was inevitable and that promot-
ing its victory would hasten "the golden age of the future."
He refused to concede that there was any logical inconsistency
in holding that Socialism was both scientifically determined
and ethically desirable, a position from which he never retreated throughout the revisionist debate of the following
decade. Eisner was, however, no logician, and he tended to
equate—or to confuse—his own idealism with the terms of
Kantian philosophy. Although he regarded German Social
Democracy as the direct heir of the *Aufklärung,* he could be
unabashedly romantic in referring to it as "a joyous ideal
and an indomitable hope, and also, if one prefers this expression, 'a new religion.' " Eisner often preferred it himself
and, moreover, insisted that "Socialism is not only the religion of the future, but already that of the present—*the religion of Socialism!*" The success of Social Democracy would,
of course, be political as well as philosophical; Eisner correctly foresaw that the day was not far distant when the SPD
would be the most numerous party in the German Reichstag.
He believed that the "dialectic of the proletarian movement"
could and should be advanced by parliamentary activity,
since "alley revolutions are a means of earlier times . . . today at best still appropriate in Russia."[15] Yet Eisner never
became a thoroughgoing revisionist. He thought Karl Marx
had been "the master of the second half of the nineteenth
century," and was sure to be "the victor of the twentieth."
He was convinced that Marxism "rested on scientific per-
ceptions . . . on whose fundamental principles there is scarcely anything essential to be altered." But Eisner reminded his
readers that Marx's accomplishment was to recognize, not to

---

[15] It is noteworthy that Eisner made this last statement two years
before the appearance of Engels' famous introduction to Marx's *Die
Klassenkämpfe in Frankreich 1848-1850* (Berlin, 1895). "Eine Reise
um die Welt in drei Tagen" (1893), "Die Tragödie des Mittelstandes"
(1894), *Taggeist,* 58-68, 83-90.

resolve the problem of class struggle. No matter what gains Socialism might attain through parliamentary success, the final and unavoidable consequence of its challenge to established authority would be a "brutal conflict." Eisner did not embrace revisionism because he could never accept its basic premise: that the passage of time and the advance of the economy were somehow working to alleviate the class struggle. As he saw it, the adherents of the ruling System and the advocates of Socialism would remain bitter and irreconcilable opponents. "No, truly there is no reconciliation between them and us."[16]

When Eisner spoke of "them," he was invariably referring to the Prussian aristocracy. To be sure, the division was between the rich and the poor, the exploiters and the exploited. But Eisner made only occasional use of the standard Marxist vocabulary. His attacks were customarily directed against the Junkers rather than the capitalists, and he confessed that a common crusade by the Socialists, Progressives, and Liberals against "the East Elbian Huns" would have his blessing, though there was little likelihood that it would ever be undertaken. The fact was that the German bourgeoisie had sold out to Bismarck: "National Liberalism has been; it is dead." Nor did Eisner think that any new independent political movement was likely to take its place. Essentially there were only two sides, not three, and there was a necessity of choice. He followed with interest and commented upon the formation of Friedrich Naumann's National Social Association. But if Eisner had only kind words for Pastor Naumann personally ("one of those few clergymen who understand their time"), he was sure that the Association could never be more than "a waiting room" before "the granite edifice of Marxism." Naumann's followers were just "lost sons of Rudolf von Bennigsen," and his movement was a bundle of self-contradiction since, in the nature of things, Socialism and

[16] "Politisches Temperenzlertum" (1894), "Der Einbund" (1896), *ibid.*, 106-114, 178-183.

Nationalism were antithetical. Naumann wanted to have Karl Marx with Karl Peters; Eisner compared this to eating sour herring with *Schlagsahne* on the dubious gastronomical logic that each tasted good separately, so they must taste twice as good together.

In discounting both National Liberalism and Naumann's version of National Socialism, Eisner reflected the surging confidence of the German Social Democrats after their electoral successes in the national balloting of 1890 and 1893. But like many of his party colleagues, whom he joined in the agitation for abolition of three-class voting in Prussia, he was affected by a sort of political myopia which caused him to read the voting returns somewhat too literally. Only the Junker and his "inane and immoral system" of class suffrage seemed to stand unshaken in the path of the Socialist onslaught. Eisner was insufficiently aware that while the German middle classes were losing parliamentary influence, they were also gaining economic power. Nor did he foresee the crucial legislative role to be played by the *Zentrum*, after 1897, as the balancer of factions in the Reichstag. As a result, Eisner tended to exaggerate the polarization of German politics and to remain preoccupied throughout his stay in Marburg with the anachronism, the "monstrous hypocrisy and audacity," of Junker domination.[17]

Eisner consequently used his pen to dissect in the same manner every major public issue of the decade. The New Course after 1890 was exposed as a continuation of the Old, with the important difference that open disaffection through the SPD had now become a virtual "counter-regime" (*Gegenregierung*). Social Democracy was the single force which had united to "negate the current world order" and which revealed the sporadic protests by the German Liberals in

---

[17] "Talarsocialismus" (1893), "Almela" (1896), "Der tolle Junker" (1897), "Nationalsociale Grundirrtümer" (1897), *ibid.*, 159-177, 184-210. See Arthur Rosenberg, *Die Entstehung der Deutschen Republik 1871-1918* (Berlin, 1930), 41-44.

matters of governmental policy to be "useless equivocation." The debate on the military bill of Chancellor Caprivi was a case in point. Only the Socialists were consistent in their opposition to a militarism which was sweeping Europe to self-destruction in "the great world war of the future." The tragedy was that it might be otherwise. It would be possible for Germany to develop instead a "real militarism" capable of carrying out "a humane mission." Eisner thereby admitted that a certain "Spartanic element" was necessary for the maintenance of any state, but he advocated that this take the form of a militia system designed to insure national independence, assist in the moral and physical training of the masses, and benefit "cultural progress." There was nothing original in Eisner's resurrection of proposals which might date back to 1807 or 1848. His plan was remarkable only for the notion that such reform was still possible, even though it would have meant an end to the aristocratic monopoly of the officer corps and, as he put it, the transformation of "*soldierly*" into "*social* militarism."[18]

It would be difficult to select a more characteristic or revealing example of Eisner's dichotomic reasoning. Besides underscoring in the most literal fashion his antipathy for the Junkers and his adulation of Social Democracy, Eisner disclosed the nature of his own commitment to the German nation. Although he took self-conscious pride in writing from an internationalist viewpoint, he was constitutionally incapable of conceiving of political problems without first positing the existence of the German Reich. In that sense—and it is well to remember that the same may be said about most of those who were soon to engage in the revisionist con-

18 "Militarismus" (1893), "Der Zweite" (1894), *Taggeist*, 13-21, 69-76. See Gordon A. Craig, *The Politics of the Prussian Army 1640-1945* (New York and Oxford, 1956), 38-53, 106-120. Eisner consciously modeled his military thinking on that of Jean Jaurès, to whom he felt "closer than to any other leader of the Socialist International." *Gesammelte Schriften*, I, 19.

troversy—his thinking owed at least as much to the tradition of German nationalism as to either Kant or Karl Marx. In his Marburg essays Eisner therefore sustained a clear distinction between the legitimate aspirations of the German nation and their perversion by its ruling clique. The majority of his articles were written for the educated and politically sophisticated, not for mass circulation. Eisner was capable of being forceful and direct in his denunciation of German *Weltpolitik*, but he more often relied on the pun, the rhetorical question, the embarrassing quotation, and the unflattering historical analogy. Had he not been the editor of a provincial newspaper, he might well have earned his living by writing for one of Berlin's political cabarets. His genuine talent for a peculiarly German style of irony was his forte as a journalist and, in 1897, his undoing as *persona grata* to the imperial censors. He had never made a secret of his distaste for Kaiser William II, but he had carefully restrained his penchant for ridicule when making obvious reference to the House of Hohenzollern. Instead, his satire was generally directed against the proliferation of pressure groups in the 1890's which served to rally popular and parliamentary support for the regime's naval and colonial policies. Eisner had at first regarded William as ineffectual and inconsequential in himself, but as a front for Junker interests and as a symbol of "the inner untruthfulness of our circumstances." He began to see, however, that the Kaiser, rather than Caprivi or Hohenlohe, was the real successor to Bismarck, and that the Kaiser's personal influence was both irresponsible and dangerous. He thereupon determined to direct his attack against the Crown and to emphasize the fact that "the battle is crystallizing around the maintenance of a certain institution of the social order."[19]

In its New Year's issue for January of 1897, the Berlin weekly *Kritik* published a parody of a supposedly fictitious

[19] "Raus!" (1895), "Eine Märzfeier" (1897), *Taggeist*, 98-105, 138-148.

Kaiser written by one "Tat-Twam." It was not long before the author was traced by the imperial police to Marburg and, after a four-hour search of his home, arrested. Eisner was aware of the risk he was running and had often complained in years past of "the sad decline of our justice." In particular, he had charged that the legal paragraphs covering *lèse majesté* were in reality no more than a disguised anti-Socialist Law. Now he was able to witness at first hand the accuracy of his own criticism. He was taken to Berlin and, on April 27, arraigned in court at a closed hearing. His defense was, if anything, more insulting than the article. He denied that he had either named or implied the identity of the present Kaiser, pointing out that the ideal qualities of the "dream figure" in his parody bore precious little resemblance to William II; at most he could be legitimately accused of overglorifying His Imperial Majesty. He did admit that he had intended his piece as a "criticism of the System" with "special reference to Germany." But he contended that this did not constitute a crime and that, in any case, "we must demand for ourselves complete freedom of criticism and defense." The case for the prosecution rested on Tat-Twam's indelicate use of the phrase "illusions of dictatorship" (*Cäsarenwahnsinn*). Eisner was persuaded that his conviction was foregone from the outset, and he was probably correct. At the trial's conclusion he was sentenced to nine months of imprisonment and on November 1, 1897, he entered the Prussian state penitentiary at Plötzensee.[20]

[20] "Ein Fäulnisprozess" (1893), "X" (1896), "Criminelle Majestätsverherrlichung" (Jan. 1897), "Herr Schönes Triumph" (Feb. 1897), "Dolus eventualissimus" (May 1897), *ibid.*, 44-55, 128-137, 212-240. Eisner's fate was by no means unique: in 1894 the historian Ludwig Quidde had been sentenced to three months in prison for an obviously satirical brochure entitled "Caligula: eine Studie über römischen Cäsarenwahnsinn." On Quidde's later political participation as a leader of the Democratic Party in Bavaria, see Chapters VI, VII.

For his career as a journalist, Eisner's internment was a great stroke of fortune, since his case naturally came to the attention of Wilhelm Liebknecht, "the old man" of German Social Democracy, the editor of the party's leading newspaper, and himself alternately a refugee and a victim of imperial justice. After serving the full term of his sentence at Plötzensee, Eisner was released on the first day of August 1898. He was interviewed by the elder Liebknecht and shortly appointed to the editorial board of *Vorwärts*. Liebknecht was openly pleased with his new protégé: "in Eisner," he wrote to Victor Adler at the beginning of 1899, "I have undoubtedly made a good choice." Already in his mid-seventies and aware of his declining faculties, Liebknecht soon turned over the actual direction of the paper to Eisner. Within a year of his release from prison, then, Eisner became the managing editor in all but title of one of Europe's most influential Socialist journals. His rapid promotion was bound to encounter opposition. To the party leaders in Berlin he was an outsider, virtually unknown and not yet affiliated with any recognizable faction. Liebknecht considered this an advantage and had hoped by Eisner's appointment to reduce friction between the "reform" and "radical" wings of the party. But Eisner was necessarily received by his new colleagues with caution and some suspicion. "We have opportunists enough at *Vorwärts*," August Bebel confided to Adler in October of 1899, "and the intellectual leader of the editorial staff, Eisner, unfortunately does not have the requisite knowledge of party history and theory; otherwise he would be a first-rate man."[21]

When Liebknecht died in August 1900, Eisner was granted

---

[21] Friedrich Adler (ed.), *Victor Adler. Briefwechsel mit August Bebel und Karl Kautsky* (Vienna, 1954), 283, 329. See the personal recollections of Friedrich Stampfer, *Erfahrungen und Erkenntnisse* (Cologne, 1957), 73-74, and Philip Scheidemann, *Memoiren eines Sozialdemokraten* (2 vols.; Dresden, 1921), I, 57-58. It was Scheidemann who introduced Eisner to Liebknecht.

several weeks of leave and given the assignment of writing his mentor's "official" biography. The task was especially delicate at that time, since no biography of a major party figure could ignore the internal schism of the SPD, recently widened and dramatized by the publication of Eduard Bernstein's *Evolutionary Socialism*. The effect of Bernstein's book, as Eisner's own career demonstrates, was not so much to introduce something new to the revisionist debate as to force the antagonists to take an unequivocal public stand—or at least to derive a plausible theory of reconciliation between reformist tactics and revolutionary objectives.[22] Eisner's essay, completed and published before the end of the year, was therefore both an exercise in hagiography and a statement of his personal position in the ideological controversy.

Eisner's treatment of Liebknecht showed that nine months in prison had done nothing to alter his views. He argued that there had developed two parallel but "irreconcilible and unbridgeable" worlds in the nineteenth century: that of the rulers and that of the ruled, of the exploiters and the exploited, the world of Bismarck and the world of Liebknecht. Each had its own history. The one was well known, full of courts and kings, diplomats and wars; the other remained still to be written. When it was—and Eisner saw his own sketch as a foreword—the past century would be seen in reality as "a time of preparation" for the great age of the proletariat, of which Liebknecht was the prophet. As such, Liebknecht had been the true mediator of Marxist teaching; above all, he had learned from Marx not to be deceived by the "concessions" bequeathed by Bismarck to the workers. Unlike more popular leaders such as Lassalle and von Schweitzer, Liebknecht had remained uncompromising in his "opposition against the

---

[22] On the course of the debate immediately following the appearance in 1899 of Bernstein's *Die Voraussetzungen des Sozialismus und die Aufgaben der Sozialdemokratie* (12th thousand; Stuttgart, 1906), see Carl Schorske, *German Social Democracy 1905-1917* (Cambridge, Mass., 1955), 16-24.

Prussian dictatorship." In recalling Liebknecht's famous observation that the Reichstag was the "fig leaf of absolutism," Eisner charged him with one tactical error: as a bitter critic of three-class voting he had at first opposed any parliamentary participation by the Socialists, not realizing that universal suffrage might eventually be used to turn out Bismarck and to further the proletarian cause. Liebknecht was later able to recognize and correct his mistake, since "his viewpoint rested on completely *correct* premises—only the conclusion was false." Eisner emphasized that Liebknecht's strength derived from his recognition that "politics is a science, in accordance with strict rules and laws," and that this enabled him to combat with equal vigor "pseudo-radical obscurities" and "momentary real-political impulses."[23]

Among the verbiage one could see that Eisner framed his treatment of Liebknecht so as to reject Bernstein's revision of Marxism without, however, identifying Liebknecht—or himself—with the faction of radicals. In point of view Eisner stood closest to the ideological patriarch of German Socialism, Karl Kautsky, who had responded to Bernstein's challenge by urging the party to keep a free hand and to reckon "with crisis as with prosperity, with reaction as with revolution, with catastrophes as with slow peaceful development."[24] During the next few years Eisner apparently came to see himself as Kautsky's counterpart, using his daily forum at *Vorwärts* to comment on the practical aspects of current events and, as a rule, leaving the more theoretical issues for Kautsky's *Neue Zeit*. But the distinction was artificial and impossible to maintain. Moreover, Kautsky never reciprocated

[23] *Wilhelm Liebknecht*, passim. This was probably Eisner's most popular writing; a second and somewhat lengthier edition was published in 1906. He also gained some attention by his caustic attack on "the Russification of official Germany" in *Königsberg. Der Geheimbund des Zaren* (Berlin, 1904).

[24] Karl Kautsky, *Bernstein und das sozialdemokratische Programm. Eine Antikritik* (Stuttgart, 1899), 166.

Eisner's estimation of their relationship, although he did initially welcome Eisner's cooperation. The first serious personal strain between the two men appeared in 1904, and it was Kautsky's subsequent abandonment of Eisner which precipitated the latter's dismissal from his editorial post during the "*Vorwärts* conflict" of 1905. This requires a brief explanation.

After the passing of Wilhelm Liebknecht, Eisner had continued as the actual manager of *Vorwärts* even though the title of editor-in-chief was formally withheld. With his patron gone, Eisner's place was no longer secure; and his position was made all the more precarious by the fact that, of the ten other members on the editorial board, five were reformers and five radicals. He had to suffer, in addition, the constant surveillance and frequent criticism of the party's executive committee in Berlin.[25] Even such correct parliamentarians as August Bebel tended to be strong programmatic radicals and to let Eisner know about it. Many party officials shared Bebel's misgivings about Eisner's competence and considered him excessively belletristic in editorial policy and performance. Consequently, emboldened by the electoral success of 1903 when the SPD amassed eighty-one seats in the Reichstag, the radicals determined to acquire control of the party's press. From their stronghold at the *Leipziger Volkszeitung* they mounted an attack against Eisner's administration at *Vorwärts* and began to agitate for a realignment of the editorial board.[26] Thus Eisner was already in a difficult situation when he became entangled in an unanticipated quarrel with Karl Kautsky.

[25] Eisner's reputation was damaged when he decided to print a charge of homosexuality brought against Friedrich Alfred Krupp. When Krupp was found dead "of a heart attack" on the day following the appearance of the article, Eisner fell into serious trouble even with his own associates. Only a blustering assault on *Vorwärts* by the Kaiser himself caused the SPD leaders to close ranks in support of their editor. Stampfer, *Erfahrungen und Erkenntnisse*, 80-81.

[26] *Ibid.*, 98-100.

Eisner and Kautsky had been on cordial but never familiar terms since the beginning of their correspondence about the turn of the century. Eisner often requested and sometimes received items from Kautsky for publication in *Vorwärts*, and he usually deferred to the opinions of his senior colleague. On one occasion, however, Eisner chose to differ. At the congress of the Second International in Amsterdam during the summer of 1904, Bebel delivered an address which was contrued by some delegates as evidence that the German Socialists preferred a monarchical form of government to a republic. He was thereupon defended in *Neue Zeit* by Kautsky, who argued that Bebel had intended no such thing and that the SPD obviously regarded a republic to be more desirable than a monarchy, since the class struggle was "most sharply and most clearly expressed" in the former. By taking exception to this view in *Vorwärts*, Eisner presumed not only to contradict Kautsky but to interpret Bebel:

> It could appear as if Bebel actually held the opinion that the classes do not come into such immediate and brutal contact in a monarchy as in a republic. Such opinions . . . Bebel neither has nor can have. . . . In no republic, therefore, is the class struggle more brutal and at the same time more absurd than in monarchical Prussia and monarchical Saxony.[27]

The issue began here and ended some months later with the question of whether Eisner could insult Kautsky in print with

[27] "Sozialdemokratie und Staatsform. Eine öffentliche Diskussion zwischen Kurt Eisner und Karl Kautsky" (1904), *Gesammelte Schriften*, I, 285-325. Eisner covered his reply with a personal letter in which he apologized for the necessity of public contradiction: "No one can sympathize with you more deeply than I that you wish to pursue science rather than polemic." Eisner to Kautsky, 31 Aug. 1904. This is taken from a file of Eisner's letters in the Kautsky Archive at the Internationaal Instituut voor Sociale Geschiedenis in Amsterdam (hereafter cited as IISG Amsterdam), "Briefe an Kautsky," D/X, No. 148.

impunity. It was soon apparent that he could not. Kautsky broke off all public exchange with Eisner and their personal correspondence perceptibly cooled.[28] In July of 1905 Kautsky wrote in confidence to Victor Adler that "the present editorship [of *Vorwärts*] is a cancer. Since I cannot reform it, there is nothing left but to discredit it."[29]

Kautsky hardly needed to raise his hand. When Eisner opposed radical demands for a mass strike in sympathy for the 1905 revolution in Russia, a renewed effort was made to force him out. In November the party's executive committee requested the resignation of two reformers from Eisner's editorial board. He and the others drew the only possible conclusion, and the "noble six" (as Bebel derisively called them) resigned at once.[30] For Eisner this marked the abrupt termination of one career and the eventual beginning of another.

Eisner in Bavaria

It is clear that for more than a decade Kurt Eisner had been undergoing an "inner migration" from Prussia. Now, as he was out of work and out of favor with the Social Democratic Party, there was nothing to hold Eisner in Berlin except some unfinished manuscripts, family obligations, and his severely abraded pride. After November of 1905 it took him barely a year to divest himself of these and, alone, to board a train for the South.

[28] "You are no longer suited to be the eulogist of my humble person." Eisner to Kautsky, 14 Nov. 1905, *ibid.*, No. 157.

[29] F. Adler (ed.), *Victor Adler*, 464.

[30] Stampfer, *Erfahrungen und Erkenntnisse*, 109-112. With some reservation, Schorske (*German Social Democracy*, 70-72) classifies Eisner as a revisionist and says that he was forced to resign because of the strike issue. Vorländer (*Kant und Marx*, 218-221) insists that Eisner was "by no means" a revisionist at the time and emphasizes his isolation in the ideological dispute as the basic reason for his resignation. Lichtheim (*Marxism*, 293-295) attempts a reconciliation of these views, but fails to weight sufficiently Eisner's personal altercation with Kautsky.

To Eisner's credit one must say that he did not allow his intense feeling of rejection to express itself in petty recriminations against his former colleagues. He had, after all, the satisfaction of believing that his career had been sacrificed for a principle, and no other belief is quite so conducive to an attitude of offended noblesse. The principle, of course, was his opposition to the Prussian ruling system, whose machinations during the Moroccan Crisis of 1905, he believed, had already confronted Europe more than once with "the immediate danger of war."[31] One of Eisner's frustrations during his last months in Berlin was to be deprived of an accessible forum for his written words, so that he was forced for the first time in his life to attempt public lecturing, an effort which brought him neither a gratifying response nor adequate remuneration. Under this stress the last bond snapped: when Eisner finally departed in 1907 he left his wife and five children behind. Whether he initially intended to send for them is uncertain; in any case he never did so, and by autumn of the following year he had broken off correspondence.[32]

It was perhaps the dominant fact of Eisner's later life that his self-imposed "exile" after the *Vorwärts* conflict was the consequence not of a diminished enthusiasm for German Social Democracy, but of an intensified disaffection for the

[31] Eisner had his charges printed as *Der Sultan des Weltkrieges. Ein marokkanisches Sittenbild deutscher Diplomatenpolitik* (Berlin, 1906), but most of the copies were not even distributed at the time. His claim that this was the first attempt by a German Socialist to relate "the *concrete* events of foreign policy" is upheld by Schorske, *German Social Democracy*, 71. Eisner also managed to have published some children's stories for adults, *Feste der Festlosen* (Dresden, 1906), in which he satirized the inequities of Wilhelmian society and justice.

[32] For a kaleidoscopic revelation of Eisner's family life, see "Abschied/Sieben Briefe an eine Freundin" and "Sinnenspiel/Aus einem Tagebuch," published from Eisner's personal "Nachlass" by Erich Knauf, *Welt werde froh!* (Berlin, 1929), 45-137. Knauf's editorial essay is unhelpful: "Kurt Eisner in seinen Werken," *ibid.*, 205-213.

Prussian state. This can be documented from a lengthy account of German history in the Napoleonic era which he delivered to the printer some time before Christmas of 1906. Its subsequent publication coincided with Eisner's departure from Berlin and showed how completely he had managed to sublimate a private hurt into a public issue. "The Prussian state pursues one single purpose: to forward the crudest material power of the Crown and the ruling Junker class in every way, unrestrained by moral scruples, national considerations, or cultural ideals."[33] As this quotation indicates, Eisner was far more interested in delivering a commentary on the politics of William II than of Frederick William III. It was not only that Eisner repeatedly insisted on the parallel of certain characters and events. His central thesis was that Germany's entire political and social structure had remained substantially unchanged throughout the nineteenth century because of the survival of Prussian absolutism after Napoleon's defeat. Eisner's history was therefore both a historical parable and an undisguised political philippic against "the Prison-State of Patriarchalism."[34] In addition, it enabled Eisner to add a last word in his unfortunate debate with Karl Kautsky on the issue of *Staatsform* in Social Democratic theory. Although the formal label given to a government was certainly inconsequential, Eisner argued, the inner character of a ruling system could not be irrelevant. Indeed, "thus considered, the form of the state is everything: it is the coercive power under which the social class struggle is carried out."

[33] *Das Ende des Reiches* (Berlin, 1907), 71-72. While still an editor of *Vorwärts* in 1905 Eisner had received an assignment to gather a collection of documents on Napoleonic Germany. After his resignation he converted this into a full-scale narrative, which his former employers published in spite of the factional dispute in the Party.

[34] This chapter title ostensibly referred to Prussia as of 1806, although Eisner frequently neglected to use the past tense. He surely deceived no one in characterizing Frederick William III as "the most utter human insignificance combined with unlimited, uninhibited omnipotence." *Ibid.*, 219.

Eisner was attempting to make two points: first, that the retarded development of the Prussian state and the simultaneous rise of German Socialism had made a direct confrontation of these two forces unavoidable, obviating the necessity for an intermediate stage of bourgeois revolution; and, secondly, that the lamentable outcome of a century ago might be repeated if the approaching realization of revolutionary ideals was again perverted by dynastic military ambitions.[35] Eisner left Prussia fearful of war, scornful of the monarchy, and apprehensive for the future of Social Democracy.

When he crossed into Bavaria in 1907 Eisner was forty years old, a small man with wispy, light brown hair, steel-rimmed glasses, and a Berlin accent; he was balding noticeably above a high forehead, and his reddish beard was already streaked with gray. Except for the few years in Marburg (when he was never far removed anyway) he had experienced very little of life outside the limits of Berlin. Now he came to Nuremberg, at the time a provincial capital of 300,000 in the midst of the Franconian countryside, a center for much of northern Bavaria's export trade and light industry. Here he accepted a position as political columnist and editor of the *Fränkische Tagespost*. Eisner sometimes dramatized to himself the notion of beginning a new life in a foreign land. If this was unduly romantic, he was certainly a long way from Berlin. While delivering a speech on "the religion of Socialism" in a predominantly Roman Catholic village near Nuremberg, he felt "depressed by the strangeness of these listeners." He was initiated into the working conditions of Bavaria's handicraft and primitive industry; after visiting a small mirror factory in Fürth he was moved to write an article on the "monstrosities of capitalism" and the need for "radical change." He was appalled by the inadequacy of rural schools and the cultural innocence of the Bavarian workers and peasants.[36]

[35] *Ibid.*, iii-viii, 127.
[36] "Kommunismus des Geistes" (May 1908), "Religion des Sozial-

Meanwhile, he set out to make his newspaper "an organ of international political enlightenment," a policy which pleased neither the provinciality of the editorial board nor the scepticism of several Social Democratic officials. While attending the 1908 party convention of the SPD in Leipzig he was lampooned by the editor of the *Leipziger Volkszeitung*, Paul Lensch, as a prophet of doom.[37] Shaken by reverberations back in Nuremberg, he was at the point of resigning when the Bosnian Crisis in October brought him some exoneration and a brief reprieve. But as the crisis passed his stock dropped again. After acquiring Bavarian citizenship he left the *Tagespost* in 1910 and moved to Munich, to try his hand once more as a free-lance writer. There he settled with Else Belli, the daughter of an old Socialist campaigner, in a tiny cottage near the Waldfriedhof in Gross-Hadern, a twenty-minute trolley-ride from downtown Munich.[38]

Eisner was back in his element: the big city. In Munich he discovered that the stories of southern *Gemütlichkeit* were only slightly exaggerated, and he found the city both lively and tolerant. Above all, the political atmosphere was congenial. Not only could he enjoy as a journalist the admirable Bavarian tradition of laxity in censorship, but he felt personally at ease with the citizenry's general attitude of good-natured hostility toward all things Prussian—even though, on occasion, that included himself. Nor was it difficult for Eisner

ismus" (Autumn 1908), "Die ewigen Arbeiter" (1909), *Gesammelte Schriften*, II, 15-38, 70-85.

[37] Eisner was still vulnerable because of the *Vorwärts* affair: see the letter from Victor Adler to Bebel (Aug. 1908) in which the former charged that Eisner "doesn't have a nose for what is rotten in the South. . . ." F. Adler (ed.), *Victor Adler*, 489. Eisner's own commentary on this incident was written in September 1918. *Gesammelte Schriften*, I, 330.

[38] Else Belli had been Eisner's colleague at the *Fränkische Tagespost*. Since his first wife refused a divorce at that time, Eisner and Fräulein Belli were not legally married until 1918. Schade, *Kurt Eisner*, 107.

to fall into step with the reformist tradition of Bavarian Socialism. He managed to win an assignment from the Party's executive committee to report on parliamentary affairs. Eisner's apprenticeship in Bavarian politics was thus completed in the press-box of the Landtag building in the Prannerstrasse, where he was often obliged to witness and comment on the daily debates. This activity, coupled with his considerable experience in Berlin, soon gave him a certain expertise and led to his appointment as a political editor with the *Münchener Post* (the Bavarian counterpart of *Vorwärts*), for which he also served as drama critic. After years of opposing three-class voting in Prussia, he naturally supported the agitation of Bavarian Socialists for a reform of their Landtag (Eisner favored complete abolition of the Upper House); and, as a confirmed Junker-baiter, he began to direct his attacks and his vocabulary against alleged collusion of Bavarian aristocracy with the "Black International."[39]

Still, it would be misleading to exaggerate the facility of Eisner's acclimatization in Munich, or to assume that he readily adopted the views of Bavarian particularism. Eisner always accepted and supported German unity, even when he most adamantly resented its ruling authority. A fifty-page essay which he published at this time on "the tragi-comedy of German Liberalism" illustrates the point very well. One of Eisner's concluding sentences might have been written by the most ardent Bavarian separatist: "the transgression of the Main border on the way to German unity could only have had the purpose of also establishing the hegemony of Prussia in the South." Yet the purpose of this essay was not to challenge the validity of Bismarck's accomplishment, but rather to criticize his methods, the spineless capitulation of his political opponents, and the authoritarian nature of Prussian domination. Bismarck's deceit was in duping the Liberals, not in coaxing the Bavarians. And the alternative to a Bismarckian

[39] "Die hohen Stühle" (1911) and "Hertling" (1913), *Gesammelte Schriften*, I, 481-508.

Germany was now a Socialist Germany, not a divided Germany. It is fair to add that this probably represented the majority view of Bavarian Socialism, as later events were to indicate.[40]

Moreover, as one might expect, Eisner never really entered the inner circle of Social Democratic leadership in Munich. He was too much the Bohemian, too much the outsider to be accepted as a party regular. He seemed to have all of the obvious attributes of an inept intellectual in politics: a didactic and sometimes patronizing moral tone, a concern for phrases rather than precincts, an inclination to scribble notes at random rather than to put away information systematically in an office file. Nor was he better suited, so far as anyone could have imagined, to be a popular political figure. In Bavaria he would never be taken for anything but a Berliner and, of course, a Jew. There was no chance of his sharing the conviviality or local humor of the average Bavarian party functionary. And his interests remained more cosmopolitan. In the late summer of 1910, for example, he traveled to Copenhagen for a congress of the Second International; there he admired the remarkable assimilation of Scandinavian Socialism, renewed his acquaintance with Jean Jaurès, and reported to his readers in Bavaria on the striking contrast between the stuffiness of Prussia and the "joy and freedom" of Denmark. He continued to follow the details of international diplomacy, and his writings were still punctuated by "inside" references to Prussian politics.[41]

---

[40] "Die Tragikomödie des deutschen Liberalismus" (1910), *ibid.*, 342-405.

[41] "Kopenhagen" (Sept. 1910), *ibid.*, II, 141-148. Jaurès had visited Eisner in Nuremberg in 1907 after the Socialist congress in Stuttgart, and the two agreed to meet again at a congress which was to have been held in Vienna in 1914. Examples of Eisner's pointedly anti-Prussian articles are "Chefredakteur Wilhelm" (Aug. 1910), "Die Meineidslinde von Essen" (Feb. 1911), "Dynastische Geschichtsauffassung" (Mar. 1911), and "Die Kabinettsorder von 1820" (Jan. 1914), *ibid.*, I, 421-431, 463-466, 509-520.

At the same time, Eisner's allegiance to the Social Democratic Party in Bavaria was never in question before 1914. He had first come to the attention of party leaders such as Adolf Müller (publisher of the *Münchener Post*) and Erhard Auer by denouncing the "personal regime" of the Kaiser at a party convocation in Munich in 1908, and there is no evidence of any altercation in the years immediately following. It was neither intended nor construed as a sign of defection when Eisner publicly criticized the Party's executive group for its placid support of "German interests" during the second Moroccan Crisis of 1911.[42] And in the next year, when he became alarmed by rumors of Russian military preparations in the Balkans, he himself began to warn of a possible attack on Germany from the East and to raise the issue of a legitimate national self-defense. Like most Socialists he was paralyzed by the news from Sarajevo. On July 27, 1914, he joined in a protest meeting and insisted that war could still be averted. But he was convinced that Russian mobilization had forced Germany to the brink, and he made no objection on August 4 when he learned that all nine of the Bavarian Socialist delegates in the Reichstag had voted with the SPD majority in support of war credits.[43] By the time the Great War came, then, Eisner had developed a habit of dissent, but not an attitude of revolution.

"Now Tsarism has attacked Germany," Eisner wrote in the first days of August 1914; "now we have no choice, now there is no looking back." But it was not long before he did look back and reconsider his spontaneous support of the po-

---

[42] "Aus der Panther-Zeit" (1911), *ibid.*, 467-480. See Schade, *Kurt Eisner*, 29-30. One of Eisner's many essays indicting the Pan-German League and the influential business interests behind German colonial adventure was later published in pamphlet form as *Treibende Kräfte* (Berlin, 1915).

[43] *MP*, 29 July 1914, No. 173. See Fechenbach, *Der Revolutionär*, 8-11, and Schade, *Kurt Eisner*, 33-35.

litical and military system he had so long opposed. In mid-December he published an article placing himself on record against Chancellor von Bethmann-Hollweg's explanation of the invasion of Belgium, that "necessity knows no law." Eisner's comparison of the German *White Book* and the Belgian *Gray Book* also convinced him that the Russian armies had not been fully mobilized until the last day of July—four days later than he had been led to believe, and (he decided) well after Germany's decision to join the conflict was irrevocable. Eisner concluded that it was actually the German militarists who had forced the issue, "and therewith the total responsibility of Russian mobilization for the outbreak of the war is objectively refuted."[44]

During 1915, therefore, Eisner admitted the necessity "to revise my opinion fundamentally." When he began to write openly of Germany's "aggressive spirit," he was notified by the *Münchener Post* that his political function with the newspaper was terminated, although he might stay on as literary critic. His articles for other journals were repeatedly suppressed by the military censor as harmful to domestic unity and the war effort, and the circulation of his *Arbeiter-Feuilleton* dropped until it was finally discontinued.[45] In effect, the war forced Eisner out of work again and reduced his personal finances to a stringent subsistence. His friends saw him

[44] "Jaurès" (1914) and "Völkerrecht" (1914), *Gesammelte Schriften*, I, 15-51. See Eisner's letter to Wolfgang Heine, 11 Feb. 1915, printed by H. von Weber, "Kurt Eisner," *Der Zwiebelfisch*, X (1919), 75-77. Eisner wrote a full account of his "conversion" in December of 1916 which was not published until after the war: "Die Mobilmachung als Kriegsursache und Anderes," *Unterdrücktes aus dem Weltkrieg* (Munich, 1919), 7-52.

[45] *Ibid.*, 20. The *Feuilleton* was a feature page which Eisner began printing before the war and distributing to various Socialist newspapers for insertion into their regular editions. Fechenbach, *Der Revolutionär*, 13-14. For examples of Eisner's drama critiques during the war, see "Strindberg nach der Höllenfahrt," *Gesammelte Schriften*, II, 327-363.

become "monkish" and "sleepless." From his cottage in the suburbs he often took the long trolley-ride into the city only to pass the day talking politics in a café and then, after stuffing a few provisions into an old rucksack, returned at night. He read incessantly, made notations for a history of the German nobility, and planned a ten-volume anthology of world Socialist literature.[46] Still at loose ends by December of 1916, he organized a small discussion group which began in the following month to meet regularly on Monday evenings at the "Golden Anchor" in the Schillerstrasse. Here a group of about thirty, most of them young, would gather to share their faith in "Socialism as the religion of the proletariat" and to hear Eisner discourse on the news of the week. This was probably the first time in his life, at the beginning of 1917, that Kurt Eisner acquired a personal following, or that he might have been called a political leader.[47]

The precise chronology of Eisner's defection from the Social Democratic majority is much more difficult to fix. It was partly an understandable consequence of his notice from the *Münchener Post* at the end of 1914. But at least one thing seems certain: Eisner's thinking in the war years was dominated more by national than by exclusively Bavarian politics. In evidence of this one can cite a long letter which Eisner sent in December of 1915 to Karl Kautsky. "At present it is

[46] In addition to Fechenbach, sketches have been written by two men who knew Eisner in Munich during the war years: Wilhelm Herzog, "Kurt Eisner," *Menschen denen ich begegnete* (Bern and Munich, 1959), 55-69; and Wilhelm Hausenstein, "Erinnerung an Eisner," *Der neue Merkur*, III (1919), 56-68. An excerpt from Hausenstein's article has been reprinted by Hans Lamm (ed.), *Von Juden in München* (Munich, 1958), 163-165.

[47] Four men have left a personal record of attending Eisner's meetings: Fechenbach, *Der Revolutionär*, 16; Oskar Maria Graf, *Wir sind Gefangene* (Munich, 1927), 437-441, 475; Erich Mühsam, *Von Eisner bis Leviné. Die Entstehung der bayerischen Räterepublik* (Berlin-Britz, 1929), 11; and Ernst Toller, *Eine Jugend in Deutschland* (2nd ed.; Amsterdam, 1936), 98.

impossible to state the truth openly," he wrote, "so I want to ease my conscience in this way." He attempted to persuade Kautsky that a Social Democratic demonstration for peace would serve the interests of the Berlin government so long as Bethmann-Hollweg was not required to define German war aims. "Since he was a prisoner of the war party in the beginning, and after all made a war which he did not want, the Chancellor is now in the clutches of the annexationists," Eisner continued, adding that "all the bourgeois parties (including certain Social Democrats) are annexationist." Any demonstration by the workers could therefore be effective only if directed against the existing regime and if "we establish its responsibility for the beginning and the continuation of the war (for purposes of expansion) and demand a new regime of peace." It followed that such a demonstration must be led by "the Social Democratic *opposition*" with the intention of turning "the *will of the masses against* the ruling war and annexation cliques." Eisner concluded that the SPD had fallen into a state of "anarchy and apathy," and that "minority action" was necessary despite appeals from the Socialist leadership for discipline, since "everyone knows anyway that an unresolved dissension of opinions prevails in the Party. There is no secret to betray."[48]

Eisner's conviction that the Social Democratic majority had become "hardly less than a governmental party" was compounded by 1917 with an increasingly radical denunciation of the government itself. In February of that year he dispatched a blistering protest against the prohibition of still

[48] Eisner to Kautsky, 3 Dec. 1915, IISG Amsterdam, "Briefe an Kautsky," D/X, No. 162. Eisner had resumed the correspondence several months previously by inquiring about the possible publication of an article in Kautsky's *Neue Zeit. Ibid.*, No. 160. Eisner's estimation of the party leadership continued to decline during 1916, and in January of 1917 he joined Kautsky at a conference of the opposition group in Berlin which signaled the beginning of a formal split. See Eugen Prager, *Geschichte der USPD* (Berlin, 1921), 124-131.

another of his articles by the military censor: "Truth is the most valuable of all national possessions. A state, a people, a system, in which the truth is suppressed or does not dare to assert itself, deserves to be destroyed as rapidly and completely as possible."[49] By this time Eisner was aware that the organization of a national protest movement by opposition Socialists was already underway. In the first week of April, financed by collections taken at the Monday evening discussions, he traveled to Gotha to meet with other dissidents from the rest of Germany. It was at this conference, on Easter of 1917, that the Independent Social Democratic Party of Germany was founded to enlist support for a peace without annexation. Eisner then returned to establish an Independent organization in Munich, of which (although he did not choose to be chairman) he became the acknowledged leader.[50]

Eisner now had a party and a program, but scarcely a popular following. Joined by a Social Democratic youth group, the gatherings in the "Golden Anchor" grew in size, but probably never attracted more than a hundred participants. And with state censorship now more tightly enforced, the only means of propaganda was the circulation of illegal pamphlets. When the Independents attempted to hold an open meeting in August, it was forbidden by the Ministry of War, and Eisner was bodily prevented by the police from speaking.[51] If the USP had any effect on Bavarian politics at this

[49] Eisner to the General Command of the First Bavarian Army Corps, 14 Feb. 1917. *Unterdrücktes aus dem Weltkrieg*, 34-37, 53-59.
[50] Fechenbach, *Der Revolutionär*, 18, and Schade, *Kurt Eisner*, 117. Eisner thought the elected leadership should be from the working class: the Munich chairman was therefore Albert Winter. The official program of the USP, of course, contained social and political proposals as well, but the major issue and the common denominator of its membership at that time was the agitation for peace. See Prager, *Geschichte der USPD*, 143-151; Paul Frölich *et al.*, *Illustrierte Geschichte der Deutschen Revolution* (Berlin, 1929), 155-159; and Schorske, *German Social Democracy*, 312-321.
[51] Fechenbach, *Der Revolutionär*, 18.

64

time, it was perhaps in providing an additional inducement for the Majority Socialists to press for parliamentary reform, in an attempt to undercut any popular appeal by the Independents. But with the conclusion of the Landtag debate on December 17, the way to reform was temporarily blocked, and the question of how best to bring effective pressure to bear against the government was reopened. In Bavaria, as elsewhere in Germany, the demand for reform had become entangled and often confused with the agitation for peace. Among Socialist party leaders and trade union representatives there was talk of attempting a general strike, though the executive committees of both the SPD and USP were at first reluctant to express dissatisfaction with a political regime on the home front at the expense of soldiers in the field. Would it not be an act of treason to strike under such conditions? In 1917 there were but few Germans who were prepared to answer in the negative, and Kurt Eisner was now one of them. In mid-December he made a quick trip to Berlin to urge Independent leaders there to hasten the call for a strike. No decision was made, but Eisner felt that a crisis was imminent. Back in Munich for the holiday, he wrote a Christmas note to Karl Kautsky's wife with the rather cheerless greeting: "we are plunging toward the abyss."[52]

There was good reason for a sense of urgency. Having abandoned the hope that Germany might win the war with its underwater fleet, General Ludendorff and his staff were already making preparations for a vast spring offensive, a last bid to drive Entente armies off the continent by working a military "wonder" in the West. With the success of the Bolshevik Revolution in November and the beginning of serious bargaining with the Russians at Brest Litovsk a month later, the prospects of another major campaign in France seemed assured—unless a significant change in Germany's

[52] Eisner to Luise Kautsky, 25 Dec. 1917, IISG Amsterdam, "Briefe an Kautsky," D/X, No. 167.

internal political circumstances should intervene. From the Reichstag and the government of Count Hertling nothing could be expected. The only possibility was direct action by industrial workers in the large urban areas. The signal came from outside Germany. At Brest Litovsk Trotsky was told bluntly that Germany had won the war in the East and that the settlement with Soviet Russia would be drafted accordingly. Thus on January 12 the last conceivable illusion that Ludendorff might settle for a peace without annexation was demolished. The news from Brest Litovsk affected Austria-Hungary first of all: four days later thousands of laborers in Vienna, Budapest, and other cities went out on strike, in effect against the annexationist policy of the German government. When the Habsburg authorities (who were equally apprehensive that negotiations might collapse because of excessive German demands) publicly endorsed the peace resolution drafted by the Vienna Workers' Council —and promised, in addition, to grant parliamentary reforms —the strike ended with an immense victory for the workers. Despite the military censorship, news of this success spread rapidly in Germany and aroused among the adherents of Social Democracy a popular enthusiasm which the leadership could not ignore. While the Majority Party still hesitated, the Independent leaders' resistance to the strike movement buckled. For the second time within a month Eisner went back to Berlin and now confirmed that a general strike was to be called in the latter part of January.[53]

The initial reaction of government officials in Bavaria was evidently (like that of the Austrians) to smother the protest with a carpet of tolerance. At the meeting in the Schillerstrasse on Monday, January 21, in the presence of police agents, Eisner announced that the ultimate intention of the

[53] Fechenbach, *Der Revolutionär*, 21. See Rosenberg, *Die Entstehung*, 190-196. For the whole question of the January strike, consult *Die Ursachen des deutschen Zusammenbruchs im Jahre 1918: Das Werk des Untersuchungsausschusses*, 4. Reihe, V, 103-108.

strike would be "to overturn the monarchy, and not only the Prussian, but to bring down militarism entirely."[54] On the following Sunday Eisner was permitted to speak in public at the Munich Colosseum to a crowd of over two hundred persons, again under police observation. Here the difference between Berlin and Munich was immediately evident. Being virtually unknown himself and having little radical tradition or organization behind him, Eisner was forced to plead for a massive demonstration as soon as possible—he could not simply announce one for the next day. The Majority Socialists in Bavaria had as yet given no indication that they would follow the precedent of their national leadership by joining the strike on the condition that it be brief and peaceful (and therefore not disruptive to the war effort). Eisner was apparently still counting on the cooperation of the SPD as he presented essentially the same moderate program upon which the two Socialist factions had agreed in Berlin and elsewhere:

1. immediate peace without annexation;
2. freedom of press and assembly;
3. termination of martial law;
4. demilitarization of industrial plants;
5. release of Karl Liebknecht and other political prisoners.

It is notable that Eisner's appeal contained neither a demand for parliamentary reform nor any hint of plans for the socialization of property or industry. At the conclusion of this assembly he was approached by a delegation of workers from the Krupp factory and invited to speak at a meeting the following day. This was the first direct political contact which Eisner and the Bavarian USP had with representatives of organized labor in Munich.[55]

Now events moved rapidly. On January 28 nearly half a

---

[54] See the detailed anonymous article based on police reports, "Vorbereitung des Münchener Munitionsarbeiterstreiks vom Januar 1918 (Nach unveröffentlichten Geheimakten)," *Süddeutsche Monatshefte*, XXI (1924), 26-32.

[55] Fechenbach, *Der Revolutionär*, 21-23.

million workers went on strike in Berlin; they were followed by thousands of others in the great industrial centers. In one of Munich's large beer-halls Eisner challenged an assembled crowd to join in the national demonstration, but speakers from the SPD were able to stall the proceedings long enough to prevent a vote. On the next morning, however, the Krupp workers balloted in favor of a strike and adopted a resolution drafted and signed by Eisner which concluded: "The struggle for peace has begun. Workers of the world, unite!" On January 30 Eisner met with labor representatives from the Rapp Motor Works and, in the evening, with a group of typesetters. He spent that night at a hotel in Munich in order to be on hand in a beer-hall early in the morning of January 31 to greet a gathering of jubilant workers. This was to be the first day of the general strike in Bavaria. Beside Eisner on the speaker's platform sat Erhard Auer, present but silent: the Majority Socialists had finally been left with no choice but the reluctant acceptance of what they preferred to call a "peaceful demonstration." At one o'clock a silent parade of Krupp workers filed through the streets of Munich. Auer was meanwhile speaking in the Mathäserbräu to another meeting of the still uncommitted laborers from the Rapp Motor Works. When he attacked Eisner as a "visionary" with "illusions of grandeur," the latter was quickly called in from the streets to confront him. In this first political duel with Auer, Eisner held the advantage and was able to win a vote in favor of the strike. A short time later he managed to stage the same performance before workers from the Bavarian Aircraft Plant. At the end of the day an estimated eight thousand workers had pledged to join in the demonstration—an inconsiderable number compared with Berlin, but a significant increase over the attendance in Munich's "Golden Anchor" a few weeks before.[56]

[56] *Ibid.*, 23-27. Eisner's own record of these last days before his imprisonment was published posthumously as "Mein Gefängnistage-

In the evening Eisner missed the last trolley out to his home in Gross-Hadern. He therefore went back to the downtown hotel where he was arrested a short time later.

Eisner was forced to spend the next eight-and-a-half months in jail. Confined at first in the Neudeck prison on the outskirts of Munich, he found himself virtually cut off from events which he had for years followed with a journalist's passion for detail. Besides letter-writing and the daily privilege of reading a newspaper, Eisner passed the spring months by editing his professional papers for publication and by completing a symbolic drama which he had begun exactly twenty years earlier in the Prussian penitentiary at Plötzensee near Berlin. Imprisonment brought at least one consolation: he now had an opportunity, rare for a man in his early fifties, for reading and retrospection. By mid-April he was still occupied and in good enough spirits to joke by mail with Karl Kautsky about a note in *Le Temps* reporting his own death. He attempted to resume work on his history of the German nobility, but soon discovered that he was impossibly hampered by the lack of available books and bibliography. He grew increasingly impatient as the summer came and he was transferred, without any notification of a change in his status, from Neudeck to cell 70 of the state prison at Stadelheim.[57] "I will soon have been sitting for half a year," he complained to Kautsky in July, "but the preliminary investigation is . . .

---

buch," *Die Menschheit*, XV (1928), 19, 27, 38, 48, 57. See Schade, *Kurt Eisner*, 45-50, for a careful reconstruction of the chronology and a brief account of the entirely peaceful demonstration in Nuremberg, the only other Bavarian city directly affected by the national strike.

[57] Eisner to Kautsky, 16 Apr. and 5 May 1918, IISG Amsterdam, "Briefe an Kautsky," D/X, Nos. 168-169. Cell 70 was later to be occupied by Eisner's own assassin, Count Arco-Valley, and in 1923 by a young putschist, Adolf Hitler. Ernst Röhm was shot in the same cell in 1934. Erwein von Aretin, *Krone und Ketten* (Munich, 1955), 229-230.

still not formally completed." He began to age noticeably and to suffer fits of depression.[58] While writing a letter in August he had to apologize for the shakiness of his script, due to the "few heavy sighs of a shut-in." With the few books which he was allowed to obtain he undertook (as he said) to follow the "Hegel-tracks" of Karl Marx. Reading in Franz Mehring's recently published biography of Marx, he lingered over the first years of exile in London. "Is not at last the politician, the fighter, the revolutionary stranded?" Eisner asked himself. "Was it not after all an abortive existence? Was it worthwhile in a stupid world to assume the unyielding task of a revolutionary and never to relent?"[59]

In spite of his recurrent self-doubt, Eisner clearly thought not. He saw Marx's life as a splendid triumph over adversity, and he liked to imagine himself as he imagined Marx: "the perfect unity of thought and deed, research and action . . . fighter and thinker." Although he had never acquired much of a taste or talent for theoretical dogmatics, Eisner was more convinced than ever that his was the *true* Marx (invariably the conviction of a party heretic). He still believed that "substantially Marx belongs to Kant," although he was now more willing to concede the importance of Hegelian influence— "much stronger than one generally assumes"—on Marx's method and style.[60] But it would be a mistake to read undue significance into such statements, or to make of Eisner a resourceful and commanding intellectual figure. For all his talk of the "scientific" aspects of Marxist thought, he had never demonstrated more than a rudimentary appreciation of eco-

[58] Eisner to Kautsky, 19 July 1918, IISG Amsterdam, "Briefe an Kautsky," D/X, No. 170. Compare the photographs of Eisner taken in January and October of 1918, reproduced in the slender selection from his literary writings, *Wachsen und Werden* (Leipzig, 1926), 61, 69.

[59] "Marx-Feier" (1918), *Gesammelte Schriften*, I, 221-239. Eisner to Kautsky, 13 Aug. 1918, IISG Amsterdam, "Briefe an Kautsky," D/X, No. 171.

[60] *Gesammelte Schriften*, II, 165.

nomics and economic theory. And, after all, only in a very general sense could his political views be identified as either Marxist or Kantian: he accepted the common notion that society was divided into "two armed camps," and he shared the fundamentally uncomplicated belief that society was wrong and that it ought somehow to be set right. There was little that was distinctive about Eisner's blend of ethical socialism and rationally qualified pacifism. He was probably justified in holding that it was he who had remained in the mainstream of German Social Democracy while the Majority Party had drifted in the currents of war.[61]

An indication of Eisner's orthodoxy was his reconciliation with Karl Kautsky after 1914. Although their correspondence remained on a formal basis, Eisner was again able on occasion to use the salutation "dear friend" instead of the customary "distinguished colleague." In editing the record of the 1904 dispute between the two men, Eisner could write in his introduction that "there exists between Kautsky and me agreement on almost all questions of political theory and practice." This assertion in 1918 serves both to locate Eisner on the political spectrum and to substantiate that the wartime schism of German Social Democracy by no means always followed the lines of the revisionist controversy a decade before. With the appearance of Independent Socialism and the Spartacist League, the word "radical" assumed a somewhat different connotation—though it should be specified that neither Eisner nor Kautsky deserved this label at any time, as Eisner's own writings and Kautsky's well-known polemic with Lenin made adequately clear.[62] The real basis

[61] This is not to deny that the SPD had already given an indication of the drift from its professed principles even before the war. "To one who has followed the evolution of Social Democracy through the prewar decade, the vote for war credits on 4 August 1914 is but the logical end of a clear line of development." Schorske, *German Social Democracy*, 285. But see A. Joseph Berlau, *The German Social Democratic Party, 1914-1921* (New York, 1949), 67-69.

[62] *Gesammelte Schriften*, I, 285. Despite the striking exceptions of men like Eisner, Kautsky, and Bernstein, the generalization stands

71

of the personal rapprochement between Eisner and Kautsky was an instinctive "centrist" position which they had shared from the beginning, even when they were at the point of mutual insult. If there was a valid distinction to be drawn between them, it derived from Kautsky's natural and more thoroughly developed internationalism. Although Eisner frequently made a display of his concern for the interests of the working classes of other nations, particularly in France, the truth was that his knowledge and conception of Socialism were indigenously German. Moreover, Eisner lacked both Kautsky's acumen as a scholar, with which he might have remedied this deficiency, and his talent for circumlocution, with which he might have made it less evident.

One further consideration must be added: the emotional stress of Eisner's prolonged imprisonment. He was now one of the few German Socialists in Bavaria who had the qualifications and the sentiments of a genuine political martyr. His political efforts had apparently ended no more gloriously than his career as a journalist. By September of 1918 Eisner still had every reason to expect that he would be kept under arrest at least for the duration of the war. One can only surmise the intensity of his frustration from the scattered notes and letters which he wrote in prison, and from the text of the experimental drama which he completed just before his transfer from Neudeck to Stadelheim. With its allegorical characters, pretentious dialogue, and idealistic theme of a "new humanity," *The Trial of the Gods* was a typical example of early German Expressionism. As a critic of the theater Eisner had gained some reputation for skill and discrimination, but as a creative writer he has remained deservedly unknown. In spite of its obvious literary flaws, however, his play may be considered as a grotesque autobiographical summary of his career and his political motivation.

---

that most Independents had earlier belonged to the radical wing of the SPD. See Schorske, *German Social Democracy*, 282-284.

Eisner's plot portrayed the opposition of a single man, the uncommonly heroic Guldar, to the naïve and incompetent ruler of an island kingdom, Prince Agab. After ascending the throne, Agab orders his people into a war whose objective he does not understand, against an enemy he does not know. Although stoned for his love of the beautiful Warana (Truth) and initially rejected by the populace, Guldar persists in his attempts to bring enlightenment to the island:

> I leapt upwards,
> Inflamed by a hitherto unfelt power,
> And ran through the streets, crying and exulting:
> "The world is rich! The world is great and bright!
> Dare, brothers, just to live; dare to think.
> To live in spirit and to create through spirit."
> They stared blankly, they smirked, sneered, reviled,
> And baited the enticer and corrupter.
> So I hated each who crossed my path.
> Yet all the more passionately I loved,
> Somewhere in the far reaches, Humanity,
> And saw not one human on earth. . . .[63]

When Guldar openly tries his courage against the power of the monarchy and the guile of Agab's wicked advisers, he is again beset by voices from the crowd: "He was not born on our island. A foreigner!" "He is a fool spurred by illusions of grandeur." Thereupon condemned by Agab to prison, Guldar asks himself if he had not indeed been a fool to flout the ruling system. The military situation meanwhile worsens as news arrives of landings by fresh enemy troops. Before the final act a pantomime takes place in which a young girl dances and the King swaggers to the music of the old Russian "Anthem of the Tsar." The stage fills with workers, whose leader suddenly sets upon the King. As the tune changes into a Slavic revolutionary march, the dancer whirls

[63] *Die Götterprüfung* (Berlin, 1920), 50.

and throws herself into the arms of an approaching worker. The King moves his feet mechanically to the music and is hooted from the stage. The curtain then rises on the last act, in which the people surge around Agab and demand peace. His crafty warlord urges them to have patience and pursue the war to final victory, but the indomitable Guldar appears to sway them to revolution: "The hour questions. The future calls. Truth commands. Idols fall. Gods are storming."[64] Guldar is proclaimed by the people as their true monarch, but he casts Agab's crown into the waves, bids mankind to live in peace, and beckons Warana to wander with him into the heavens.

This was pure melodrama. But these were the images in Kurt Eisner's mind when the unexpected news came that he was to be released from prison.

[64] *Ibid.*, 99, 123-124, 140, and passim.

CHAPTER III

The November Revolution

A COMBINATION of circumstance and calculated maneuver enabled Kurt Eisner to leave Stadelheim on October 14, 1918, and return to Munich. At last surrendering to his prolonged disability, Georg von Vollmar had resigned from public office and requested that he be formally replaced. The man chosen to lead the Social Democratic Party in Bavaria was Erhard Auer who, as Vollmar's administrative assistant, had been his *de facto* successor for some time. It was then a matter of course that Auer should also be selected as the Majority candidate in the by-election to fill Vollmar's vacant seat in the Reichstag. The election was to provide the SPD with an opportunity to win a massive vote of public confidence in its traditional stronghold, Munich's second precinct. In such a test of party prestige there could be little question that Auer would win by a convincing margin. With nothing more to lose than an election, the Independent Socialists nominated Eisner—and then began accusing the regime of blocking the democratic process by keeping in prison a man who, after nearly nine months of "investigation," was still unconvicted of an alleged crime. By deciding to release Eisner, the government hoped to envelop him and his party in an open electoral procedure which was thought to have two distinct advantages: it could be easily supervised, and it was bound to fail.

This was to be but the first in a series of miscalculations which led to the revolution in Bavaria. Behind them all was the same faulty premise: that the situation was well in hand. It was not so much that the authorities underestimated the strength of radical agitation, but they made the more fundamental mistake of confusing the passivity of the populace with loyalty to the status quo. As the crisis approached the regime appeared to take all the proper precautions. Genuine political reforms were debated and enacted, security regulations were tightened, the cooperation of Socialist party and trade union officials was obtained. The Bavarian government faced the possibility of revolution with eyes wide open, and yet there was no more than token resistance when the revolution occurred barely three weeks after Eisner's release from prison.

Reform or Revolt?

Munich was a different city from the one which Eisner had left in January. The confidence and high spirits on the home front which had buoyed Ludendorff's drive in the West had been, like the military offensive, broken. The news of impending defeat and the imminent necessity of seriously compromised negotiations had been taken especially hard by a people long kept ignorant of the facts and then suddenly confronted with them. It was not only a universal weariness with the war effort. "In October of 1918," one Liberal writer admitted, "we finally considered ourselves, *everyone without distinction of party*, deceived and duped." Announcements of the contact between Max von Baden and President Wilson were posted on every street-corner, while in the city's giant beer-halls public debates and sporadic rioting had been touched off by Walther Rathenau's plea for a *levée en masse* to keep German armies in the field. Among the dissatisfied there was open talk of "swindle" and, as officially reported to Berlin, an intensified attitude of "wearied disgust" toward the Empire (*Reichsverdrossenheit*).[1] It was in this atmos-

---

[1] Treutler to Hertling, 1 Sept. 1918, NA Washington, Bayern 50, XV, UM 73/771-773. Ernst Müller-Meiningen, *Aus Bayerns schwersten Tagen* (Berlin and Leipzig, 1924), 24. See Rathenau's speech of 7 Oct. 1918, "Ein dunkler Tag," *Nach der Flut* (Berlin, 1919), 49-51. For the reaction in Munich, see Graf, *Wir sind Gefangene*, 536-537; Bonn, *So macht man Geschichte*, 185-188; and Karl Alexander von Müller, *Mars und Venus. Erinnerungen 1914-1919* (Stuttgart, 1954), 246, 250-253, 257-262.

phere of recurrent discontent that the election was to be contested—and never completed.

To succeed in the gamble which it was admittedly taking by allowing Kurt Eisner to campaign under these circumstances, the Bavarian government was counting heavily on the restraining influence of the Social Democratic leadership. A great deal therefore depended on the personal popularity and political strength of Erhard Auer. In physique, temperament, background, and career, he was abundantly endowed to be Eisner's opposite number. Auer was a big man. He had a huge frame, large hands, and widely set eyes. As a politician he had been able to convert a number of personal misfortunes into political assets. Born illegitimately and raised as an orphan by the township of Passau, he could properly claim to be a true son of Bavaria and an unreserved advocate of social welfare legislation. Precociously concerned with the lot of rural laborers while working as a farmhand, he had attempted at the age of fifteen to form an organization of peasants; for this he received the black mark of a short detentionary sentence in his police dossier, but a bright note of commendation in Socialist hagiography. After serving in the regiment of the Royal Guard, stationed at the *Türkenkaserne* in Munich, he had settled in the capital city to become a salesman, a local politician, and in 1907 a Social Democratic member of the Bavarian Landtag. His career as a party functionary was interrupted by the war, during which he served briefly with infantry forces in Belgium and with the German occupation in France. By 1917 he had returned to Munich and resumed his activities in party and Landtag. There he proved to be more of a stand-in than a real replacement for Vollmar, lacking both the latter's urbanity and his ability as a debater. Yet he soon became the leading spokesman for his faction in the parliament and co-author of the Auer-Süssheim bill for legislative reform. By 1918 he was consequently acknowledged as Vollmar's heir apparent.[2]

[2] See Wilhelm Hoegner, "Erhard Auer," *90 Jahre SPD in München*

On the day before Eisner's release from prison, a convocation of the Bavarian SPD met in Munich. By then it had become acceptable among party officials to speak of "the revolution," although opinions naturally varied as to the meaning of the term. At this meeting the issue was brought into the open by a delegate from Nuremberg, Ernst Schneppenhorst, who openly advocated "the elimination of the monarchy" and indicted the Wittelsbachs along with the Hohenzollerns for prolonging the war. Whereas there was general agreement on the necessity of the Kaiser's abdication, no Majority Socialist had yet dared to suggest in public that the Bavarian King shared equal responsibility and should therefore be forced to relinquish his Crown. In the controversy which followed Erhard Auer raised, as expected, the voice of restraint: "We are living through the greatest revolution which has ever occurred. Only the form is now different; different because other forms are possible . . . through the discipline of the working population, because it is possible to achieve in a legal way that for which we have striven for decades."[3]

Two things were characteristic of this statement, and were to be typical of Auer from this time until the revolution was an accomplished fact: the notion of a gradual and entirely peaceful transition which had already commenced, and an unmistakable ambiguity as to its objective. With his confidence in organization and his repeated appeals to Socialist solidarity, Auer betrayed throughout the persistent mentality of a party functionary. Neither then nor later did he attain

---

(Munich, 1959), 10-11. This sketch is amplified in Hoegner's autobiography, *Der schwierige Aussenseiter. Erinnerungen eines Abgeordneten, Emigranten und Ministerpräsidenten* (Munich, 1959), 17-18.

[3] *Protokoll über die Verhandlungen des 14. Parteitages der Sozialdemokratischen Partei Bayerns am 12. und 13. Oktober 1918 in München*, 165-174. Schneppenhorst was later to become the Bavarian Minister for Military Affairs and a key figure in the proclamation of the Soviet Republic; see Chapter X.

the stature of his predecessor as a leader, and this fact must be put in the balance with others in weighing the reasons for the onset and the course of the revolution.

The program which the Bavarian SPD carried into the electoral campaign directly reflected Auer's personal ambivalence. The Party resolved to support "the transformation of Germany into a *Volksstaat* with complete self-determination of the people in nation, state, and city." Since it was well known that "*Volksstaat*" was the generally accepted Socialist euphemism for a republic, this was presumably a demand for the Kaiser's abdication. But the terms of the statement might have been fulfilled just as well by a constitutional monarchy as by a republic, providing that "the people" so determined; and it was conspicuous that no precise reference was made to the future of the Wittelsbach dynasty. Still more significant was the failure of the SPD to specify what action might be considered within the bounds of legality in case of resistance by the established regime to the proposed "transformation." Means and ends were therefore equally obscured by the phraseology. The same was true of Auer's major campaign addresses. He again referred to "the greatest revolution of world history," and he extolled the discipline with which it was already being accomplished. He spoke grandly for a "peace of understanding" and made a statesmanlike plea for "a regime which is really the representative of the people." He was persistent in his denunciation of "the hegemony of Prussia which . . . was and is the misfortune of Germany." But he wavered between demanding that "the present system must be discarded root and branch" (in reference to Berlin), and cautioning that the SPD was "no organization of dreamers" who expected by force "to make for everyone overnight a heaven out of a vale of tears."[4]

[4] Erhard Auer, *Das neue Bayern. Politische Reden* (Munich, 1919), 9-27. See Hermann Müller-Franken, *Die November Revolution. Erinnerungen* (Berlin, 1928), 11.

Eisner's oratorical performance during the campaign was in consciously studied contrast. After spending several days in seclusion at his cottage in Gross-Hadern, Eisner made his first public appearance on October 23. With his whitened hair long and unkempt, he now had the aspect of a prophet. "You see me just as Stadelheim gave me back to freedom!" He spoke without equivocation of an impending revolution and of the need to overthrow established authority by whatever means were necessary. He compared his personal martyrdom to the well-fed respectability of his political opponent. A vote for Auer, he insisted, would mean a continuation of the war effort and hence a sanction for mass murder. But, he prophesied, "the revolution will put this election to shame." As Eisner made the rounds of the beer-hall gatherings from day to day, it became evident beyond a doubt that he intended Munich, and not just Berlin, to be the capital of a socialistic republic. "The electoral rallies of the USP in which Eisner spoke became propaganda meetings for the coming revolution."[5] By carrying reports of these speeches, in effect, the newspaper press was printing a daily record of seditious threats. It seems incredible that Eisner was not sent straight back to Stadelheim.

The personal relationship and the contrast between Eisner and Auer was to remain a central theme of the revolution in Bavaria. For the time being, as in January, Eisner continued to hold the initiative. So long as the war continued and the fate of the Bavarian monarchy remained unsettled, Eisner's appeal was clear and urgent. Since he was willing to accept, indeed to advocate, both military defeat and the termination of the monarchy, the terms "peace" and "republic" as Eisner used them were largely unambiguous—until they were re-

---

[5] Fechenbach, *Der Revolutionär*, 33; Graf, *Wir sind Gefangene*, 537-538. See Schade, *Kurt Eisner*, 50-52, and Georg Escherich (ed.), *Von Eisner bis Eglhofer. Die Münchener Revolution von November 1918 bis zum Zusammenbruch der Räteherrschaft* (Munich, 1921-1922), No. 1, 13.

alized. Confronted with this, Erhard Auer was necessarily put on the defensive. Nothing would have been more out of keeping with the tradition of the Bavarian SPD than its leader's pose as a radical revolutionary. Eisner represented no established tradition, and it was not difficult for him to hold tradition at fault for every discomfort. But Auer felt that he had a responsibility to more than his own conscience —and his conscience, in any case, was bent on reform rather than revolution.

The question of constitutional reform had already been twice postponed, first by the outbreak of war and again in January of 1918 by the failure of the general strike. During the final year of the war, the momentum of the reform movement was only gradually regained, and not until the first days of November did it culminate in legislative action. Since a belated effort by the "old regime" to assuage public discontent through reform seems to follow so closely the classic pattern of revolutionary development, one is bound to inquire as to its significance in this case.

The heart of the reform issue before January had been the demand to abrogate or drastically abridge the power of the Bavarian Upper House. The Social Democrats were particularly keen on this, but it was they who had suffered most, in a parliamentary sense, from the debacle of the strike; as the other factions saw it, the whole disagreeable affair could be blamed on the failure of the SPD leaders to keep their party membership intact and in line. With the Socialist ranks somewhat in disarray, then, it took the reformers several months to mount another campaign, and not until the middle of April did the constitutional affair again enter "an acute stage."[6] This time the course of reform was set on a new

[6] Treutler to Hertling, 23 Apr. 1918, NA Washington, Bayern 61, VII, ACP 339/583-584. See Gregor Schmitt, "Auf dem Weg zur Revolution von 1918 in Bayern. Parlamentarische Reformversuche

tack. On April 18 the Social Democrats and the Liberals combined to present in the Finance Committee of the Lower House a motion in favor of popular election to that chamber on the basis of proportional representation. Instead of continuing a frontal assault on a prominent bastion of hereditary privilege, the reformers thereby shifted the attack toward what seemed a more vulnerable flank.

The timing could not have been less favorable. The German spring offensive had begun just weeks before and had already opened two wide breaches in the British lines. Ludendorff's troops were threatening Paris and preparing to launch a major offensive in Flanders. It hardly seemed the moment to attach great importance to procedural maneuvers in a committee room of the Bavarian Landtag. Yet the reform proposal did receive due consideration. The arguments against the measure were presented by the leader of the Center Party, Heinrich Held. It was his contention that a system of proportional representation would have two disadvantages: it would destroy the traditional relationship between the various social groups and their parliamentary representatives, and it would consequently tend to place political control in the hands of the professional party politicians. The Center Party was willing to make a concession, however, by permitting the introduction of a proportional system in several of Bavaria's largest cities: on the basis of the 1910 census, one parliamentary representative might be chosen for every 42,000 citizens. Since the Social Democrats were already well represented in these areas anyway, they properly regarded this as falling short of a significant reform and pressed their motion that the arrangement be extended to the entire state. They were, in short, demanding nothing less than a thoroughgoing act of reapportionment to redress the political imbalance between city and countryside. To change the electoral procedure

---

vor der Novemberrevolution," *Zeitschrift für bayerische Landesgeschichte*, XXII (1959), 498-513.

in only a few urban areas would not basically affect the under-representation of the cities in the Landtag, nor would it, of course, pose a threat to the domination of Bavarian politics by the Center Party.

The Bavarian government predictably sided with the latter. Minister of the Interior von Brettreich announced the regime's intention to proceed with utmost caution, on the principle that what is efficacious in a small area might not be suitable for a large one (the inverse of a precept sacrosanct in Bavaria since German unification). He also suggested the danger of defaulting the administration of public affairs to the professional politicians and warned against overweighting the influence of the big cities. The government was therefore prepared to consider the introduction of a proportional system only in "certain electoral districts," although—and this was the clinching argument—it was questionable in the Minister's mind that any constitutional revision should be undertaken in time of war.[7] With that, reform was effectively blocked for a third time, and the matter progressed no further until late in the summer when the first reports arrived of German military setbacks along the Marne.

As political crisis succeeded military crisis, the position of the SPD was progressively strengthened. Thus, the more the Bavarian government was forced to rely on Social Democratic organization for the maintenance of law and order, the more adamant became the Party's demands for constitutional reform. The price of cooperation was concession. Moreover, there was now "entirely outspoken dissatisfaction not only with the Bavarian regime, but also especially with the person of His Majesty the King."[8] The usual charge

[7] Treutler to Hertling, 25 Apr. 1918, NA Washington, Bayern 61, VII, ACP 339/584. *Verhandlungen der Kammer der Abgeordneten des Bayerischen Landtags, Stenographische Berichte*, XIX (27 May–2 Aug. 1918), Nos. 473-476, 203-272. After the defeat of the SPD-Liberal motion, the proposal of the Center Party was adopted.

[8] Treutler to Hertling, 1 Sept. 1918, NA Washington, Bayern 50, XV, UM 73/771-773.

against Ludwig was not that he was responsible for bringing war and disaster close to Bavaria, but that he was powerless to avert them; it was therefore high time that the form of the Bavarian ruling system be brought into line with the reality, and that a parliamentary regime be granted full discretionary powers. Unnerved by the swell of opposition, the government prepared to take the necessary steps to secure the monarchy and to stabilize the regime. On September 2 the King officially requested that reform be enacted and a new coalition cabinet composed to include both the Center and the Social Democratic Party. This announcement preceded by more than a month the formation of a national coalition government in Berlin under Max von Baden. Yet it was not until October 16 that the Bavarian Chamber of Deputies finally met in special session to debate the question of constitutional reform.[9]

In opening the proceedings, Prime Minister von Dandl made it clear that the Crown was merely suggesting reforms which it had long foreseen to conform with the interest and wishes of the Bavarian people. Speaking for the Center Party, Heinrich Held announced that he was prepared to support reform provided that it preserved and indeed strengthened the monarchy. The implication that reform was only to be granted from above, by the grace of the monarchy and for the benefit of the monarchy, aggravated resentment against the regime. Liberal delegates were frankly peeved, and the Social Democrats pointedly refused to participate in inter-party conferences. But such behavior on either side could be explained as a normal part of a negotiating process in which the conclusion was essentially foregone.[10] Through two weeks

[9] Ernst Theo Rohnert et al., Bayern in Geschichte und Gegenwart (Munich, 1956), 175-176.

[10] Treutler to Max von Baden, 26 Oct. 1918, NA Washington, Bayern 50, XVI, UM 73/780-781. Schulthess' Europäischer Geschichtskalender, 1918/I, 389-390. Müller-Meiningen makes the (unlikely) conjecture that the SPD was delaying in the expectation

of formal debate the Lower Chamber deliberated on the principal questions at hand: status of the Upper House, electoral distribution and procedure, composition of the cabinet. On November 2 the measure was passed and Ludwig dutifully announced that a "new order" was to reign in Bavaria. Under the amended constitution, the King would approve but not dismiss the ministry; the Upper House would delay but not veto legislation. A new proportional voting system was to be introduced and a new cabinet, including two Social Democratic ministers, was to be inaugurated.[11] The most conservative press called it "a problematical experiment," while the Majority Socialists hailed the beginning of "a new era of Bavarian constitutional and administrative life."[12] Whatever their individual interpretations of the King's declaration, all of the traditional parties of Bavarian politics were prepared to accept the new regime, if not to declare themselves entirely satisfied with it.

This was a genuine and significant political reform of the Bavarian state. It had the support of every important faction from one end of the party spectrum to the other, and it marked the mutually satisfactory conclusion of a fair polit-

---

that "something big" would occur. *Aus Bayerns schwersten Tagen*, 45.

[11] "Eine königliche Kundgebung über die Neuordnung in Bayern," *MZ*, 3 Nov. 1918, No. 302. *Verhandlungen der Kammer der Abgeordneten des Bayerischen Landtags, Stenographische Berichte*, XX (16 Oct.–7 Nov. 1918), No. 488, 5-11; No. 494, 95-96. The Upper House, which had completed its final session on August 2 with three cheers for King Ludwig, was scheduled to meet and sanction the new reform program on November 8. *Verhandlungen der Kammer der Reichsräte des Bayerischen Landtags, Stenographische Berichte*, V (28 Sept. 1917–2 Aug. 1918), No. 72, 420. See the summary in *Schulthess*, 1918/I, 408-410.

[12] "Die Parlamentarisierung in Bayern," *BV*, 4 Nov. 1918, No. 256. "Das Neue Bayern," *MP*, 4 Nov. 1918, No. 257. Meanwhile, the Liberal newspapers and the semi-official journal of the Center Party, *Bayerischer Kurier*, were cautiously optimistic about the reform and its acceptance.

ical bargain between the strongest of them. The only recognizable dissenters were to be found among the most rabid monarchists, who were scattered and unorganized, and in a small group of the more radical Independents around Kurt Eisner. Any open opposition to the new parliamentary regime could only have come from one or the other of these two sources. Logically such opposition should have broken harmlessly against the great mass of supporters for the November 2 settlement. How was it then still possible for a revolution to succeed? One explanation is simply that most people did not have time to comprehend the importance of the reforms. If it was not a case of too little, it was certainly too late. Most of the visible signs of the old regime, moreover, were left in full view. For most Bavarians the King was the symbol and the Upper House the embodiment of traditional authority—they were both to remain. The new cabinet would be led by the same Prime Minister, and the Center Party would retain an absolute majority in the Chamber of Deputies, at least until new elections were held at some undesignated time in the future. No one could yet anticipate how soon or to what degree the proportional system would alter the character of parliamentary representation, what party coalitions would be formed, or how this would actually affect the character and performance of the government. In the past five years there had been many official promises and explanations. So far as most people were concerned at the moment, until it was put into practice the new constitution was only a scrap of paper.

But there is a still more fundamental explanation. Constitutional reform could not end the war.

The safety of Bavaria's southern frontier and the structure of the German Reich were put in question simultaneously by the collapse of the Habsburg Empire. The initial reports in mid-October that the Dual Monarchy was prepared to sue for a separate peace had set off a wave of alarm in Bavaria, and had prompted the government to dispatch its best available troops to the Tyrolean border to check any possible invasion from the South. On October 27 Austria-Hungary left the war and the citizens of Munich heard for the first time the awful scream of an air raid siren. During the days that followed, the population was kept on edge by rumors of surprise bombing attacks and the impending intrusion of enemy troops onto Bavarian soil. Then, on the first day of November, news reached Munich that the Habsburg dynasty had been overthrown. This was, as the *Münchener Zeitung* editorialized," a decisive moment for the entire German nation."[13]

It would be overwrought to speak of panic, but it is accurate to say that these events more than offset the intended effect of the constitutional reform. They gave the King's proclamation the appearance, not altogether inaccurate, of a last minute improvisation. And this, in turn, once again placed the supporters of the "new order" on the defensive. In what was ostensibly an election speech at Munich's huge Theresienwiese on the morning of November 3, Kurt Eisner denounced the reform as insincere and insufficient. "Across the border we greet the new Austrian Republic," he declared, "and we demand that a Bavarian regime instituted by the people proclaim peace together with the German republicans of Austria in the name of Germany, since neither the will nor the power exists in Berlin to reach an immediate peace." Facing Eisner in a public debate, Erhard Auer retorted that the Independents were evidently prepared to sanction a "demolition" of the German Reich, something which would be "insane and criminal." The line between them was never more sharply drawn. Whereas Auer was attempting to retain sup-

---

[13] "Die Revolution in Oesterreich-Ungarn," *MZ*, 1 Nov. 1918, No. 300. "Zur Beruhigung," *BV*, 2 Nov. 1918, No. 255. See K. A. von Müller, *Mars und Venus*, 260, and Graf, *Wir sind Gefangene*, 535-536. Formally speaking, a republic was not established in Austria until November 12. For the chronology of events in Vienna after October 27 see *Schulthess*, 1918/I, 82-107.

port for a constitutional monarchy, Eisner was urging open defection and a political revolution.[14]

November 3 was a more decisive moment than anyone in Bavaria realized. In Munich the Independents were able to rouse their gathering on the Theresienwiese into a noisy demonstration at the prison in Stadelheim, where they demanded—and were granted—release of three prisoners still under arrest for their part in the January strike. But the most significant event of that Sunday was the outburst of rioting by sailors in Kiel, in which several were killed and nearly thirty wounded. Following as it did the upset in Vienna, the Kiel mutiny was to be the final signal for revolution in Munich, as elsewhere in Germany. Events could not be localized in 1918 any more than they were in 1914. Yet it is doubtful that news of the mutiny reached Munich before the early morning of November 5, after concrete plans for a coup d'état had almost certainly been laid by Eisner and his associates. Events were already taking their own course in Bavaria. Even an ailing professional anarchist, living in a small Bavarian village far from the pulse of political activity, could write confidently to a friend: *"avant nous le déluge."*[15]

In the dusk of the evening of November 5 Eisner made his way to the Hackerbräu, the modest beer-hall at the northern end of the Theresienwiese. To his surprise he heard no loud

[14] This part of Eisner's statement was adopted in the form of a resolution by the Munich USP. Reprinted in *Dokumente und Materialien zur Geschichte der deutschen Arbeiterbewegung*, Reihe II ([East] Berlin, 1957), II, 280. For a record of the debate, see "Waffenstillstand, nationale Verteidigung und Münchener Arbeiterschaft," *MP*, 5 Nov. 1918, No. 258.

[15] Gustav Landauer to Luise Dumont-Lindemann, 4 Nov. 1918. Martin Buber (ed.), *Gustav Landauer. Sein Leben in Briefen* (2 vols.; Frankfurt a.M., 1929), II, 289. The excursion to Stadelheim is described in detail by Fechenbach, *Der Revolutionär*, 35-37. On Kiel see the contrasting views of Gustav Noske, *Von Kiel bis Kapp* (Berlin, 1920), 10-24, and Frölich *et al.*, *Illustrierte Geschichte der deutschen Revolution*, 185-190.

talking and laughter as he entered; he encountered only a waitress who said that the scheduled political rally had been greatly overcrowded and had moved out onto the adjoining meadow. Literally groping his way in the dim light until he found the giant statue of Bavaria which dominates the entire field, Eisner was greeted by a gathering of supporters and curiosity-seekers. Fired by the reports from Kiel, the enthusiasm of the crowd was such that Eisner was scarcely able to deliver his speech. He asked for patience and, to prove that his intentions were serious, he swore a formal oath "that Munich shall arise in the coming days." According to one witness Eisner went so far as to specify that those who wanted action would need to wait no more than forty-eight hours.[16]

Eisner was later to boast that "on Monday we discussed the matter and on Thursday it was all taken care of."[17] Although the conspirators did not leave a convenient transcript of their preparations, there is enough evidence to substantiate Eisner's claim. On the preceding Sunday, November 3, Eisner had departed from Munich immediately after speaking on the Theresienwiese (leaving the march on Stadelheim to his lieutenant, Felix Fechenbach). He spent that afternoon at Pfaffenberg in Lower Bavaria, the home of the blind leader of the Bavarian Peasants' League, Ludwig Gandorfer. Independently of Eisner, Gandorfer had circulated a pamphlet on the last day of October demanding the deposition of the Bavarian regime. No record exists of the conversation between the two men, but it is not difficult in the light of subsequent events to establish its substance. As Munich was completely dependent on the surrounding countryside for provisions, it was essential that a contact with the peasantry be secured by any regime which hoped to govern from the capital. In the

---

[16] Compare the accounts of Fechenbach, *Der Revolutionär*, 37; Graf, *Wir sind Gefangene*, 542-543; Müller-Meiningen, *Aus Bayerns schwersten Tagen*, 29; and Escherich, *Von Eisner bis Eglhofer*, No. 1, 13.

[17] Bonn, *So macht man Geschichte*, 190.

case of a successful coup in the city, Gandorfer's cooperation would supply the needed contact outside. Eisner must have unfolded his plan for revolt, solicited Gandorfer's support, and obtained his blessing.[18]

By that Monday, then, Eisner was able to begin a series of secret conferences with a number of influential individuals in Munich. A visitor from Berlin found him at his cottage in Gross-Hadern that evening conferring with two professors from the University of Munich. He was also in contact with Edgar Jaffé, associate editor (with Werner Sombart and Max Weber) of the internationally known *Archiv für Sozialwissenschaft und Sozialpolitik*. At the same time, Eisner was able to resume contacts with a few labor leaders from Munich's major industrial plants who had supported him in the strike attempt in January. To these men, a witness recorded, Eisner gave "precise instructions." Finally, he was assured of participation by a number of men wearing the field-gray uniforms of the German army. One of them, Fechenbach, was living at Eisner's home, while others were in strategic positions at some of the large military barracks in the city. This was the group—probably no more than two dozen men in all—who agreed to follow Eisner's lead.[19]

As for the overwhelming majority of Munich's 600,000 citizens, there can be little doubt that they wanted, as the

[18] Fechenbach, *Der Revolutionär*, 33, notes that the son of Karl Liebknecht stayed at the Gandorfer farm after his father's imprisonment in 1915.

[19] Scattered remarks on Eisner's preparations can be gathered from Bonn, *So macht man Geschichte*, 191; Fechenbach, *Der Revolutionär*, 37-39; and Herzog, *Menschen denen ich begegnete*, 60-61. Herzog claims to have seen Professor Friedrich Wilhelm Foerster at Eisner's cottage, but Foerster (while admitting to contact with Eisner just before the January strike) implies that he was in Switzerland in the first weeks of November. Foerster, *Mein Kampf gegen das militaristische und nationalistische Deutschland* (Stuttgart, 1920), 20. For Foerster's subsequent role as the Bavarian minister in Switzerland, see Chapter IV.

emissary of the federal government had reported back to Berlin, "nothing more than peace."[20] Capitalizing on this fact, Eisner challenged Erhard Auer to stage jointly a gigantic demonstration for peace on the Theresienwiese on November 7. Although he had misgivings, Auer recognized that he could not well associate himself with those who still advocated "national defense" and opposed the armistice proceedings. He therefore consented. The placards which appeared throughout Munich on November 6, signed by both Auer and Eisner and calling for a demonstration on the next day, represented the first instance of public cooperation between the two Socialist factions in Bavaria since the formation of the Independent Party in 1917.[21] Neither Auer nor the Bavarian government was blind to the risk involved, but they remained confident that the situation was under control.

On the afternoon of November 6 the outgoing cabinet met with the new "reform" cabinet under the chairmanship of Prime Minister von Dandl, one of the two ministers slated to retain his post. One cabinet was a lame duck; the other was not to assume office until November 8. Both were understandably concerned about administrative transition at such a critical time. "There are restless and unreliable elements even in the Bavarian Army," admitted Minister of War von Hellingrath. "But, gentlemen, you may be entirely reassured. The Army as a whole is still securely in our hands. Nothing is going to happen." There was, nevertheless, some sentiment that Eisner should be arrested immediately, instead of being allowed to play out the dangerous role of bearded prophet. Erhard Auer took the floor: "Let's not continually have this talk about Eisner; *Eisner is taken care of.* You can be sure of that. We have our people in hand. I am going to march

---

[20] "The deep longing for peace" was a recurrent theme of the minister's communiqués. Treutler to Max von Baden, 7 Oct. 1918, NA Washington, Bayern 50, XVI, UM 73/775-776. Müller-Franken, *Die November Revolution*, 15.

[21] "An die Bevölkerung Münchens," *MP*, 6 Nov. 1918, No. 259.

with the parade myself. Nothing is going to happen."[22] Despite these assurances, the regime made specific preparations in the event of violence, alerting troops stationed in the city and arming them with rifles and tear gas. The Chief of Police, the Military Commandant of Munich, and the General Commander of the First Bavarian Army Corps reported that they were standing by.

The Munich Putsch

November 7 was a warm autumn day in Munich. In the morning Minister of the Interior von Brettreich released an official announcement which was printed on the customary rectangular sheets and placarded throughout the city. In large black letters the populace could read that they would find "against any caprice or violence the ADEQUATE PROTECTION which the whole people expects from its regime."[23] After a private conference with Erhard Auer at noon, von Brettreich felt able to assure an anxious inquirer by phone that "Eisner will have his back against the wall this afternoon." Minister of War von Hellingrath repeated his own confident views at the late morning session of the Committee of Finance. Meanwhile, Eisner was quietly holding a final briefing session with several leaders of the Independent Socialist Party.[24]

At one o'clock most of Munich's shops and businesses closed. The city was outwardly calm and, after finishing lunch, King Ludwig went for his afternoon constitutional in the

[22] Cited by Müller-Meiningen, *Aus Bayerns schwersten Tagen*, 30-31. See K. A. von Müller, *Mars und Venus*, 264.

[23] "An die Bevölkerung Bayerns" (7 Nov. 1918, 10:30 A.M.), *Bekanntmachungen*, F. Mon. 3179. This citation refers to an unpublished collection in the Münchener Stadtbibliothek, Monacensia Abteilung, of over two hundred official announcements, uniformly printed throughout the entire period of the revolution; the code number is that currently employed by the library itself.

[24] K. A. von Müller, *Mars und Venus*, 265. Fechenbach, *Der Revolutionär*, 39.

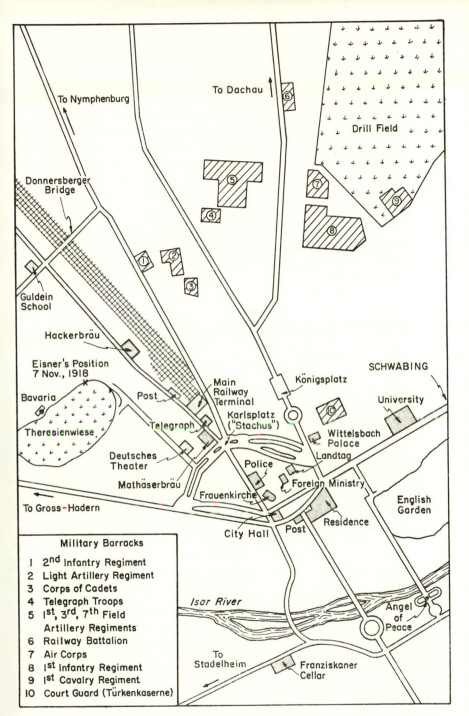

MUNICH IN 1918

English Garden. Between 2 and 3 P.M. the Theresienwiese began to fill with workers, most of them union members marching in rank from their respective factories. Until the war Munich had not had industry enough to support a large working population, but now the meadow was filled with workmen from the munitions, metal, and airplane works, as well as those from the new Krupp plant. Milling among the crowd was another strange element for landlocked Bavaria: a large number of sailors who had arrived in Munich on the previous Sunday. A thousand men were to be transferred from the Pola shipyards to Kiel and Wilhelmshaven, but had been detained in Munich because of the mutiny in those ports. Although all military personnel stationed in the city were under strict orders to remain in their barracks, many field-gray uniforms were also in the crowd; some were on furlough from the front and others had defied orders to stay away from the demonstration. To complete the picture one must add the *Oktoberfest* element, that assortment of beer-hall perennials, Schwabing *literati*, students, miscellaneous women, and youngsters of all sizes which appears at every large public gathering on the Theresienwiese.[25]

Shortly after three o'clock the scheduled speeches began. A dozen leaders of the two parties spoke, most of them ranged at intervals along the slope which transverses the western edge of the meadow. Right in front of the statue of Bavaria stood Erhard Auer. He followed the plan agreed

[25] Max Siegert, *Aus Münchens schwerster Zeit. Erinnerungen aus dem Münchener Hauptbahnhof während der Revolutions- und Rätezeit* (Munich, 1928), 7. For descriptions of the Theresienwiese on November 7 by witnesses, see Müller-Meiningen, *Aus Bayerns schwersten Tagen*, 31; Graf, *Wir sind Gefangene*, 549-550; K. A. von Müller, *Mars und Venus*, 265-266; Herzog, *Menschen denen ich begegnete*, 61-62; Fechenbach, *Der Revolutionär*, 39-40; and Hoegner, *Der schwierige Aussenseiter*, 13. See also the secondhand contemporary accounts recorded by Erich Kuttner, *Von Kiel bis Berlin* (Berlin, 1918), 22-24; and Lujo Brentano, *Mein Leben im Kampf um die soziale Entwicklung Deutschlands* (Jena, 1931), 352.

upon with Eisner: to speak for twenty minutes or so, then call for adoption of a resolution against "national defense" and favoring the democratization of administration and the suffrage.[26] If anything could be called suspect it was the frequent waving of red flags and the call for soldiers to gather around Eisner. The Independent leader was to be found far from the center of things. Eisner's position down in the northwest corner, just opposite the Hackerbräu, was strategically chosen. Behind the Hackerbräu, across the railroad tracks, lay the military barracks. Well after Auer, across the meadow, had called for a show of hands and had proposed a march into the city, Eisner continued to speak to his excited followers, announcing that the time had come for action. With him was Ludwig Gandorfer, who promised that the workers and soldiers could count on support from the peasants. Then Felix Fechenbach stepped forward in uniform, holding a red flag and shouting for action. The crowd around Eisner began to move, but not to follow the great mass led by Auer and a band of musicians, who were already marching down the Landwehrstrasse and into the city. Wheeling in the opposite direction, Fechenbach pointed toward the Guldein School, a temporary barracks and munitions depot at ten minutes' walk from the mob's position on the meadow. Arm in arm Eisner and Gandorfer marched ahead with Fechenbach and Hans Unterleitner, a Bavarian locksmith and Independent Socialist who had been arrested with Eisner in the January strike. One witness was close enough to observe that Eisner was noticeably pale. Behind him, the crowd laughed and talked and swore.[27]

[26] A text of the resolution was subsequently printed, *MZ*, 9 Nov. 1918, Nos. 307-308. The spirit in which the SPD entered the demonstration may be read in the editorial of its party journal, "Eine Feierstunde," *MP*, 7 Nov. 1918, No. 260.

[27] For eyewitness accounts of the march, see Graf, *Wir sind Gefangene*, 551-556; Fechenbach, *Der Revolutionär*, 40-42; and Herzog, *Menschen denen ich begegnete*, 62-63. Forty years have

At the Guldein School Fechenbach and another soldier forced their way in and held an obstinate officer at bay while the others helped themselves to arms. The guards, instead of opposing the soldiers, the women, and the others behind Eisner and Gandorfer, chose to join them. This school building, improvised as a military compound, was only the first link to snap in the chain of governmental security preparations. Moving across the Donnersberger Bridge the crowd divided and entered the two clusters of military posts. The pattern was the same: a delegation entered the barracks and announced the revolution while the mob waited outside. Then a window opened, a red flag was let out, and a hoarse cry proclaimed peace and the Republic. Opposition was met only at the *Türkenkaserne*, barracks located closer to the center of town, fifteen minutes from the others. But the outburst of tear gas and stray bullets was quickly suppressed by the revolutionaries, and the last major military outpost in the city defected from royal authority.[28]

All of this activity had occurred in one section of the city. Elsewhere everything had taken an orderly course. The thousands who followed Auer had paraded across the heart of the business district and made a great deal of harmless noise before dispersing at the *Friedensengel* on the Isar. The timing, even if not entirely predictable, could scarcely have been better. In the Prannerstrasse, the Landtag quietly closed a formal debate on the question of the potato shortage and

---

considerably dulled Herzog's recollection of the details. See also Immanuel Birnbaum, "Vor 40 Jahren: Revolution in München," *Süddeutsche Zeitung*, 8 Nov. 1958, No. 268.

[28] For the most detailed contemporary account of the day's movements, see "Die Ereignisse in München," *MZ*, 9 Nov. 1918, Nos. 307-308. The itinerary of Auer's parade was: Landwehrstrasse, Sonnenstrasse, Karlsplatz, Lenbachplatz, Maximiliansplatz, Briennerstrasse, Residenzstrasse, Maximilianstrasse, and along the Isar to the *Friedensengel*.

adjourned at 6 P.M. An alert correspondent for the *Frank-furter Zeitung* learned of Eisner's coup and called the Ministry of the Interior. There was no truth to such rumors, he was assured by von Brettreich; Eisner had been arrested right after the demonstration and was "already under lock and key."[29] In fact the royal government knew well enough that the situation was out of hand, but it was still not clear what would happen. Eisner had apparently disappeared and armed soldiers were wandering into the center of the city.

More than one person who lived through this day in Munich has argued that a purposeful counterstroke in the evening would have ended the revolution. While this is probably true, it begs the question. The revolution overthrew a regime which had demonstrated to most of its citizens no purpose except self-preservation, and few were willing to bleed for that after four years of war. One looks in vain for a focus of authority—and it is certain that Eisner made at least this basic calculation before attempting to direct an uprising. No one thought to consult with old King Ludwig, who had been called back from his walk and now huddled in the royal Residence with his ill wife. The power of the old cabinet was largely abrogated, and the new had yet to assume its duties. The state bureaucracy was all too bureaucratic in its willingness to serve any constituted authority. Military officials were left entirely helpless, as the Minister of War had to admit, by the defection of troops stationed in Munich. As it was clearly a revolt against the state, city officials felt that events were outside their competence unless significant support came from the Prime Minister; and he could scarcely expect city police to attempt a show of force against the Bavarian Army. The only real organized power left in Munich was represented by the trade unions, and union members were not prepared to rescue a dynasty which had thrived on class privilege for

[29] Fritz Wahl, "Rätezeit in München," *Gegenwart* (Frankfurt a.M., 1956), 15-16.

centuries and had finally agreed to reform less than a week before.

At 8 P.M. royal ministers von Dandl and von Brettreich went to see the King and admitted that His Majesty's life might be in danger. Within an hour Ludwig and his family had escaped from the city by private automobile, still confident they would be called back in triumph when the crisis had passed.[30] Across the Isar Kurt Eisner was waiting in the Franziskaner Cellar, a large and relatively quiet beer-hall to which he had somehow made his way in the confusion. His intention cannot be established with certainty. It may well be that he himself feared a counterstroke of some sort in the late afternoon and was intending to wait until his reappearance could be useful. In any case, it seems certain that he did not anticipate the precise location and timing of events after the initial march to the Guldein School. It was rumored that he was to speak that evening at the Franziskaner Cellar, but upon hearing that the main body of soldiers had moved into the Mathäserbräu in the center of Munich, he went to offer them his leadership.[31]

The Mathäserbräu was not only the largest beer-hall in the city—it had the distinction in 1918 of being also the rowdiest. Just off the "Stachus" (*Karlsplatz*), this severely plain structure occupied a central position among Munich's state and city administrative buildings, scarcely five minutes from the nexus of post, telegraph, and railway centers. When Eisner arrived after dark, a large meeting of soldiers was already in session in an assembly room on the second floor.

[30] Compare the account of Joseph Benno Sailer, *Des Bayernkönigs Revolutionstage* (Munich, 1919) with *König Ludwig und die Revolution. Neue Beiträge zur Vorgeschichte der Bayerischen Revolution* (Munich, 1921).

[31] The confusion of the afternoon is only too well reflected in the accounts of it. See Graf, *Wir sind Gefangene*, 556-557; Müller-Meiningen, *Aus Bayerns schwersten Tagen*, 32-36; K. A. von Müller, *Mars und Venus*, 270-272; and Herzog, *Menschen denen ich begegnete*, 63.

He himself joined (or perhaps hastily organized) a group of workers in a ground-floor dining hall. Here Eisner was designated First Chairman of the Council of Workers, probably the first elective office he had held in his life. He and other members of the *Arbeiterrat* then met in conference with leaders selected by the *Soldatenrat* upstairs. The Council of Workers and Soldiers was thereby constituted and the revolution was in business.[32] The Council took three immediate steps. The first was to authorize truckloads of armed soldiers to cruise about the city through the night, enforcing order when necessary. The second was to dispatch contingents of soldiers to stand guard in front of the major public buildings and to take over centers of transportation and communication. From the strategic position of the Mathäserbräu this was quickly accomplished. Finally, the order was given to seize the major newspaper and publishing houses and to print an announcement that the Council of Workers and Soldiers had been established to replace the old regime. Dated "Thursday, November 7, 1918, 11 o'clock," this yellow placard was the first printed document of the revolution. It ended with a stock revolutionary phrase, "Long live freedom! Down with the dynasty!" and was signed simply by the *Arbeiter- und Soldatenrat*. Eisner was not yet the recognized leader of the revolution.[33]

[32] Elected as vice-chairman of the Council of Workers was Hans Unterleitner, who was later to become Eisner's son-in-law. The course of proceedings in the Mathäserbräu has been confirmed by an interview held with Unterleitner after his emigration to the United States by Harold J. Hurwitz, *The Bavarian Revolution and its Significance for the Sociology of Revolution and of National Development* (unpublished thesis; Bates College, 1946), 198-199.

[33] "Bewohner Münchens!" *Bekanntmachungen*, F. Mon. 226. The exact sequence of events cannot be fixed beyond doubt. Stationmaster Siegert notes that the main railway terminal was seized by soldiers at 8:12 P.M., but this probably preceded the "official" seizure by the delegation from the Council of Workers and Soldiers. *Aus Münchens schwerster Zeit*, 13.

Even before any announcement of the Council's existence could be published, the final step in the seizure of power was in progress. Escorted by an armed guard of sixty men, the Council and a band of admirers marched from the Mathäserbräu across the Promenadeplatz and into the Prannerstrasse, where the Landtag building stood dark and vacant. Rousing a custodian to open the doors, the crowd poured into the chamber of the Lower House and took places behind the deputies' desks. At 10:30 p.m. Eisner stood at the presidential podium—his hair awry, his shirt open at the collar—and rang for order. In the name of the Council of Workers and Soldiers he proclaimed the end of the Wittelsbach dynasty and the foundation of the Bavarian Republic. "Now we must proceed to building a new regime. . . . The one who speaks to you at this moment assumes that he is to function as the provisional Prime Minister." Enthusiastic applause assured the speaker that his assumption was justified. Kurt Eisner had become head of the Bavarian state.[34] In the early hours of the morning he finished composing a proclamation for the press, and then napped on a red plush sofa in the Landtag building.[35] While Eisner slept trucks patrolled the city, a red flag was hoisted from the towers of the Frauenkirche, and a bright red poster was printed and distributed throughout Bavaria:[36]

[34] Herzog, *Menschen denen ich begegnete*, 64-68. This version is not reliable on all points of sequence, although the description of the scene in the Landtag building is generally corroborated by Fechenbach, *Der Revolutionär*, 43-44; and Wahl, "Rätezeit in München," *op.cit.*, 15-16. Both were present. See Wahl's contemporary report to his newspaper, "Aufstand in München," *Frankfurter Zeitung*, 8 Nov. 1918, No. 310.

[35] "Aufruf aus der Nacht zum 8. Nov. 1918." Reprinted in Eisner's *Die neue Zeit*, I, 5-7. Eisner signed this proclamation as the "First Chairman of the Council of Workers, Soldiers, and Peasants."

[36] "Volksgenossen!" *Bekanntmachungen*, F. Mon. 3379.

Proflamation.

Volksgenossen!

Um nach jahrelanger Vernichtung aufzubauen, hat das Volk die Macht der Zivil- und Militärbehörden gestürzt und die Regierung selbst in die Hand genommen. Die Bayerische Republik wird hierdurch proflamiert. Die oberste Behörde ist der von der Bevölferung gewählte Arbeiter-, Soldaten- und Bauernrat, der provisorisch eingesetzt ist, bis eine endgültige Volksvertretung geschaffen werden wird. Er hat gesetzgeberische Gewalt.

Die ganze Garnison hat sich der Republikanischen Regierung zur Verfügung gestellt. Generalkommando und Polizeidirektion stehen unter unserem Befehl. Die Dynastie Wittelsbach ist abgesetzt.

Hoch die Republik!

Der Arbeiter- und Soldatenrat.

Kurt Eisner.

Proclamation
FELLOW CITIZENS!

In order to rebuild after long years of destruction, the people has overthrown the power of the civil and military authorities and has taken the regime in hand. The Bavarian Republic is hereby proclaimed. Elected by the citizens and provisionally instituted until a definitive representation of the people is created, the Council of Workers, Soldiers, and Peasants is the highest authority. It has lawgiving power.

The entire garrison has placed itself at the disposal of the republican regime. The General Command and the Police Presidium stand under our direction. The Wittelsbach dynasty is deposed.

Long live the Republic!

The Council of Workers and Soldiers.

Kurt Eisner.

"What yesterday was still an almost politically indifferent military movement in northern Germany has overnight become a political convulsion in Munich. . . . A new age has come."[37] In most of the city such an age was scarcely apparent to the citizens who had arisen early that Friday morning. Only the absence of a morning newspaper might have suggested to those in the residential areas that something extraordinary had occurred the night before. The *Münchener Neueste Nachrichten*, alone of the city's major dailies, was able to print its regular edition under the stipulation that it reproduce the official proclamation of the new Republic on the first page. As a consequence, numerous members of the royal Chamber of Deputies were no better informed than other Munich residents as they attempted to enter the Landtag building for the scheduled morning session. They first learned of their unemployment when halted at the doors by soldiers wearing red armbands and cockades.[38]

Externally the city was unusually quiet, except for the truckloads of armed guards which clattered through the streets, more a source of disturbance than of order. Red flags began to appear during the morning on various public buildings, banks, and the large department stores—all guarded by armed soldiers. On the windows of some of the small and elegant shops the word *Hoflieferant* had been rubbed out or

[37] *Frankfurter Zeitung*, 8 Nov. 1918, No. 310.
[38] "An die Bevölkerung Münchens!" *MNN*, 8 Nov. 1918, No. 564. On the general surprise in Munich, see Müller-Meiningen, *Aus Bayerns schwersten Tagen*, 29-30; Brentano, *Mein Leben*, 352; Bonn, *So macht man Geschichte*, 191; and Friedrich von Müller, *Lebenserinnerungen* (Munich, 1951), 206-209. See also the reaction (in Berlin) of Bavarian-born Ernst Troeltsch, *Spektator-Briefe: Aufsätze über die deutsche Revolution und die Weltpolitik 1918/1922* (Tübingen, 1924), 23. Upon learning of the revolution, many citizens of Munich heard Eisner's name for the first time. One of them adds: "It was not yet entirely clear to me what Councils of Workers and Soldiers signified." Constance Hallgarten, *Als Pazifistin in Deutschland* (Stuttgart, 1956), 35.

plastered over.[39] People were seen to congregate in front of the bakery shops in bread lines, an unaccustomed sight for a Friday. In the avenues the great statues of the Wittelsbach princes stood undisturbed. At worst, public buildings, monuments, and churches were desecrated only by red or yellow placards bearing announcements of the new regime. Cases of plundering were reported, and sometimes confirmed, but violence never threatened the city's composure. The coup d'état in Munich had been relatively quiet and completely bloodless.[40]

The events of November 8 were decidedly anticlimactic after the suspense of the previous day. Yet one of them was hardly less crucial for the successful accomplishment of the revolution. Some time during the morning hours Kurt Eisner contacted Erhard Auer and urged him to join in a coalition government, "with the explanation [as Auer later testified] that I should establish order, since otherwise the anarchy would become unmanageable for him."[41] Convinced that it was already too late for the revolution to be undone, Auer agreed. Auer's attitude toward the revolution has subsequently become the subject of extensive political polemic, even

[39] "By Royal Appointment." This inscription (it should be noted for the Freudians) had been printed on the shop window of Eisner's father in Berlin. See Graf, *Wir sind Gefangene*, 559-560, and Paul Gentizon, *La révolution allemande, novembre 1918–janvier 1919* (Paris, 1919), 11-12, 26.

[40] The account of Müller-Meiningen ("vampires of the revolution," "virtuosi of plunder") is overdrawn at this point. *Aus Bayerns schwersten Tagen*, 44-45. See "Die Samstag-Ereignisse in München," *MZ*, 10 Nov. 1918, No. 309. On Sunday a crowd of 3000 watched a soccer match in Schwabing without incident. "Der Sonntag," *MZ*, 11 Nov. 1918, No. 310.

[41] *Die Attentate im Bayerischen Landtag. Der Prozess gegen Alois Lindner und Genossen vor dem Volksgericht München* (Munich, 1919), 77. It has been impossible to uncover any contemporary written record of this contact. For whatever reason, neither man chose to make public reference to the circumstances of their agreement except on the occasion cited here.

though the historical record is fairly conclusive. In the weeks before November 7 he had stated his views clearly and often. He had anticipated gradual and peaceful acquisition of equal rights by the working class, but he never intimated that substantial parliamentary reform was not feasible within a constitutional monarchy. He had openly criticized Eisner for stirring "radical" (that is, republican) agitation. In agreeing to participate in the demonstration on the Theresienwiese, he had hoped to assuage such agitation, and was confident that he could do so. When Eisner's coup nevertheless succeeded, Auer consulted with ministers of the royal government and discovered that military and administrative support of the monarchy had collapsed. He is said to have held that the old regime could have been saved had royal officials kept their nerve and had five hundred troops in Munich remained loyal.[42] What action or attitude Auer might have taken during the evening of the Munich Putsch if the five hundred had stepped forward is an academic and essentially unhistorical question. On November 8 he issued, in behalf of his party, a straightforward account of his position: "Under the pressure of the terrible duress in the German Fatherland, without our cooperation [*Zutun*], yesterday's demonstration arose to a political deed of which all segments of the population must take account."[43] He had neither advocated nor agitated for a republic; the parliamentary reforms which he sought could have been realized as well under a limited monarchy. For

---

[42] The phrase "five hundred reliable troops" first appeared in an account of the conference between Auer and von Brettreich (which took place about midnight of November 7-8 in the Ministry of the Interior) by Michael Doeberl, "Weltkrieg und Revolution," *BSZ*, 8 Feb. 1919, No. 38. It has been repeated in differing versions. See Victor Naumann, *Dokumente und Argumente* (Berlin, 1928), 412-413, and Hoegner, *Die verratene Republik. Geschichte der deutschen Gegenrevolution* (Munich, 1958), 33.

[43] "An die organisierte Arbeiterschaft Münchens," *MP*, 8 Nov. 1918, No. 261.

Erhard Auer the revolution was not so much undesirable as it was unnecessary. But when it came, he supported it.[44]

Late in the morning of November 8, Kurt Eisner presented himself at the Ministry of Foreign Affairs on the Promenadeplatz. The conversation there between former Prime Minister von Dandl and the still unshaven Eisner has not been recorded, but obviously one was unable to bargain and the other unwilling.[45] By noon the Landtag building was stirring with activity, and at 3:38 P.M. the first plenary session of the Provisional National Council of the Bavarian People's State was opened (so the transcript reads) "by the chairman of the Council of Workers and Soldiers, Kurt Eisner." For a man who had just lost a lot of sleep, his brief speech was surprisingly literary. He spoke with confidence of a "radical transformation of the constitution and entire life of Bavaria," and he promised to represent a new order which would be both stable and democratic. Only such a government could hope at last to gain "a peace of understanding," Eisner said, since it was common knowledge that Woodrow Wilson would not deal with the autocrats of the old system still ruling in Berlin.

> But now that a revolutionary regime has arisen in Bavaria whose impelling forces have fought German military policy in a lonely and dangerous opposition since the beginning of the war, we may trust that such a regime can awaken

[44] Auer's deportment has been challenged, for opposite reasons, by both Bavarian conservatives and German communists. He was berated for being naïve and ineffectual—i.e., for not doing enough to prevent the coup—by Professor Doeberl, "Exkurs zur Geschichte des Münchener Putsches vom 7./8. November 1918," *Sozialismus*, 170-173; and he has been severely criticized of late by a Leipzig historian for doing everything within his power to save the monarchy. Hans Beyer, *Von der Novemberrevolution zur Räterepublik in München* ([East] Berlin, 1957), 2-12.

[45] See Escherich, *Von Eisner bis Eglhofer*, No. 1, 15. Eisner himself proudly related that he was "without collar, still dirty from the night of revolution." *Die neue Zeit*, II, 27.

a different impression in the American president and induce a more conciliatory attitude.

Eisner closed by promising that a National Assembly would be called "in times of more peaceful development" to draft the definitive form of the Republic; for the moment, however, it would be the task of the people to rule directly through the "elemental impulse" of the revolutionary councils. The session was adjourned after several announcements from the rostrum[46] and the acclamation of a virtually all-Socialist cabinet:

Prime Minister	Kurt Eisner (USP)
Foreign Affairs	Kurt Eisner (USP)
Interior	Erhard Auer (SPD)
Education and Culture	Johannes Hoffmann (SPD)
Justice	Johannes Timm (SPD)
Finance	Edgar Jaffé (USP)
Military Affairs	Albert Rosshaupter (SPD)
Social Welfare	Hans Unterleitner (USP)
Transportation	Heinrich von Frauendorfer (no party).[47]

It is important to give more than passing reference to Kurt Eisner's first formal speech as leader of the Bavarian Republic because it set, in at least two respects, the tone of his regime: it was a statement both essentially moderate and full of ambiguity. In this, his remarks were a faithful amplification of the cryptic official proclamation issued that same day, and a preface for the much longer "Program of the Ba-

[46] *Verhandlungen des provisorischen Nationalrates des Volksstaates Bayern im Jahre 1918-1919. Stenographische Berichte Nr. 1 bis 10* (8 Nov. 1918–4 Jan. 1919), No. 1, 1-5. One of the announcements was made by Eisner personally: that a Council of Peasants (*Bauernrat*) would be joined to the Council of Workers and Soldiers.

[47] The presence of one non-Socialist "*Fachminister*" was supposedly to symbolize the cooperation of the state bureaucracy with the new regime. On Frauendorfer's subsequent opposition to Eisner, see Chapter V.

varian People's Regime" published a week later.[48] Throughout one sees Eisner's concern to balance order and progress—in other words, to stabilize without thwarting the "elemental impulse" of the revolution. To do so meant that Eisner would have to find some way in which to combine the traditional structure of executive and legislative authority with the new organs of revolutionary initiative. The fundamental problem created by the revolution, therefore, was the reconciliation of a parliamentary system with the innovation of revolutionary councils.

Eisner's promise to honor the right of a duly elected National Assembly to decide the permanent form of the republican state was a distinct concession to traditional procedure. Only the question of proper timing seemed to be left in doubt, since it was not yet clear when a "more peaceful development" could be expected. In the formal Program of November 15 Eisner was to address himself more explicitly to the problem of governmental structure by providing for the establishment of a *Nebenparlament*. Presumably intended to replace the Upper House, this would be a representative body composed from the various revolutionary councils and other "vocational organizations" in Bavaria.[49] If it can be assumed that Eisner thereby foresaw a legislative function for the council system, the precise meaning of "*neben*" in this context was still uncertain. What would be the relative authority and special functions of the Bavarian Chamber of Deputies and a corresponding organization of councils? What would be the

[48] Eisner, *Die neue Zeit*, I, 20-29. Escherich notes that the program "found approval not only in Munich, but also in large circles in all of Bavaria." *Von Eisner bis Eglhofer*, No. 1, 17.

[49] Judging from the transcripts of the cabinet meetings (recorded in shorthand by Staatsrat Josef von Grassmann), Eisner was none too precise in attempts to explain his conception of a *Nebenparlament* to his ministerial colleagues. These transcripts are on file in the Bayerisches Geheimes Staatsarchiv (cited hereafter as BGS Munich): *Ministerratsprotokolle*, 15 Nov. 1918, NG 2/1-2/2.

Kurt Eisner I.

"My predecessor, Ludwig I, made Munich the most beautiful city in Germany. I will make it the freest."

Simplicissimus, XXIII (1919)

principle and proportion of representation in each house? And what would be the relationship of such a bicameral legislature to the executive branch of the republican government? These were the questions which the revolution, by its success, had posed. For the time being, however, they seemed not to matter greatly, and there is no evidence that the absence of clear answers in Eisner's first official pronouncements aroused any public indignation.

Once accomplished, in fact, "the revolution" became a charmed phrase whose potency depended largely on its imprecise definition. During the first weeks of November Eisner enjoyed enormous prestige. He was personally unknown, but "the revolution" was everywhere accepted. All of the major political groups in Bavaria were quick to align themselves "on the basis of the facts," even though the facts were still only vaguely apparent. Most of those who objected were silent.[50] It was a phenomenon which could not last, and it did not last after Eisner was forced to commit himself on controversial matters of domestic and foreign policy. But whatever might become of the revolution, the coup d'état had been a success.

[50] The protest of Crown Prince Rupprecht on November 10 was not published until December 24. It went unanswered by Eisner, as did the formal objection on November 12 by former President of the Chamber of Deputies von Fuchs. Texts are to be found in *Schulthess*, 1918/I, 467, 476.

CHAPTER IV

Problems of Peace and Order

THE most arresting fact about the overthrow of the Wittelsbach dynasty, of course, was the almost effortless way in which it was accomplished. The revolution was the result of a total paralysis of governmental authority. Otherwise the calm acceptance throughout Bavaria of a regime led by a former Berlin journalist, a man released from the state penitentiary less than a month before, would have been inconceivable. Not only did Munich remain quiet in the weeks which followed, but the wave of resistance which might have rolled in from the countryside failed to break over the capital city. There was something undeniably bizarre about the Eisner government in a traditionally conservative and Roman Catholic state. Yet, for the moment at least, the apparent incongruity with Bavarian tradition mattered much less than compatibility with political circumstances in Germany as a whole. The proclamation of the German Republic in Berlin two days after the Munich Putsch served as nothing else could have done to ratify the revolutionary action in Bavaria. The end of the Second German Reich was no more seriously contested than the disappearance of the First. The Bavarian monarchy was but one of more than a dozen hereditary establishments which were terminated that week, and none of them was any more ably defended.

It would be inaccurate as well as facetious, however, to say that the *Zeitgeist* was once again on the side of the big battalions, since the same condition which enabled the republican regimes to be so swiftly established was also a threat to their survival. Military discipline, bureaucratic order, and the cooperation of the peasant and laboring population were equally necessary to end the lapse of administrative authority and to restore public confidence. With a single exception (Frauendorfer) not one member of Eisner's cabinet could

110

claim as much as a day of executive experience in the Bavarian government, apart from the office of a party functionary. Collectively and individually, therefore, they were at first dependent on the services of hundreds of individuals throughout the state whose identity they did not know and whose political sympathies they had no time to question. The Eisner regime consequently began with high ideals and dramatic gestures, but also with all the petty and serious compromises necessary to keep the administrative machinery of the government intact.

Domestic Policy: the Initial Weeks

The first plenary session of the Provisional National Council had left unsettled the fundamental question of sovereignty. Presumably the highest authority of the Bavarian state was the Council itself, since sovereignty had been transferred to it from the deposed monarchy by the direct action of the Council of Workers and Soldiers in Munich. But there were two difficulties in regarding the Provisional National Council as the highest embodiment of political authority in Bavaria. In the first place, although Kurt Eisner had been elected Prime Minister by this Council, as one observer put it, "the Council itself had been elected by no one."[1] The choice of delegates had been obscure and arbitrary, and not even Eisner was prepared to contend that the result had been "democratic." Just prior to the approbation of Eisner and his cabinet, moreover, the Provisional National Council had elected its own Presidium headed by a Majority Socialist, Franz Schmitt. In accepting his post, Schmitt had even referred to himself—probably unconscious of the implications—as "President of the Council of Workers and Soldiers."[2] To the problem of representation, then, was added the question of priority. Was the original Council of Workers and Soldiers synonymous

[1] Müller-Meiningen, *Aus Bayerns schwersten Tagen,* 46.
[2] *Verhandlungen des provisorischen Nationalrates,* No. 1, 3.

with the subsequently constituted Provisional National Council, or was one subordinate to the other? And which was the superior officer, the President of the Provisional National Council or the Prime Minister whose mandate was presumably derived from that Council? These questions mattered in a political situation which demanded immediate and perhaps drastic action.

Without recalling either council to obtain a formal enabling act, Eisner released a statement on November 10 which was intended to settle all questions of competence for the time being:

> Through the resolutions of the provisional assembly of the councils of workers, soldiers, and peasants, the executive power has passed into the hands of the cabinet of the Bavarian People's State. Henceforth no decrees have the power of law which are not issued by the cabinet of ministers. . . . Within a few days everything will take its accustomed course.[3]

On November 14 the semi-official *Bayerische Staatszeitung* announced the plan of representation whereby the Provisional National Council would be legally constituted. It later proved to be the case, however, that the Council was not called back into session until December 13, well after most of the crucial issues had already been decided and acted upon. It was thus only as a forum for the public appointment of the new cabinet and for Eisner's first speech as Prime Minister that this body had any importance in the inauguration of the new government.[4]

---

[3] "Im Namen des bayerischen Volksstaates!" *MZ*, 10 Nov. 1918, No. 309. Eisner himself argued that the cabinet could not be responsible to the Provisional National Council. *Ministerratsprotokolle*, 11 Nov. 1918, BGS Munich, PA, VII, 104a. This citation refers to a file of abstracts based on the original notes recorded in the cabinet meetings by Staatsrat von Grassmann. The file of abstracts will be cited only, as in this case, when the original notes are missing from the portfolios of Grassmann's more detailed transcripts.

[4] *Schulthess*, 1918/I, 429. The original plan called for 50 delegates

Eisner was not the first ruler to call a representative body into session for the sole purpose of being legitimized by it. After the secrecy and intrigue of the revolution itself, he was determined to be as open and respectable as possible, to inspire public order and confidence by his example. The most notable manifestation of the new Prime Minister's theatrical flair was the *Revolutionsfeier* of November 17, a formal celebration in the National (formally "Royal") Theater. Instead of splendid uniforms, royal sashes, and décolletés, the audience displayed dark business suits, red ribbons, and modest propriety. Bruno Walter led a symphonic orchestra in Beethoven's "Leonore Overture." Then the curtain rose on an immaculate Kurt Eisner, dressed in a black frock coat, his hair and beard trimmed for the first time in months. He spoke of the revolution as of a holy relic, the first revolution in history "which unites idea, ideal, and reality." The mistakes and guilt of the past must be admitted, he said, as "we seek a new form of democracy. . . . Let us forget what was, and trust what is to be." After a reading from Goethe, a rendition of the "Egmont Overture," and an aria from Handel's "Messiah," the program closed as the audience solemnly rose to sing the last verse of Eisner's own "Hymn of the Peoples." One theatrical director thought the evening so successful that he urged Eisner to repeat the program for the children of Munich.[5]

---

each from the councils of soldiers, workers, and peasants; 30 from the former Landtag faction of the SPD; 5 each from the Bavarian Peasants' League and the trade unions; and 3 from the Liberal Union. By the time the Provisional National Council actually met, this number (193) had been expanded to 256 delegates in order to accommodate more trade union members and representatives of "vocational organizations." For a complete listing, see *Verhandlungen des provisorischen Nationalrates*, xiii-xvi.

[5] "Ansprache anlässlich der Revolutionsfeier im Nationaltheater am 17. November 1918," reprinted by Eisner, *Die neue Zeit*, I, 30-35. See Josef Hofmiller, *Revolutionstagebuch 1918/19* (Leipzig, 1938), 59, 67, 81; and "Revolutionsfeier des Soldaten-, Arbeiter- und Bauernrates," *MZ*, 18 Nov. 1918, No. 317. A copy of the official program,

Technical questions of competence and public demonstrations of respectability do not assure public order, nor did the new regime suppose any such thing. In the early morning hours of November 8, a young lieutenant had entered Munich from his post at Schleissheim to investigate reports of the revolution. Before the night was out, he had been given the grand title of "Commander-in-Chief of the Bavarian Army" and, as his first duty, the somewhat more modest task of securing a guard for the Landtag building, where Eisner slept. The chaotic state of military security was reflected in the proclamation issued by Lt. Kurt Königsberger and countersigned by Eisner. All troops were urgently requested to return to their quarters, to desist from and prevent plundering, and to secure order by undertaking the election of councils in the barracks (*Kasernenräte*). Elected representatives would then meet in an executive council and gain the best interests of the troops through proper (but unspecified) channels. A host of other proclamations gave miscellaneous instructions on the election of councils, warned against misdemeanors, and exhorted that strict discipline be observed. Eisner personally appealed to the workers to organize in the shops and to provide "a number of trustworthy, energetic men for the maintenance of order." The council system in Munich was thus first conceived as a means to prevent further disturbance, not to mobilize the forces of revolution.[6]

On November 13 it was publicly announced as a matter of fact by the new Minister for Military Affairs, Albert Rosshaupter, that Lt. Königsberger had fulfilled his duty of re-

---

with the text of Eisner's "*Gesang der Völker*" on the back, is extant: *Flugblätter*, F. Mon. 2564. This citation refers to the large collection of miscellaneous pamphlet literature of the revolution located in the Münchener Stadtbibliothek, Monacensia Abteilung; the code system is (unfortunately) the same as that employed by the library for the collection of *Bekanntmachungen*.

[6] "Oberkommando der bayerischen Republik," *Bekanntmachungen*, F. Mon. 3184. "An die Arbeiter Münchens," *ibid.*, F. Mon. 3315.

storing order and had resigned as Commander of the Army. Henceforth this power would reside in the Ministry, to be exercised by Rosshaupter himself. All Munich police and "security forces" were, by decree, likewise brought under the direction of the new regime. The confusion had been extraordinary, with various units operating their own patrols under separate regulations and from different beer-halls and barracks. Six signatures were finally required on the governmental order to regulate the situation. Even so, the absence of a more clearly defined and unified command continued to hamper the housing, feeding, and demobilization of the thousands of troops which poured through Munich in November and December.[7]

It is necessary to point out here that the regulation of military affairs in Bavaria remained largely a formality. The Eisner regime had no better guarantee of loyalty from the men in uniform than had its predecessor. In reality, the headquarters of the three Bavarian army corps stationed at Munich, Nuremberg, and Würzburg were virtually autonomous and uncommitted politically. There were at first few important changes in military command at the top level, apart from Rosshaupter, and his position was obviously no more secure than that of the regime itself. Nor was there any new military force created by the republican government powerful enough to assure its existence. In the first weeks after the revolution this did not seem a matter of great concern for Eisner or his ministerial colleagues, since the armistice agreement at Compiègne had forestalled any possibility of foreign invasion and the threat of Bolshevism still appeared quite remote. It was not until late in December that the failure of the new regime

---

[7] *Schulthess*, 1918/I, 479. In the collection of *Bekanntmachungen*, see "Der Sicherheits-Dienst der Hauptstadt München," F. Mon. 3314; "Alle Einwohner Münchens," F. Mon. 3305; and "Alle Einzelposten und Strassenpatrouillen," F. Mon. 3197. Regulations for the regular army troops were also issued: "An die Soldaten und Offiziere," BGS Munich, PA, VII, 104.

to assert more decisive control over the military situation became a pressing issue, and that belated plans were laid—inside and outside the cabinet—to organize a more effective security force.[8]

The character of the new regime and the extent to which its first efforts were dictated by the need for order were evident in one clipped statement of the official proclamation of November 8: "All bureaucrats are to remain at their posts." The question of whether to retain the state's civil service was never posed; it was solely a matter of how it could be arranged without difficulty and delay. All bureaucratic and military officials had been under sworn oath of allegiance to the Bavarian monarchy. Some of them initially refused to consider this oath void, but were nevertheless quickly persuaded to accept another oath which specified that their service to the republican government would be conducted "with reservation of our conscience" (*unter Wahrung unserer Gesinnung*). The bureaucratic machinery consequently continued to function without interruption, but also without significant reform. The old slate of ministers had been cashiered for a new, but the administration which these men were to direct remained almost totally unchanged. It is this fact rather than any delirious enthusiasm for the People's Republic which probably explains the swift acceptance of the revolution by one sector of the public after another: bureaucrats, officers, teachers, transportation workers, labor union leaders, and all the rest.[9] Even King Ludwig, withdrawn to a private estate near Salzburg, cooperated nobly, if unwittingly. Wishing to save his sub-

[8] "Die Neuordnung im bayerischen Heere," *Politische Zeitfragen,* 1919, VIII-IX, 128-129. For the sequel, see Chapter VI.

[9] *Ministerratsprotokolle,* 9 Nov. 1918, BGS Munich, PA, VII, 104a. A typical example of initial acceptance by the bureaucracy was the "Empfang der Abordnung der Vertreter der Vereinigten Verbände des Personals beim Herrn Verkehrsminister am 13. November 1918," BGS Munich, GN 29.

jects from undue embarrassment, on November 13 he released all officials and officers from their personal oath of loyalty to his royal person. Eisner conveniently interpreted and published this announcement as the monarch's formal recognition of his abdication.[10]

There was one completely new ministry represented in the republican cabinet—although it was not exactly a republican innovation, since the Ministry of Social Welfare had been one of the reforms proposed under the old regime before November 7. A cluster of serious internal problems faced Bavaria as a result of the war, the revolution, and the crowding of workers and soldiers in Munich and other urban centers. "Social welfare," then, presumably indicated the government's concern that its citizens were at least housed and fed. And yet, without established policy or bureaucratic machinery, the work of the man who directed this ministry, Hans Unterleitner, was disorganized and largely ineffectual. His position in the cabinet was really that of a minister without portfolio—and without budget—and his activities were invariably of an emergency character, such as the requisitioning of public buildings for temporary housing. The actual execution of the social welfare program in Munich, where it counted most, was in fact left to the city's magistracy.

In a formal meeting at the Munich *Rathaus* on November 12, the city council (*Magistrat*) heard a motion by Majority Socialist Eduard Schmid which proposed a "simplification" of civic administration, a gradual reform appropriate to the new political situation, and the prompt establishment of "the necessary contact with the proper officials of the People's State." Lord Mayor von Borscht concurred that such a motion was required by the municipality's delicate position, and

[10] "Thronverzicht König Ludwig III," *Bekanntmachungen*, F. Mon. 3301. Eisner's interpretation was made the more plausible by the announcement of the abdication of the King of Saxony on the same day in Dresden. *Schulthess*, 1918/I, 479. Ludwig himself did not give up hope of restoration of the monarchy before his death in 1921.

Schmid—as if to allay fear that radicalism was about to invade the *Rathaus*—noted that the magistracy "should not at first be influenced by the operations of the Council of Workers and Soldiers." Two days later a new steering committee was accorded full power to act in behalf of the City of Munich in matters of social welfare.[11] Politically speaking, this represented a transfer of plurality from the Catholic Center to the Socialists. But not one Independent Socialist sat on the steering committee, which thereby avoided intrusion from Unterleitner and could devote itself without interruption to the problems of housing, provisioning, and demobilization. This was but one instance of the general tendency of Eisner's regime to affect only superficially the organization and administration of public affairs.

One can see in this illustration, moreover, the limitations of any one man or small group of men in executing a reform program without the positive and active support of a mass following. To carry off an armed putsch in a moment of political and military collapse was one thing; to alter basically the structure of a whole administrative system was another. Kurt Eisner had no real choice in the matter. Without a huge party organization behind him, he could not have replaced the old bureaucracy with loyal functionaries even if he had wished to do so. His latitude of movement was constantly restricted by the cautious reluctance of the Majority Socialists as well as the restrained but apparent hostility of the Church and the Center Party. At the first serious affront to either, his leadership was certain to be challenged. Eisner's promise to effect a "radical transformation of the constitution and entire life of Bavaria" was therefore not in his power to fulfill—unless he received enthusiastic support from the Majority Socialists, who possessed the extensive organization which he lacked. This, as it turned out, was not forthcoming. It was

---

[11] "Plenarsitzung des Magistrats vom 12. November 1918" and "Schaffung eines Arbeitsausschusses der Gemeindekollegien," *MGZ:S*, 16 Nov. 1918, No. 92.

thus the failure of the two Socialist factions to form a genuine political coalition which, above all, precluded any thoroughgoing administrative purge in Bavaria.

Outside of Munich as within, the end of the Wittelsbach dynasty created only a temporary confusion of allegiance, even though the revolution had been a greater surprise elsewhere than in the capital. "Cooperation between countryside and city" was the official phrase, often repeated, to encourage rural support in maintaining food stocks in the urban centers.[12] During the otherwise perfunctory initial session of the Provisional National Council, a brief flurry of debate had been touched off by leaders of the Bavarian Peasants' League (*Bauernbund*), who opposed relying on the Catholic-dominated Bavarian *Bauernverein* to rally the peasants to cooperate with the new regime. The League would guarantee "that the provisions come in," one of its leaders promised, if only the regime would assure order and prevent plundering.[13] It was well known, however, that the League represented only a fraction of the Bavarian peasantry, whereas the *Bauernverein* might claim to speak for at least half of the non-urban population. There were, in addition, those non-Catholic landowners affiliated with the *Bund der Landwirte*. Eisner's regime faced the dual problem of avoiding any open conflict between these interest groups which might endanger the supply of agricultural products, and of securing the support of individual farmers for the innovation of the peasants' councils. The solution, in brief, was to give the Peasants' League a free hand in the organization of peasants' councils without allowing the League exclusive prerogatives in the regulation of provisions. The necessities of order thus took effective

[12] See the "Aufruf vom 8. November 1918. An die ländliche Bevölkerung Bayerns." Reprinted by Eisner, *Die neue Zeit*, I, 17-19. This was signed jointly by Eisner and Ludwig Gandorfer.

[13] *Verhandlungen des provisorischen Nationalrates*, No. 1, 5. Speakers for the League were Ludwig Gandorfer and his brother Karl.

precedence over the "interests" of the revolution (that is, any fundamental reform of Bavaria's agricultural system or rural political structure) even at the topmost level of administration. The regime secured at least the passive support of all the major interest groups only at the price of avoiding infringement on their respective spheres of influence.[14]

Of equally great interest to both town and country in all of Germany was the question of socialization. This had been a subject for speculation and dogma among the theorists of Social Democracy for decades: to what extent should the state take over the means of production, eliminate capitalism, and redistribute profit? It was generally agreed that the great landed estates should be divided among small independent farmers, but the practical question of just what was "great" had never been decided. The program of the new Bavarian Republic promised the redistribution of land, but offered no definitions. In industry the government proposed the seizure of large mining interests, the increased usage of water power, and an extensive program of electrification. These areas were esteemed "ripe" for socialization, probably because governmental regulations concerning fuel supplies had been widely introduced in the war economy. "We speak, however, in complete frankness," the regime's program explained, "that it seems to us impossible, at a time when the productive power of the land is nearly exhausted, to transfer industry immediately to the possession of society. There can be no socialization when there is scarcely anything to be socialized."[15] In Bavaria, then—as in Berlin, where the Socialist coalition government was facing similar problems—socialization was

[14] See Schlögl, *Bayerische Agrargeschichte*, 566-571, and Wilhelm Mattes, *Die bayerischen Bauernräte. Eine soziologische und historische Untersuchung über bäuerliche Politik* (Stuttgart and Berlin, 1921), 36-50. There were two other farm organizations of note—the *Landwirtschaftlicher Verein* and the *Deutscher Bauernbund*—but neither played an important political role during the Eisner regime.

[15] Eisner, *Die neue Zeit*, I, 24-25.

postponed to an indefinite future date. The capitalist structure of the economy was not to be seized at once from the top, but would be stabilized and "ripened" from below through the councils of workers, soldiers, and peasants. Workers were asked, in the meantime, to be content with concessions which the trade unions had long demanded: the eight-hour day, increased unemployment insurance, and improved working conditions. While the "democratization of the whole people" was proceeding in this manner, Eisner announced, socialization must be prepared on an international scale. It was a utopian vision which seemed mystically to unite those of Wilson and Lenin: "We thus believe that not until after the peace, when the united League of the world's democracies has been constituted, can the indispensable socialization be executed through the decisive influence of the newly resurrected power of the proletarian International [and] the cooperative effort of the peoples of the earth."[16]

The Bavarian revolution had begun as a classic example of successful intrigue by a minority in the capital city, and it remained an affair in which the revolutionary impetus was dependent on that city. By choosing to press neither a program of socialization nor of collectivization, the Eisner regime forfeited the possibility of making the revolution more than a change of ministerial personnel. How receptive the Bavarian people might have been to such programs in 1918 will never be known, as their receptivity was not put to a test. The initiative had to come from Munich, and it was never generated. Long after the fact, it is tempting to conclude that a more forthright radical stand by the new government would only have brought it all the sooner to grief. But this is an assumption, after all, which rests on a conjecture about mass psychology, and it is no more provable than the contrary

[16] *Ibid.* For divergent views of German Social Democracy and the question of socialization, see Rosenberg, *Geschichte der Deutschen Republik* (Karlsbad, 1935), 37-43; and Stampfer, *Die vierzehn Jahre der ersten deutschen Republik* (Karlsbad, 1936), 72-74, 129-133.

121

view which emphasizes the flexibility of public opinion at that time as a result of the revolutionary dislocation. To guess how "the mass" might have reacted to a less defensive approach by the regime is idle and irrelevant. The point is that accumulated pressures within the government were sufficient to stifle even the proposal, not to mention the experiment, of immediate and genuine revolutionary change.

By the middle of November revolutionary governments were already well established everywhere in Germany. Despite the evident variety of institutional forms and of more or less radical leadership, most parts of the nation had in fact shared a common experience: the same shocked acceptance of military defeat, the same tardy and ineffectual attempts to rescue the old ruling system, the same indications of mass confusion and political naïveté once the new order was proclaimed, the same preoccupation of neophyte republican officials with the restoration of public discipline. As in Bavaria, the changes effected elsewhere during the first days were usually cautious and, insofar as the actual administrative structure of government was concerned, superficial. The November revolution was a changing of the guard but not of the garrison.

Yet the relatively isolated and quite unique character of the revolutionary movement in Bavaria should be emphasized. In part this was a natural function of geography: reports of a mutiny in Kiel understandably had less of an impact on Munich than rumors of collapse in Vienna and the resulting exposure of Germany's southeastern frontier. Furthermore it was, as suggested, a matter of chronology: since Munich was the scene of the first successful coup d'état in Germany, the revolution in Bavaria was seemingly self-generated and could for several months appear to be self-sufficient. But there were also certain inherent political factors which, in combination, distinguished Munich at the outset from the other important centers of the German revolution. By comparing

Munich with Berlin in particular—for it was in Berlin that the general pattern of the 1918 revolution would be determined—these factors become immediately apparent.[17]

In its composition, for example, the Bavarian cabinet of ministers was not unlike the council of People's Commissars (*Volksbeauftragten*) in Berlin, each representing a tenuous balance between Majority and Independent Socialism. But the numerical distribution of seats in the two executive bodies was much less significant than the nature of the coalitions behind them. In Berlin the Majority Socialists—Ebert, Scheidemann, and Landsberg—directed the new regime, while the Independents—Haase, Dittmann, and Barth—merely complied. In Munich, by contrast, it was Kurt Eisner who had achieved recognition as the chief minister, whereas Erhard Auer and the Social Democrats were required to accommodate themselves at first to the terms of the coalition. Moreover, the fact that Eisner could legitimately claim to have *seized* power was not only his single important qualification for holding office in the Bavarian government; it also distinguished him from the entire Socialist leadership in the German capital. His position consequently had a direct sanction which none of the Berlin Commissars could invoke. Eisner had actually carried out a putsch in the streets on November 7; Scheidemann announced one from a balcony forty-eight hours later. Eisner had immediately and openly declared himself as a republican; Ebert and his colleagues hesitated before abandoning the possibility of serving a constitutional monarchy instead. Thus the first incision of the revolution in Bavaria, so to speak, was cleaner and more decisive. And the character of the ruling coalition therefore

---

[17] For a carefully structured analysis of the various revolutionary occurrences throughout Germany (including Bavaria, which he calls "einen ausgesprochenen Sonderfall"), consult the brilliant work of Eberhard Kolb, *Die Arbeiterräte in der deutschen Innenpolitik 1918-1919* (Düsseldorf, 1962).

differed in accordance with the influence of the man who had applied the blade.

Another distinctive characteristic of the Bavarian situation was the deepened hostility between the Socialists, the victors of the revolution, and the Catholics, the defeated. This was, of course, attributable to the abruptly altered circumstances of a state previously dominated by a Catholic political establishment. To put as baldly as possible the difference between Munich and Berlin in this regard, King Ludwig was a Roman Catholic whereas the Kaiser was not. As a consequence, the foundation in 1918 of a republic in Bavaria unavoidably sharpened the local conflict between the two great mass movements of the time. The Bavarian Liberals might remain ambiguous toward a Socialist revolution; but Catholic clergymen and Center deputies were bound to resent it. This direct challenge to the political entrenchment of the Church—even though without the religious overtones to be described adequately as anti-clericalism—was not nearly so evident outside of Bavaria. It is true that Catholic politicians elsewhere deferred to Socialist leadership immediately after the revolution and stayed for the most part (Erzberger was a striking exception) in the background. But there was no fundamental impediment to a Socialist-Liberal-Catholic coalition in Berlin, where the Conservatives could be more properly and conveniently associated with the fallen House of Hohenzollern. The revolution in Bavaria therefore rested from the beginning on a much narrower base and, without the assurance of firm Catholic support, was more liable to topple under extreme duress.

In the given circumstances, however, the stability of republican authority in Munich was much less seriously threatened than in Berlin. Throughout most of northern Germany there was a clear and present danger of further revolution. In southern Germany, with the possible exception of Stuttgart, no such danger was apparent. Whether due to the absence of a vigorous radical tradition, to the rural structure of society, or just to the disinterest of Bolshevik agents in the less industrialized and presumably less "promising" areas of Germany, the Eisner regime enjoyed a temporary security which the Ebert government did not. Berlin passed almost immediately from the crisis of the November revolution to a decision as to its character—with the outcome resting frankly on military authority. The passage to decision was much less rapid in Munich, where there was neither the same urgency nor a comparable authority. Unlike Ebert, the Bavarian Prime Minister had no secret telephone connection to *Reichswehr* headquarters as, for the time being, he had no need of one. There was another reason: Eisner was much less intent than Ebert on restricting the power of the revolutionary councils.

It was obvious to everyone that the councils were an important but still indeterminate political factor. In one form or another they had appeared everywhere in Germany and were, in many areas, yet to be reckoned with. In Berlin the executive organ (*Vollzugsrat*) of the council system represented a standing challenge to the authority of the six Commissars—in reality, that is, to the political advantage of the Social Democratic Party. Along with a few other northern cities, notably Bremen, Berlin had a strong and established radical wing of Independent Socialism which maintained close contact with urban workers located in the major industrial plants. Led by the so-called Revolutionary Shop Stewards (*Obleute*), whose chairman was Richard Müller, this faction embodied a plausible alternative to the regular party leadership. The tension in Berlin was therefore heightened from the beginning by the choice between cooperation and obstruction. For this situation there was no real parallel in Munich until some time later. The improvisation of a Revolutionary Workers' Council failed to provide a counterpart to Müller's group; and the Bavarian USP, such as it was, stood united behind Eisner. His personal relationship with the councils was also a unique one. They had provided his route to power: he had first of all become a council leader and only then the

Prime Minister of the Bavarian state. His initial appeal to the councils was consequently based on the claim that he was their man. Whether this would prove in time to be an advantage or a disadvantage was another matter, but it did create a pattern of negotiation in Munich fundamentally different from that in Berlin.

Underlying all of these considerations was the fact that Munich was, after all, only a provincial capital. That Berlin was indisputably the first metropolis of the German nation was recognized not only by most Germans but, a fact equally important for the moment, by the Entente. What happened in Munich could not have had the same decisive meaning for the entire Reich as did the development in Berlin. This was certain to hold true so long as Germany remained unified, so long as no concerted attempt was made in southern Germany to reverse the verdict of 1870. Bavarian particularism therefore seemed to be one of the crucial question-marks of the revolution. Yet, for all the attention and speculation attached to it, the potentiality of an active separatism was not to become a significant factor during the revolutionary period. The principal reason for this was quite simply that traditional Bavarian particularism had also been monarchist, and was therefore undercut in 1918 by the very fact of the revolution. The threat of secession, then, was necessarily limited in November to a political gambit of Eisner's personal diplomacy.

Foreign Policy: the Break with Berlin

As premier of the new Republic, Kurt Eisner wore several political hats in various styles. He was leader of the Independent Socialist Party, chairman of the Council of Workers, Soldiers, and Peasants, and chief executive of the provisional cabinet of ministers. Since the latter body had constituted itself as the supreme authority of the state, it was in every respect proper that Eisner should designate himself as the Prime Minister of Bavaria. At the same time, he was his own foreign minister, and it was probably indicative of

126

his estimation of that office that his official letterhead read: "Foreign Ministry and Prime Ministry of the Bavarian People's State." International diplomacy had long been the central theme of his journalism, and he frankly regarded himself as an authority on the subject. The initial proclamation of the Republic, Eisner's first speech as Prime Minister, and the program of the new regime had all expounded Eisner's view of the international situation and his determination to take an energetic part in securing a just peace for Germany.[18]

The reasoning behind this policy was elaborated on November 10 in an appeal from the Bavarian government "to all the regimes and peoples of America, France, England and Italy, [and] to the proletariat of all lands." Bavaria, the message read, led by men who had opposed German militarism since the outbreak of hostilities, had swept away all those who "bore and shared responsibility" for the World War. A *Volksstaat* had been created in Bavaria, a paragon for the rest of Germany which might inspire "for the first time a real inner unity" of the Reich. Only the unduly severe armistice terms of the Entente powers threatened the high ideals and hopes of the revolution. Although it would be quite proper to punish the guilty—the militarists and the autocrats of the old system—it could hardly be the Entente's intention that such punishment should fall on a people struggling to sustain a new democracy. "The League of Nations, which has become the common ideal of humanity, can never come into being if it begins with the extirpation of the youngest member of democratic culture."[19]

[18] At a session of the soldiers' councils in late November, Eisner referred to himself as an "expert in the field of foreign policy." *Verhandlungen des provisorischen Nationalrates*, Beilage III, 53.

[19] "Kundgebung der Regierung des bayerischen Volksstaates vom 10. November 1918." Text published by Pius Dirr (ed.), *Bayerische Dokumente zum Kriegsausbruch und zum Versailler Schuldspruch* (Munich and Berlin, 1922), 26-27. Collected by a special committee of the Bavarian Landtag, this volume contains a generous selection

This reference to the League, and the deliberately grandiose tone which enveloped it, betrayed the significant calculation of Eisner's foreign policy. This was an appeal not only to four governments and millions of workers, but to one man: Woodrow Wilson. The explanations for such a public appeal are several. It was certainly one more example of Eisner's penchant for dramatic gesture. It was also an act of self-interest: any sort of recognition by the Entente would mean legitimation for the revolution and prestige for its leader. It was, at the same time, an expression of Eisner's genuine belief, shared by many Bavarians, that Berlin had been discredited within the Reich and abroad, and that leadership might well have to originate elsewhere in Germany. Moreover, the appeal had a basis in the hard facts of economic life for a nation defeated, short of supplies, and facing the problems of demobilization and incessant radical agitation. Eisner's letters show that he had weighed all these considerations.[20] But the factor which seems to have counted most was the advice of three men who had little more in common than a knack for telling Eisner what he wanted to hear.

The most curious of these men was the Reverend George D. Herron. After marrying into a fortune and retiring from his professorship at Grinnell College in Iowa, Herron had come to Geneva to enjoy life in the circles of international pacifism which congregated in that city before 1914. As the war began and the list of his acquaintances grew, he showed himself to be intransigently opposed to the "Prussian peril," completely humorless, and evangelically American. Finding the Europeans insufficiently impressed with America's in-

---

of papers from Eisner's Foreign Ministry. The original documents are to be found, among others, in BGS Munich, PA, VII, 100 and 106.

[20] See especially Eisner's confidential note of November 12 to Professor Foerster, *ibid.*, 28-29. See also the capable report of "The Dresel Mission," *Papers relating to the Foreign Relations of the United States. The Paris Peace Conference, 1919* (Washington, 1924), II, 130-153.

comparable moral stature, Herron wrote a book which made him known throughout Central Europe: *Woodrow Wilson and the World Peace*.[21] His message was simple—that only Wilson could save the world—and many believed. Despite his repeated denials, the legend grew that Herron was an intimate friend of the President and that a word from him was worth at least that of an under-secretary in the United States Department of State. While Herron's reputation as Wilson's confidant flourished, those who wanted to talk of peace sought him out. During 1917 and 1918, Herron became involved in a remarkable cloak-and-dagger affair involving nearly every belligerent government in Europe.[22]

One of those who came to Herron, and brought others to him, was a professor of pedagogy at the University of Munich, Friedrich Wilhelm Foerster.[23] Also a well-known pacifist, Foerster had become Herron's friend even before the war, and had later provided most of Herron's contacts with German and Austrian negotiators, both official and unofficial. Although Foerster knew that Herron was only a private citizen and that he had never actually met President Wilson, he

[21] See the study based on Herron's private papers by Mitchell Pirie Briggs, *George D. Herron and the European Settlement* (Stanford, Calif., 1932), 26 and passim. A book even appeared in Czechoslovakia by Stephen Osuský under the (here translated) title, *George D. Herron, Wilson's Man of Confidence during the War* (Prague, 1925). See also Herron's *Germanism and the American Crusade* (New York, 1918) and *The Defeat in Victory* (London, 1921).

[22] Herron's biographer did not have access to all of the government documents now available which enable one to follow these secret negotiations in detail. *Papers relating to Foreign Relations, 1918* (Supplement 1), I, 65-67, 82-105, 119-123, 147-149, 173, 217-219, 267, 276-279. See Heinrich Benedikt, *Die Friedensaktion der Meinlgruppe 1917/18* (Graz and Cologne, 1962), 116-175, 192-212, 273-277.

[23] Foerster published his own account of his role as Eisner's adviser in *Mein Kampf gegen das militaristische und nationalistische Deutschland*, 20-34. He adds only confusion in his much later *Erlebte Weltgeschichte 1869-1953* (Zürich, 1953), 211-214.

also knew that the American legation in Bern had become aware of Herron's activities and was relying on him as a source of information. It was probably also known to Foerster that messages from Herron were relayed by the legation directly to Secretary of State Lansing, and that the President himself had been more than once confronted with Herron's questions.[24] Because the State Department had made clear that its official policy was to deal only with authorized representatives of the German government, talks with other agents through the Foerster-Herron contact had broken down in the autumn of 1918.[25] But with the sudden success of the revolution in Munich, the situation was significantly altered. When Foerster met with Herron a few days thereafter—to ask that Eisner's appeal be forwarded directly to Wilson—he spoke to the American in his new capacity as the envoy of the Bavarian Republic in Switzerland. Herron complied.[26]

[24] Documentation on Herron's contact with Wilson may be found in Ray Stannard Baker, *Woodrow Wilson, Life and Letters* (8 vols.; New York, 1927-1939), VIII, 245, 259, 280-281; *Papers relating to Foreign Relations*, 1918 (Suppl. 1), I, 286, 290; and Herron, *The Defeat in Victory*, 194-209. Wilson personally wrote to Herron only once. The matter was closed after Wilson expressed (10 Aug. 1918) the hope that "Herron will not go any further with these conversations," lest he "make the impression that he had means of knowing what sort of proposals would be acceptable to us."

[25] American Secretary of State Robert Lansing had restated the policy frequently and said (13 Aug. 1918) that continuation of Herron's activity could only "prejudice matters rather than promote them." *Papers relating to Foreign Relations*, 1918 (Suppl. 1), I, 31, 67, 188-189, 282. On the collapse of talks with another Bavarian representative, *ibid.*, 122-123, 217-219, 229, 260, 297.

[26] See the exchange of telegrams between Eisner and Foerster (11-14 Nov. 1918), *Bayerische Dokumente*, 28-30. Eisner dispatched a copy of the appeal directly to Herron with a note: "I beg you to send the following manifesto to President Wilson and the governments of France, England, and Italy, and to diffuse it in the Swiss press. . . ." Herron immediately wrote to Wilson: "You are the only source of faith the German people have left in the world. Especially this

Eisner had thus entered into his foreign policy with the best of intentions and on the basis of what he had reason to believe was sound advice. Several messages directly from Herron and constant encouragement from Foerster persuaded him that his appeal was wise and would not go unheeded. "You can be sure beyond the shadow of a doubt," Herron telegraphed on November 14, "that if you succeed in establishing at once a real democratic regime in Bavaria and the other German states, the President will be the first one to bring to you all possible sympathy and help."[27] Foerster reported that he was in touch with "leading men of the Entente states," among them "the most intimate confidant of Clemenceau." The appeal had made a "great impression" in Switzerland, he assured Eisner, and the prospects for some mitigation of the armistice terms were improving. Foerster appended a word most gratifying to Eisner's ego: "As the finest reward for all your efforts, you may have the satisfaction that you have saved Germany in this moment, since previous proclamations from Berlin have been unable to arouse any confidence."[28]

The assertion by Foerster that efforts of the government in Berlin to speak for the Reich had been in vain was corroborated by Eisner's third adviser, his appointee as Bavarian

---

Bavarian group believes in you above all else. . . ." He requested that the President offer "some word of assurance" to Eisner. Quoted from the Herron Papers by Briggs, *George D. Herron*, 64-65.

[27] Herron's promise, of course, was irresponsible. *Bayerische Dokumente*, 30-31.

[28] *Ibid.*, 31, 33-39. Foerster was apparently referring to an appeal by Secretary of State Solf from the German Foreign Office to Lansing on November 10. *Schulthess*, 1918/I, 460-461. "At the moment it is of great political importance," Foerster wrote to Eisner on November 21, "to make it clear to the Entente, precisely because it regards Berlin with the greatest mistrust . . . that Bavaria will decisively influence the progress of political development in Germany." *Bayerische Dokumente*, 49.

minister to Berlin, Dr. Friedrich Muckle. According to Muckle, the new federal government was a regime of incompetent *petits bourgeois*. The authority of Friedrich Ebert was so seriously threatened by radical agitation, Eisner was told, that his position was both unstable and basically reactionary, necessarily resting on "a whole line-up of the worst representatives of the old system." Bavaria had little to gain by unqualified support of Berlin. Should reaction gain the upper hand in the national capital, the spirit of revolution could only be dampened in southern Germany. But if radicalism should win out in the North, the sole result would be an intervention by the Entente which would cast Germany "to the deepest depths of humiliation." To avert this dilemma, Muckle advised three steps: "the immediate publication of secret documents, arrest of those guilty [for the war], introduction of a federal court [to try them]."[29] Eisner should at once undertake "to cleanse the government of all ineffectual elements." Such a policy would both eliminate reaction and forestall radicalism. Should Berlin fail to respond to the Bavarian demands, Muckle concluded, *"we must at least threaten the secession of the South.* Prussia has plunged us into the misfortune of the war; it should not force us even deeper into the chasm out of which we are attempting to make our way."[30]

Muckle's report reached the Bavarian Foreign Ministry on November 19. Eisner scarcely hesitated before deciding to follow the suggested steps. On November 21 he demanded through Muckle that the Berlin regime immediately release documents dealing with the outbreak of the war, and he requested that Muckle be named to the Armistice Commission, the body delegated by Berlin to negotiate directly with the

[29] This advice coincided with that which Eisner had received from Herron two days before: "Above all I urgently advise you to persuade as many German states as possible to follow your lead, and secondly, to undertake the first steps to a full and open confession of the guilt and misdeeds of the German regime at the beginning of the War. . . ." *Ibid.*, 39-40.

[30] *Ibid.*, 43-45.

Entente.[31] On the morning of November 23 Eisner left by rail for Berlin to attend a conference of the German states. With him he took a folder of official documents: reports from the Bavarian delegation in Berlin during July and August of 1914. Four of them—abridged—were released that evening, and published widely throughout Germany and in the Entente capitals the next day.[32] The contents of the documents indicated, as the *Münchener Post* summarized them, that German and Bavarian officials had been well informed after Sarajevo, but had done nothing to prevent the "dangerous game" played at Vienna in late July 1914. From government officials came denials that Germany had wanted war, but no suggestion that the documentary account of the "Blank Check" to Austria was not genuine. When the *Reichskonferenz* was called into session on November 25, Kurt Eisner was the most controversial figure in German politics.[33]

The conference itself was an exercise in rhetoric. First, Friedrich Ebert repeated the official formula of the Berlin government: the executive of the German Republic was constituted in the six People's Commissars whose mandate was derived from the workers and soldiers; this arrangement was of course provisional, pending the election of a National Assembly, "which we are determined to call together as soon as possible." Then Secretary of State Wilhelm Solf spoke for the Reich's Foreign Office. Because of France's obvious intention to promote a division of the German states, he said, it was imperative that Berlin alone represent a united German front in foreign affairs. Independent action, such as "the pub-

---

[31] *Ibid.*, 46. See Klaus Werner Epstein, *Matthias Erzberger and the Dilemma of German Democracy* (Princeton, 1959), 284-301.

[32] The original texts of the documents were later reprinted by Pius Dirr side by side with the portions released by Eisner, as "Die Veröffentlichung vom 23. November 1918 und ihre urkundlichen Unterlagen," *Bayerische Dokumente*, 3-16.

[33] "Reif für den Staatsgerichtshof!" *MP*, 25 Nov. 1918, No. 275. For a summary of press and official reaction in Germany, see "Nach der Enthüllung," *Bayerische Dokumente*, 51-65.

lication of one-sided accounts from federal or state documents," must be considered "intolerable." Solf's estimation of French policy was seconded by Matthias Erzberger, chairman of the Armistice Commission, who reported on the severity of French demands in Alsace-Lorraine and the Rhineland. Eisner was next to speak; his remarks were personal and, it must be said, vicious. Men like Solf and Erzberger were typical of those "compromised" by their association with the Kaiser's regime; for the good of Germany, they would do well to follow their lord into exile. The Entente would clearly deal only with those who had nothing to do with the old system, with "men at the top in Germany who enjoy the confidence of the people." There could be little question whom Eisner would have nominated as he concluded by demanding that a new commission of the "uncompromised" be constituted to represent Germany before world opinion.[34]

As the conference proceeded Eisner stated his case more insistently, warned of a separatist movement in the South "stronger than ever," and contended that the National Assembly should be constituted on the Bavarian model of representation through councils of workers, soldiers, and peasants. But it was all for the morning papers. There were scattered voices of support, notably from Karl Kautsky, but not one of Eisner's proposals came to a vote. With a resolution of unity and a repetition by Ebert of the same formula with which the conference had begun, the final session was adjourned. Eisner returned to Munich and notified Berlin the next day that "the Foreign Ministry of the People's State of Bavaria refuses all intercourse with the present representatives of the [German] Foreign Office."[35]

[34] A complete record of the proceedings was published as "Eine deutsche Bundesstaatenkonferenz," *MP*, 26-27 Nov. 1918, Nos. 276-277. Portions of the official transcript, which differ only slightly, may be found in *Bayerische Dokumente*, 66-71.

[35] *Ibid.*, 72. Brief accounts of the conference are given by Stampfer, *Die vierzehn Jahre*, 70, and Schwend, *Bayern zwischen Monarchie*

Less than three weeks after becoming premier of the Bavarian Republic, Eisner had drawn the discernible lines of a foreign policy. In its broadest objective—to secure for Germany a peace with honor—the policy was identical with that pursued in Berlin. But for the Ebert government it was an embarrassment that Eisner presumed to have any foreign policy at all, since its very existence predicated Berlin's incompetence to speak for the entire German nation. To be sure, there was something slightly ludicrous about Eisner's formal proclamation of a diplomatic rupture, but if it made a rather bad joke, Ebert was no less liable than Eisner to be made the butt of it. The official reaction of the central government was to deal with Eisner by ignoring him. The lone casualty among the "compromised men" of the old regime was Secretary Solf, the former director of German colonial affairs who was already under attack and who might well have been forced out anyway.[36] The criticism of Erzberger was ill-considered and ineffectual. And the prospect of a public commendation for Eisner's diplomatic efforts from the American government never materialized.

Judged by any pragmatic standard, there is no question that Kurt Eisner's venture in international statesmanship was a failure. He was unable to attain any of the objectives which he apparently sought: some sign of diplomatic recognition from Woodrow Wilson, an important realignment at the German Foreign Office, and a ground swell of favorable public opinion in Bavaria. The third disappointment was perhaps only a consequence of the first two, although to the extent that public sentiment was controlled by and expressed through

---

und Diktatur, 50-51. Also see the section on "Kurt Eisners 'Grosse Politik' " by Erich Otto Volkmann, *Revolution über Deutschland* (Oldenburg, 1930), 89-91.

[36] According to his wife's diary, Solf returned from the conference "entirely broken." Cited by Eberhard von Vietsch, *Wilhelm von Solf. Botschafter zwischen den Zeiten* (Tübingen, 1961), 212-220.

professional political leaders and their party press, the unfavorable reaction to Eisner's personal initiative in Berlin was predictable. In the first place, it was Eisner alone, in his dual capacity as Prime Minister and Foreign Minister, who had undertaken to defy the Berlin government. The other members of his cabinet had not been consulted, even though Eisner, speaking in the name of the Bavarian state, had necessarily implicated the entire regime. It was therefore a manifest violation of the spirit of the coalition agreement with the Majority Socialists. In addition, Erhard Auer and his party colleagues had every reason to regret the discomfort caused the national leadership of the SPD by Eisner's impertinence. Since the Majority Socialists now dominated the Berlin government, they were naturally least likely to be well disposed toward encouragement of Bavarian particularism. If the SPD leaders could be considered closest to Eisner in domestic policy, then, they were at the moment furthest from him in foreign policy. Precisely the inverse was true of the other major political power in Bavaria, the Catholic Center, which had been traditionally associated with a "federalist" (states' rights) position in German affairs. Most Catholic leaders could easily agree with Eisner on a policy of decentralized authority in the Reich, but they were also the most dismayed by Eisner's putsch and the consolidation of a Socialist coalition in Bavaria. There was consequently no real prospect that Bavarian conservatives would suddenly rush to Eisner's support merely because of his performance in Berlin. And nothing of the sort occurred.[37]

It could be argued that Eisner had calculated as much before going to Berlin with his brief case of documents, and that he had hoped by his publications to appeal over the heads of the politicians directly to the people. This was a political style of which he was capable and which was logically suited for a minority leader. But it is necessary to strike

---

[37] For a further discussion of the Bavarian political parties, see Chapter VI.

a balance between the element of calculation in Eisner's motives and his well-developed sense of ethical idealism. Eisner was not a pragmatist. Even after there was no longer any doubt as to the damaging political consequences of his action, he never felt that he had made a mistake. He had genuinely believed the advice which he received from Herron, Foerster, and Muckle, and he considered it his ethical duty to publish what he regarded as the truth of German war-guilt. In short, Eisner was an honest and incurable do-gooder. He miscalculated not so much the political reaction as the people's capacity for contrition. He expected them, in effect, to repent of a sin which they would not acknowledge, documents or no. The subsequent charge that Eisner had purposely slanted his publication of the diplomatic dispatches in the process of abridging them was therefore erroneous, and not only in its estimation of Eisner's intentions (by implying a calculated fraud). It also stressed unduly the importance of the documents themselves. Eisner's real offense was not the means of his action, but that he acted at all.[38]

For the blurred distinction between the appearance and the intention of his foreign policy Eisner himself was partly to blame. Ever since the final weeks of the war there had been rumors of a movement to separate Bavaria from the Reich in order to join with German Austria in a new southern federation. Feelings against Prussia (including, of course,

[38] Supported by the testimony of several distinguished historians (Fischer, Montgelas, Lepsius, Thimme, Delbrück, etc.), a court later declared Eisner's action to have been a "deliberate falsification." Only Professor Ludwig Quidde dissented, arguing that Eisner had been acting as a publicist, not a scholar (when asked why he did not print the texts unabridged, Eisner had replied that "the press suffers from a shortage of space, so that the release, which is rather lengthy, would probably not be published verbatim"). *Die Kriegsschuldlüge vor Gericht. Bericht um die Eisnerschen Dokumenten-Fälschungen am Amtsgericht München I, 27. April bis 11. Mai 1922* (Leipzig and Munich, 1922), 54-57, 83-85, and passim. It is ironic that this volume is edited so as to underscore statements derogatory of Eisner.

Eisner's own) were unquestionably strong in Bavaria and, as already indicated, they had served to heighten the emotional pitch which made the coup d'état in Munich possible. Eisner not only neglected to disassociate himself from the outburst of Bavarian prussophobia, but he had ostentatiously raised the specter of separatism as a threat to the Ebert government at the *Reichskonferenz* in Berlin. Then, by severing diplomatic relations with such a flourish, he created the impression that he was actually espousing or, at least, intentionally abetting the separatist cause—an impression which has persisted, but is nevertheless false. Eisner wanted to lead the German Republic, not to destroy it.[39] The known facts point away from any separatist intention on Eisner's part and toward a desire to include Austria in an enlarged German Reich, within which Prussia could be counterbalanced without being excluded. Both Eisner's writings before becoming the Bavarian Prime Minister and his actions subsequently—the diplomatic rupture notwithstanding—attested to this line of reasoning.

By contrast, a notable corollary of Eisner's foreign policy was his explicit disavowal of Russian Bolshevism. He had been repeatedly informed by Professor Foerster that he could hope to obtain diplomatic recognition and economic support from the American government only if he made a vigorous public statement of his opposition to the ambitions of international Communism. "A Bolshevik regime would be denied any support," Foerster had written on November 16; "I believe that a public declaration which . . . contains a rejection of Eastern methods will be of most extraordinary importance."

[39] Eisner also hoped thereby to tip the balance of the Socialist coalition in Berlin to the Independent leaders. On November 27 he telegraphed Muckle: "Please report immediately to Haase: I suggest Reichspresidium for negotiations with Entente seat Munich: Haase, Dittmann, Kautsky, Eisner, Mühlon." BGS Munich, PA, VII, 105. See the comments of Müller-Meiningen, *Aus Bayerns schwersten Tagen*, 78, and Schwend, *Bayern zwischen Monarchie und Diktatur*, 58.

Shortly after his return from Berlin, Eisner made just such a declaration by explaining that the Entente

> is afraid of Bolshevism, just as we are afraid here. This fright has developed because we have formed councils of workers, soldiers, and peasants and thus, in this respect, imitated the Russian example. . . . [But] we have neither used Russian methods nor are we pursuing Russian objectives. There is no Russian Bolshevism in Germany, perhaps with the exception of a few visionaries.[40]

The sincerity of this statement, and of similar remarks made by Eisner during his premiership, has been challenged more than once. It has been suggested that his public repudiation of Bolshevism was a matter of temporary political expediency, and that Eisner either had Bolshevik sympathies from the outset or came under Bolshevik influence after the revolution had begun.[41] After nearly half a century, not a single scrap of evidence has been produced to substantiate this charge. Moreover, Eisner's entire biography testifies against it. Ever since he had been a young reporter, Eisner had regarded Russia as a distant land from which a politically sophisticated and culturally superior Germany had little or nothing to learn. In all his published commentary on the politics of the Second International before the war, there was not the slightest hint of accord with the Leninist position. At the Gotha conference of the USP in 1917 Eisner had openly opposed the radical wing of the Independent Party (then

[40] *Bayerische Dokumente*, 33-39. *Verhandlungen des provisorischen Nationalrates*, Beilage I, 5-6.

[41] Like the question of Auer's reaction to the Munich Putsch, the issue of Eisner's relationship to Bolshevism has been a political hassle between Bavarian conservatives and German communists. See Doeberl, *Sozialismus*, 42-46, 53, and Beyer, *Von der Novemberrevolution*, 12-19. An attempt to reconcile these views and place the problem in context has been made by Helmut Neubauer, *München und Moskau 1918/1919. Zur Geschichte der Rätebewegung in Bayern* (Munich, 1958), 15-22.

called the *Gruppe Internationale*) on the grounds that extreme leftist tactics would split rather than unite the German workers. Some time later, after visiting one of Eisner's discussion meetings in Munich, the anarchist Erich Mühsam recorded with unconcealed disgust that "Eisner was, as a result of his bourgeois mentality, an enthusiastic panegyrist of Kerensky. . . . The passage of the Bolsheviks through Germany meant a betrayal to him, a proof that Lenin and Trotsky were pawns of Ludendorff." And in the summer of 1918, upon hearing of the negotiations at Brest Litovsk from his prison cell, Eisner wrote to Karl Kautsky inquiring if his information about the treaty was correct: "If it is, then there could certainly be no more possible divergence of opinion about the Bolsheviks."[42] There is still no proof that Eisner later changed his mind, and quite a bit to suggest that he did not. In evaluating the inception of his domestic and foreign policy, then, it is possible to take at face value his stated assumption that "there is no prospect that the Russian Revolution will be imitated by the German proletariat, least of all to the degree of the Bolsheviks."[43]

The fact that the uprising in Munich had occurred on the first anniversary of the October Revolution in Russia is striking but coincidental. The timing of the Munich Putsch was

[42] Prager, *Geschichte der USPD*, 146. Mühsam, *Von Eisner bis Leviné*, 11. Eisner to Kautsky, 19 July 1918, IISG Amsterdam, "Briefe an Kautsky," D/X, No. 170.

[43] Eisner, "Die Bolschewiki und die deutsche Sozialdemokratie," *Die neue Zeit*, II, 48-54. On December 12 Eisner said: "Here we have no need of revolutionary help from the Bolsheviks . . . we will make our own revolution." *Ibid.*, 33. Speaking a week later to a meeting of the Munich chapter of the Spartacus League, he repeated this view and (according to a Liberal newspaper which otherwise opposed his regime) "professed himself to be an opponent of Bolshevism." When he then charged that Spartacist leader Max Levien had also long believed in the "uselessness" of Bolshevism, a near riot ensued. Above the confusion Eisner shouted: "Not one word further will you hear from me in any of your meetings," and left the room. "Eisner bei den Spartacusleuten," *MZ*, 30 Dec. 1918, No. 349.

contingent on too many other factors: Ludendorff's failure and departure, the armistice negotiations between Wilson and Max von Baden, the collapse of the Dual Monarchy, the mutiny in Kiel, the overconfidence of Erhard Auer and the Bavarian royal ministers—all of which bore much more directly on the success of the revolution in Bavaria than did the dubious example of Lenin's subversion of the Kerensky government in Petrograd a year before. Nor, as this chapter indicates, were the initial policies of the Eisner administration directly influenced by events so far removed as the conduct of the Bolshevik regime in Russia. Yet in one respect the Russian precedent did have a significant effect on the form of revolutionary activity throughout most of Central Europe, and Bavaria (as Eisner himself admitted) was no exception. The ubiquitous appearance of the councils of soldiers and workers in 1918 was the one true innovation of the revolution.[44] The question of Eisner's personal affinity or alleged contact with Soviet leaders in Moscow is therefore only a particular aspect of the much more extensive problem of the total impact of the successive Russian revolutions. Whatever case may be made for the indigenous character of the "council theory" (*Rätegedanke*) in Germany, the fact remains that these organizations were directly and consciously related to the Russian soviets.[45] In their inception the Ba-

[44] As suggested previously, a unique feature (in Germany) of the Bavarian revolution was the widespread organization of peasants' councils. The dissatisfaction of the Bavarian peasantry during the war years is discussed in Chapter I, the attempt to extend the council system in Chapter V.

[45] This question has also acquired political overtones. Historians of the DDR insist that all credit is due Lenin and the responsiveness of German workers to their Russian comrades. See Albert Schreiner and Günther Schmidt, "Die Rätebewegung in Deutschland bis zur Novemberrevolution," *Revolutionäre Ereignisse und Probleme während der Periode der Grossen Sozialistischen Oktoberrevolution 1917/18* ([East] Berlin, 1957), 231-308. Historians of the Bonn Republic tend to stress the national origins of the German councils in previous labor organizations. See Walter Tormin, *Zwischen Räte-*

varian councils were no more a product of Bolshevism than the soviets had been in 1905. But in the given political circumstances of November 1918, no responsible public official could mistake the potential importance of the revolutionary councils as organs of radical influence. The future orientation of domestic and foreign policy in Bavaria was consequently dependent on the development of the council system.

diktatur und sozialer Demokratie. Die Geschichte der Rätebewegung in der Deutschen Republik 1918/19 (Düsseldorf, 1954), 126-138. Both of these studies have now been superseded by that of Kolb, *Die Arbeiterräte in der deutschen Innenpolitik,* 56-70 and passim, and Peter von Oertzen, *Betriebsräte in der Novemberrevolution* (Düsseldorf, 1963).

CHAPTER V

Council System and Cabinet Crisis

ONCE back at his office in the building of the Foreign Ministry, where a portrait of King Ludwig still hung ostentatiously above his desk, Kurt Eisner was confronted with a disarmingly ambitious agenda. He was committed to three major speeches within two weeks: to a joint session of the various Munich councils on November 28; to the initial meeting of the Bavarian State Soldiers' Council (*Landessoldatenrat*) two days later; and to the corresponding session of the Bavarian State Workers' Council (*Landesarbeiterrat*) on December 9. The deliberations of these groups were to be followed by the reconvocation of the Provisional National Council, supposedly to be the pro tempore governing body of Bavaria, on December 13. Since representation in the latter assembly might well depend on the character of the preliminary meetings, it was apparent that Eisner would need to sell his political wares at each session if he wished the councils to be, as he had predicted, the "elemental impulse" of the revolution. His first action was to meet privately with the executive committee (*Vollzugsausschuss*) of the Munich Council of Workers and Soldiers on November 27. Eisner had retained nominal chairmanship of this group, composed for the most part of those who had actively abetted him in the seizure of power three weeks before. They were, as he correctly surmised, still inclined to be like-minded in their support of him. Out of this meeting came a public declaration, addressed to the revolutionary councils of Berlin:

The executive committee of the Council of Workers, Soldiers, and Peasants ascertains with indignation, in light of the negotiations of the conference of representatives of the German Republic, the shocking fact that the compromised representatives of the previous system—Messrs. Erzberger,

Solf, David, and Scheidemann—are still exercising decisive influence, especially in foreign policy. We demand the immediate removal of these counter-revolutionary elements and call upon the Council of Workers and Soldiers in Berlin to effect by all means the fall of a regime which continues to provide an influential position for such persons.[1]

By anticipating the three council sessions in Munich with such a public statement, in effect signed in their name, Eisner and the executive committee probably hoped as much to influence the Bavarian council delegates themselves as to impress Berlin. It was another evidence of something which Eisner alternately tried to deny and to combat: his recognition of the newspaper as a dictator of public opinion.

The fact that Eisner could devote more of his attention to the operation of the councils was some indication that he considered the revolution to be safely established. The problem now was to keep it moving. But, certainly not by coincidence, this was just the moment at which outspoken opposition to his leadership began to mount. Frankly displeased by the accusation that party colleagues such as Philip Scheidemann and Eduard David were reactionaries to be dispensed with, the Social Democratic *Münchener Post* said its first harsh word about Eisner's premiership in reference to his maneuver to prescribe the policy of the councils: "From secret diplomacy we have now come to secret rule, an unworthy and absolutely unbearable circumstance."[2] At the same time, stories were circulating about a speech which Eisner had made to a council executive group in Berlin just before his return to Munich. He was reported to have said

---

[1] *Bayerische Dokumente*, 72. The *Vollzugsrat* of the Berlin councils voted to request the removal of Erzberger and Solf, but not of Social Democrats Scheidemann and David. *Ibid.*, 82.

[2] "Konterrevolutionäre Elemente," *MP*, 29 Nov. 1918, No. 279; and "Hinter geschlossenen Türen," *MP*, 30 Nov. 1918, No. 280.

that the system of councils would need to be consolidated to serve as "a substitute for bourgeois parliamentarianism which has become bankrupt," and that there could be no purpose in a nationally elected constituent assembly until a "new spirit" had permeated German politics. "The enthusiasm of Mr. Eisner for the National Assembly," commented one Liberal newspaper in Munich, "is thus exceedingly mild, and will perhaps diminish even further."[3]

It is fair to conclude, then, that Eisner was already aware of the interrelationship of his foreign policy and the question of the revolutionary councils in Bavaria. And he saw the critical importance of the proposal for the immediate election of a National Assembly, which he tended to equate with the domination of German affairs by Berlin. As an alternative, Eisner hoped for time to nurture the "new democracy," while realizing that this concept would need to be more exactly defined and tailored to appeal to the councils. Whereas the councils had first been organized to maintain the new order, now the new order would need to be systematized so as to maintain the councils. Since the *ad hoc* character of Eisner's thinking on this question necessarily had to take account of such elements of a system as were already established, it is important to consider the structure which had been developing in Bavaria during the initial weeks of the revolution. By doing so, one can understand the limitations of Eisner's policy concerning the councils and appreciate the character of the opposition which he was to encounter.

The Councils of Soldiers, Workers, and Peasants

Revolutionary councils were formed in every major city of Bavaria within days after the coup d'état of November 7. But by no means every municipality had an incompetent or unpopular administrator, nor was there everywhere a group

---

[3] "Eisner im Berliner Vollzugsrat," *MZ*, 26 Nov. 1918, No. 325; and "Eisner und die Nationalversammlung," *MZ*, 29 Nov. 1918, No. 328.

of revolutionaries decisive and forceful enough to impose themselves on the representatives of the old regime. The form and importance of the councils consequently differed widely from city to city: in Augsburg a council of workers and soldiers seized complete authority; in Nuremberg a strong council was compelled to tolerate a strong mayor; and in heavily Catholic Regensburg the mayor was able to maintain his prerogatives and to dominate the local councils.[4] It is possible to record with assurance that, by the end of November, there was some sort of council organization in virtually every township (*Gemeinde*) in Bavaria; one may therefore presume the existence of at least six to seven thousand separate bodies in the entire council system.[5] These councils were composed in

[4] On Augsburg see Ernst Niekisch, *Gewagtes Leben. Begegnungen und Begebnisse* (Cologne and Berlin, 1958), 38-41; on Nuremberg, Otto Gessler, *Reichswehrpolitik in der Weimarerzeit* (Stuttgart, 1958), 108-112; and on Regensburg, Richard Müller, *Vom Kaiserreich zur Republik* (2 vols.; Vienna, 1924-1925), II, 64. For a general view of the improvisation and spread of revolutionary councils throughout Germany, see Kolb, *Die Arbeiterräte in der deutschen Innenpolitik*, 83-113.

[5] Between July and September of 1919 an extensive survey of council organization and activity was conducted by the Ministry of the Interior (then under Fritz Endres). The resulting collection of council papers and bureaucratic reports has been placed on file in the Bayerisches Hauptstaatsarchiv (to be cited as BHS Munich). Consult the bibliography for a complete listing. Several of the provincial reports specify that councils existed "in nearly all townships," of which there were almost 8000 in 1918. The district and local reports tend to confirm this, as for example in the case of one district in Lower Franconia in which councils had been formed "in 48 of 50 townships." "Bezirksamt Marktheidenfeld . . . an die Regierung, Kammer des Innern in Würzburg. 24. VII. 1919. Betreff: Die Arbeiter-, Bauern- und Soldatenräte." BHS Munich, M. Inn. 54190. As the Rhenish Palatinate was immediately occupied by Entente troops, the councils there were soon curtailed by French military authorities. *Die Pfalz unter französischer Besatzung. Kalendarische Darstellung der Ereignisse vom Einmarsch 1918 bis November 1924* (Munich, 1925), 7-11.

every conceivable manner and represented a wide spectrum of political persuasion. With a few exceptions the councils had little influence or contact outside of their separate localities, and for that reason the term "council system" may be somewhat misleading.

Since all the councils were genuinely revolutionary in the sense of being without precedent in Bavaria, there was abundant confusion in terms of function as well as organization. No word was more frequently used by critics of the council system than "encroachments" (*Übergriffe*), and yet until there was a definition of the councils' power and a consensus as to their jurisdiction, such criticism was necessarily gratuitous—unless one expected the old regime to remain entirely unaltered by the revolution. Every duty and privilege appropriated by the councils was necessarily an encroachment on the previous system; the question was, to what extent was such an appropriation sanctioned by the fact of the revolution? This was not the sort of question which permitted an abstract answer. The function of the individual councils, like their form, thus emerged uncertainly and variously according to the varieties of political experience. It is well to keep this qualification in mind while considering the general structure and development of the three branches of the council system.

The soldiers' councils rapidly assumed a form similar to the cadres of the existing military establishment. For each unit of the Bavarian Army a representative council body was established as a counterpart. The first element, constituted during the night of revolution in Munich, had been a sort of extemporaneous general staff, designated simply as the Council of Soldiers. From this central authority originated, on November 8, instructions that each military post was to select a barrack council (*Kasernenrat*) of ten soldiers: "These assume direction of the barracks. Their instructions are to be followed implicitly."[6] When a measure of order had been

---

[6] "Soldaten Münchens!" *Bekanntmachungen*, F. Mon. 3197. The structure of the Bavarian Army is detailed in the *Hof- und Staats-*

restored in the city, further regulations were issued in an attempt to establish the rudiments of a council system for all of Bavaria. Instructions on November 13 specified: 1) that besides the barrack councils, there were to be councils in the military hospitals to represent the wounded (*Lazaretträte*); 2) that trustees were to be elected to councils at the division level (*Garnisonräte*, as they were later called); 3) that all soldiers' councils "were to find their culmination in a Steering Committee" (*Vollzugsausschuss*); 4) and that the Steering Committee, in turn, would delegate two plenipotentiaries (*Bevollmächtigte*) who would "work together in the most intimate contact" with the Minister for Military Affairs.[7] Signed by Eisner, Military Minister Rosshaupter, and Chairman of the Steering Committee Fritz Sauber, these regulations actually legislated a cleavage in the council structure, since the original Council of Soldiers automatically became the Steering Committee; it was not elected from below by the other council groups.

The functions allotted to the soldiers' councils by the regulations of November 13 were sufficiently vague to offer the councils a hope of grandeur and yet to withhold any real authority. The barrack councils were granted the right to hear complaints, recommend promotions, request the removal of junior-grade officers, and to "assist" in army command posts. But the last word in every case was accorded to the Ministry for Military Affairs, where the presence (without prescribed powers) of the council plenipotentiaries might or might not be of substantial importance. As it turned out, there soon developed "fundamental differences" between Albert Rosshaupter and the council representatives assigned to his ministry.[8]

---

handbuch des Königreichs Bayern für das Jahr 1913 (Munich, 1913), 270-294.

[7] "An die Armee des Volksstaates Bayern," BHS Munich, M. Inn. 54199.

[8] Mühsam, *Von Eisner bis Levíné*, 6. Attached to Rosshaupter's

The lot of the common soldier was changed only insofar as he might wear an open collar, slouch against a wall or munch a sandwich while on guard duty, and refuse to salute an officer in the street. In recognition of the times, officers were at first required to remove all medals and shoulder insignia. They were requested by the government to place themselves at the disposal of the new regime, and the councils were instructed to accept the authority of any ranking military personnel who did not violate the spirit of the revolution: "the officers come not as your superiors, as before, but they come as SOLDIERS!"[9] Yet it was a distinction without a difference. A French newspaper correspondent even claimed to have heard officers addressed by enlisted men as *"Oberkamerad."*[10] Incidents of insubordination were generally confined to the first few days of the revolution; the authority of the officer corps was thereafter upheld by the Minister for Military Affairs and grudgingly conceded by council leaders. Although certain council groups gained political importance in Munich, most of the others enjoyed at most a brief opportunity to be insulting with impunity.

The files of council documents show, paradoxically, that most of the "encroachments" by soldiers' councils were not in areas where large military units were stationed (and where discipline was thus likely to be more tightly enforced). Complaints were, however, frequently submitted from scattered localities in which a small garrison either invaded the offices

---

ministry as a representative of the workers' councils, Mühsam found the soldiers' councils "for the most part entirely reactionary." *Ibid.*, 28. Rosshaupter had made his own view clear to the cabinet right from the outset: "In military affairs the officers should decide; the soldiers' councils ought rather to be active in social matters." *Ministerratsprotokolle,* 9 Nov. 1918, BGS Munich, PA, VII, 104a.

[9] "An die Offiziere!" *Bekanntmachungen,* F. Mon. 3306. "Soldaten!" *Ibid.,* F. Mon. 3311.

[10] Gentizon, *La révolution allemande,* 13. See also his chapter entitled "Le nouveau régime et l'armée," *ibid.,* 83-93.

of a mayor or bureaucratic official, or peremptorily assumed command of food provisioning, housing, and the like. It was the wish to deal with this sort of situation, rather than to create a council system as such, which first induced governmental regulation of council activity. On November 21 Erhard Auer dictated a memorandum for Albert Rosshaupter in which he took note of the "numerous complaints" about the soldiers' councils and requested that Rosshaupter issue specific regulations designating their relationship to civilian administrative officials:

> In this connection it is to be emphasized that no executive power resides in the soldiers' councils. They are therefore to avoid any interference in state or municipal administrative activity. As a matter of principle, the execution of laws and other legal injunctions will be, now as before, carried out by the incumbent offices and authorities. At the most, soldiers' councils can . . . cooperate in the maintenance of peace and order and in the fulfillment of other incidental duties.[11]

In Auer's view, then, the role to be assigned to the councils was an exceedingly circumscribed one. His position as Minister of the Interior and leader of the Social Democratic Party was soon to make this view of decisive importance for the development of the council system.

Before another week was out Rosshaupter had delivered the requested regulations. Aside from an introductory statement about the councils as the inculcation of the "new spirit," they were brief and precise. Special prominence was given to the right of an enlisted man to file a grievance against a superior; "nevertheless . . . the duty to obey is neither cancelled nor suspended." Nor were the councils, under any circumstances, empowered to depose and replace an officer. It

[11] "An das Ministerium für militärische Angelegenheiten. München, 21. November 1918. Betreff: Soldatenräte," BHS Munich, M. Inn. 54199.

150

was furthermore stated explicitly that "intrusion into non-military affairs . . . is not authorized. The connection of the council organization with the general political direction of the state is to occur exclusively through the State Soldiers' Council and through the delegation in the provisional parliament." Subsequent observations by soldiers' delegates at council meetings in Munich were to make clear that the regular administrative staff of the army was thereafter able to prevail over council representatives.[12] Moreover, demobilization soon began to cause a slow attrition of soldiers' councils, and that unceasingly extolled objective of the revolution, universal disarmament, was a constant moral impediment to any claim of permanence. By the end of November, therefore, the vital impetus of the council system had already passed from the soldiers' councils to the workers' councils.

Just as the soldiers' councils reflected the structure of the Bavarian Army, the workers' councils naturally developed an anatomy like that of the state bureaucracy. In neither case, it is worthwhile to note, did the Russian example constitute a precedent except in some vaguely inspirational way. Without predetermined plan, guiding hand, or even governmental directive, local councils were formed in one community after another as if they had been infected by a communicable and highly contagious disease. There is, of course, sufficient evidence of conscious attempts by council members in one locality to organize sister councils in adjacent regions, but the sudden appearance of workers' councils throughout Bavaria was too swift and too widespread to have been directed from Munich. Nor did the extremely chaotic result testify to an organized program. One can only suggest some theory of simultaneous discovery, and record that decades of

[12] "Vorläufige Verordnung für die Soldatenräte," 29 Nov. 1918, BHS Munich, M. Inn. 54198. A mine of information for a study of the emergence of the soldiers' councils is the *Verhandlungen des provisorischen Nationalrates*, Beilage II, 13-126.

indoctrination through the Social Democratic Party and months of agitation by various radical groups in Germany had not been entirely wasted on the Bavarian working population.

That the system of workers' councils took the form of the existing bureaucratic apparatus is more easily explainable and demonstrable. It was characteristic of the workers' councils either to force out local officials entirely or (more often) to effect an administrative *modus vivendi* with governmental bureaucrats. With its seat in a town hall or district office, a workers' council would normally seek to dictate or oversee bureaucratic functions. The result was a plethora of "township councils" (*Gemeinderäte*) and "district councils" (*Distriktsräte* or *Bezirksräte*), but a total absence in the first weeks of any councils corresponding to the highest administrative unit of the Bavarian state, the province (*Kreis*). This was so because the administrative headquarters of provinces were all located in their respective provincial capitals, where local councils immediately established priority. With possibly one exception, the provincial council "committees" (*Kreisausschüsse*) never formed an important or coherent part of the council hierarchy.[18]

Munich was a special case. Like the Steering Committee of the soldiers' councils, the Central Workers' Council (*Zentralarbeiterrat*) was a creation of the first day of revolution in the capital. During the initial week, this body was roughly synonymous with the Revolutionary Workers' Council (RAR), a group evolved from the original Council of Workers elected in Munich's Mathäserbräu on November 7. The

---

[18] The first and only important provincial executive committee was formed in Augsburg on November 27; it immediately protested Auer's domination of the workers' councils and berated the *Zentralarbeiterrat* in Munich as unrepresentative of the council system. "Kreis-Ausschuss der Schwäbischen Arbeiterräte. An den Bayerischen Ministerpräsidenten, München. Augsburg, den 28. November 1918. Betreff: Beschlüsse der Schwäbischen Arbeiterräte," BHS Munich, M. Inn. 54199.

RAR immediately undertook a vigorous program of organizing "shop councils" (*Betriebsräte*) in Munich's industrial quarters; these were to be the urban counterparts of the township councils elsewhere. The result was somewhat too successful for the interests of the RAR. The Munich shop councils dispatched procedural questions in a minimum of time and then elected their own Munich Workers' Council (MAR). Controlled by trade union leaders, this body thereupon claimed to be the legitimate representative of the city's proletariat and, on November 14, forced the RAR to agree that: 1) the membership of the RAR would be limited to fifty; 2) the RAR would join with the 550 delegates of the MAR; and 3) from this body a new Central Workers' Council would be elected; of its fifty members, ten could be appointed by the RAR as representatives of "those who have magnificently assisted at the peak of the revolution."[14] Within the system of workers' councils in the city of Munich, then, the "revolutionaries" were formally in a minority of eleven to one; whereas within the central council body ostensibly representing all of Bavaria, they were outnumbered by only five to one. The terms of this agreement emphasized two characteristic features of the system of workers' councils: the exaggerated political importance of the Munich councils compared with the provincial, and the disproportionate prominence of RAR members within council gatherings in the capital.

If regulation of the soldiers' councils was clearly the province of the Minister for Military Affairs, it was not at first certain who should be the corresponding governmental administrative officer for the workers' councils. On November 7 Kurt Eisner had been elected leader of the Council of Workers, but upon becoming Prime Minister, he had preferred to

[14] "Ergebnis der Verhandlung der von den Gewerkschaftsführern am 14. November 1918 gewählten kleinen Kommission (Schieffer, Ischinger, Huber) mit Kurt Eisner betreffend der Besetzung des Arbeiterrates in München, den 14. November 1918, nachts 10 Uhr 10," BGS Munich, MA 1943, I.V. 378.

assume personal direction of foreign affairs rather than to occupy himself with the detailed operations of bureaucratic machinery. Eisner had the sort of mind which conceived of political activity in terms of speeches and proclamations; this was to be characteristic of his entire Prime Ministry and, as a case in point, of his relationship to the councils. During November an immense volume of correspondence passed through Eisner's office.[15] Nearly all of it was handled directly by his two private secretaries, who prided themselves on answering every letter regardless of how inconsequential the contents. Much of this correspondence—perhaps one-fifth— had to do in some way with the council system, whether from individual councils announcing their activities or from municipal and bureaucratic officials requesting a statement of policy about the council system. The evidence indicates that Eisner himself intervened only occasionally in these matters, and that he generally chose to refer them to the Ministry of the Interior. When Eisner did send instructions to council groups, it was usually in order to grant them "the right of control" (*das Kontrollrecht*) over the affairs of bureaucratic officials.[16] The ambiguity of this expression prevented it from ever being admitted to the official vocabulary of governmental regulations for the council system, since it left unsettled the awkward question of who was to have the last word in case of dispute. It did imply that the bureaucrats were to stay in office, but failed to specify in what sense their activity was to be subject to "control" by the councils.

Trained as a party functionary, Erhard Auer knew better than Eisner that a bureaucracy depends as much as any army

[15] See the bibliography for a listing of the political documents and correspondence of the *Nachlass Eisner*, BGS Munich. Several cartons of Eisner's personal and literary papers were returned to his family in 1948, present whereabouts unknown. *Ibid.*, PA, VII, 115.

[16] See, for example, the "certification" given by Eisner to the council at Lindau, 21 Nov. 1918, BHS Munich, M. Inn. 54199.

on a definitive chain-of-command. While Eisner was writing an occasional letter to council leaders, Auer sent out over six hundred messages to government officials and revolutionary councils in all of Bavaria.[17] By following this correspondence from day to day, it is possible to see the formulation emerging which, by November 21, became a form letter. It was essentially the same statement which Auer recommended to Rosshaupter for the soldiers' councils, and it bears repeating: "The councils of soldiers, workers, and peasants possess no executive power. They are therefore to avoid any interference in state or municipal administrative activity. As a matter of principle, the execution of laws and other legal injunctions will be, now as before, carried out by the incumbent offices and authorities."[18]

When the "Provisional Regulations for the Workers' Councils" were issued on November 26, it was this formulation which was ratified despite the vapid assurance that, for the time being, the councils represented "the basis of the new system of administration." The regulations made no mention of any "right of control."[19] Although Eisner had privately stated that he wished "to centralize the contact with the workers' councils in his person," the system quickly fell under the supervision of Erhard Auer.[20] Eisner's influence was therefore restricted primarily to personal contacts with council leaders and public appearances at council meetings in Munich.

[17] See Auer's statement to the State Workers' Council in Munich on December 10. *Verhandlungen des provisorischen Nationalrates,* Beilage III, 195-197.

[18] Cited, as an example at random, from Auer's notification "An das Bezirksamt Mindelheim. München, 21. November 1918. Betreff: Befugnisse der Soldaten-, Arbeiter- und Bauernräte," BHS Munich, M. Inn. 54199.

[19] "Provisorische Richtlinien für die Arbeiterräte," 28 Nov. 1918, BHS Munich, M. Inn. 54190.

[20] *Ministerratsprotokolle,* 20 Nov. 1918, BGS Munich, GN 2/1-2/2.

The peasants' councils had neither the obvious structure nor the initial revolutionary impetus of the soldiers' and workers' councils. One of the most revealing documents of the revolution was a brief note written out by Eisner on November 9: "Mr. Ludwig Gandorfer of Pfaffenberg is empowered to invite fifty members of the Council of Peasants to the Provisional National Assembly."[21] The instructions were nonsensical, but quite clear. There was no Council of Peasants at the time, but Eisner plainly wanted his colleague to create one. When Gandorfer was killed in an automobile accident on the next day, during an excursion into the countryside to enlist support, this responsibility passed to a hastily organized Central Peasants' Council (*Zentralbauernrat*) in Munich. Within a week, Gandorfer's younger brother Karl was able to establish his dominance in this body. As he represented the more radical wing of the Bavarian Peasants' League, Karl Gandorfer's leadership was regarded as an affront by the much larger and more conservative Bavarian *Bauernverein*.[22] The latter at first refused any cooperation in the formation of peasants' councils, and the task of organization was therefore undertaken largely on the personal initiative of the younger Gandorfer and his friends. As a result, the peasants' councils most often assumed the character of local party cells of the Peasants' League and were numerous only in those regions where individual leaders of the League were influential.

Since one of the first problems of the new regime was to establish order in the distribution of foodstuffs, the workers' councils soon took a direct interest in securing rural support for the council system. There were frequent instances of peasants' councils formed by workers' councils, and of joint

[21] Quoted by Mattes, *Die bayerischen Bauernräte*, 114.

[22] See Karl Gandorfer's testimony in "Bericht über die Vollsitzung des Landesbauernrates am 15. August 1919 in der Residenz zu München," BHS Munich, M. Inn. 54196. Also consult the excellent analytical and statistical account in Mattes' chapter, "Die Ursachen der Gründung der Bauernräte," *Die bayerischen Bauernräte*, 66-93.

workers' and peasants' councils. In some cases conservative farm organizations such as the *Bauernverein* and the *Bund der Landwirte* established peasants' councils themselves in order to prevent the intrusion of representatives from the Peasants' League. One result of all this manipulation by existing quasi-political organizations was to create a decided disproportion of structure and significance between north and south. The peasants' councils were stronger in the provinces of Upper and Lower Bavaria and Swabia, weaker in the three provinces of Franconia and the Upper Palatinate.[23] The same rule-of-thumb was thus applicable to the peasants' councils and to the councils of workers and soldiers: the greater the proximity to Munich, the more obvious the impact of the revolution.

The Central Peasants' Council was without a doubt the least prominent and the least effective politically of all the council executive bodies in the capital city. It was not only assailed by the conservative opponents of the Peasants' League, but its legitimacy was challenged by local and district councils who resented not having had a voice—or a representative—in its formation.[24] The entire system of peasants' councils, moreover, soon came under the jurisdiction of the Ministry of the Interior. Karl Gandorfer repeatedly attempted to have a new cabinet post created, a "Ministry of Agriculture," to be filled by a member of the Peasants' League— presumably himself. In this he was publicly supported by

[23] *Ibid.*, 61. See Schlögl, *Bayerische Agrargeschichte*, 572-573.

[24] Typical of council complaints was this message: "The chairman explained to us that the 50 members of the Central Peasants' Council were already appointed. We do not recognize this arbitrary selection because it originated only at the wish of a few peasants' councils and its selection did not occur through the district delegates." "Der Bezirksbauernrat Lindau. An das Staatsministerium des Innern. Lindau, 13.12.1918," BHS Munich, M. Inn. 54199. Eisner nevertheless upheld the *Zentralbauernrat*'s claim to leadership. "Kurt Eisner. An den Bezirksbauernrat Lindau. München, den 17.12.18," BGS Munich, MA 1943, I.V. 378.

Eisner, but frustrated each time by Erhard Auer. Auer's ostensible reason was the puny membership of the Peasants' League compared with that of the *Bauernverein*.[25] He might have added two further considerations: that he did not wish any additional support for Eisner in the cabinet, and that he did not care to install Gandorfer as the final authority for the affairs of the peasants' councils. The system was consequently characterized by the political apathy of the rural population toward the Central Peasants' Council and, at the same time, by the extreme interest of the Ministry of the Interior in circumscribing its actual political power.

Structurally the peasants' councils followed the general pattern of the workers' councils, but lagged in coherence and spirit. There was no recorded instance of a peasants' council turning out a local official at the point of a gun. Meetings of peasants' councils were in most cases limited to small gatherings on market days. The most obvious shortcoming of the "system" was the lack of communication. There was never a concerted attempt to enforce a unified policy on the district and local councils, whose only regular instructions from Munich council leaders came in the form of announcements in newspapers. Conversely, there was no pattern of regular report from the districts to the Central Council, whose functions were limited to three: acting as a clearing-house for rural complaints, organizing the sale of horses by the Bavarian Army during its demobilization (granted as a personal favor by Eisner to Karl Gandorfer), and representing the peasants' interests at council meetings in Munich. The "Temporary Regulations for the Peasants' Councils" of November 26 did no more than repeat the formula already established for the soldiers' and workers' councils.[26]

[25] *Ministerratsprotokolle*, 3 Dec. 1918, BGS Munich, GN 2/1-2/2.
[26] "Vorläufige Richtlinien für die Bauernräte," BHS Munich, M. Inn. 54190. On the sale of horses, see the report of Karl Gandorfer, *Verhandlungen des provisorischen Nationalrates*, No. 6, 174-176.

It was certainly more than a coincidence that the provisional regulations for all three branches of the council system were issued simultaneously. The designing hand was that of Erhard Auer, and the design in each case was to bar the councils from executive power at every level of administration. At the same time, the process of filling the lacunae of the council system was just beginning: both the creation of councils in townships where they did not already exist and the election of intermediary councils to span the structural gap between local and central council bodies. The bureaucracy was even instructed to supervise the elections, doubtless on the theory that a properly nominated council would be more inclined to respect regular administrative procedure than one organized by a radical-minded council agent from Munich. The total effect of the regulation and expansion of the council system was to call attention to the fact that the state government was thereby incurring a financial obligation of considerable proportion. In turn, this set in motion an effort, directed from Auer's ministry, to tighten the government's financial controls over the councils. Thus even while the number of individual councils was being increased during early December, the system as a whole was examined with an eye to reducing it in size, cost, and influence.[27]

The terminal date of this development was to be December 17. By then governmental regulations included three important specifications: 1) that soldiers' councils were to be completely divorced from workers' councils and paid for exclusively from the military budget; 2) that the peasants' councils were to be united whenever possible with the workers' councils and regarded, if separate from workers' councils, as "honorary" (i.e., non-remunerative) bodies of public service; 3) and that therefore, only workers' councils were to depend on state funds for compensation. Each of these stipulations had an implication which might not have been obvious at

[27] For a consideration of the financial problems of the government, see Chapter VII.

first glance, since they 1) eliminated the combined soldiers'-and-workers' councils, generally the earliest and most radical of council bodies; 2) ended any claim to autonomy of the system of peasants' councils and thus assured their control by the Ministry of the Interior; and 3) effectively reduced the workers' councils to an adjunct of the bureaucracy while assigning to them only perfunctory bureaucratic duties. It is noteworthy that the only italicized sentence of the "Organization and Prerogatives of the Workers' Councils" of December 17 was *"The workers' and peasants' councils and their committees possess no executive power."*[28] It needs no further explanation that those who looked to the councils as the basis of a new principle of democratic government watched their development during early December with increasing apprehension.

The Problem of Parliamentarianism

The revolution had postponed but not cancelled the political contest between the Majority Socialists and the Independents. After three weeks of informal truce, the temporarily repressed opposition between the two factions began to re-emerge in the form of a coalition crisis. This first serious test of the new regime was a result of the increasingly divergent conduct of domestic and foreign policy. The regulations governing the council system issued on November 26 had been formulated on the personal initiative of Erhard Auer, whereas the diplomatic wrangle with Berlin was generally regarded, for better or worse, as Kurt Eisner's private affair. Neither had received the full and formal approval of the entire cabinet.[29] By examining the records of the cabinet meetings on November 26 and 27, one can see that these two

[28] "Organisation und Befugnisse der Arbeiterräte," *BSZ*, 19 Dec. 1918, No. 295.

[29] Eisner was not present in the cabinet meeting at which the text of the council regulations was approved. *Ministerratsprotokolle*, 25 Nov. 1918, BGS Munich, GN 2/1-2/2.

issues were far from being unrelated—that their juxtaposition implied, in fact, a contradiction—and that their resolution could not long be delayed. The point at which they converged was the question of the National Assembly.

It was Eisner's view that the Berlin government wished "to return as rapidly as possible to the old conditions, against which the workers' and soldiers' councils are justifiably offering resistance." He was convinced that the councils were a guarantee against counter-revolution on the one hand, and against Bolshevism on the other. As for the latter, he told the cabinet, the real danger was not from the councils, as many claimed, but from "the paid agents of the Russian soviets." Eisner argued that the German people could not afford to wait for all the legalistic formalities which the convocation of a National Assembly would require, but must act directly to save the nation from extremism. A display of popular support for the revolutionary leadership through the councils would have this effect, he said, since "Wilson will deal with any regime which has the masses behind it." In Eisner's opinion, therefore, it was patently untrue that the National Assembly was a necessary presupposition of effective diplomacy. "You must have confidence in me."[30]

The tone of Eisner's explanation to the cabinet was pleading and personal; it was not a formal demand for a vote of confidence, and no such vote was taken. Various ministers expressed a feeling of disquiet: about the strictly personal character of Eisner's action, about possible reprisals from Berlin, about the endangered unity of the German nation, and about the enormous costs of supporting the council system— all, in the opinion of Auer and his Social Democratic colleagues, manifestations of instability to which a National Assembly might put an end. Eisner replied to each point, but at length only to the final one. Although it was true that the soldiers' councils would "gradually disappear," the peasants' councils must be maintained "to achieve the liberation of the

[30] *Ibid.*, 26-27 Nov. 1918.

peasants from the former system . . . from the *Zentrum*."
And as for the system of workers' councils:

> We cannot eliminate them now, or else we will have Bol-
> shevism. . . . For the time being they are a sensible ar-
> rangement. [I am] therefore also an opponent of the im-
> mediate convocation of the National Assembly. The people
> must be allowed to express themselves. For the transition
> period—that is, at least one year—this organization should
> remain. Whether the inner transformation will succeed is
> the question.[31]

It is probably impossible in retrospect to do more than
Eisner ever did himself during his Prime Ministry: to define
precisely what he meant by an "inner transformation." But
it is at least clear that he wished to delay the establishment
of parliamentarianism in Bavaria, if not in all of Germany,
long enough to institutionalize the original impetus of the
revolutionary councils. For the moment he did not elaborate
on the form or the function which he envisaged for the council system, nor did he specify what its relationship should be
to the executive, legislative, and bureaucratic institutions of
a parliamentary democracy. There is nothing to indicate, in
fact, that he had made any systematic attempt to consider
these questions. Yet two things are immediately striking
about Eisner's conception of the councils: that he wanted to
maintain them in addition to traditional parliamentary institutions (recalling the proposal for a *Nebenparlament*); and
that he regarded them as an alternative rather than as a means
to Bolshevism. In the briefest terms, these two points constituted the essence of Eisner's political thinking during his term
as the Prime Minister of Bavaria.[32]

For their part, the Social Democratic ministers lacked any
well-considered ideological reason for rejecting out of hand

[31] *Ibid.*

[32] For the subsequent development of Eisner's theoretical views,
see Chapter VII.

the council idea. They could point out the questionable logic of urging immediate action through the councils to save Germany from radicalism while, at the same time, requesting a year of grace for the councils to become adequately established. But logic was by no means the sole basis of their disinclination to grant Eisner's appeal for support. It was equally important that they shared neither his malice toward parliamentarianism nor his optimistic estimation of the council system as the practical instrument of a "new democracy." They were therefore determined to press for parliamentary elections at the earliest feasible date and to insure bureaucratic control over the operation of the councils. This was the crux of the ensuing governmental crisis.

At the outset Eisner appeared to be comfortably in command of the situation. It has been already noted that his initial action after returning from Berlin was to gain, in private, the approval of a council executive group for his diplomatic enterprise. His first public appearance was on November 28, when he spoke to a joint session of council delegates from the city of Munich. He was obviously enjoying a flush of confidence that day as he told the assembly that "in Bavaria ninety-five per cent of the people stand behind us." His remarks appropriately fell into two parts: a defense of his policy vis-à-vis Berlin and a testimonial of his personal dedication to the idea of the councils. Since he repeated much of what he had already told the cabinet of ministers, it is sufficient to give one citation:

> Gentlemen! I speak to you, to the councils of workers, soldiers, and peasants. But I do not in the least doubt that there are already today wide circles which are only waiting to put aside these corporations of the people, wrought out of the revolution. In the Reich as in the individual states, the call for a National Assembly is dictated only by the hope, through the National Assembly, to eliminate the immediate organic participation of the masses.

163

The council gathering was obviously impressed, and responded by giving unanimous approval to the resolution of its executive committee endorsing Eisner's opposition to Berlin.[33]

It would seem that Eisner had thereby gained a solid block of support in the Bavarian capital, but it is difficult to determine what importance should actually be attached to such a vote of confidence. It is undoubtedly true that the council members could agree that Eisner should "search for peace" and that former representatives of the Kaiser's court should not represent Germany in the armistice negotiations. But subsequent debates in council sessions were to show that many council leaders were not restricted to such a primitive formulation of the issues. It is also true that the November 28 meeting of the Munich councils probably represented the greatest possible concentration of "radical" opinion in Bavaria. But if radicalism was to be defined as opposition in principle to the parliamentary system of representation, the records of Eisner's regime show that only a small minority of council members, even in Munich, was genuinely radical in this sense. It must therefore be concluded that most of those voting in support of Eisner's foreign policy were unaware of its total implications for Bavaria's internal development; and that the others chose not to oppose Eisner exclusively on the grounds of his tactics in defying Berlin when a more fundamental matter of principle was at stake. It was a question not only of how well the people were represented at the moment, but of what was to be the ultimate basis of representation. The importance of the internal crisis which followed was that it made this issue a matter of common knowledge and concern.

By proposing the delay of a constituent assembly, Eisner had publicly exposed himself to the charge that he intended to impede the parliamentary process, or even to replace it with a new concept of democracy based on the council sys-

[33] *Verhandlungen des provisorischen Nationalrates*, Beilage I, 1-6.

tem. His address at the opening plenary session of the Bavarian State Soldiers' Council on the last day of November was hardly designed to allay suspicion. Eisner told the delegates that he wished to speak of "the inner foundation of the new democracy . . . the councils of workers, soldiers, and peasants." He spoke at length, and repeated himself often. Despite its forensic deficencies, the speech did make unmistakably clear Eisner's intention that parliamentary procedure should be modified as well as supplemented by the council organizations.

> We do not want to create a formal electoral democracy in which a slip will be thrown into the ballot box every three to five years and then everything will be left to the leaders and representatives. [That] is actually the opposite of a democracy. The new democracy should be such that the masses themselves directly and continuously assist in the affairs of the commonwealth. . . . The restitution of parliamentarianism in the old style means the elimination of the councils of workers, soldiers, and peasants. This I will attempt to prevent so long as I have the power to do so.

The rest of Eisner's remarks were largely theatrical. He garnished an account of his trip to Berlin with bits of dialogue between himself, Erzberger, and Solf. "These gentlemen made the war," he reiterated, and "are guilty for the prolongation of the war." He also chided those who had first encouraged him to assert Bavarian leadership in the Reich and then attacked him for being a separatist. His own position, he claimed, was clear and unchanged. "I will be against centralism in foreign politics, in domestic politics, and in party politics as long as I live. . . . I see the restitution of Germany in the unfolding strength of her members, not in their amputation."[34]

The debate which followed Eisner's speech, and centered on it, lasted through four days. The transcript of these sessions

[34] *Ibid.*, Beilage II, 13-23.

165

is the record of a rapid deterioration of the Prime Minister's position and of his confidence. The keynote of opposition was struck by Erhard Auer, who referred to Eisner and the council system in all but name when he warned that "a dictatorship can and must not exist in a free people's state." In an equally obvious criticism of Eisner's foreign policy, Auer explicitly described Bavaria as "an inseparable member of the German Reich." As the debate proceeded it became clear that an informal alliance had arisen between the provincial delegates, who objected to domination of the executive committees by the Munich councils, and those within the Munich councils who spelled out Auer's inference that Eisner might be an anti-parliamentarian. Eisner twice returned to the podium in self-defense and, in fact, showed an unusual extemporaneous flair. He admitted that an "exclusive predominance" (*Alleinherrschaft*) of Munich had unavoidably prevailed in the first days of the revolution, but he stated categorically that "there is no dictatorship." As for the parliamentary issue, the National Assembly in reality posed "no problem at all," since it would be convened once the "necessary preparations" had been taken; it must be the "crown" of the revolution, he said grandly, but not the foundation.[35]

But equivocation was useless. When the afternoon session of November 30 became a shambles of personal invective, Eisner admitted frankly that "I very much regret this debate." Meanwhile, pressure was brought to bear on Eisner from two other sources. The Union of Bavarian Transportation Personnel issued a formal declaration on the morning of December 1, stating that continued cooperation with the regime was contingent on a reaffirmation of its previously stated intention to hold elections for a National Assembly as soon as possible. "Delay," the Union warned, "means dis-

[35] *Ibid.*, 24-55.

order and dissolution, anarchy and civil war."[36] Another challenge to Eisner's authority was delivered simultaneously by the release of a statement from Professor Foerster, in Munich on leave from his diplomatic post in Switzerland, entitled "The Untenability of the Present Political Situation in Bavaria." Foerster stated that he had been deeply disappointed by developments in Munich which, if continued, could only lead to a preponderance by the one class of society represented in the revolutionary councils.

> That a true democratic representation of the interests and rights of *all* classes will not thereby be secured is clear beyond doubt. *But Eisner does not at all want such equality.* . . . He has lost all faith in the bourgeoisie. *And therefore he is struggling desperately against the National Assembly.*

As one who knew intimately the international situation, Foerster concluded, he must warn that there could be no hope of a reasonable settlement with the Entente until a reliable regime was empowered to speak for all of Germany. Only through the National Assembly could this be possible.[37]

With that, three major props of Eisner's regime were all but swept away. Voting on procedural matters in the State Soldiers' Council indicated that its Steering Committee had lost control of the assembly. A crucial sector of the bureaucracy threatened an insubordination which could paralyze the whole economy, even in the unlikely event that there would be no other defections within the administration. And the whole substance of Eisner's foreign policy had been publicly challenged by the man on whose advice and consent it had been primarily based. This was the situation on the morning

[36] "Das bayerische Verkehrspersonal für die Nationalversammlung," *MZ*, 2 Dec. 1918, No. 331.
[37] "Die Unhaltbarkeit der gegenwärtigen politischen Lage in Bayern," *MP*, 2 Dec. 1918, No. 281.

of December 2 as the assembly of soldiers' councils reconvened to await a report from the cabinet. While the delegates marked time, the ministers met secretly in Eisner's office. Unknown to the press and to the council representatives, Erhard Auer had resigned as Minister of the Interior. His resignation, of course, would mean the end of any political coalition between the Social Democratic Party and Eisner's Independent Party. And since the majority of council representatives were also members or supporters of the SPD, it was possibly a mortal blow to the council system in Bavaria as well. Eisner did the only thing he could: he begged Auer to reconsider and to accept a "compromise." When Auer consented and the ministers began to hammer out the details of a settlement, the cabinet meeting lasted on through the afternoon.[38] The council delegates were restless and had to be twice adjourned. At 5:20 P.M. the ministers at last filed into the chamber and sat while Eisner read without comment a unanimous declaration of the cabinet. The statement was punctuated by an occasional *"bravo"* or *"sehr gut"* from the audience as it promised both revolutionary progress and administrative order, a curb to centralization and unity with the Reich, the introduction of socialistic measures and a continuation of free enterprise, maintenance of the councils and reaffirmation of parliamentary procedure. On each point there

[38] Minister of Justice Johannes Timm and Minister of Transportation Heinrich von Frauendorfer joined Auer in threatening their resignation. The minutes of the December 2 meeting are unfortunately missing from the file of Grassmann's notes (it is impossible to determine beyond a doubt who removed this record or for what reason), but the transcript of the following day's proceedings begins with this notation: "Auer, Timm, and Frauendorfer had declared their resignation, then conditions." *Ministerratsprotokolle*, 3 Dec. 1918, BGS Munich, GN 2/1-2/2. Auer was the only one to make a public statement on the matter: "After I had relinquished my office on Monday, December 2, 1918, Mr. Eisner urgently requested me to continue the conduct of my office as Minister of the Interior." "Meine Absetzung," *MP*, 7-8 Dec. 1918, No. 286.

was evidence of give and take between Eisner and Auer. Only one proposition was unqualified, and only this assertion was ostentatiously applauded by the assembly of council delegates: "the people's regime of Bavaria will honor its pledge to convoke the National Assembly as rapidly as possible."[39]

Each of the ministers followed Eisner in turn, promising support of the cabinet's resolution and outlining the policies and problems of his particular ministry. The total effect was to restate without ambiguity the provisional character of the Eisner regime and to preclude any foreseeable threat to the parliamentary principle. It was a scarcely mitigated defeat for Eisner's concept of a "new democracy" as a system of direct representation through the councils of soldiers, workers, and peasants. This was not necessarily tantamount to a renunciation of the council system as a subsidiary of the executive and administrative structure of the state, but the sense of the cabinet's declaration was certainly to underscore the word "subsidiary." Bavaria thereupon entered a phase of preparation for electoral contests to determine the proportion, not the principle, of parliamentary representation.

If Kurt Eisner was not at liberty after December 2 to challenge the parliamentary principle, he did continue to hope that his conception of a "new democracy" could be ratified by parliamentary means. His ultimate objective—to integrate the council system with the traditional branches of government—thus remained fixed, though imprecisely defined. Since it was still questionable as to how rapidly it would be possible to stage the popular elections, Eisner could persist in advocating that they be deferred until the "new spirit" had been secured in Bavaria. But it was a matter—as he recognized—which now lay beyond his control.[40] Short of an attempt to

<hr>

[39] "Eine programmatische Erklärung des Ministerrates," *Bekanntmachungen*, F. Mon. 3386.

[40] Announcement that elections for the German National Assem-

impose a personal dictatorship by declaring martial law and Bavaria's secession from the German Reich, both absurd and improbable courses, Eisner had no realistic alternative to participation in an electoral process in which he had little prospect of success. While it is probably true that he overestimated the extent of his popular support, it can hardly be argued that Eisner expected a plurality of the Socialist vote, much less an absolute majority of the total electorate. The most he could do was to stall for time and hope for the best.

The Majority Socialists, however, were unwilling to tolerate any more of Eisner's procrastination. At a cabinet meeting just three days after the coalition settlement, Erhard Auer moved that January 12, 1919, be designated as the date for statewide elections to the Bavarian Landtag. In countering this proposal and arguing for a delay in balloting, Eisner warned that the cabinet could not afford to give the impression of ruling against the councils, lest it thereby provoke a "second revolution." This was an injudicious moment to wave a red flag. The ensuing quarrel between Eisner and several of the other ministers demonstrated that the coalition crisis was actually far from resolved.

One of the important but intangible factors influencing the conduct of the regime was the climate of feeling among its leaders. The personal strain within the cabinet was never recorded in the press, seldom evident in official pronouncements, and only vaguely understood outside of the administration itself. Nor did a single member of Eisner's cabinet later publish a memoir. It is therefore worthwhile to repro-

---

bly would take place on January 19, 1919, was made official in Berlin by the Ebert government on November 30. *Schulthess*, 1918/I, 529-530. Eleven days later Eisner told a meeting of leftists in the Wagnerbräu that "the National Assembly is an accomplished fact. If the proletariat now prevents the National Assembly, this will mean the bankruptcy of the proletariat." "Die Radikalen," *MZ*, 12 Dec. 1918, No. 341.

duce at some length the only direct evidence of the bickering and backbiting which was henceforward to undermine the effectiveness of the republican government. After Eisner's rejoinder to Auer, the transcript of the December 5 cabinet session (here slightly abbreviated) continues in the staccato style of the recording secretary:

TIMM: A workers' council cannot stand beside an authorized [parliamentary] representation with machine guns. That is anarchy. . . . Then we need no popular representation at all. There is either one or the other.

FRAUENDORFER [to Eisner]: You are no statesman, commit blunders, are an anarchist. Don't take everything for granted, I warn you. You are no statesman, you are a fool!

EISNER: I have also done my job. You are no politician. . . .

FRAUENDORFER: Everyone says that you are not able to govern. . . .

EISNER: Public opinion is a matter of indifference to me. . . . You are for elimination of the councils of workers, peasants, and soldiers.

TIMM: Yes, if there is order in state and Reich.

AUER: If the Republic is secured. . . .

TIMM: Is it your view that if the National Assembly is unacceptable, then the soldiers should disband it again?

EISNER: No, but under the circumstances a new revolution would occur. The voters must have the possibility of bringing pressure on the parliament. If the new National Assembly concurs with the general disposition [of the people], no one will have an interest in agitating against this parliament. . . . But if it does not perform its task, then we will have a means of pressure in the masses. We want to protect the present accomplishments [of the revolution].

HOFFMANN: We are mired in an internal conflict. The criticism that anarchistic and Bolshevistic methods have been employed here is not justified. The revolution has created an urge for organization. Soldiers' councils will disappear without a trace. The workers' councils will [remain as a] product of the revolution.

FRAUENDORFER: I understood E's statement [to mean] that, in addition to the parliament, the councils should remain as constitutional [i.e., legislative] organs. That is not possible. Sovereignty lies in the parliament. It can recognize them as advisory bodies. The Council of Peasants is the most ridiculous product [of the revolution]. There are only 10,000 peasants. E. is an idealist, has no sense of reality. We are being ruined by bad management. You have given the impression of Bolshevism. I cannot tolerate the consolidation of the councils. Otherwise I will resign [since] that will lead to the ruin of our Fatherland.

EISNER: AR [workers' councils] will exercise only advisory and controlling function, excluding legislation. That would be Bolshevism. . . . I want no restriction of the parliament through the AR. . . . I am against the dictatorship of the councils and for the sovereignty of the parliament.

ROSSHAUPTER: SR [soldiers' councils] . . . will disappear.

JAFFÉ: The ASR should develop themselves further as advisory bodies. . . .

TIMM: No one has the courage to abolish them.[41]

This glimpse into the inner sanctum of the Eisner regime affords the basis for a number of conclusions about its personalities and problems. His position weakened by the December 2 settlement, Kurt Eisner was now noticeably less bold: witness his candid admission that the councils should be permitted to have no legislative function whatsoever. Nor did he receive any real support from the other Independent ministers. Hans Unterleitner was not present at this meeting, and he seldom demonstrated enough strength of character or intellect to have offered Eisner much assistance anyway. Finance Minister Edgar Jaffé actually had little in common

[41] *Ministerratsprotokolle*, 5 Dec. 1918, BGS Munich, GN 2/1-2/2.

with Eisner except a penchant for abstractions. He continued to favor the original proposal for a *Nebenparlament* of the councils, but his insistence on this scheme even after Eisner was forced to abandon it made Jaffé's contribution to the USP more a matter of confusion than of clarification. At the same time, although they had managed to seize the initiative, the four Social Democratic ministers were not entirely united either. In criticism of Eisner, Timm was the most adamant, Hoffmann the least. Auer and Rosshaupter were still composed and generally conciliatory, although the former was beginning to lean increasingly in the direction of Timm.[42] Auer's restraint was determined in part by his basic agreement with Hoffmann that the councils were a natural product of the revolution and should be properly regulated rather than abruptly dismissed: hence his reluctance to initiate an open split with Eisner on the council question. As the only non-Socialist in the cabinet, Heinrich von Frauendorfer obviously did not share Auer's scruples. It was the threat of a strike by his transportation personnel which had been a decisive factor in compelling Eisner to accept the new coalition agreement; and his continued presence in the cabinet, combined with his influence on other bureaucratic officials in Munich, was to remain a constant source of internal pressure on the policy of the administration. Considering such pressure and the composition of the cabinet as a whole, it is not surprising that the December 5 meeting was adjourned with a decision to adopt the date originally proposed by Auer for the parliamentary elections.

The seriousness of the dissension and the details of the dispute in the cabinet were unknown outside of a discrete circle of government officials. Yet the general fact that Eisner had been constrained to make an important concession on December 2 and that he had already lost the power of decision over the scheduling of the elections was, at best, a very

[42] For the consequences of Auer's changing position, see Chapter VI.

173

badly kept secret. It was this knowledge, coupled with the apprehension in some quarters about the future of the council system, which produced the first serious recurrence of radical discontent since the night of the Munich Putsch. A new mood of belligerence became evident on the evening of December 5 at an open meeting in the Wagnersaal, where a political address in favor of the National Assembly by Max Weber was repeatedly interrupted from the floor until the speaker was unable to continue. Twenty-four hours later a night of rioting and confusion showed that the street was once again a political factor. Apparently without pre-arrangement, two separate public meetings erupted into the city in a spirit of protest. A party of nearly three hundred men broke into the residence of Erhard Auer, roused him out of bed, and obtained his written resignation at the point of a gun. Meanwhile, anarchist Erich Mühsam and another group seized several of Munich's leading newspapers, assumed editorial control, and granted ownership to the astonished typesetters. Alerted by police officials, Eisner personally appeared at various newspaper offices and persuaded Mühsam and his accomplices to leave in good order. He then confronted a crowd of Auer's assailants and told them that, although their action "was certainly well intended and certainly occurred out of love for me," it was nevertheless "not good." After the mob had dispersed at his request, Eisner visited the shaken Auer and they quickly agreed that the statement of resignation should be publicly revoked.[43] Despite his unconcealed sense of gratification for the unsolicited support, Eisner's deportment that night was surely more than a calcu-

---

[43] According to the official version, four newspaper offices were occupied during the night: *Münchener Neueste Nachrichten, Bayerischer Kurier, Münchener-Augsburger Abendzeitung,* and *Münchener Zeitung.* Mühsam was directly involved in at least the latter two instances. "Demonstration gegen die Presse," BGS Munich, PA, VII, 79. Auer's own account of his experience appeared in "Meine Absetzung," *MP,* 7-8 Dec. 1918, No. 286.

lated gesture of self-interest, and showed his genuine concern to maintain the law and order of the Republic. By 4 A.M. the affair was settled and the city was quiet. The newspapers resumed publication the next day and Auer returned to his desk at the Ministry of the Interior.[44] But it was clear that radicalism in Bavaria had assumed a political importance not to be measured solely in electoral statistics.

[44] In the cabinet Timm and Hoffmann agreed in demanding the arrest of Mühsam and others, but Eisner objected: "There was nothing at all serious behind the affair, nothing serious. Even Mühsam was not in favor of [the incident at Auer's residence, which was] rather in the spirit of mardi gras." *Ministerratsprotokolle*, 7 Dec. 1918, BGS Munich, GN 2/1-2/2. The regime did no more than issue a reprimand to the rioters: "Die bedauerlichen Ausschreitungen der letzten Nacht," *Bekanntmachungen*, F. Mon. 3198. Such "Presseputsche" occurred in several German cities in December. See Kolb, *Die Arbeiterräte in der deutschen Innenpolitik*, 312-315.

CHAPTER VI

Party System and Bürgerwehr Crisis

NOVEMBER and December were months for the reappraising, regrouping, and usually renaming of Bavaria's political organizations. With the important exception of the Social Democratic Party, the revolution had resulted in a brief hiatus for every one of the traditional parliamentary formations in Bavaria. Since Munich has been the crucible of the revolution, it was outside the capital city, in one or another of the major provincial centers, that those parties which reluctantly accepted or passively rejected the revolution were reconstituted. If point of origin or reorganization were the sole criterion, one might attempt a classification of the "bourgeois" parties founded away from Munich (notably the Catholic-dominated Bavarian People's Party [BVP] and the Bavarian affiliate of the liberal German Democratic Party [DDP]) and the "leftist" factions conceived and centered in the capital (the SPD, Kurt Eisner's Independents, and the Communist Party of Bavaria). The traditional theoretical distinction between Right and Left, however, proved to have little practical bearing on the politics of revolution in Bavaria during the winter of 1918-1919. No doubt there was increasing hostility between city and countryside after November 7, but it was not to be traced accurately along party lines, nor did it suggest any other tidy formula which could adequately reflect the complexity of the electoral campaign.

Despite the general acceptance of the revolution, tradition and organization gave every advantage to the parties already well established under the old regime. The largest of these were the BVP and the SPD, and it was in reality between them that the election was contested. Since neither was certain to receive an absolute majority in Bavaria's unwieldy multi-party system (thirteen parties were entered in all), the claim of the DDP to be a "third power" could not be ignored and later proved to be justified. There was no real doubt that the preponderance of votes would fall to these three parties once the electoral procedure was begun—it was only a question of distribution. The USP never had a chance at the polls, Eisner's informal pact with the Bavarian Peasants' League notwithstanding, so that his party's only hope was to attract enough votes to make its participation in a governmental coalition indispensable. The Munich chapter of the Spartacus League (not officially designated as the KPD until after December 31) followed the lead of its national organization by refusing to participate in the election, both as a measure of protest against the procedure itself and in the practical calculation that its chances would be negligible.

Starting after December 5, the campaign lasted more than six weeks, terminating with the balloting of January 19 for delegates to the German National Assembly in Weimar. This vote followed by one week the election of the Bavarian Landtag, the returns being much the same. Surveying this period as a whole, it is possible to observe three determining political developments which made the party system and the electoral results what they were. It became clear, first of all, that Kurt Eisner could not hope to command any widespread support either from the electorate or from the leadership of the SPD, with the result that the Majority Socialists sought an alliance with the DDP both as a matter of political preference and as an act of self-interest. Secondly, although the BVP could establish itself as the largest single party, its effective power was circumscribed by the decision of the Democratic Party to join with the SPD, thereby leaving the political representatives of Bavarian Catholicism in virtual isolation and creating a serious imbalance between their numbers and their ability to influence administrative policy. In an inverse sense, thirdly, there also developed an imbalance between the parliamentary importance and the actual influence of Bavarian Communism. In fact, the reaction of the other parties to the radical slogan of "all power to the coun-

177

cils" best served to gauge the impact of the revolution on the Bavarian political system.

In reviewing these developments it is important to keep in mind an intangible sense of political intoxication. Only a few weeks had passed, after all, since an armed putsch had suddenly dislocated a ruling tradition of long standing. Politicians and voters alike were still suffering from a loss of equilibrium, as if stunned by a first shock to the inner ear and thus all the more vulnerable to another. The confusion of emotion, apathy, and apprehension is the part of any political campaign which no amount of analysis based on party platforms and electoral orations can adequately convey—all the more so, then, in the unnerving proximity of war and revolution.

The Political Realignment

Until December 2 the name which had been automatically associated with the revolution in Munich was that of Kurt Eisner. It was he who had "made" the revolution and become its leading statesman. It was he who had represented Bavaria in Berlin and in the forum of the international press. His leadership had been accepted or at least tolerated even by those who objected to the very idea of a socialistic republic, not to speak of how it was conducted. In a willing suspension of disbelief most Bavarians had briefly come to think of Eisner as the Prime Minister, and to remember less well that he was the leader of only a tiny dissident faction of Social Democracy. But when it was announced that parliamentary elections were to be held in January,[1] it did not require a long memory to recall the days before November 7 when Eisner had been hopelessly outmatched in an electoral contest against Erhard Auer. With a tradition of

[1] "Wahlproklamation," *Bekanntmachungen*, F. Mon. 3195. The available secondary literature on the Bavarian political parties during the revolution is discussed in the bibliographical essay.

fifty years, an extensive and efficient party organization, and the support of an established trade union movement, the SPD might once again look forward to an electoral test with some confidence. It remained, of course, a matter of conjecture to what extent the Majority Party would dominate the Socialist vote in Bavaria, and it was uncertain what the proportion of that vote would be in the final tabulation of ballots cast for all parties. But it appeared reasonable to assume that Kurt Eisner's name would be less prominent in a listing of party leaders than on the roster of Bavarian ministers.

The USP had been the creation of a small group of Socialist defectors in Munich and Nuremberg. As such, the party's appeal was limited primarily to those in urban areas who shared the view that a vote for the SPD was a ballot for reaction. The political campaign conducted by the Independents in Bavaria was to be largely under the banner of Eisner's name and his policies. They claimed particular credit for the inauguration of the revolution, the introduction of woman suffrage, the eight-hour day, and a host of other benefits still only vaguely realized but undoubtedly to be gained only through Independent Socialism.[2] The leadership of the USP, like the party itself, was essentially a small and synthetic clique without the experience, the organization, or the intimate contact with Bavarian life which might have made it a serious political contender. Yet it was characteristic of Independent orators to insist that the revolution was not at an end, that social revolution must follow political coup, and that only the same quality of leadership could ensure equal

[2] See "Die politischen Parteien in Bayern" (2. Folge), *Politische Zeitfragen*, 1920, X-XI, 145-176. This is the major published collection of the political pamphlets dealing with the revolution in Bavaria: see the List of Official Documents and Papers Cited. The principal unpublished collections are the *Flugblätter* in the Münchener Stadtbibliothek, Monacensia Abteilung, and the portfolios from the Rehse Archive located at the Library of Congress in Washington, D.C. (to be cited hereafter as LC Washington, RA).

success in both phases. No matter what the result of the elections might be, they claimed, "the future belongs to the Independent Socialist Party."[3]

The partnership of the USP with the Bavarian *Bauernbund* is worth mentioning for two reasons: because the modest electoral success of the BBB (the League's party designation) gave some indication as to the slight changes which the revolution brought to voting patterns in the rural areas, and because this alliance both complemented and betrayed the urban character of the USP's political support. The BBB had been a party to the revolution only in the person of its wartime leader, Ludwig Gandorfer, for several years a personal friend of Eisner. Following his accidental death two days after the Munich Putsch, Gandorfer's leadership had been passed to his like-minded but less forceful brother Karl and to the more moderate Georg Eisenberger. These two had thereupon undertaken an industrious program of recruitment in which the newly created peasants' councils were often indistinguishable from regular chapters of the BBB.[4] Both were against something—strict controls of the war economy and Roman Catholic domination of rural politics—rather than for any sweeping concept of a "new democracy." It was probably this pragmatic and local bent of political mind, and a campaign based on back-porch conversations rather than stirring orations from the podium of council sessions in Munich, which was to make the BBB more successful at the polls than the Independent Party itself.

From the outset, then, the prospects of the SPD seemed significantly better than those of the USP. Social Democracy had attracted more than 27 per cent of the popular vote in Bavaria before the war, and the Majority Party had every reason to expect that its position in the state (as in the rest of Germany) had been further enhanced by the course of

[3] Speech by Josef Simon, 17 Dec. 1918, *Verhandlungen des provisorischen Nationalrates*, No. 4, 75-79.

[4] Mattes, *Die bayerischen Bauernräte*, 84.

events since the last general election in 1912. The SPD could now claim to be the party of continuity, an assertion buttressed by the uninterrupted support of the Free Trade Unions, a potent electoral factor both within and outside Munich. Since the SPD stood to profit equally from discredit of monarchism and distrust of radicalism, it ostentatiously assumed a posture of proper balance between order and progress. By emphasizing the role of protector, if not indeed proprietor, of the revolution, Erhard Auer and his party found it increasingly advantageous to suggest that Eisner and the Independents were in some sense unbalanced and eccentric, a charge near enough to the truth to be credible.

Socialist unity was an image piously invoked on occasion by both parties but initially unacceptable to either. Eisner liked to speak of November 7 heroically as a "stroke of hussars," or fondly as "my revolution."[5] He found it important to emphasize this repeatedly, since his message to the voters was based on the proposition that those who had instigated the revolution should continue to lead it. But as the campaign proceeded and the sessions of revolutionary councils in Munich became more and more obviously forums of debate for political parties, Eisner's interpretation of the November days was challenged with increasing vigor. Although he could not deny Eisner's accomplishment as a putschist, Erhard Auer did argue that the revolution had long been prepared by the Social Democratic Party, that its bloodless execution was due to the discipline imposed by the Majority Party on the workers, and that its continued success depended on the immediate contact with the working class provided by his party

[5] *Verhandlungen des provisorischen Nationalrates*, Beilage III, 129. Eisner also liked to relate that he had carried off the revolution "with a dozen little men and women." Quoted from Alfred Steinitzer, *Bajuwarische Bilderbogen* (Munich, 1921), 40-41. See the interview with Eisner on December 29 by the American representative Ellis Loring Dresel, *Papers relating to Foreign Relations*, 1919, II, 150.

organization and the Free Trade Unions.[6] Eisner was unable to regard such campaign talk as other than an attack on his personal leadership—as in fact it was. He countered by charging that the SPD had never believed its own shibboleths, that it had cooperated with the old regime and lifted not one finger to bring the new, and that Auer was perpetuating an old Social Democratic habit of talking Left and turning Right; the revolutionary impetus had thus been necessarily created within the Independent Party and infused into the revolutionary councils.[7] After the Bavarian Provisional National Council was finally called back into session in Munich on December 13 (for the first time since November 8), the lines of this dispute were drawn and redrawn in public debates, lead editorials, and reams of pamphlet literature. The total effect was to force the two Socialist factions further apart, the one falling back on its broad party and trade union support, the other taking up a position based on revolutionary "elites" and the council system.

As the SPD turned its back on the USP it faced the DDP. The most prominent of the several splinter groups claiming to be heirs of the tradition of Liberalism, the Democratic Party launched its campaign in Bavaria at a rally in Nuremberg on December 22.[8] The membership included delegates

[6] "That this victory could be thus achieved without blood is due only to the splendid organization and iron discipline of German Social Democracy." Auer, *Das neue Bayern*, 6.

[7] It is indicative that, despite Eisner's frequent promises to the contrary, the USP began publishing its own newspaper on December 20. The masthead of the *Neue Zeitung* initially bore the inscription "Unabhängiges Sozialistisches Organ unter ständiger Mitarbeit von Kurt Eisner." The first issue featured an article by Eisner in which he attacked the bourgeois monopoly of the Bavarian newspaper press. "Presse," *NZ*, 20 Dec. 1918, No. 1.

[8] The party had been formed within two weeks after the Munich Putsch. "Die deutsche Volkspartei in Bayern," *MZ*, 18 Nov. 1918, No. 317. "Tagung der Deutschen Volkspartei in Bayern," *MZ*, 23 Dec. 1918, No. 352. See Gessler, *Reichswehrpolitik*, 53-54.

from the Association of Liberal Unions of Munich, members of the old Progressive Party, and representatives of the German Peasants' League (*Deutscher Bauernbund*). The title first chosen for this formation, the "German People's Party in Bavaria," soon proved to be unfortunate in light of the nomenclature adopted by the various national parties; but it did serve to underscore the fact that the DDP, more than any other party in Bavaria, tended to look northward for its intellectual orientation. The national leadership—men like Max Weber, Hugo Preuss, Ernst Troeltsch, and Friedrich Meinecke—not only brought the greatest acumen to theoretical considerations, but as a practical matter they were thoroughly dedicated to the unity of the German Reich.[9] This was the touchstone of the alliance which now developed between the DDP and the SPD. In Bavaria as well as Berlin, the two parties could agree that the consequences of Eisner's personal diplomacy had been extremely unfortunate. It noticeably pricked Eisner's vanity as much as it delighted the Majority Socialists when a Democratic spokesman, Professor Ludwig Quidde, publicly confronted the Prime Minister with the remark: "Oh, what an illusion and what a fantastic idea: to be able from here in Bavaria to bring peace to the German Reich!"[10] The fact that Erhard Auer and his colleagues con-

[9] See, for example, Max Weber, "Deutschlands künftige Staatsform," *Gesammelte Politische Schriften* (2nd ed.; Tübingen, 1959), 436-471. "Deutsche Volkspartei" was the title adopted by supporters of Gustav Stresemann following his "exclusion" from the DDP. It was the latter group with which most Bavarian Liberals became affiliated. Only a smaller, more conservative wing was organized in support of Stresemann's faction as the *Nationalliberale Landespartei in Bayern*, the program of which may be read in *Politische Zeitfragen*, 1919, II, 32-35.

[10] *Verhandlungen des provisorischen Nationalrates*, No. 4, 78-79. In addition to being a lecturer at the University of Munich and a spokesman of the Democratic Party (of which Georg Hohmann was the chairman), Quidde was an internationally known pacifist who had been in contact during the war with Foerster and Herron in Switzerland.

tinued to sit in the Eisner cabinet caused the Democrats to break ranks with the SPD on only one occasion: the DDP joined with the BVP on December 20 in a formal protest to the regime over the repeated interruptions of political rallies by radicals in Munich. Shortly thereafter the Democratic leaders openly regretted the action insofar as it implied any cooperation with or support of the BVP.[11] In most of its electoral propaganda the DDP tried to make a place for itself between the two larger parties, but in reality most Bavarian Liberals were prepared to come to terms with Social Democracy once the votes were counted.[12]

The pattern of alliance and antagonism among the four parties thus far discussed (USP, BBB, SPD, DDP) was nicely illustrated by the debate over socialization. Kurt Eisner's original position on this question had been stated in the "Program of the Bavarian Republic" as early as November 15: "There can be no socialization when there is scarcely anything to be socialized." This initial reaction had come at a time when the Prime Minister's principal concern was to restore order and to establish confidence in his regime.[13] In theoretical terms it had been based on the claim that such a view represented the true Marx: that the transmutation of the economy to socialism would occur as the inevitable culmination of capitalistic development rather than through the sudden manipulation of the modes of production at a time of military collapse. This remained Eisner's policy until late in December, when he decided that a more positive proposal to implement a program of socialization might have a salutary electoral appeal. Even so, for those radicals who were at that

[11] "An die provisorische Regierung," *MZ*, 20 Dec. 1918, No. 349. For an example of the DDP's subsequent repudiation of any cooperation with the BVP, see Quidde's statement of December 30, *Verhandlungen des provisorischen Nationalrates*, No. 7, 203-210.

[12] See the "third power" conception of Dr. Heinz Potthoff, "Wen wählen wir am 12. Januar?" *MNN*, 4 Jan. 1919, No. 6.

[13] See the section on "Domestic Policy" in Chapter IV.

time urging a sweeping plan of "full socialization" (*Vollsozialisierung*), Eisner's belated enthusiasm must still have seemed faint indeed. "You know," he told a gathering of council delegates on December 30, "I am not of the opinion that one can socialize all of industry today. . . . Political forces can be overthrown, but no economic organization can be erected through revolution." The transfer of ownership from private hands to state control (*Verstaatlichung*) was therefore proposed by Eisner only in the case of certain basic industries and utilities.[14]

Probably the decisive reason for the moderation of the USP in this matter was its need to court the electoral favor of rural voters. From its inception the USP had been a party of protest, against the war and against Majority Socialism. But an expression of dissatisfaction with the SPD by some workers and soldiers in the urban centers would not necessarily gain support in the countryside, and Bavaria was still a rural state. To the question of how to attract voters outside of Munich, the Independents devised three solutions. The first was to search out local candidates in farm areas who were neither Catholics nor Majority Socialists, and who were yet popular enough to contend the election.[15] A second was to put up Eisner himself as a candidate, announce his arrival at a rural township well in advance, then have the Prime Minister make a sortie from the capital in his official limousine to stage one grand appearance, in hopes of awing the populace sufficiently to leave a favorable impression at least until election day.[16] The third technique, as noted, was to main-

---

[14] *Verhandlungen des provisorischen Nationalrates*, No. 7, 228. See the proposals for thoroughgoing socialization made in January by Otto Neurath, *Bayerische Sozialisierungserfahrungen* (Vienna, 1920), 2-4. Neurath was to appear with his plans again two months later: see Chapter IX.

[15] This proved successful in only two instances, both in Upper Franconia.

[16] See, for example, "Kurt Eisner in Ingolstadt," *NZ*, 7 Jan. 1919,

tain the closest possible alliance with the BBB. Harmony with the Peasants' League, however, prescribed a compatible view of the farm question, and the leaders of the BBB were frankly opposed to any extensive plan for the collectivization or rationalization of agriculture. Their own program went no further than to favor state development of water power and rural electrification, and to recommend the confiscation of a few large landholdings to be redistributed among small independent farmers.[17] The maintenance of the USP-BBB coalition therefore required a common opposition to immediate measures of radical socialization.

In strictly economic terms no better case for the socialization of "ripe" industries could be made in January of 1919 than in November of 1918. It was transparently the evolution of political rather than of economic conditions which had determined Eisner's decision to encourage a program of socialization. And the general reaction to his program was correspondingly political—and negative. The response of the SPD disclosed a great deal about the cautious and essentially conservative nature of the Majority Party, which had always claimed to advocate socialization, and whose positive cooperation at this time might have made the success of such a program a genuine possibility. It is perhaps a sufficient commentary to note that the rebuff to Eisner could be phrased as a paragon of orthodox Marxism: "Social Democracy will not support the experiment of a leap into the socialist society, but will encourage the further development of the capitalistic economy toward the socialistic."[18] Actually, except for the use of the active voice (Eisner would never admit that he consciously intended to aid the development of capitalism),

No. 12, and "Ministerpräsident Eisner in Wunseidel," *NZ*, 10 Jan. 1919, No. 15. A critical account of one such occasion is given by Müller-Meiningen, *Aus Bayerns schwersten Tagen*, 109-110.

[17] "Programm des Bayerischen Bauernbundes," *Politische Zeitfragen*, 1920, X-XI, 148-149.

[18] "Und Walther Rathenau sprach," *MP*, 28-29 Dec. 1918, No. 302.

this position was not unlike that of the USP. But the difference was evident enough in the contrast between Eisner's tone of perpetual apology for his party's moderation and the almost strident boastfulness of the SPD that it would tolerate no tampering with the structure of the Bavarian economy, least of all under the administration of a financial and technological illiterate such as Eisner.

In theory, socialization was the one important issue which represented a basic source of disagreement between the SPD and the DDP. It remained, however, a difference more theoretical than actual. Since the Majority Socialists admittedly wanted "no proletarian class program," their party could be counted on to proceed gingerly and selectively in any attempt to socialize industry or agriculture.[19] For their part, the Democrats repeatedly emphasized their opposition to "the socialization of all the modes of production," though the party's leadership did formally favor governmental regulation of any industry which perpetuated "exploitation for the benefit of private interests."[20] The net effect of opposing socialization while endorsing it in certain instances was essentially the same as favoring socialization while permitting it only in specified sectors of the economy. The divergence between the DDP and the SPD was therefore only one of vague and extremely distant objectives. Both parties were satisfied with that, and were content to leave the question of what was ultimately desirable to the German National Assembly and the Bavarian Landtag.

As the other major political contestant, the Bavarian People's Party had an unparalleled electoral advantage, but also the liability of that advantage. The official support of the

[19] "Die Volksregierung der Schaffenden," *MP*, 11 Nov. 1918, No. 263. See the article by Erhard Auer, printed as a campaign pamphlet, "Von der Alleinherrschaft zur Freiheit durch das Volk," *Flugblätter*, F. Mon. 2686.
[20] "Aufruf der Deutschen Volkspartei in Bayern" (17 Nov. 1918), *Politische Zeitfragen*, 1920, XII-XIV, 159-161.

Roman Catholic Church assured the BVP of a plurality in the balloting, but prevented the party from utilizing its strength to secure a workable coalition with any of the other major factions. An effort to block the restoration of Catholic political domination in Bavaria was the one thing upon which both Democrats and Socialists of every persuasion could agree. From the speaker's rostrum and in the press a proposal was advanced for reform of the public school system, an attempt to restrict clerical supervision and to revise the materials and methods of instruction. A bill to this effect was drafted by the Majority Socialist Minister of Education and Culture, Johannes Hoffmann, approved by the cabinet, and—needless to add—vigorously opposed by the Catholic hierarchy.[21]

In siding with the hierarchy the BVP as much as confessed one of the two fictions with which it was forced to live during the Eisner administration. The first was that the BVP was not really a Catholic party at all, but a forum for all religious faiths and conservative political convictions. It was emphasized that this was a new party which had loosened its formal ties with the national Catholic party, the *Zentrum*, to which the leadership of the BVP had belonged almost without exception. The historical basis of this claim was the fact that a movement for separation from the national party had actually preceded the revolution. Moreover, the impetus for reorganization after November 7 had come not from the old party headquarters in Munich, but from the Regensburg stronghold of the Bavarian *Bauernverein*. The faction formed in Regensburg on November 12 under the auspices of Sebastian Schlittenbauer and Georg Heim, president of the *Bauernverein*, was then presented as a *fait accompli* to the former

---

[21] Hoffmann announced that his bill would mean "an end of the Church-and-Center state of Bavaria." *Verhandlungen des provisorischen Nationalrates*, No. 5, 102. *Ministerratsprotokolle*, 16 Dec. 1918, BGS Munich, GN 2/1-2/2. "Eine Verwahrung der bayerischen Bischöfe," *BK*, 20 Dec. 1918, No. 353. See Michael Kardinal Faulhaber, *Deutsches Ehrgefühl und Katholisches Gewissen* (Munich, 1925), 21-22.

leadership at the Leohaus in Munich three days later. Rather than split the Catholic bloc between town and country, the birth of a new party was accepted and authorized by the Bavarian *Zentrum*'s "Committee of Nine" and by "the responsible representatives of all pertinent professional organizations." Yet the criterion of what was "pertinent," despite protestations to the contrary, was still Roman Catholicism.[22]

The second fiction was that the BVP did not desperately want the return of the monarchy. In reality most Bavarian Catholics shared the feeling not only that something had been lost in the revolution, but that its restoration mattered greatly —and that "something" was still epitomized for the BVP by the House of Wittelsbach. To be sure, its official program spoke of the Republic as "a given historical fact," but it added pointedly that the party was "basically not in accord with the way in which it was brought about." And the leading Catholic journal stated this view even less cautiously: "No man can demand that we turn our backs today on that which we honored yesterday, that we burn our banners instead of just rolling them up."[23] Like the SPD and the DDP, the first demand of the BVP was for free elections and the immediately subsequent convocation of parliamentary assemblies. But alone of the major parties the BVP held the view that the ultimate form of the Bavarian state was still an open question.

[22] "Die bayerische Volkspartei besteht!" *BK*, 18 Nov. 1918, No. 321. Of the 58 BVP delegates elected to the Landtag in January of 1919 (thus, not including the Rhenish Palatinate), only three were not Roman Catholic; and twenty-two had been members of the *Zentrum*'s Landtag delegation before the revolution. Biographical sketches can be found in *Politische Zeitfragen*, 1919, III-IV, 65-76. The most conservative non-Catholic party of any consequence is described briefly by Werner Liebe, "Die Bayerische Mittelpartei (DNVP)," *Die Deutsch-Nationale Volkspartei 1918-1924* (Düsseldorf, 1956), 38-42.

[23] "Das allgemeine Programm der BVP," *Politische Zeitfragen*, 1919, I-II, 3-6. "Freistaat Bayern," *BK*, 9 Nov. 1918, Nos. 311-312.

The monarchy as such does not contradict the concept of democracy. . . . Of course, a restitution of the monarchy in the old form and integrality of power seems out of the question, [but] Ludwig III was no despot. . . . He will doubtless himself never again wish to remount the throne unless he is called by the consensus of the Bavarian people. . . . *Here the party does not decide, here decides the majority of the people.*[24]

The Bavarian People's Party may have been, then, broad-minded in religion and eminently fair-minded in politics, but it nevertheless represented in the elections of 1919 the interests of Catholic monarchism. And therein lies the basic explanation for the extraordinary vigor with which two slogans were infused into the electoral campaign: *Los von Berlin* and *Bayern den Bayern.*[25] It is unnecessary to recall all the reasons and ramifications of the first. In part it was strictly election propaganda, intended to focus all the discontents of the past and fears of the future on the BVP's major opponent at the polls. It could be argued that Bavaria had been dragged into the war because of Berlin's incompetence, and that she might now be plunged into Bolshevism by Berlin's impotence. The Bavarian People's Party—and, the party claimed, the Bavarian people—had little in common with the Socialist regime in the German capital, and was "fed up with being ruled from Berlin."[26] Although most of the party's leaders made a public ceremony of confessing only "federalist" inclinations, their personal feelings were in fact distributed along the continuum of federalism, particularism, and separatism. The most notable and subsequently notorious exam-

---

[24] "Die Bayerische Volkspartei und die Verfassungsfragen in Bayern und im Reich," *Politische Zeitfragen*, 1919, I-II, 16-21. This formulation was apparently based on an article by Georg Heim, "Die neuen Richtlinien für unsere Politik," *BK*, 20 Nov. 1918, No. 323.

[25] "Free from Berlin" and "Bavaria for Bavarians."

[26] *Politische Zeitfragen*, 1919, I-II, 6. See Josef Held, *Heinrich Held. Ein Leben für Bayern* (Regensburg, 1958), 29-32.

ple of the latter was Georg Heim, who had published an editorial just before the cabinet crisis of December 2 entitled "Eisner's Erring Ways and Bavaria's Future." Heim's proposals for a "Greater Bavaria," whose northern frontier would in effect restore the Main border ante 1870, were never adopted by the BVP, and were later equivocated by Heim himself, but they doubtless expressed the speculations if not the desires of more than a lunatic fringe of the party's membership.[27]

Lest the BVP appear in any way to support the personal diplomacy of Kurt Eisner, the second slogan was introduced as something of an antidote for the first. Although the BVP would have been the first party to wish Eisner's removal from office, it had openly followed the Prime Minister's attack on Berlin with malicious delight. But this threatened to become too much of a good thing when Eisner traveled to Stuttgart on the day after Christmas to attend a meeting of southern German states. The premiers of Baden, Württemberg, and Hesse could agree with Eisner that Prussia must no longer be allowed to dominate the Reich, but the Bavarian Prime Minister's suggestion that concrete measures be undertaken to create a united southern balance against Prussian hegemony came to nothing. The Catholic press in Munich could only admit its sympathy with Eisner's effort and its regret that he had failed to obtain more positive results.[28] Such failure, how-

[27] "Eisners Irrgänge und Bayerns Zukunft," *BK*, 30 Nov.–1 Dec. 1918, Nos. 333-334. Heim proposed a political and economic union of southern Germany with the Vorarlberg, Tirol, Steiermark, and Upper Austria (not including Vienna); Trieste would become an accessible free port. Heim made no secret of having contacts with French authorities interested in his ideas. For the most extreme criticism of Heim, implicating others as well, see Walther F. Ilges, *Die geplante Aufteilung Deutschlands. Enthüllungen über die französisch-bayerischen Pläne zur Zertrümmerung des Reiches* (Berlin-Charlottenburg, 1933), 1-19.

[28] "Bayern," *BV*, 2 Jan. 1919, No. 1. A text of the vague agreement reached in Stuttgart can be found in "Süddeutschland und das

ever, could easily be explained to the electorate: Eisner was not a true Bavarian and he was therefore incapable of truly representing Bavarian interests—hence, "Bavaria for Bavarians." It is unfortunately necessary to add that, although there was a certain impeccable logic to this, the argument was not always allowed to rest on logic alone. Beneath the campaign slogans was a distinct smudge of anti-Semitism not soon to be erased in Bavarian politics, and for that the Catholic press of the Eisner period must bear—by no means alone—a burden of responsibility. In all fairness the party's official position should be quoted, even though its precise tone was seldom maintained.

> The Bavarian People's Party knows no difference between Germans and Bavarians of Jewish faith and Germans and Bavarians of Christian faith. . . . For the Bavarian People's Party racial affiliation (*Rassenzugehörigkeit*) also plays no role. . . . The Bavarian People's Party values and honors every honest Jew. . . . But what must be fought are the numerous atheistic elements of a certain international Jewry with predominantly Russian coloring. . . .[29]

As the campaign proceeded it was not clear which sort of Jew Eisner was considered to be, but it was always apparent

---

Reich," *MP*, 2 Jan. 1919, No. 1. Eisner's proposals were called an "excursion in the clouds" by Württemberg's Prime Minister Wilhelm Blos, *Von der Monarchie zum Volksstaat. Zur Geschichte der Revolution in Deutschland insbesondere in Württemberg* (2 vols.; Stuttgart, 1922-1923), II, 78-82. But the meeting understandably aroused French interest and memories of Napoleon's Confederation of the Rhine. "Entente des Etats du Sud," *Le Temps*, 3 Jan. 1919, No. 20999.

[29] "Bayerische Volkspartei und Judentum," *BK*, 6 Dec. 1918, No. 339. The *Bayerischer Kurier* was notably more responsible throughout than the Catholic daily, *Das Bayerische Vaterland*. Eisner made a public statement to the effect that "although he had no connection with Judaism in a ritualistic sense, he was nevertheless proud to be a Jew." "Wahlnachrichten," *NZ*, 8 Jan. 1919, No. 13.

in BVP literature that he was a Jew. As such he was suspect, if not of representing alien interests, at least of protecting them. In this guise and others, the specter of a dark Bolshevik conspiracy was constantly being conjured up to public view, until it grew out of all proportion to its actual size.

To be precise, there was no Communist Party in Bavaria before the first day of January 1919. There is little else that can be said with precision about the development of radicalism in Bavaria after November 7, since neither its strength nor its importance was strictly measurable. One cannot help being struck by the initial confusion of leftist issues and personalities, a testimony to the fact that a genuine radical tradition began to be created in Bavaria not until after the Munich Putsch.[30] But the absence of established radical parties and party allegiances before November 7 was only one aspect of the confusion. Another was the development of the council system, which had been explicitly intended to cross party lines and to win the support of all those who emphasized that the revolution must be social as well as political in nature.

A number of the radicals, moreover, had an instinctive and inveterate distaste for organization as such. Of these the best known was Gustav Landauer, recognized throughout Germany as a gifted scholar (he had published on subjects as varied as Meister Eckhart, Shakespeare, and Walt Whitman) and as a theoretical anarchist.[31] Left at loose ends by the

[30] None of the men who were later to become prominent as leaders of Bavarian radicalism—Mühsam, Landauer, Toller, Levien, Leviné, etc.—had assisted Eisner in the November revolt. Mühsam, the only one of these who had been in Munich at the time, later made the inconsequential claim that it was he who had first proclaimed the Republic on November 7 from the back of a truck. *Von Eisner bis Leviné*, 12.

[31] Landauer's most influential book was his *Aufruf zum Sozialismus* (2nd ed.; Berlin, 1919). See the treatment of his theoretical views by Martin Buber, *Paths in Utopia* (London, 1949), 46-57. Also

war, living in a small Swabian village and waiting to return to some metropolitan cultural center when conditions and finances would allow, he was called to Munich in mid-November by a characteristic personal note from his friend Eisner: "Come as soon as your health permits. What I want of you is that, through forensic activity, you will cooperate in the reformation of spirits." But once in the capital and initiated into the political situation as a member of the Revolutionary Workers' Council (RAR), Landauer had his most serious misgivings confirmed: "the damned National Assembly means the perpetuation of the foulest party politics."[32] It was doubtless for this reason that he felt increasingly out of harmony with Eisner's leadership and gravitated toward his fellow anarchist, Erich Mühsam. It was Mühsam who had gained entry into the RAR for Landauer and other radicals who drifted into Bavaria during the first days of the revolution: "The condition was simply the will to carry the revolution further to the accomplishment of socialism on the basis of the concept of councils (*Rätegedanken*)."[33] When not heckling moderate speakers in council assemblies, the RAR was usually to be found meeting comfortably in the private dining-room of a beer-hall. Here strategy was planned, resolutions passed, texts for handbills composed, and quantities of beer consumed. By the end of November, an adjoining room came to be occupied by the Union of Revolutionary Internationalists of Bavaria (*Vereinigung Revolutionärer Internationalisten Bayerns*). The VRI was entirely Mühsam's crea-

---

see the biographical sketch in Escherich, *Von Eisner bis Eglhofer*, No. 2, 27-28.

[32] Buber (ed.), *Gustav Landauer*, II, 296-297. Landauer and Eisner remained close personal friends—their families spent Christmas together at Grumbach—but Landauer continually urged Eisner to take a more radical course. *Ibid.*, 341-342, 350-351, 354-355, 364-365.

[33] Mühsam, *Von Eisner bis Leviné*, 14. See the sketch of him in Escherich, *Von Eisner bis Eglhofer*, No. 2, 26-27.

tion, a sort of rump faction which regarded itself neither as a political party like the USP nor a council body such as the RAR. The platform of the VRI was wonderfully imprecise, demanding no less than "the salvation of the world in the renaissance of a radical and concessionless socialistic-communistic International." It thereby hoped to spread "the example which our Russian comrades have given to us." The VRI was, however, no Leninist party. Mühsam wished to avoid any "quarrel on questions of organization" and consistently refused to solicit membership.[34] Several delegates of the RAR, who felt too strongly about opposition to parliamentary elections to accept Eisner's "compromise" on December 2, joined the VRI *faute de mieux*. Otherwise the enrollment was scant and the financial support limited to passing the hat at public meetings. The VRI's only notoriety resulted from the rioting during the night of December 6-7 and Mühsam's attempt to "socialize" several of Munich's newspapers. When confronted with the public reprimand issued to the rioters by the government, Mühsam was singularly unrepentant.[35] But there were others who took more seriously the failure of an unrehearsed radical putsch.

On December 11 the first Bavarian chapter of the Spartacus League was founded in Munich, the result both of initiative taken by a Bavarian radical, Hans Kain, and of instructions carried from the League's Berlin headquarters by a young man named Max Levien. Tall and fair-haired (a French journalist noted that he was "more slavic than semitic" in appearance) and a fluent speaker in five languages including his native Russian, Levien looked the part neither of a Bol-

---

[34] VRI *Flugblatt*, 30 Nov. 1918, reprinted by Mühsam, *Von Eisner bis Leviné*, 14-15. On November 18 he had published a pamphlet under the banner head of his defunct journal *Kain*, employing the characteristic slogan "the spirit is everything." LC Washington, RA, "Flugblätter der Revolutions– und Rätezeit," II. The journal resumed irregular publication in a new format three weeks thereafter as the organ of the VRI. *Kain*, 10 Dec. 1918, No. 1.

[35] Refer to the conclusion of Chapter V.

shevik revolutionary nor a Bavarian *Stammtischler*. Yet he was evidently thought by the Spartacus League to be the best available man to unite the internationalist and the local elements of potential radicalism in Munich. With Kain he had at least one thing in common: the realization that the revolutionary councils would never be a significant factor in Bavaria unless an organized and disciplined party consciously set out to win the Bavarian laboring classes for Communism. Levien consequently began appearing at meetings of the VRI and advocating a union of the two radical groups. Like Rosa Luxemburg he believed that any further act of revolution could only result from the spontaneous enthusiasm of the masses; but he also shared her view that the proletariat must be enlightened and instructed to recognize the revolutionary moment when it should come.[36]

Events in Berlin settled the organizational issue and set the course of Bavarian radicalism. On December 19 the first National Congress of Workers' and Soldiers' Councils rejected, by a vote of 344-98, a motion which would have recognized the council system as "the basis of the constitution of the socialistic Republic" and would have ascribed to the councils "the highest legislative and executive power."[37]

[36] On the origins of the Spartacus League in Munich, see John Raatjes, *The Role of Communism during the Munich Revolutionary Period, November 1918–May 1919* (unpublished diss.; University of Illinois, 1958), 57-60. Levien's birthplace was given as Moscow in a police circular (8 May 1919), reproduced by Rudolf Schricker, *Rotmord über München* (Berlin, 1934), 152. Before a turn in the German army during the war, he had been a student in Zürich and, while there, an acquaintance of Lenin. See the interview granted by Levien to Paul Gentizon, "Le mouvement bolsheviste à Munich," *Le Temps*, 12 Mar. 1919, No. 21067.

[37] *Allgemeiner Kongress der Arbeiter- und Soldatenräte Deutschlands vom 16. bis 21. Dezember im Abgeordnetenhause zu Berlin: Stenographische Berichte*, 31-32, 49-50, 142, 150. Two Bavarian delegates spoke, one for (Fritz Sauber) and one against (Ernst Niekisch) the motion. See Niekisch, *Gewagtes Leben*, 43-45, and R. Müller, *Vom Kaiserreich zur Republik*, II, 203-219.

196

For the Spartacus League this was a bitter defeat. Since 1917 its leadership had been advocating that absolute authority be invested in the council system. Now the National Congress itself had declared its subservience to the National Assembly, to traditional parliamentarianism.[38] In the final days of December Levien traveled to the national conference of the Spartacus League in Berlin. There the conference delegates condemned the action of the National Congress of Councils and reaffirmed the League's demand that supreme political power be embodied in the council system. Over the protest of Rosa Luxemburg and Karl Liebknecht, the League then resolved by a ballot of 62-23 not to participate in national and local elections. At the same time the League officially adopted its new title as the Communist Party of Germany (KPD).[39]

When he returned to Munich at the beginning of January, then, Max Levien was the leader of a party but not a candidate for office. He was almost immediately successful in persuading the VRI into a merger, although Erich Mühsam himself was consistent to the end and refused to become officially a member. He and Levien were to be "co-leaders," and party declarations were at first jointly signed by the KPD and VRI; but Mühsam's group and his policy of non-organization had become superfluous. The VRI was soon disbanded, and in mid-January the KPD became the acknowledged political representative of radicalism in Bavaria.[40] Thereafter the radicals were called to rally under the Communist banner of "all power to the councils of workers, soldiers, and peasants."

[38] "Selbstmord des Rätekongresses," *RF* (Berlin), 20 Dec. 1918, No. 35. This decision led directly to the withdrawal of the USP from the Berlin coalition government. See Kolb, *Die Arbeiterräte in der deutschen Innenpolitik*, 197-216.

[39] "Konstituierung der Kommunistischen Partei: Die Reichskonferenz des Spartakusbundes," *RF* (Berlin), 31 Dec. 1918, No. 45.

[40] Mühsam, *Von Eisner bis Leviné*, 16-17.

The Crisis of Christmas Week

Christmas Day of 1918 passed quietly in Munich. The weather was crisp, the sidewalks were crowded with strollers, and the city appeared much as it had before 1914. Neither the war nor the revolution had left much physical trace. Even the red banner which had flown from the former royal Residence since November 7 had been recently replaced—without ceremony—by the traditional blue-and-white colors of state. In the evening the streets were dark and quiet, the shop windows unlit, the public buildings, cinemas, theaters, and concert halls closed and cold as a result of the coal shortage.

But a certain malaise was real if unseen. As a visible symptom one might have noticed the passage of a military patrol or the posting of a freshly-printed yellow placard with its disconcertingly bold headline: "Street-fighting in Berlin." With the casualties in the German capital reported to be nearly a hundred, the contrasting calm in Munich seemed improbable and even ominous, and it appeared doubtful that the January elections would be allowed to come and go unchallenged. For some, the nervous tension could express itself during the holiday week by what more than one observer considered a neurotic fit of dancing—as if one dared not wait another fortnight for the official inauguration of the carnival season. The weeks which followed were to raise further the pitch of this tension, and to release the first shock of physical violence in Munich.[41]

The success of Kurt Eisner's regime in wresting political and military authority from the House of Wittelsbach had been due in large measure to the inadequacy of the monarchy's security forces in Munich. In an attempt to profit from its own experience, the new cabinet decided not to

[41] "Strassenkämpfe in Berlin," *Bekanntmachungen*, F. Mon. 3220. "Die Weihnachtsfeiertage," *MZ*, 27 Dec. 1918, No. 354. Hofmiller, *Revolutionstagebuch*, 111, 119, 126. The *"Tanzwut"* in Munich even became a subject for discussion in the cabinet. *Ministerratsprotokolle*, 3 Jan. 1919, BGS Munich, GN 2/1-2/2.

leave law enforcement in the Bavarian capital to the police force alone, but to delegate responsibility for the city's security to three new agencies. The first was a sort of praetorian guard, the Munich Military Police, organized on the first day after the revolution. Placed under the direct command of the Minister for Military Affairs, this force numbered no more than 140 men.[42] The assignment to form a second security force was granted to a local condottiere, Alfred Seyfferitz, on November 22. By the beginning of 1919 his "Republican Security Troops" had become a paramilitary unit (similar to the Free Corps sponsored by the Berlin government) of nearly 1500. Since Seyfferitz and his staff also took both pay and orders from Albert Rosshaupter, these troops were regarded as completely loyal to the government.[43] The third force was that represented by the Munich soldiers' councils, the elected or appointed representatives of military units stationed in the city. As the councils were financed with funds budgeted for the Bavarian Army, their chain of command was also formally channeled through Minister Rosshaupter. In terms of coherence and reliability, however, the soldiers' councils were an unknown and even uncounted quantity, and were consequently of uncertain status as an instrument of security. It was this uncertainty which became the basic element of the plan to organize a *Bürgerwehr*.

The conception of a "civilian militia" was not new to Germany. An organization known by that name had been "one

---

[42] "Aktennotiz," BHS Munich, Abt. IV (formerly *Kriegsarchiv*), II Mob 10, Bd. I.

[43] "Ministerium f. mil. Angel., Armee Abteilung. An das Gen. Kdo. I A.K. u. a. Betreff: Republikanische Schutztruppen," 23 Jan. 1919, *ibid.* A later report by Rosshaupter (11 Feb. 1919) set the strength of this group at 1800 men. Similar organizations were formed in Passau, Rosenheim, Augsburg, Nuremberg, and Fürth. *Darstellungen aus den Nachkriegskämpfen deutscher Truppen und Freikorps*, IV: *Die Niederwerfung der Räteherrschaft in Bayern* (Berlin, 1939), 3-4.

of the chief gains of the March revolution" in 1848.[44] Given such a tradition, it might not have been thought inappropriate or extraordinary that a governmental decree should be released two days after Christmas which proposed the formation of a *Bürgerwehr*. Yet this decree resulted in the most sensational incident since the Munich Putsch. The impetus to form a militia system directed from Munich had come from two sources dissimilar in motivation and enthusiasm. One was the legitimate concern of several members of Eisner's cabinet that the existing security system, which would necessarily rely heavily on the soldiers' councils in case of emergency, was incoherent, insufficient, and not altogether trustworthy. Both Erhard Auer and Minister of Justice Johannes Timm had frankly expressed their misgivings about the councils in cabinet meetings; Auer had even gone so far as to release orders to several rural townships in Bavaria to establish "local guards, civilian militia, etc.," and had authorized the distribution of small arms for this purpose.[45] The measure had earlier aroused little comment. But now the news of open street-fighting and governmental crisis in Berlin led Auer and Timm to endorse a plan to create a *Bürgerwehr* in Munich, presumably to guard the capital during the electoral period as well as to provide a unified command for all militia forces in Bavaria.

The other impetus had come from a former officer of the Bavarian Army, Rudolf Buttmann. After choosing to change into civilian clothing on November 8 rather than endure the insults of enlisted men on the street, he had soon begun to gather a group of men (as he later boasted) "who were all determined to carry out a counter-revolution." As a means to this end, Buttmann's group decided to urge the formation of a *Bürgerwehr*, by which they meant a conservative force

---

[44] Craig, *The Politics of the Prussian Army*, 122.

[45] See, for example, "Vom Vollzugsausschuss des Bezirks Miesbach-Tegernsee. An das Ministerium des Innern. Betreff: Ortswachen, Bürgerwehr," 9 Dec. 1918, BHS Munich, M. Inn. 54199.

against, and eventually to supplant, the soldiers' councils. In search of support Buttmann made the rounds in Munich—trade union leaders, police officials, and the Minister for Military Affairs—none of whom offered him any real encouragement. Commandant Dürr, in charge of coordinating the security forces under Rosshaupter, gave Buttmann the most categorical refusal: "You counter-revolutionaries ought to be put against the wall."[46] Buttmann's followers were consequently forced to defer, but not to abandon, their plans. And here matters stood until the Christmas holidays and the alarming news from Berlin.

When the cabinet reconvened on December 27, a few hours after the publication of the *Bürgerwehr* decree signed by Auer and Timm, both Eisner and Auer were still occupied at the conference of southern states in Stuttgart. Rosshaupter had just returned from Berlin and was personally convinced that the Ebert government had the military and political crises in hand. But his warning that the decree was sure to arouse mistrust among soldiers stationed in Munich came too late. Since the decree had been sponsored by the ministries of Interior and Justice rather than voted on by the entire cabinet, Timm was left in Auer's absence to defend it. He described the *Bürgerwehr* as a formation of "trade union troops" intended to insulate Munich against the "waves" of radicalism from Berlin. He failed to mention whether he and Auer were at least indirectly aware of Buttmann's activities or whether a moment had been purposely chosen for the decree when Eisner was not in the city. In any case, formal approval had been obtained neither from the Chief of Police, the Commandant, the Social Democratic Party, nor the Free Trade Unions. It was, then, clearly the unilateral initiative of two cabinet

[46] Rudolf Buttmann, "Erinnerungen aus der bayer. Revolution," *Illustrierter Beobachter*, XX (1927), 282-286. According to Buttmann, Rosshaupter had promised him arms for a *Bürgerwehr* on November 29, but reneged in December.

members supported by a coterie of bureaucratic and civic leaders. This was not, it should be made explicit, the Buttmann group.[47]

Rosshaupter's warning proved entirely justified. Representatives of the soldiers' councils met that same day and declared their opposition to the decree, calling the plan for a *Bürgerwehr* "a great danger for the revolution, since the public peace will be thereby endangered and a civil war could thus easily ensue." Auer's ministry was informed that the local councils would take orders only from executive committees of the council system and from Commandant Dürr—a scarcely ambiguous threat of insubordination.[48] On the following day the incident became a scandal. At the Hotel Vierjahreszeiten a meeting of Buttmann's group was broken up by the Munich Military Police: twenty men were arrested and charged with gathering arms and plotting a counter-revolution. And the suspicion was aroused that Auer and Timm had been conspiring with Buttmann to remove Eisner from office by force of arms. Whatever their personal motivations, they had committed a political blunder which left them momentarily without public support. In the State Soldiers' Council radical leaders were able to press the matter to the point of a vote demanding that the two ministers resign from the cabinet. After the revelation of the Buttmann conspiracy, even the Social Democratic Party washed its hands of the *Bürgerwehr* affair and stood by as Auer returned to Munich to be either a villain or a dupe.[49]

[47] *Ministerratsprotokolle*, 27 Dec. 1918, BGS Munich, PA, VII, 104a.

[48] "Landessoldatenrat Bayern, Vollzugsausschuss. An das Ministerium des Innern," 28 Dec. 1918, BHS Munich, M. Inn. 54199.

[49] See the account sympathetic to Buttmann by Rudolf von Sebottendorff, *Bevor Hitler kam. Urkundliches aus der Frühzeit der Nationalsozialistischen Bewegung* (Munich, 1934), 64-70, and the more sober evaluation of Bernhard Zittel, "Rätemodell München 1918/19," *Stimmen der Zeit*, CLXV (1959), 25-43. The relation of this incident to the origins of National Socialism has been care-

Under these circumstances the secret meeting of the cabinet on December 29 had particular significance. The transcript of this session discloses both the basis on which the *Bürgerwehr* crisis was resolved and the aggravated personal strain among the ministers. An initial airing of the facts in the case established that an armed coup d'état had in reality been Buttmann's ultimate intention; and, willingly or not, Auer and Timm were now implicated. The former protested that he was being made a "scapegoat," and that "if the facts are true, if I have become the victim of a cruel ruse, I am naturally prepared to draw the consequences. . . . I am ready to disappear." Although they would not hear of his resigning, colleagues in Auer's own party showed little more sympathy in private than in public for his action. The result, said Albert Rosshaupter in reference to the stand of the soldiers' councils, had been foregone: he had therefore refused to sign the decree and, in any case, he held a *Bürgerwehr* to be "superfluous." With such a statement coming from the man charged with the responsibility for military security, it was clear that the situation in the cabinet was precisely the reverse of that on December 2. Now Auer found himself isolated and forced to back down on a critical matter of policy, while Kurt Eisner was able to dictate the terms of a compromise. He could warn that the "strong ferment" among the Munich workers due to unemployment had been further stirred by Auer's imprudence. "They will break loose if something doesn't happen, and an attempt might be made to establish a dictatorship of the workers' and soldiers' councils. Whether I can prevent that, I do not know. . . ."

Eisner thereupon demanded that Auer publicly retract his signature and renew his allegiance to the regime; in return, the Prime Minister would personally defend him before the

---

fully explained by Reginald H. Phelps, " 'Before Hitler came': Thule Society and Germanen Orden," *The Journal of Modern History*, XXXV (1963), 245-261.

councils. The bargain was a hard one, and Auer was by no means eager to accept it. He would do so and remain in office, he explained, only because the elections were but two weeks away. A statement of compromise was subsequently agreed upon, after Johannes Hoffmann had summarized the sense of the meeting: "Everyone should make an effort to suppress his differences of opinion, above all in public. The Auer-Eisner antagonism must no longer be so in evidence; otherwise we shall arrive at the state of things in Berlin."[50]

With that, the issue was ostensibly settled. But Auer's political opponents could hardly have been expected to let the matter drop. On December 30 the cabinet appeared before the Provisional National Council, then in its last week of existence, much as the ministers had appeared at the congress of Bavarian soldiers' councils on December 2. As might have been anticipated, an obvious and rather theatrical attempt was made to humiliate Auer. The chief spokesman for his critics was Ernst Toller, an excitable and effective young speaker, who insisted on the absolute incompatibility of "revolution and bourgeoisie." Whoever hoped to combine them, he said, "is either naïve or dumb." The rebuttal was necessarily lame: Auer maintained his innocence of any counter-revolutionary intent and accused his opponents of playing with words by misconstruing *Bürger* as "bourgeois" instead of "civilian." The assembly was not satisfied (Gustav Landauer led a chorus of "*genügt nicht!*"), and Auer's discomfiture was continued through a day of debate. It was not difficult, then, for Kurt Eisner to assume an air of magnanimous pardon when he rose to read the statement of compromise. He itemized the cabinet's decisions to: 1) disavow the *Bürgerwehr*, 2) admit that Auer and Timm had been "under erroneous presuppositions," 3) protect the revolution, and 4) prevent the further distribution of arms.

Eisner then begged all members of the Provisional Na-

[50] *Ministerratsprotokolle*, 29 Dec. 1918, BGS Munich, GN 2/1-2/2.

tional Council to overlook personal differences and to unite in support of the cabinet: "it is, after all, a Social Democratic regime." Eisner's theme was restated by Toller in closing the debate on January 2 with a motion for "a united front . . . and thoroughgoing socialization." The measure was adopted, 112-11. The slogan of an *Einheitsfront* was thereafter to be the keynote of Eisner's personal leadership.[51]

To recount the details of the *Bürgerwehr* crisis is significant for two reasons of unequal importance: the effect which it had on the subsequent political alignment, and the negligible difference which it made in the electoral contest. An explanation of the second is more apparent than of the first. The extreme delicacy of the personal situation in the cabinet was still known only to a small circle within the government. In public the ministers had managed to maintain the façade of harmony, although Auer's undisguisable embarrassment and his antipathy for Eisner were no secret. It is, moreover, doubtful that the spectacle in the Provisional National Council actually had much effect on the personal views of its members, nearly all of whom already had a firm political commitment. It seemed perfectly consistent to reproach Auer (as his own party did) for one rash action, and yet to continue to support his general political position. And it made more sense to think him the dupe rather than the villain. The rationalization of Auer's part in the *Bürgerwehr* incident was simple and impeccable: why should he have conspired against a government of which he was almost certain to gain legal control within two weeks? There was not and has never been a convincing answer to this question, and it makes nonsense of subsequent invective against Auer as an "enemy of the working class." Auer wanted to insure the elections, not to instigate a counter-revolution.

[51] *Verhandlungen des provisorischen Nationalrates*, No. 7, 185-236; No. 8, 237-259. When the vote was taken 133 delegates were absent; the abstentions thus exceeded the plurality for the motion.

But if the *Bürgerwehr* crisis was to have no discernible effect on the electoral results, it did weigh in the balance of political power. In the first place, it made the continuation of a Socialist coalition as intolerable for the SPD as it was indispensable for the USP. "The Auer-Eisner antagonism" of which Hoffmann spoke was now in the last stages of petrification. Political opposition had been hardened by personal feelings. Erhard Auer was committed to oppose Eisner as a leader, the USP as a party, and the council system as an autonomous form of government. The reason he had given for withholding his resignation unmistakably indicated that his willingness to endure two more weeks of the coalition was based solely on the calculation that he would be able to manage without it thereafter. For Eisner the situation was the contrary—and that was the sense of the proposal for a united Socialist front. He could not dispense with the cooperation of Auer's party because he had nowhere else to look for sufficient support. Now (with the elections approaching) more than ever, he needed an alliance which could be called "Social Democratic."

It is necessary in this connection to mention parenthetically the "Basic Law of the Bavarian Republic" published on January 4, 1919. The *Staatsgrundgesetz* deserves attention as a legal curiosity as well as a document of the united front. It provided that Bavaria should thenceforth be a republic, a member of the "United States of Germany," and a democracy governed jointly by a unicameral legislature and a cabinet of ministers. The latter reserved "the highest executive power" and the right to demand a referendum within four weeks on any bill passed by the parliament. "Should the people's vote decide against the Landtag, it is to be dissolved. But should it be decided against the cabinet of ministers, the latter must resign" (Article 6). The remainder of the provisions made a liberal dispensation of basic rights, including woman suffrage, and specified the abolition both of aristocratic titles and of ecclesiastical authority in the public schools—all issues upon

206

which Socialists of any stripe could substantially agree. The most controversial provision was contained in Article 17: "Until the final settlement of the constitutional draft, which must be laid before the Landtag immediately after its convocation, the revolutionary regime exercises the legislative and executive power." By virtue of this paragraph Eisner's regime could "legally" retain sovereignty in Bavaria even after the Landtag had been elected and convened. This could only obtain, however, provided that a united front was successfully maintained and the ministerial cabinet was not dissolved from within.[52]

Outside of the provisional government, the effect of the *Bürgerwehr* crisis was to tie the hands of the conservatives and to free those of the radicals. Support of the militia idea could now be interpreted as distrust of the soldiers' councils in particular and of the entire council system in general. Any further oratory or action against the councils thereafter was to be immediately branded as reactionary, and any attempt to strengthen security forces was labeled a counter-revolutionary plot. Even the legitimate fears of responsible people had thus been made *a priori* suspect. It should be kept in mind that these fears were to be fed every day for months, and that a growing sense of political frustration was the inevitable result. And now this fact was compounded with the anxiety, provoked by the Basic Law, that even the elections could not restore normalcy to Bavarian politics, regardless of who was victorious. "This," wrote DDP leader Ludwig Quidde, "is downright monstrous."[53]

The radicals, on the other hand, were free to say and to do as they pleased with virtual impunity, being opposed neither by the force of a militia nor by the undivided resolution of the Bavarian government. The first warning of this came on New Year's Eve, when Munich was harassed all

[52] "Staats-Grundgesetz der Republik Bayern," *Bekanntmachungen,* F. Mon. 3205.
[53] "Zum neuen Staatsgrundgesetz," *MAA,* 11 Jan. 1919, No. 15.

night by gangs of drunken soldiers and shooting on the streets. There was more noise in a single evening, one newspaper observed, than the city had heard during four years of war. The disturbance followed a mass meeting the previous night in which several speakers had openly advocated the "arming of the proletariat."[54] Such radical spirit was particularly dangerous at a time when the political campaign was most intense. After Christmas there were as many as twenty separate political rallies in Munich on a single evening.[55] On January 7 the situation for the first time became critical: a demonstration for higher unemployment compensation met on the Theresienwiese, marched to the Ministry for Social Welfare, then broke into a riot which lasted several hours. Two people were killed, and the regime was in serious trouble. The cabinet met to hear a sober warning from Commandant Dürr: "It is not a matter of simple demonstrations, but of actual putsch attempts. We can no longer offer a guarantee for the safety of the city. The police force is no longer sufficient and the troops will no longer cooperate if they are compelled to remain under such tension. . . ."[56]

In view of this situation it was apparent that the *Bürgerwehr* compromise had settled little. Certainly it had not secured the city against armed violence. In a series of secret meetings the cabinet deliberated on a course of action. Despite Chief of Police Staimer's warning that a choice was essential, Kurt Eisner wished neither to restrict the right of assembly nor to permit the use of weapons by government forces. When both Dürr and Staimer threatened to resign, however, the cabinet made a hasty decision: orders were issued to arrest Max

[54] "Kommunistische Hetze," *MNN*, 2 Jan. 1919, No. 2. "Die Neujahrsnacht in München," *MAA*, 2 Jan. 1919, No. 1.

[55] "Massenversammlungen in München," *MNN*, 4 Jan. 1919, No. 5.

[56] *Ministerratsprotokolle*, 9 Jan. 1919 (morning), BGS Munich, GN 2/1-2/2. "Die Demonstration vom 7. Januar," *Bekanntmachungen*, F. Mon. 3203. "Eine Arbeitslosen-Demonstration mit blutigem Ausgang," *MNN*, 8 Jan. 1919, No. 9.

Kurt der Kleber

"The people didn't make me the premier, so they can't depose me, either."

Simplicissimus, XXIII (1919)

Levien, Erich Mühsam, and eight other radical leaders, to be held on suspicion of creating public disorder. It was an attempt to detain these men until after the elections and, by implication, to blame them for the rioting of the unemployed. But as Eisner admitted two days later, "the prerequisite of our action was lacking."[57] As the ten were all council members, the cabinet's action was again interpreted as an attack on the council system. News of the arrest only brought another demonstration, another riot, and more casualties: six dead and fifteen wounded. This time the march had been on Eisner's ministry, where a jeering mob armed in part with hand grenades and machine guns stood by as a sailor climbed into Eisner's second-story window and obtained the release of the ten prisoners. The Republican Security Troops were present, but were not ordered to intervene. The outcome was that the KPD could celebrate its first tangible triumph in Munich, and the prestige of Eisner's regime suffered one more trouncing.[58]

The unwillingness or inability of Kurt Eisner to take decisive action following the *Bürgerwehr* crisis, at a time when the most elementary rules of statecraft demanded it, has been the theme of most of the criticism leveled against his premiership. He has been accused of being either a hopeless idealist, a Bolshevik, or both. But his idealism was of a certain type; and he was certainly no Bolshevik. His personal experience as a journalist twice imprisoned had made him a fanatical believer in the freedom of public expression. His long-stand-

[57] *Ministerratsprotokolle*, 9 Jan. (afternoon) and 11 Jan. 1919, BGS Munich, GN 2/1-2/2. Although Eisner insisted that there be "no restriction of the freedom of assembly and speech," he told the cabinet: "Levien has illusions of grandeur, colossal conceit. There is no good will there."

[58] "Mitbürger! Wieder ist Blut geflossen!" *Bekanntmachungen*, F. Mon. 3223. "Demonstration der Kommunisten," *MP*, 11-12 Jan. 1919, No. 8. "Bolschewistische Umtriebe in München," *MAA*, 11 Jan. 1919, No. 15. The latter article is indicative of the popular tendency to see a conspiracy behind every radical outburst.

ing convictions as a Kantian and his years of opposition to the war had made him a compulsive opponent of armed violence in any form. He failed to take sufficient security precautions in Munich not because he wished to aid the Communists, but because he did not believe he had the right to suppress them. His regime was contending with a subtle and complex problem, one which every Western parliamentary democracy has since been forced to meet in one form or another. For many states with a long parliamentary tradition and a relatively insignificant fringe of radical agitation, the solution has been less difficult than it was in Germany during the Weimar Republic. The majority of unemployed workers and soldiers in Munich in 1919 was by no means communist. It was a mass of the disappointed and the displaced, for the most part with legitimate grievances. That a man of Eisner's background and temperament did not move against these people with military force is not, then, surprising. What is surprising—and for this he can be fairly censured—is that he continued to believe that all the conflicting elements in the Bavarian body politic could be peaceably, reasonably, and genuinely reconciled. It was this belief which persuaded him to remain in office at a time when he would have done better to resign.

CHAPTER VII

The Statistics of Deterioration

MORE than three million Bavarians went to the polls on Sunday, January 12, to elect representatives to the first parliament of the new Republic. Contrary to expectation, the heavy balloting was conducted in seven provinces without a notable incident of public disorder. Whatever else the electoral returns might have demonstrated, they did show the assumption of an overwhelming majority that Bavaria would resume parliamentary government. The character of that government, the drafting of a republican constitution, the establishment of decorum and precedent would presumably all be determined by the Landtag-elect. Apart from which faction or coalition actually "won" the election, then, this much seemed certain simply from the procedure of balloting itself: most Bavarians were prepared to accept and support a unicameral legislature based on a multi-party system and directed by a responsible cabinet of ministers. When the voting of the succeeding Sunday, January 19, produced nearly identical results, it could be concluded as well that the electorate desired its representatives to participate in the German National Assembly, though the precise nature of Bavaria's relationship to the Reich was a matter still to be settled.

For Kurt Eisner and his party the elections proved to be a political disaster. After January 12 the days of his prime ministry were numbered; only the number remained an uncertainty. The longer he retained his office, the more heavily the electoral totals would weigh against the stability of his regime and the more difficult it would become for any successor to strike a new political balance. If this had been strictly a political matter, just an inconvenient delay in transferring authority from one regime to another, the consequence might have been no more serious than the usual disability of a lame duck administration to innovate policy or initiate legislation.

The paralysis in the executive arm of government, however, occurred just as the Bavarian economy was approaching a crisis.

Until January the economic situation had been disturbing: prices were rising, buildings were left unheated for lack of fuel, there were shortages and privations that touched everyone. On the second day of the New Year, for example, the city magistracy of Munich was forced to advertise the "Last Public Sale of Vegetables." Citizens were instructed not to fail to purchase from the municipality's final stocks of cabbages and carrots, since "before spring further delivery of vegetables is scarcely to be expected."[1] But in the course of that month the situation began to deteriorate alarmingly as it became more than a question of private discomfort: the Bavarian state itself was on the verge of economic stagnation and financial ruin. If the causes were not immediately evident, the practical results were soon manifest and, in part, measurable. The most obvious and indicative economic factor bearing on the existence of the Eisner regime was the sudden increment of unemployment. Following the rioting of January 7, when a crowd of unemployed workers and soldiers in Munich was able to wrest a promise of compensatory concessions from the Minister for Social Welfare, the critical juncture of political and economic crises was clearly no coincidence. Not only was Bavaria slipping rapidly into a slough of insolvency as a result of the exorbitant compensation payments, but the growing mass of unoccupied and dissatisfied workers represented a last resort for those who refused to recognize the elections as a mandate for the parliamentary system. By the end of January there had developed, in short, a distinct and direct threat of anarchy.

The Parliamentary Elections

The number of ballots cast for candidates to the Bavarian Landtag on January 12 virtually trebled the total recorded

[1] "Letzter Volksverkauf von Gemüse," *MAA*, 2 Jan. 1919, No. 2.

in the last previous general election of 1912. The polling locales were literally crowded with people who had never voted before. If the revolution had failed to bring a "new democracy," it did produce a new electorate. As a result of the new electoral law adopted in December, which established woman suffrage and reduced the minimum voting age from 26 to 21 years, about seven voters in ten were making their first trip to the polls. In retrospect it is no more difficult to locate these initiate voters than it was, in most cases, to distinguish them in the crowds on that Sunday afternoon in 1919. The greatest novelty, of course, was the appearance of a female electorate: wives and widows, the ladies of fashion, peasant women in their Sunday dress, the long files of robed nuns. In all, the 1,832,048 women voters accounted for 53.4 per cent of the total electorate. It is impossible (despite the remarkable exertions of the Bavarian State Statistical Bureau) to fix precisely the number of males voting for the first time, though it can be fairly estimated at nearly three-quarters of a million. The majority of these were young men: both those who had reached voting age since 1912 under terms of the old suffrage, and those newly enfranchised by the reduction of the minimum age. In fact, a whole new generation—every man and woman under 33 years of age— had become eligible to vote and now comprised about one-third of the Bavarian electorate.[2]

The actual balloting, nevertheless, ran remarkably true to form. By Monday morning the first electoral returns were tabulated and published: the SPD gained an early lead in Munich, but reports from outside the capital indicated (as expected) that the BVP would take and hold a slight plurality. By January 14 the results were virtually final and this pattern was confirmed. Traditionally the voting in Bavaria had tended to follow confessional lines. The extent to which the tradition

[2] The analysis here and following is based on the *Statistisches Jahrbuch für den Freistaat Bayern 1919*, 578-589.

was upheld can be indicated by a closer look at the rivalry of Majority Socialism and Catholicism in the various provinces:

	Population in 1910	Catholics (per cent.)	Protestants (per cent.)	BVP	SPD
Upper Bavaria	1,511,952	91.1	7.4	268,085	274,394
Lower Bavaria	724,331	98.9	1.0	114,003	73,216
Rhenish Palatinate	937,085	44.3	54.1	124,207	170,216
Upper Palatinate	599,461	91.8	7.9	160,787	69,499
Upper Franconia	661,862	42.8	56.7	87,902	108,231
Middle Franconia	931,691	27.0	70.9	60,273	209,189
Lower Franconia	710,943	80.4	17.7	172,390	97,833
Swabia	809,966	86.0	13.3	157,463	108,068
Bavaria (total)	6,887,291	70.6	28.2	1,145,110	1,110,646
Munich (total)	607,592	82.3	14.4	85,949	161,132

Only in the immediate proximity of the capital was Socialism able to break the confessional barrier. In fact, by subtracting the municipal returns from those of the province of Upper Bavaria, it is obvious that the BVP managed to hold its own everywhere except within the city limits of Munich. It is equally apparent, however, that many Bavarians outside of Munich saw no practical incompatibility between professing Catholicism and voting for a Socialist party: witness Swabia, for example, where the confessional ratio was greater than five to one while the electoral margin was well under two to one.

In general, the success of the SPD was undiminished by the split of the Socialist vote. This was true even of the urban centers, as the returns from Munich's twelve urban electoral precincts illustrate:

Total Votes	Precinct	USP	BBB	SPD	DDP	NLB/ BMP	BVP	Other
23,220	I	713	9	6,232	6,859	559	8,544	304
25,617	II	1,687	13	12,204	4,301	376	6,652	384
21,206	III	709	11	6,629	6,181	337	7,115	224
22,675	IV	735	32	7,781	5,518	685	7,430	494
31,075	V	1,672	44	12,039	8,300	741	7,402	877
47,981	VI	2,753	56	22,444	10,073	873	10,147	1,635
38,315	VII	1,042	65	19,193	6,653	435	10,190	737
29,785	VIII	2,017	39	18,363	3,021	200	5,885	260
30,969	IX	1,724	16	17,020	4,833	301	6,732	343
30,784	X	2,193	31	18,115	3,728	193	6,155	369
24,201	XI	1,332	14	11,940	3,921	252	6,362	380
31,089	XII	1,754	29	15,403	5,101	362	8,008	432
356,917		18,331	359	167,363	68,489	5,314	90,622	6,439

The SPD thus carried ten of the twelve precincts, most of them handily. Only in the third precinct would the addition of the Independent votes have altered the result in favor of the Majority Socialists. It is more appropriate to conclude that the SPD was prevented from sweeping all twelve precincts by the strong showing of the Democratic Party, rather than by the division in Socialist ranks.

The cumbersome and unduly involved system by which the apportionment of parliamentary seats was calculated is too complex to be described in full here. The electoral law provided, in the words of its framer, "a system of individual election with a competition of lists." The entire state was divided into constituencies. The parties were able to enter only one candidate in each constituency, but the same name could be entered in several. The number of individual candidates therefore varied from the 108 offered by the BVP to the single entrant of a few inevitable "crank" parties. The voter had to select a single name and thereby give his ballot to the party list of his chosen candidate. The seats were then assigned under a method of proportional representation, with the distribution of remainders calculated on the highest average.[3] Suffice it to say that both the theory and practice of this procedure were a mystery to the voters themselves, and that a simple system of proportional representation would have yielded virtually the same results for the parties. The only apparent reason for abandoning the electoral system of 1912, a *scrutin d'arrondissement*, was to prevent the BVP from gaining a large number of constituencies with only narrow pluralities. This much was accomplished.

Party	Popular Vote	Percentage	Landtag Seats	Percentage
BVP	1,193,101½	35.0	66	36.6
SPD	1,124,584	33.0	61	33.9
DDP	477,992	14.0	25	13.9
BBB	310,165½	9.1	16	8.9
NLB/BMP	196,818½	5.8	9	5.0
USP	86,254½	2.5	3	1.6
Other	20,627½	0.6	0	.0

The objective of "individual election" was presumably to ensure the maximum effectiveness to individual political figures who were well known. This enabled the established parties to make use of attractive local candidates, but it also permitted a lesser party to enter its "champion" throughout the state. It is impossible to assess the actual difference which this arrangement made, except that it failed to be of any significant advantage to Kurt Eisner and the USP. Personally Eisner received nearly a quarter (17,302) of his party's votes, but to do so it had been necessary for him to enter the lists in thirty-nine constituencies. He was awarded over five hundred ballots in only three. By contrast, Erhard Auer outpolled all other individual candidates by commanding 40,269 votes in only five constituencies, and like his party he scored heavily in Munich. If Eisner was soundly defeated, the other Independent cabinet ministers were humiliated: Edgar Jaffé gained 2331 votes, and Hans Unterleitner only 946. The

---

[3] "Wahlordnung für den neuen bayerischen Landtag," *Gesetz- und Verordnungsblatt für den Volksstaat Bayern*, 14 Dec. 1918, No. 84.

STATISTICS OF DETERIORATION

USP leaders more particularly associated with the council system fared still worse: Ernst Toller received 834½ votes; Fritz Schröder, 597½; Fritz Sauber, 534½; and Gustav Landauer (who entered in the town of Grumbach as a personal favor to Eisner), 92.

THE LANDTAG ELECTIONS OF 12 JANUARY 1919

	USP	BBB	SPD	DDP	NLB/BMP	BVP	Other	Total
Upper Bavaria	21,732	100,306	290,535½	97,045½	6,486	289,418	8,379½	813,902½
Lower Bavaria	1,210½	95,922½	77,390½	16,495	315½	119,702½	694½	311,731
Upper Palatinate	1,083½	13,836	73,224	18,484	2,270	172,440	1,466½	282,804
Upper Franconia	32,813½	3,099	107,784½	50,319	32,334	90,809½	2,427½	319,587
Middle Franconia	14,893½	4,483½	206,345	135,806	70,466	61,083	2,562½	495,639½
Lower Franconia	3,711	2,714½	110,239	56,300½	3,578	179,571½	3,072½	359,187
Swabia	3,336½	89,804	97,531½	48,064	2,131	158,328½	2,024½	401,220
Rhenish Palatinate*	7,474	——	161,534	55,478	79,238	121,748½	——	425,472½
BAVARIA (totals)	86,254½	310,165½	1,124,584	477,992	196,818½	1,193,101½	20,627½	3,409,543½

* Balloting delayed until 4 February 1919

THE ELECTIONS FOR THE GERMAN NATIONAL ASSEMBLY OF 19 JANUARY 1919

	USP	BBB	SPD	DDP	NLB/BMP	BVP	Total
Upper Bavaria	39,719	88,552	274,394	87,600	9,483	268,085	768,454
Lower Bavaria	483	86,901	73,216	12,127	——	114,003	286,730
Rhenish Palatinate	7,229	——	170,216	59,417	88,352	124,207	449,421
Upper Palatinate	2,031	15,388	69,499	18,234	——	160,787	265,939
Upper Franconia	35,278	——	108,231	50,739	29,486	87,902	311,636
Middle Franconia	18,454	——	209,189	125,505	71,807	60,273	485,228
Lower Franconia	15,616	——	97,833	52,223	5,714	172,390	343,776
Swabia	3,895	84,386	108,068	42,198	2,431	157,463	398,460
BAVARIA (totals)	122,705	275,227	1,110,646	448,043	207,273	1,145,110	3,309,644

The USP totals contrasted embarrassingly with those won by leaders of the other parties. As anticipated, the BVP had the most balanced electoral response, boasting a score of candidates who amassed 19,000 votes or more. One Democratic candidate challenged Auer's individual preeminence with more than 39,000 votes, but the DDP returns were generally inferior to those of the two largest parties. The BBB had done surprisingly well as a party, but the fact that the leader of its conservative wing, Georg Eisenberger, earned more support than Karl Gandorfer (21,462 to 18,376), and that both had outpolled Eisner, made this of mitigated significance as a vote of confidence for "the revolution."[4]

When the electoral statistics became known, it still remained to be seen what the parties themselves would make of them. In a multi-party system it is not unusual, by some strange calculation, for each party to see its own victory indubitably confirmed by the results of an election. Kurt Eisner might have been thought the last to make such a claim. He was in fact among the first. On the morning after the Landtag election, the *Neue Zeitung* published an appeal "To all Socialists!" signed by Eisner and the executive board of the USP. Since the war was ended and the revolution successful, they declared, any reason for dissension among Socialists was past, "and thereby the restoration of a unified party has become possible and necessary." It would be the objective of this reunited party "to give Germany and the world an example of how the transition to a socialistic society can be achieved."[5] On January 14 "invited" members of the workers' and soldiers' councils met in the Deutsches Theater. Here Eisner termed the results of the election "surprisingly favor-

---

[4] Statistics on individual candidates are taken from Joseph Würsdörfer, "Die Wahlen zum Bayer. Landtag am 12. Januar 1919 und ihr Ergebnis," *Politische Zeitfragen*, 1919, III-IV, 41-76. Würsdörfer also discusses the system of apportionment in detail.

[5] "An alle Sozialisten!" *NZ*, 13 Jan. 1919, No. 17.

able." It was his view that there could be "only a socialistic or a bourgeois regime." This would mean, of course, the exclusion of both the BVP and the DDP from the governing Socialist coalition. At the same time, all those radicals who relied on violence as a political means must also be excluded: "there can therefore now be no cooperation with the Spartacists." Between the extremes, Eisner concluded, a Socialist coalition (presumably including the BBB along with the SPD and USP) should concentrate on two immediate objectives: securing a place within the Bavarian constitution and political structure for the council system, and taking the first important steps in a program of socialization.[6]

If it was Eisner's intention in this speech to throw down some sort of political gauntlet, the Social Democrats refused to pick it up. In the first place, they charged that the council meeting at the Deutsches Theater had been stacked in favor of the USP delegates, "a large part" of whom had Bolshevik sympathies. The SPD could offer cooperation only with those who openly disavowed such leanings and who ceased to think "that the transition of capitalist society to the socialistic can only follow the way of the dictatorship of the proletariat," a way which would lead instead to "the destruction of the state [and] the elimination of parliamentarianism." The *Münchener Post* also cited the precedent of Berlin, where the Christmas crisis had ended in a definitive SPD-USP split and the resignation of the latter from the governmental coalition: "Scheidemann, Haase, Ledebour, and Liebknecht are supposed to become socialistic brothers! A fully utopian, but unfortunately widely circulated idea in the leading Independent circles." As a resolution adopted by the SPD's executive committee stated it, the question of a united Socialist front was not something to be settled in a rump session of council representatives in Munich, but by a formal caucus of the Majority Party. Although the SPD might not be opposed to a

[6] "Sozialistische Einheitsfront," *MP*, 15 Jan. 1919, No. 11.

reconciliation in principle, the "real" united front was, after all, the Social Democratic Party itself.[7] Within the SPD only a small faction, led by Ernst Niekisch of Augsburg, favored an *Einheitsfront* as Eisner had proposed it.[8] The party as a whole concurred in Erhard Auer's reading of the electoral returns; it was he who spoke the last word at a political rally on January 16: "a class can predominate but not govern— only an organization can govern." And that was plainly his own party.[9]

The confidence with which the SPD rejected Eisner's offer of a united front was justified only because the party was certain of an alternative. The grounds for certainty became solid enough when the leading Democratic journal, the *Münchener Neueste Nachrichten*, editorialized as follows: "The total result of the election gives the German Democratic Party (DDP) a decisive position in the constituent parliament: together with the Social Democratic Party it represents a reliable, progressive democratic majority."[10] The Democrats also joined with the SPD in criticizing the procedure in the Deutsches Theater, charging that sanction of the united front on Eisner's terms would mean an "absolutism of the councils in Bavaria." The DDP even hoped to wean the BBB away from its coalition with the USP by encouraging the more conservative Eisenberger wing to abandon the Gandorfer-Eisner alliance. To the Eisenberger group the DDP could submit two cogent arguments: that the real basis of Gandorfer's influence rested on the peasants' councils rather than the Peasants' League, and that the BBB and the Democratic Party shared a common opposition to the authority

[7] See the series of SPD editorials: "Einigungsbestrebungen," "Die Einheitsfront," and "Die eingebildete und die wirkliche Einheitsfront," *MP*, 14-16 Jan. 1919, Nos. 10-12.

[8] "Sitzung der Fraktion am 14. Jan. 1919," BHS Munich, ASR 3.

[9] "Die Bedeutung der Wahlen zur Deutschen Nationalversammlung," *MP*, 17 Jan. 1919, No. 13.

[10] "Der Ausfall der Landtagswahlen," *MNN*, 13 Jan. 1919, No. 19.

outside Munich of the BVP. The result was to pose an attractive and feasible alternative to Eisner's united front in the form of a centrist coalition of SPD, DDP, and BBB.[11]

In either case the Bavarian People's Party was sure to be excluded. The statistics showed that the BVP had kept a plurality but lost its predominance. Even if the Catholic party could succeed in holding the National Liberals and the Bavarian Middle Party firmly in its orbit, the BVP would fall far short of mustering a Landtag majority. Nor could the BVP any longer hope to control the Bavarian delegation to the German Reichstag. Without a major parliamentary ally, the leaders of the BVP were left to find some consolation and infinite pleasure in Eisner's predicament. If it was not clear in the Catholic press which party had won the election, there was no doubt as to who had lost it: "A man, a Jew, who still flusters after the Berlin putschists, should no longer stand at the head of a *Volksstaat* whose voters have just prepared for him a crushing defeat."[12]

Overlaying the entire political campaign was the question of the council system. The electoral returns can perhaps be best evaluated in terms of this issue, since the council question was unerringly "the measuring rod of revolutionary radicalism."[13] By such a standard, the parliamentary elections had apparently administered a sound thrashing to the Bavarian radicals. Kurt Eisner's party had been the only one officially committed to an important and permanent role for the revolutionary councils. Yet, for a variety of reasons, it would be fallacious to conclude that less than 3 per cent of the Bavarian population favored the councils and that the rest wished to see them done away with. After all, the election

[11] "Räteabsolutismus in Bayern," *MAA*, 15 Jan. 1919, No. 22. "Kunstgriffe," *MNN*, 16 Jan. 1919, No. 25.
[12] "Kurt Eisner," *BV*, 16 Jan. 1919, No. 12. "Ist Herr Eisner Bolschewist?" *BK*, 23 Jan. 1919, No. 23.
[13] Zittel, "Rätemodell München 1918/19," *op.cit.*, 30.

was not a referendum. The issue had not been put to the voters in terms of a clear choice, and there is no reason to believe that the electoral statistics literally reflected such a choice.

The elections did have the effect of defining more clearly the role of the Communist Party in Bavaria. Technically speaking, there had been nothing illegal before January in open opposition to the re-establishment of parliamentary government. By definition the "radicals" were anti-parliamentarians, and had every right to be such so long as there existed no legally constituted parliament. During the campaign the attitude of the radicals had been one of defiance. They spoke frequently, at length, and often harshly against the "farce" of party politics. Since (with few exceptions) they refused to participate in the elections, they reserved the privilege to ignore the results. "The revolution," warned Erich Mühsam, "shall not allow itself to be voted down."[14] But the results, of course, could not be ignored. January 12 might not have changed the attitude of the Bavarian radicals, but it did change the status of Bavarian radicalism, since any future effort to block the parliamentary process became *a fortiori* an act of subversion against the state. At this point—less than two weeks after the foundation of the KPD—it apparently occurred to no one to argue that membership in the Communist Party was in itself seditious. This would depend on how intransigence was translated into policy.

It required only a few days for the KPD to make its policy known. Any illusions which the party leaders might have had before January 12 about supporting Kurt Eisner and his united front in order to prevent Erhard Auer from capturing the premiership were entirely shattered. As things stood, it seemed only a matter of days until Eisner would voluntarily resign or be forced out by the Majority Socialists. Since the effect of the campaign and of Eisner's maneuvers immedi-

[14] *Verhandlungen des provisorischen Nationalrates*, Beilage III, 149.

223

ately thereafter had been to identify his party with the council system, it was now mandatory for the radicals to deny that the defeat of the USP had anything to do with the question of the councils. And the most likely place to do that was from within the council system itself. The signal for just such a campaign was given at the Deutsches Theater on January 15. A meeting of council delegates was opened by Gustav Landauer's demand that the radicals also be included in the united front. In the midst of "great agitation" Eisner attempted to defend his exclusion of them. He said that he would "stand and fall with the workers', soldiers', and peasants' councils," but that he could not endorse the threat of armed force; nor could he hope, as a practical matter, to gain the cooperation of the SPD if he made such an endorsement. When the meeting then lapsed into disorder, several Independents exchanged insults with radical leaders Mühsam and Max Levien. In the confusion a reporter was able to record only that Eisner was charged with perpetrating "vulgar lies." Other Independent leaders such as Ernst Toller, who represented both the USP and the council system, attempted to save the situation, but a falling-out between the Communists and the Independents was, under the circumstances, unavoidable.[15] The immediate result of the Landtag election was thus to leave the USP more isolated and the KPD more adamant. On the Wednesday after election day the first issue of the Communist *Münchener Rote Fahne* appeared with the slogan: "DOWN WITH INTERNATIONAL CAPITALISM! ALL POWER TO THE COUNCILS OF WORKERS, PEASANTS, AND SOLDIERS!"[16]

Neither willing to join with the Communists nor able to align with the Majority Socialists, the USP had reached a theoretical as well as a practical impasse. As he campaigned, it had mattered more to Kurt Eisner that his ideas on the council system be attractive than that they be precise. It be-

[15] "Die sozialistische Einheitsfront," *MP*, 16 Jan. 1919, No. 12.
[16] "Proletarier aller Länder vereinigt Euch," *MRF*, 15 Jan. 1919, No. 1.

comes increasingly apparent, as one follows his reasoning through page after page of transcript, that his party's program was made to be "sold" rather than systematized. Eisner himself spoke of the councils variously as "the basis of all future political development," "the parliaments of the manual and also of the intellectual workers," "the immediate democratization and politicization of the masses," "the moral force of the masses," "the instruments of political life," etc. Prior to the revolution not a single line of Eisner's writings had been devoted to an attempted definition of the council idea. His statements on the subject during December and January were anything but coherent, though one could be sure that he attached great importance to the councils and expected the system to be the basis of his "new democracy." Yet he saw himself as a model of consistency:

> I have not changed at all; I have gone ahead in my way clearly and without ambiguity, and I have said after the announcement of the National Assembly just as before: the foundation is not constituted by bourgeois parliamentarianism in its outward formality, but by the democratic organizations. Herewith I stand and fall. If it does not succeed, then the revolution has been in vain.[17]

The truth was that Eisner's views had been undergoing a gradual but discernible change. He had first expected the councils to assume a legislative function, to supplement if not to supplant the Landtag, to be some sort of *Nebenparlament*. His party lieutenant, Edgar Jaffé, had explicitly referred to "this new parliamentary formation," and had speculated that it might be "a second member and perhaps—it depends on how it operates—a more important member" of the legislative branch of government. Between the Landtag and this new chamber derived from the council system (that is, based on occupations rather than geographical districts),

[17] *Verhandlungen des provisorischen Nationalrates*, No. 2, 11; No. 4, 63-70; Beilage III, 131-133.

225

there would be a "noble competition," Jaffé predicted, to be won by the body which best served the general interest.[18] It was this conception which Eisner and his party reluctantly abandoned after the political campaign began and which they now dropped altogether once the electoral returns were in. Instead, the USP began to insist that the councils must be preserved in a *bureaucratic* capacity, as an adjunct of the executive branch. Eisner thereafter spoke less often and less violently against "bourgeois parliamentarianism," and began to save his choicest phrases of vituperation for the reactionary bureaucracy of the old system which, as he saw it, had remained in power in spite of the revolution and continued as the chief obstruction to a genuine democracy.[19] This line of reasoning enabled the Independents to accept the electoral verdict without abandoning the councils to the absolute domination of the Landtag. It also meant that not a single member of the newly-elected parliament would be seated on a platform of "all power to the councils."

From the outset Erhard Auer and the SPD had refused to admit that any permanent legislative functions should be

[18] *Ibid.*, 142-143.

[19] Apart from the opposition of the major political parties to any legislative function for the councils, a more prosaic reason may be offered for the shift in Eisner's position. During the initial weeks of the revolution his office had been flooded with letters from countless individuals and groups offering their services to the new regime. The former were politely but invariably refused, whereas the latter were frequently invited to join in the formation of a *Nebenparlament*. To house these groups, the Deutsches Theater was rented: here met, at one time or another, the Association of Fruit and Vegetable Dealers, the League of Socialist Women, the Council of Intellectual Workers, and the Union of Restaurant Personnel—all, among others, legitimate members of the *Nebenparlament*. By the end of December Eisner had so often used this device to gain supporters (and to rid himself of supplicants) that it was useless as a coherent representative organization. See, for example, "Staatsministerium des Aeussern. An die Vereinigung der Obst- und Gemüsehändler," 4 Dec. 1918, BGS Munich, PA, VII, 84.

granted to the council system. Auer's regulation of the system had been consistent with this policy, as the administrative impotence of the council organization by mid-January testified. Like Eisner, but for the somewhat different reasons noted before, Auer had been exceedingly reluctant to define his party's plans for the council system. As a rule he avoided using the term "council" in public, and once suggested openly that "a better form and perhaps a more accurate nomenclature are to be found." In his speeches during and immediately after the election, Auer was willing to concede only two specific functions to the councils, both of them relatively nominal: combatting black market operations and administering unemployment insurance. Beyond these, his only concrete suggestion was for "*berufsgenossenschaftliche Selbstverwaltungsorganisationen der Arbeiter und Arbeitsgeber.*" Such an unyieldingly germanic formulation is not easily anglicized. Auer apparently thought that in a "better form" the council system would not represent the workers alone, but would rather unite labor and management in administrative organizations designated on the basis of, and designed to deal with, common professional interests. About priorities there could be no real question: "the State has to be the overseer, to make sure that the organizations of self-administration function in accord with the principles laid down by it."[20]

Such a proposal was more than just a watering-down of the council idea as it was understood by the radicals and many of the Independents. It meant that within the councils the weight of the workers was to be balanced by their employers, and whatever remained of the council system was to be under the strict surveillance of the parliamentary government. If the electoral returns were now translated into a new governing coalition of the SPD and DDP, as seemed likely, this was the probable future of the council system. Auer's scheme bore more resemblance—doubtless consciously so—

[20] *Verhandlungen des provisorischen Nationalrates*, No. 2, 13-22.

227

to the Bavarian "labor cooperatives," formed shortly after the revolution, than to the existing council bodies.[21] The result of its practical implementation would be simply an extended and formalized system of voluntary collective bargaining, the principle of which had already been accepted by both the Christian Trade Unions and the Free Trade Unions. It goes without saying that the SPD was a long way from supporting the idea of "revolutionary" councils. Yet Auer's carefully guarded ambiguity, not to say obscurity, in referring to the future of the council system—a matter in which his would presumably be the most important single voice—betrayed his recognition that the mystique of the revolution was still attached to the councils. It thus remained appropriate even after the elections for Majority leaders to pledge solemnly to preserve "the gains of the revolution," regardless of their actual plans for the council system.

Even the Democratic Party, the bourgeois party *par excellence*, declined to go on record in favor of the outright abolition of the councils. This was partly out of deference to the SPD, partly in the belief that the council system could be quietly but effectively quashed in the new parliament. Before the elections the DDP had served as a sort of super-ego to the council system. A handful of Democratic delegates had been permitted to sit in the Provisional National Council, where they took their assignment seriously and played an oratorical role quite out of proportion to their numbers. In fact, it was a Democratic delegate, Professor Ludwig Quidde, who had drafted the "Statute and Agenda of the Provisional National Council," the only document which undertook to give shape to the structure and proceedings of that body.[22] But

---

[21] See Hoegner, *Die verratene Republik*, 34-35. For a discussion of the *"Zentral-Arbeitsgemeinschaft"* formed on a national basis under the leadership of Carl Legien, see Erich Eyck, *Geschichte der Weimarer Republik* (2 vols.; Zürich and Stuttgart, 1954-1959), II, 146-147.

[22] "Entwurf einer Satzung und Geschäftsordnung des provisorischen

for Quidde and the other Democrats, the revolution had resulted in an extra-legal situation which was tolerable only as a "transition . . . to a genuine and free *Volksstaat*." For the DDP there was never any alternative to a government dominated completely by the Bavarian Landtag and the German National Assembly. "By comparison, the councils of workers and soldiers are the one-sided representation of certain classes of the people . . . which must bow to the will of the people as it is expressed in the elections." By commanding nearly 15 per cent of the electorate, therefore, the leaders of the DDP were in a position to see that the view of their party and "the will of the people" were not far apart. Specifically, they would be able to block any plan (even had the SPD favored one) to create a bicameral legislative system in which, as Professor Quidde put it, the second chamber was designed to obstruct the first. From the idea of a *Nebenparlament* the Democratic Party could not admit "that anything lasting and useful will ever result." So long as the DDP held the electoral balance of power, then, the councils might continue to exist, but it was improbable that they would ever have more than a secondary role in the Bavarian bureaucracy.[23]

Alone of the major parties, the BVP made a public issue of its opposition to the councils. The party as such naturally did not have—or wish—any part in the council structure, but it had in reality also been represented in the Provisional National Council through a delegation of five from the Christian Trade Unions. Before the elections one of these delegates had already frankly stated that "in the form and in the function in which the council system now exists, it has in the future no justification and no value." If the councils were to be "politicized," he said, then they should be called "socialist councils" (*Sozialistenräte*) and paid for by those they

---

Nationalrates des Volksstaates Bayern" (12 Dec. 1918), *Verhandlungen des provisorischen Nationalrates*, Beilage IV, 206-211.
[23] *Ibid.*, No. 4, 50-56.

229

represented, rather than be supported by the Bavarian state."[24] Since the result of the elections gave the BVP neither a majority nor the expectation of forming a ruling coalition, there was no reason for the party to alter its stance in the direction of a compromise. On the last day of January the executive committee of the BVP met to adopt and announce the following declaration: "The legally elected Landtag is sovereign in its activity and is to be immediately convened to assume its legislative functions. The arbitrarily composed parliament [Provisional National Council] as well as the partially chosen councils of soldiers, workers, and peasants will have, after the consummated election of the people's representatives, no further justification for existence."[25]

It is impossible to restrain a speculation on what-might-have-been had the SPD successfully formed a governing coalition before the end of January. On the basis of what is known, this is likely to have been a centrist rather than a leftist coalition. If so, Kurt Eisner would have been forced into a prominent but ineffectual opposition, such as was already the case for the leaders of Independent Socialism in Berlin. The total effect would have been to bring Bavaria back into step with the rest of Germany and to assure Bavaria's support of and participation in the Weimar Republic. But the fact is that such expectations were not immediately realized. It is plausible that most Bavarians, in reading and discussing the electoral returns, had no inkling that these statistics were any evidence of "deterioration." They were wrong—and it was not long before they realized it. The elections established no new regime; they only paralyzed the one in existence. The elections therefore did not lead to order; they only provoked disorder.

The Economics of Unemployment

The shortage of adequate employment for its population was a problem naturally and especially acute during the first

[24] See the speech by Rudolf Schwarzer, *ibid.*, No. 5, 121-123.
[25] *Politische Zeitfragen*, 1919, I-II, 28.

months of the revolution in Munich, Bavaria's only real metropolis. The immediate sources of unemployment in the capital were close enough to the surface to be seen with the naked eye. The inevitable regimentation of the war years had increased in importance and size the administrative functions of the state government located in Munich. Despite the severe attrition of Bavarian troops in combat (which took an estimated 13,600 citizens of Munich alone), the population of the city had increased steadily since 1914 and was approaching 650,000 by 1919. For the period immediately following the Armistice it is proper to speak of overpopulation, due in the main to the problems created by the demobilization of manpower and the reconversion of wartime industry.

The return of Bavarian troops from the front had begun in force during late November and continued unabated throughout January. Munich was both a major processing center for those being mustered out and an attraction for discharged veterans at loose ends. Civic officials had made every effort to meet the problem of crowding, assuming it to be temporary, by requisitioning school buildings, hotels, and beer-hall cellars, and by beginning on November 26 to organize a program of quartering in large private homes.[26] By mid-December Munich already had one hundred barracks and temporary dormitories, housing 50,000 men in groups of 60 to 3000.[27] The return of additional troops during the Christmas holidays and thereafter stretched the city's facilities and tolerance to the limit. It is therefore not difficult to appreciate the importance of this mass in terms of political instability and economic liability.

[26] "Plenarsitzung des Magistrats vom 26. November 1918," *MGZ:S*, 30 Nov. 1918, No. 96; "Sitzung des gemeindlichen Arbeitsausschusses vom 28. November 1918," *MGZ:S*, 7 Dec. 1918, Nos. 97-98; and "Meldungen der Wohnungen mit mehr als 6 Wohnräumen," *MGZ:B*, 19 Dec. 1918, No. 103. See Michael Gasteiger, *Die Not in München* (Munich, 1923), 5-6. Gasteiger estimates that 50,000 persons entered the city to take up permanent residence right after the war.

[27] "Sitzung des gemeindlichen Arbeitsausschusses vom 11. Dezember 1918," *MGZ:S*, 18 Dec. 1918, No. 101.

The manufacture of munitions and of metal products were the principal wartime industries to have been established in Bavaria. It was the former which posed the most serious problems, both industrial and moral. Whereas a factory specializing in metal parts could, for instance, be retooled to produce bicycles, the conversion of a ballistics industry meant a major readjustment of machinery and skills. The sudden cessation of production entailed a hiatus of several months at least. The continuation of production, however, implied a defiance of the disarmament clause of the armistice agreement, as well as an implicit negation of the aims of the revolution. When the question was raised in the Bavarian cabinet, it was disclosed that a suspension of the munitions industry would put a minimum of 8000 workers out of a job in Munich alone.[28] No action was taken—a decision which even the councils did not protest. A message from council officials in Berlin to leaders in Munich urged that unemployment was by all means to be avoided: "Therefore do *not* demand at any price the immediate stoppage of war production! You will thereby make countless comrades breadless."[29] As a consequence, the manufacture of munitions continued in Bavaria for more than two months after the armistice. For Kurt Eisner it was a gnawing political and moral dilemma, but not until mid-January did he finally order that the small arms industry be suspended by the end of that month.[30] The decision came late. In the meantime Munich had literally become an arsenal; and now thousands of workers were to be turned out onto the streets where the chances of spontaneous combustion were greatest.

The question of financial compensation for the unemployed

[28] *Ministerratsprotokolle*, 29 Nov. 1918, BGS Munich, GN 2/1-2/2.

[29] "Beauftragter des Vollzugsrats des Arbeiter- und Soldatenrates beim Demobilmachungsamt. An den Arbeiter- und Soldatenrat in München," 26 Nov. 1918, BHS Munich, ASR 20.

[30] It is doubtful that Eisner any longer had a choice, since Bavaria had barely enough raw materials to maintain even essential industries.

had been discussed in the cabinet as early as November 19, and a nominal program of compensation was adopted by the magistracy of Munich exactly one week later.[31] But until Christmas the official number of jobless was insignificant. This was due to the slowness of demobilization, the willingness of returning soldiers to enjoy a few weeks of paid vacation in uniform, and a regulation that no firm with over ten employees could release a worker with less than four weeks notice. The first real "taste" of compensation was an enforced one, following an order from Berlin that all large industries in Germany were to be laid off for the Christmas week. Two-thirds of the compensation was to be paid by the municipal governments, the rest through the states. To help defray this expense in Bavaria, a sum of 20 million marks was transferred from the *Reichsbank* to the state government, of which two million were allotted to Munich.[32] Civic officials were disturbed both because of the financial strain and because they had not been consulted on the matter. At a plenary session on Christmas Eve the magistracy considered a resolution to refuse compliance. The principal advocate of non-compliance was Stadtrat Kronenberger, the mayoralty's financial expert: "If the regime does not yet realize it, it must be said in all openness that the city has come to the limit of its financial resources, and that every further step in this direction must lead to economic ruin. . . ." But political rather than financial considerations prevailed—notably the fear that the city government might simply be replaced by a state commissioner who *would* comply—and many Mu-

---

[31] *Ministerratsprotokolle*, 19 Nov. 1918, BGS Munich, GN 2/1-2/2. "Plenarsitzung des Magistrats vom 26. November 1918," *MGZ:S*, 30 Nov. 1918, No. 96. This program was officially begun on December 1 in compliance with instructions from the Bavarian Ministry for Social Welfare. "Erwerbslosenfürsorge," *MGZ:B*, 3 Dec. 1918, No. 97.

[32] "Telegramm-Abschrift. Reichsschatzamt, Berlin. An Aeusseres Ministerium, München," 3 Jan. 1919, BGS Munich, PA, VII, 102.

nich residents thus received something for nothing for the first time in their lives.[33]

During the first week in January the number of those asking for unemployment compensation nearly doubled: the official figure in Munich stood at 18,000 on the morning of January 7. And the pressure for increased compensation had risen accordingly. To meet this demand the rate of compensation for the city of Munich had already been raised from five to six marks a day for a single man.[34] The concession nevertheless failed to prevent a demonstration on the Theresienwiese favoring still higher rates. By the time the day was out, the Minister for Social Welfare had been forced to agree to a new formula: 8 marks a day for every man, 2 marks for a wife, 2 marks for every child over seventeen, and 1 mark for every child under seventeen. The cost of unemployment compensation again doubled within a week, and the number of those requesting compensation began to mount sharply.[35]

An examination of certain key sectors of the economy shows that Bavaria was already a state living beyond its means. The transportation system, for example, had been seriously disrupted by the war. It had operated with a deficit of 90 million marks in 1918 and was expected to lose another 170 million in 1919. The conditions of the Armistice threatened to make a bad matter worse by requiring that the state give up nearly half of its locomotive equipment. By mid-December Bavaria still "owed" the Entente powers 146 heavy

[33] "Plenarsitzung des Magistrats vom 24. Dezember 1918," *MGZ:S*, 3 Jan. 1919, No. 1.

[34] This compared favorably with the rate in other large German cities: Berlin 4, Frankfurt 4.5, Cologne 4.6, and Stuttgart 6. "Sitzung des gemeindlichen Arbeitsausschusses vom 7. Januar 1919," *MGZ:S*, 10 Jan. 1919, No. 3. "Sitzung des gemeindlichen Arbeits- und Demobilmachungsausschusses vom 8. Januar 1919," *MGZ:S*, 14 Jan. 1919, No. 4.

[35] "Satzung der Stadtgemeinde München über Erwerbslosenfürsorge" (14 Jan. 1919), *MGZ:B*, 17 Jan. 1919, No. 5.

machines, and the indulgence of the French and the British could not be hoped for indefinitely. Another one-third of Bavaria's railway locomotives were no longer operational, a figure which had never exceeded 18 per cent before the war. What transportation facilities remained had been temporarily confiscated or clogged by demobilization. Despite the stimulus of the war economy, shipment of freight had increased only 30 per cent since 1913. Even so, provided that the problems of reconversion could be solved, the flow of goods might have been adequate to sustain Bavarian industry had it not been for one basic fact: Bavaria had been entirely cut off from the major source of its fuel supply.[36]

From the Saar the city of Munich had previously obtained 95 per cent of the coal used in the production of gas. Without this fuel the entire beer industry was threatened with closure. The government had been forced to seek vastly increased shipments from Silesia and Bohemia, but had met with only moderate success. By the New Year, according to an economic adviser of the Commission on Demobilization, Bavaria was receiving an average of 5000 tons of coal a day, whereas the minimum requirement for its industry was 15,000 tons: "That this situation must lead to catastrophe within a short time is obvious." Kurt Eisner's personal economic consultant, Professor Lujo Brentano of the University of Munich, came to the same conclusion: the coal supply was "absolutely insufficient to ensure the continued operation of Bavarian industry." A third expert testified before a committee of the magistracy that Munich had only enough coal in stock to last until early February, even under enforcement of the most stringent controls. Despite measures such as rationing, black-out, and restriction of street-car service, the situation

[36] "Bericht vom Verkehrsministerium," 21 Dec. 1918, BHS Munich, ASR 19. See also the "Memorandum Furnished by the Bavarian Minister of Transportation (von Frauendorfer)," *Papers relating to Foreign Relations*, 1919, II, 168-172.

became progressively worse and the price of fuel, when it could be obtained, prohibitive.[37]

Retail Commodity	Inflation July 1914-November 1918 (percentage)	Inflation July 1914-November 1919 (percentage)
Flour	75	400
Milk	90	172
Butter	65	150
Eggs	136	216
Pork	120	485
Sugar	120	340
Beer	21	71
Men's bootery	284	1180
Men's clothing	275	400

Inflation affected private and public sectors of the economy alike. A book which had sold for 1.80 marks during the war cost 6 marks by January of 1919; and a bottle of *Deidesheimer Herrgottsacker* had gone up from 1.90 to 5.10 marks in the same period. If "luxury" items were dispensable, housing was not. Building costs in Munich, it was disclosed in bidding on a schoolhouse contract, had risen nearly 250 per cent since 1913; and building materials were either not available or could be imported only with extreme difficulty.[38] To encourage public housing projects, the Berlin government had offered to pay

[37] "Die Demobilmachung des Volksstaates Bayern," 28 Dec. 1918, BHS Munich, ASR 20. See the letter from Brentano to Eisner, 13 Dec. 1918, *Mein Leben*, 358. Also see the Arzberger report, "Sitzung des gemeindlichen Aktionsausschusses vom 28. November 1918," *MGZ:S*, 7 Dec. 1918, Nos. 97-98. Frauendorfer told the cabinet that Bavaria had received only 9258 tons of coal from Bohemia in the period from January 9 to January 23, an average of barely 600 tons a day. *Ministerratsprotokolle*, 23 Jan. 1919, BGS Munich, GN 2/1-2/2.

[38] Hofmiller, *Revolutionstagebuch*, 133, 143. "Bericht Dr. Wadlers an Eisner betrifft 'die Wohnungsfrage' vom 21.1.1919," BGS Munich, PA, VII, 109. For a detailed statistical analysis, see "Preissteigerung der wichtigsten Lebensmittel und Rohprodukte vom Juli 1914 bis November 1919," *Statistisches Jahrbuch 1919*, 601.

$\frac{3}{6}$ of the cost, with the state bearing $\frac{2}{6}$ and the city $\frac{1}{6}$. But the only significant project of this type undertaken in Munich was not expected to be completed before the end of February, at a total cost of 300,000 marks. Since this was under the auspices of the Ministry for Social Welfare, the government's policy was to keep rents low. In view of the inflation of costs on building materials, private construction firms understandably had no interest in low-rent building projects. Social policy and economic reality were at odds.[39] The result was no construction, no employment in construction, and no housing for the unemployed.

To meet its own bills and to stimulate the economy, the Bavarian government adopted a free money policy—or rather intensified the policy that had originated in the latter war years. One of the regime's first actions, on November 11, had been to increase the circulation of "war emergency currency" (*Kriegsnotgeld*) from 90 to 110 million marks.[40] In addition, Munich had its own emergency currency. Just at the time when unemployment was becoming obviously acute, on January 14, the Lord Mayor announced the release of one million marks in newly printed 50-mark bills. And yet while prices rose, salaries did not. The average daily wage of an unskilled worker in Munich in mid-January was only 9-10 marks, and of a skilled worker, between 12 and 16 marks. Since a small family of four could expect to receive 12 to 14 marks a day under the formula of unemployment compensation agreed to by the government on January 7, it paid only the highly skilled to continue working. And even the real wages of the skilled laborer, measured in terms of actual buying power, were seriously jeopardized by the inflation.[41]

[39] *Ministerratsprotokolle*, 22 Nov. 1918, BGS Munich, GN 2/1-2/2. "Sitzung des gemeindlichen Arbeitsausschusses vom 7. Januar 1919," *MGZ:S*, 10 Jan. 1919, No. 3. The basic monthly rent for a unit of three rooms and kitchen was to be only 53.50 marks.

[40] *Ministerratsprotokolle*, 11 Nov. 1918, BGS Munich, PA, VII, 104a. See "Unsere Valuta vom Juli 1914 bis November 1919," *Statistisches Jahrbuch 1919*, 602.

[41] "Sitzung des gemeindlichen Arbeits- und Demobilmachungs-

As the cost of living was rising, so was the cost of government. "The deficient condition of state finances," Minister of Finance Jaffé admitted on December 28, "requires painful thrift." This statement had special significance since it was made in reference to the council system. Jaffé was announcing the regime's decision to limit the government subsidy of council members to 5 marks a day. Payment was to be made only to members of workers' councils as compensation for working time lost in service for the council system. Soldiers engaged in council work would continue to draw their regular pay, financed through the military budget; peasant council representatives were to receive no compensation unless they were members of joint workers' and peasants' councils, as specified in the regulations of December 17.[42] Until late December, then, the financing of the council system had been costly and chaotic. Exact bookkeeping had been impossible, although Erhard Auer had estimated that the system was costing the Bavarian government 500,000 marks a week and would ultimately represent an expense of 40 million marks a year. These figures by themselves were sufficient to make the council system a political issue as well as a significant economic factor. Those who opposed the council system claimed that it was an unnecessary luxury, an inefficient appendage of government which virtually doubled the cost of the bureaucracy. Supporters of the council system, among them Jaffé, challenged Auer's figures and claimed the councils to be the true bearers of the revolution (and thus presumably "priceless" in any case).[43]

---

ausschusses vom 8. Januar 1919," *MGZ:S*, 14 Jan. 1919, No. 4. "Ausgabe städtischen Kriegsnotgeldes," *MGZ:B*, 17 Jan. 1919, No. 5. See Gasteiger, *Die Not in München*, 7-9.

[42] "Staatsministerium der Finanzen. Bekanntmachung, die Kosten der Arbeiter- und Bauernräte betreffend," *BSZ*, 31 Dec. 1918, No. 303.

[43] *Ministerratsprotokolle*, 25 Nov. 1918, BGS Munich, GN 2/1-2/2. *Verhandlungen des provisorischen Nationalrates*, Beilage III, 200.

Unemployment in Munich: January-February 1919

I. THE NUMBER OF UNEMPLOYED

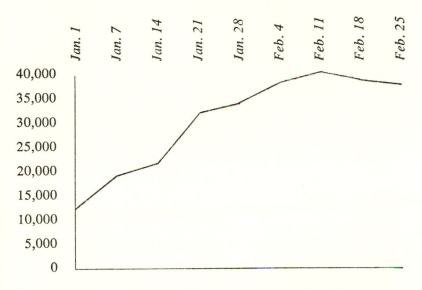

Both arguments were gratuitous, since no one knew precisely how much the councils were costing. The point was, as both sides realized, that the councils as they were constituted in January represented merely another form of unemployment compensation. Bavaria was paying enormous, if indeterminate, sums of money to council members for performing largely redundant tasks. These men were, as Albert Rosshaupter complained in a cabinet meeting on January 23, coming to think of their council positions as occupations.[44] This would be justifiable only if the councils were an integral part of the state and were permitted to assume legislative or bureaucratic functions which would permit economies elsewhere. As no more than a hidden form of unemployment compensation, the council system was an intolerable economic

[44] *Ministerratsprotokolle,* 23 Jan. 1919, BGS Munich, GN 2/1-2/2.

II. THE EXPENSE OF UNEMPLOYMENT COMPENSATION

(THOUSANDS OF MARKS PER WEEK)

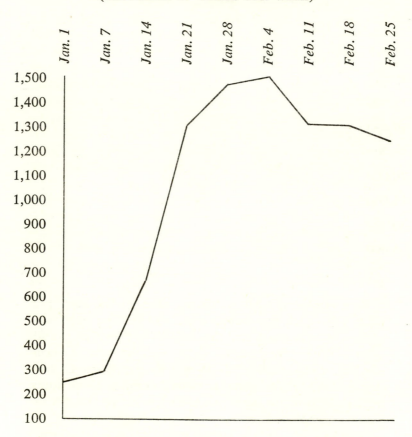

burden for the Bavarian state. The conclusions to be drawn from the economic facts thus seemed to correlate with the political development: either the councils had to establish themselves as a useful part of the governmental structure, or they would be hard put to justify and maintain their existence (except in some very restricted form) after the convocation of the Landtag.

The figure budgeted by the cabinet on January 18 for the financing of unemployment compensation was 15 million marks. Until that week a total of less than 1,500,000 marks had been paid out as compensation. Thereafter, however, this sum was barely enough to underwrite compensation claims for a single week. The concessions made by Minister Unterleitner under pressure of the mob on January 7 were formalized in a statute one week later.[45] This coincided, certainly not by accident, with the sharp rise in the curve of unemployment in Munich; and that, in turn, forced up the cost correspondingly. The economic and political crisis in Munich thereby reached a peak in the first days of February: over 40,000 unemployed were drawing compensation amounting to nearly 1,500,000 marks a week.[46]

This was the state of the economy in Munich between the election and the convocation of the Landtag: pressing problems of demobilization and reconversion, stagnation in key sectors such as construction, devaluation of the mark, spiraling unemployment, and the mounting cost of compensation and the council system. When placed beside the electoral returns, the economic facts warranted and were increasingly to provoke a massive discontent. Although the Eisner regime could not fairly be blamed for creating these circumstances, there was no longer any reason to suppose that it could, as then constituted, succeed in coping with them.

[45] "Satzung der Stadtgemeinde München über Erwerbslosenfürsorge" (14 Jan. 1919), *MGZ:B*, 17 Jan. 1919, No. 5. *Ministerratsprotokolle*, 18 Jan. 1919, BGS Munich, GN 2/1-2/2.

[46] The preceding graphs are based on the weekly reports published in *MGZ:S*, 8 Jan.–8 Mar. 1919, Nos. 2-19. The slight amelioration in mid-February was due rather to more efficient bookkeeping than to any perceptible economic improvement. In all of Germany there were more than a million unemployed by the end of February, the heaviest concentrations outside of Munich being in Berlin (estimated at 250,000) and Hamburg (70,000). See Kolb, *Die Arbeiterräte in der deutschen Innenpolitik*, 318-321.

CHAPTER VIII

The End of the Eisner Regime

THE outcome of the parliamentary elections and the increasing distress of the Bavarian economy had the effect of intensifying the political polarization which had been in progress at least since the beginning of December. In two respects the viewpoint represented by Kurt Eisner and the USP was fading from the political spectrum: the effort to achieve a reconciliation of the Socialist factions in a united front, and the attempt to establish a compromise of virtual parity between the parliamentary and council systems. If anything, it was the parliamentary front which was united. Although the Majority Socialists were certain to encounter vigorous opposition from the Bavarian People's Party in the new parliament, they could also expect the support of the BVP in upholding parliamentarianism. But the same circumstances which favored the consolidation of parliamentary authority also encouraged the activation of radicalism. For those who still dissented, time was pressing. If they hoped to take advantage of Eisner's political weakness and his deference toward the revolutionary councils, it was obviously in their interest to do so before the Landtag could be called into session.

A survey of the extant documents dealing with the council system in Bavaria shows beyond dispute that nearly all of the individual councils had, by the middle of January, directly or indirectly submitted to the authority represented by the Ministry of the Interior and the Ministry for Military Affairs. Examples of "encroachments" by council representatives in local affairs of state were still numerous enough, but there was no serious question by this time of the appropriate ministry's authority as the supreme arbiter of disputes between the councils and civic or bureaucratic officials. It is also demonstrable that Erhard Auer and Albert Rosshaupter had set a clear precedent of deciding in favor of the latter.

And the fact is that resistance to this authority from within the council system was remarkably feeble. *De facto* if not *de jure*, then, the ministerial regulations of December 17 had become the law governing the councils. As it had been granted neither indispensable legislative functions nor significant bureaucratic duties, the council system had become neither indispensable nor significant in the processes of government.

The councils had, however, retained political importance as symbols of the revolution. Whatever the reality might have been in terms of specific powers, the councils still represented a strong emotional factor—a factor which had to be respected by the parliamentary parties, and which might yet be exploited by the radicals. This helps to explain the origin and the effectiveness of a new movement which called itself "Left-Socialism." It was a phenomenon limited primarily to Munich and centered at first in the workers' councils. In both cases the reason was the same: the essence of the movement was the preparation for direct action against the Landtag. Munich was the obvious place for such agitation, and the workers' councils there were the most radically inclined of the entire council system.

As the threat of radicalism mounted steadily through January and into February, the pressure for some decisive action was felt by those who sensed that Bavaria might be slipping toward anarchy rather than approaching the inauguration of a stable parliamentary regime. Kurt Eisner responded by attempting one last gesture to regain support for his personal leadership; the Social Democratic ministers, by arranging for the unimpeded transfer of administrative authority to themselves; a band of sailors, by making a show of arms; and a young reserve officer, by deciding to take the matter into his own hands. All of them were to be unsuccessful.

The Radical Threat

Until the beginning of 1919 the Munich Workers' Council had been distinguished by neither the energy nor the importance of its activities. It is correct to say that the MAR remained a negligible political factor until January 6, when its executive committee (*Vollzugsrat*) organized a meeting to deliberate on the theme of "workers' council and political situation." The focus of the meeting was the so-called Kröpelin motion. This was in actuality no motion at all, but a warning to the government: "The Munich Workers' Council will summon its entire strength that it might continue in existence after January 12 and that its prerogatives remain intact in full measure for the future. Any limitation whatsoever of these prerogatives will be rejected by all means as reactionary, and the Munich working people will intervene united against such an attempt."[1]

The author of this paragraph was Carl Kröpelin, a young member of the RAR and one of the outspoken advocates of the council system. The sense of his "motion" was an attempt to establish through the MAR a precedent which would be valid for the entire council system. But as the MAR was constituted at that time, it was not regarded by Kröpelin and several other council leaders as an adequate instrument with which to force the council issue. A study of successive transcripts of the meetings of the executive committee during January shows the basis of their concern. There was no apparent sense of just what the MAR's prerogatives were. Its membership was constantly engaged in a round of procedural questions, punctuated by speeches on the need for clarity, for better contact with councils outside of Bavaria, for a council journal, for more frequent meetings, etc. Worse, in Kröpelin's view, was the MAR's apparent conception that it was waging an essentially legal battle, as if its sole purpose were to secure for the council system a paragraph in the Bavarian constitution.[2]

---

[1] "Münchener Arbeiterrat. An den Minister des Aeussern," 6 Jan. 1919, BGS Munich, MA 1943, I.V. 378.

[2] The files of the minutes of the *Vollzugsrat* are incomplete, albeit

The approaching restoration of the Landtag had thus brought Kröpelin and others like him to realize that prompt action must be taken by the councils or they would soon face extinction. At a time when most Bavarians were again turning their full attention to party politics and parliamentary coalitions, a group of determined council leaders therefore began deliberating how they might best gain control of the council system and secure its position within the state. The decisive moment in the formation of this group, which adopted the name "Left-Socialist Workshop" (*Linkssozialistische Arbeitsgemeinschaft*), came on the day before the Landtag election. In a large committee room of the Landtag building, a gathering of nearly one hundred council representatives— most of them from the MAR—heard the reading of a memorandum from Carl Kröpelin. It was in tone like a missive from St. Louis to the Crusaders: "Our sacred duty is to put aside all incidental and petty interests in Munich and Bavaria and to gather all proletarian and socialistic comrades, and thereby to create a compact, responsible proletarian mass." The Workshop was to be a united front with a difference. Its purpose would be to appeal "to all Socialists and to comrades of the extreme Left" who believed the councils to be "the most suitable bodies" to carry out the objectives of the revolution. By placing exclusive emphasis on the council system, the "petty interests" of the political parties were to be attenuated.[3] If members of the Workshop could agree on this, the question remained: just how far left was "Left-Socialism" to be?

The question was raised and answered by Max Levien, who came to the Workshop as a guest and left as a leader. The chairman of the Bavarian Communist Party accomplished

---

substantial enough to disclose its character before February 21. They are to be found in BHS Munich, ASR 2, 3.

[3] "Sitzung der linkssozialistischen Arbeitsgemeinschaft des MAR im Finanzausschusszimmer am Samstag den 11.1.19," BHS Munich, ASR 25.

this feat in three steps. He first asked that he be admitted to the meeting, if not as a Socialist, then as a representative of the RAR. The Workshop agreed and, in fact, adopted a resolution never to mention the word "Spartacus" at any of its meetings. Levien followed this initial success with a lecture on power politics. The future of Bavaria, he contended, would not be decided alone by "weapons of criticism." Whatever the ostensible outcome of the *Bürgerwehr* incident, it had demonstrated Erhard Auer's realistic and ruthless appreciation of military power. The councils could not afford to share the "dangerous illusion" of Kurt Eisner that things would somehow work out by themselves in spite of the parliamentary elections. "If one wishes to triumph, then one triumphs not with the ballot but with power. . . . Comrades, we absolutely must obtain and secure [our] authority. The regime has no authority . . . it is not taken seriously—it is ridiculed!" Levien's message was presently restated by Erich Mühsam in one sentence: "power belongs to the councils" (*den Räten gehört die Macht*).[4]

Levien's third maneuver was to present the Workshop with three carefully drafted resolutions: 1) opposing the cabinet's arrest of radical leaders and condemning any further measures to suppress the right of demonstration; 2) praising the "heroic courage" of the workers who had defied the regime in Berlin and demanding the resignation of Majority Socialists Ebert, Scheidemann, and Noske; 3) protesting the Bavarian Basic Law both because it was promulgated without consultation with the councils and because it "eliminates from all discussion, as a matter of principle, the question of a council government." It is not certain that the members of the Workshop realized the full implications of these proposals. For his part, Levien was undoubtedly conscious that he was urging: 1) the unrestricted right of radical agitation; 2) the replacement of the German national government by a more leftist one; and 3) the transformation of the Bavarian coun-

4 *Ibid.*

cils into soviets, that is, into organs of governmental control. Again it was Mühsam who did not mince words: "When I advocate that all power be placed in the hands of the councils, I do so in the belief that a good seed is present in the Munich Workers' Council." He was quite correct. The Levien resolutions were approved by the Workshop—the "good seed"—by a vote of 84-5.[5]

The step from the Kröpelin motion to the Levien resolutions was a big one in the radicalization of the Munich Workers' Council. Heretofore most members of the MAR who had radical leanings were motivated by no more than a vague wish to "save the councils." Levien and Mühsam were able to articulate this feeling, to admonish that a genuine compromise with parliamentarianism was impossible, and to place in the foreground of debate the contention that the councils must either rule or be ruled. The impact of the Workshop on the council system as a whole was almost immediately visible. The meetings of the various executive bodies in Munich during January began to have a noticeably more radical tone; and some council leaders who had previously wavered in their sympathies between the USP and a less restrained radicalism began to incline leftward.

Both of these developments were apparent at a session of representatives from the combined Bavarian councils on January 21. In a debate on the form in which the council system might be most effectively perpetuated, the delegates were faced with two specific proposals: either the councils must entirely replace the bureaucracy, or they must constitute a sovereign legislative body (something more than just a

[5] *Ibid*. Among the unsigned papers of the Workshop in the same portfolio is a draft of the "Richtlinien für die künftige sozialistische Politik." Especially characteristic is Article 3 of this document (my italics): "The Landtag is sovereign as a legislative body as soon as it has secured its basic right through the revolutionary constitution, [which is] presented by the socialistic regime [and] *which is to be ratified by the councils of workers, soldiers, and peasants.*"

Nebenparlament) which could prescribe the nature of laws to be approved only as a matter of formality by the Landtag. In either case the assumption was that the councils might become the dominating element in the governmental structure of the state, and not just one branch among several in its administration. No decision was reached, but it was evident that the council delegates were facing up to concrete possibilities. Of all the delegates, it was Ernst Toller who spoke the most radical word. Although still a leader of the USP, he chided the council members for remaining too inhibited by the parliamentary principle: "Basically the Landtag and the councils are contradictory." Toller was not alone in beginning to think in these terms and in urging others to do likewise.[6]

On the first day of February the Munich Workers' Council held its ninth plenary session. It was the occasion for a scene much like the one which had occurred in the Left-Socialist Workshop three weeks before: the meeting began with the admission of Max Levien and three other Communist leaders to the MAR, and ended with Levien and Erich Mühsam insisting that "all power, in Germany just as in Russia, belongs to the councils of workers, peasants, and soldiers." The announced theme for discussion was "council organization and parliament." The moderate council delegates, of course, stressed the "and." The radical opposition followed the Left-Socialist line: that no compromise was possible and that any attempt to abolish the councils would only provoke a "second revolution." Levien listed among the objectives of the council system "the dictatorship of the proletariat," and Mühsam added a warning that the Landtag must act with the approval of the councils or "we will send it packing" (*von uns nach Hause gejagt*). When Hans Unterleitner charged that there were "criminals" among the Communists, the meeting broke

[6] "Aktionsausschuss-Sitzung der A. S. u. B. Räte Bayerns am Dienstag den 21. Jan. 19 vormittags 9 1/2 Uhr," BHS Munich, ASR 4.

into one of those near riots which had become an institution at political gatherings in Munich.[7]

The result of such tactics in the MAR proved to be less conclusive than in the Workshop, since no vote could be taken in the ensuing confusion. But the Communist leaders had at least gained a permanent forum within the MAR, and they had used it at the first opportunity to deliver an ultimatum to the regime and the Landtag. In light of the increasing unemployment in Munich and the progressively bolder swing of radicalism in the council system, the threat of a second revolution could neither be made nor taken lightly.

The activation of the radical movement and the successful penetration of the Communist Party into the council system had not been unnoticed. Despite their unfortunate experience before the elections, governmental security officers Dürr and Staimer again recommended to the Bavarian cabinet on January 20 that Max Levien be arrested. The recommendation was supported by Erhard Auer but opposed by Kurt Eisner, who insisted that the police must first obtain "incriminating evidence." No action was taken at the time other than to put Levien under surveillance.[8] The security problem soon became more urgent, however, when the cabinet learned that Left-Socialism was beginning to infect not only the workers' councils, but the Munich Soldiers' Council (MSR) as well. The leader of the MSR was Fritz Sauber, one of the Independent Socialists who had been defeated disastrously in the elections and who had since come to accept Levien's either-or estimation of the council question. Confronted with news of "massive agitation" by radical leaders within the Munich military barracks, the cabinet had once again to deliberate on the limits of democratic toleration. The result was the same. Although Eisner would admit that Sauber was "playing

---

[7] "Münchener Arbeiterrat," *MAA*, 2 Feb. 1919, No. 56.
[8] *Ministerratsprotokolle*, 20 Jan. 1919, BGS Munich, GN 2/1-2/2.

a dangerous and ambiguous role," he contended that police action without actual proof of sedition would only provoke more violence: "I want to have no fighting among the soldiers." Strong words by Auer and Johannes Timm were not enough to bring about unanimity in the cabinet or Sauber's arrest.[9]

On February 6 Albert Rosshaupter appeared at a meeting of the Bavarian State Soldiers' Council. The delegates had assembled to debate on the new regulations governing military affairs recently issued from Berlin and to be enforced by the state government. It was the contention of some radical leaders from the MSR that the strict application of these regulations would destroy the soldiers' councils and re-establish the absolute authority of the officer corps. Speaking to this charge, Rosshaupter made a distinction between purely military functions, which the soldiers' councils might hope to retain, and political activity: "I have always stressed with great emphasis that the political assignments of the soldiers' councils can be *only of a temporary nature.* . . ." This statement provoked a formal protest from the executive committee of the soldiers' councils and a demand from Erich Mühsam (who had been admitted to the sessions as a representative from the MAR) that Rosshaupter resign.[10] Although Mühsam's motion was defeated, the protest from the council leaders was made public. It stressed that Rosshaupter's position directly contradicted the original purpose of the councils, and it took note of Kurt Eisner's pledge that he would "stand and fall" with the council system.

> We believe that not only Mr. Eisner will fall with the councils, but that the great idea of the revolution, the socialization of the state, will collapse. To prevent this we advocate

[9] *Ibid.*, 21 and 23 Jan. 1919.
[10] "Bayerischer Landes-Soldatenrat," *MP*, 6 Feb. 1919, No. 30. Since the SPD journal printed complete transcripts of council meetings in Munich during February, it will be uniformly cited in this chapter.

the continuation of the workers' and peasants' councils as economic bearers of the revolution and the continuation of the soldiers' councils as co-determining factors of the executive power.[11]

Even allowing for the inexactitude of the resolution's terminology, the cleavage between the view it expressed and that of Rosshaupter was obvious. Every event that followed was in some sense a restatement of this basic incompatibility.

On the next day Max Levien was suddenly arrested and sent to the prison at Stadelheim on the outskirts of Munich. The circumstances of Levien's second arrest are not clear, nor are they especially important in themselves. When a delegation led by Erich Mühsam protested to Minister of Justice Timm, and warned that this action might well provoke an open revolt, Timm denied knowledge of the charges against Levien and told the delegation to see an attorney.[12] Whether the action had been carefully planned or not, it was as badly mishandled as Levien's first arrest before the Landtag elections. After three days of legalistic postponement, no "incriminating evidence" was produced against Levien and no Social Democratic minister would assume responsibility for his arrest, even though they were all known to favor it. As a consequence, it required no more than a *coup de théâtre* to secure Levien's release on February 11. A band of soldiers and workers marched out to Stadelheim, met the prisoner at the gate, and accompanied him back to Munich, where an extraordinary plenary session of the MAR was "fortuitously" in progress. Levien entered with members of his entourage waving a red flag behind him. The regime could hardly have done more to help the Communist Party to prominence.[13]

[11] "Zur Frage der Soldatenräte" and "Landes-Soldatenrat," *MP*, 6-7 Feb. 1919, Nos. 30-31.

[12] "Demonstration für das Rätesystem?" *MP*, 10 Feb. 1919, No. 33. *Ministerratsprotokolle*, 12 Feb. 1919, BGS Munich, GN 2/1-2/2.

[13] "Stürmische Vorgänge im Münchener Arbeiterrat," *MP*, 12 Feb. 1919, No. 35.

The march on Stadelheim could be said to have had a certain symbolic significance, since the Independent Socialists had organized a similar march just four days before the Munich Putsch and had obtained the release of three political prisoners. If this historical parallel was overlooked, another was not: the MAR meeting to which Levien came had been convened to consider the proposal for a mass demonstration on the Theresienwiese. Among the specific objectives of the demonstration were to be the perpetuation of the council system and the recognition of political immunity for council delegates. Speaking for the proposal, Gustav Landauer charged that Erhard Auer was planning a bourgeois coalition and the dismissal of Eisner and the other Independent ministers from the cabinet. This would, he claimed, remove the last hindrance to the extinction of the councils: "The council system must be the cornerstone of the new constitution. The German people forward to world revolution!" When a spokesman of the SPD attempted to plead for confidence in Auer, he was interrupted by catcalls and whistles, and was unable to continue. In protest, the Social Democratic and Free Trade Union delegates left the hall. Rather than allow the meeting to be dissolved, Landauer hastily climbed up onto the speaker's table and instructed radical partisans in the gallery to come down and take the place of the departed council members. In the rump session which followed, the Left-Socialists had no difficulty in gaining an overwhelming majority for the proposal. It was agreed that the demonstration would take place on the following Sunday, February 16.[14]

By the beginning of February, then, the radicals were successful in literally taking over the MAR and in proceeding unobstructed in their program of direct agitation against the convocation of the Landtag. The polarization between parliamentarianism and radicalism was well advanced, and the basic issue of the revolution was quite differently defined than

[14] *Ibid.*

it had been before the Munich Putsch. Put somewhat too neatly, the parliamentarians now hoped to take advantage of the electoral results in order to cope with the economic and political crisis, whereas the radicals wished to exploit the crisis as a means of preventing a parliamentary settlement. The difficulty with such a formulation is that it stresses the purely negative intention of the radical program. In fact, both sides claimed to favor a positive "democratic" solution, a semantic impasse which has since become only too familiar. And in both cases the evaluation of the situation was the same: it had become a matter of necessity to be either for or against parliamentary government—that is, stated inversely, for or against replacing parliamentarianism with a form of direct representation based on a system of revolutionary councils.

The first heavy snowfall of the winter covered Munich and most of Bavaria during the first week of February. Public transportation was temporarily disrupted and the pace of public activity necessarily slackened. For Munich it was an exceptionally quiet week, with very few political meetings and not a single riot. For the first time since November, Bavarian newspapers were filled primarily with reports from other European capitals. In Paris the Peace Conference was in its third week, and in Berlin preparations were concluded for the convocation of the German National Assembly in Weimar on February 6. In both of these cases, the efforts of Kurt Eisner to secure a leading role for the Bavarian Republic had failed. The men whom Eisner had repeatedly challenged, and whom his publication of documents was intended to discredit, were everywhere in authority as representatives of the Berlin government. So far as the German delegation to Paris was concerned, it did not greatly matter: since the terms of peace were to be dictated by the Entente in any case, the presence of a Bavarian delegation could have meant no more than a few newspaper clippings.

253

But the failure of Eisner's "foreign policy" in Berlin was to have more tangible consequences in Weimar. Eisner had again traveled to the German capital on January 25 to a second conference of German states; there he proposed that the National Assembly be convened in Würzburg, and he tried to rally the southern states against the constitutional draft of Hugo Preuss, the formidable advocate of centralized national government. Both plans were frustrated. When the National Assembly met as scheduled, it immediately voted to proceed on the basis of the Preuss program; and after the election of Majority Socialists Friedrich Ebert and Philip Scheidemann as President and Chancellor respectively, the course of the "Weimar" Republic was clearly set in the direction of an *Einheitsstaat*.[15] The flurry of dispatches and telegrams from Eisner's office was of no avail. The Bavarian postal service, transportation system, and diplomatic corps were all to pass quickly under national control—and even that last bastion of Bavarian autonomy, the beer tax, was in serious jeopardy.[16]

Kurt Eisner went neither to Paris nor to Weimar. Instead,

[15] Hugo Preuss, "Denkschrift zum Entwurf des allgemeinen Teils der Reichsverfassung vom 3. Januar 1919," *Staat, Recht und Freiheit. Aus 40 Jahren Deutscher Politik und Geschichte* (Tübingen, 1926), 368-394. Eisner's opposition to Preuss was, as usual, *ad hominem*: "I warn you. If you come before the National Assembly with this constitutional draft, you will arouse a spirit of revolt." "Aufzeichnungen über die Besprechungen im Reichsamt des Innern vom 25. Januar 1919 über den der verfassunggebenden deutschen Nationalversammlung vorzulegenden Verfassungsentwurf," BGS Munich, PA, VII, 85. Eisner outlined his Würzburg proposal in an exchange with Prime Minister Blos of Württemberg, *ibid.*, 102, 115.

[16] For example, the message of Eisner to Berlin, 28 Jan. 1919, *ibid.*, 85. Eisner personally instructed Minister von Preger (who had replaced Muckle at the Berlin post) to vote against the Preuss draft. "Volksstaat Bayern, Ministerium des Aeussern. An Bayerische Gesandtschaft, Berlin, Betreff: Reichsverfassung," 30 Jan. 1919, BGS Munich, GN 15. Consult Werner Gabriel Zimmermann, *Bayern und das Reich 1918–1923* (Munich, 1953), 31-44. For the sequel, see Chapter IX.

he boarded a train heading southward into Switzerland, and arrived in Bern by February 3 in time for the opening of the first postwar congress of the Second International. Of all the capital cities where Eisner could have spent that week, Bern might well have seemed the least likely. Yet, as he realized, Bern represented Eisner's only chance somehow to revive the mystique of the first days of his regime. If he could at last become the spokesman for all of Germany—or, at least, for all of German Socialism—he calculated that he might yet maintain his premiership in Bavaria. Despite everything that pointed to the contrary, Eisner still believed this to be possible, and he was convinced that it was necessary (as he openly said) to save Bavaria from Bolshevism.[17]

It was an irrational calculation, one which is difficult to comprehend or to justify by any unprejudiced standard. Eisner was constitutionally unable to concede that the Landtag elections had represented the real voice of the Bavarian people; to him it seemed rather that a small clique of professional politicians was attempting to force him from office. He could consequently hope to strike a moral tone in Bern which would evoke popular enthusiasm, and thereby force the politicians to accede to the continuation of his leadership. Eisner was not the only political figure of his day to appeal over the heads of national and party leaders to the people. Nor was he the only one to learn that apparent public success abroad does not necessarily alter political realities at home. Eisner was loudly and warmly applauded by the Second International for his frank admission of German war-guilt, for his attack on the militarism and bureaucratization of the imperial system, and for his intervention in support of the immediate return of all war prisoners without regard to nationality. The French and English delegations were delighted, and saw in Eisner a representative of the "good" Germany. But most German Socialists at Bern—Karl Kautsky and Hugo Haase

[17] Anette Kolb, "Mit Kurt Eisner und Hugo Haase in Bern," *Kleine Fanfare* (Berlin, 1930), 180-186.

were the only noteworthy exceptions—thought Eisner's *nostra culpa* to be, rather, a national disgrace.[18]

Back in Munich, the reaction of the parliamentary leaders was unanimously negative. The Bavarian People's Party had already demanded Eisner's resignation; it was now joined by the Democratic Party, whose journal called the extension of Eisner's term "unthinkable" and his prompt withdrawal from office "a political necessity." The Social Democratic Party was formally more cautious, but hardly less obvious in its criticism: the *Münchener Post* insisted that Eisner had gone to Bern as the representative of two per cent of the electorate, not as the Prime Minister of Bavaria.[19] The significance of this remark was made clear when Erhard Auer announced that the Landtag would convene on February 21. Even had Eisner remained in Munich, there was little he could have done to discourage Auer's initiative. Eisner was in no sense the master of the political situation: he had neither the strength required to remain the leader of a parliamentary system, nor was he willing to use the force necessary to establish a soviet system. Given the circumstances and the nature of his own conscience, he could move neither forward nor backward, neither to the left nor to the right.

Immobilized himself, Eisner was also unable to attract others to his scheme of a united Socialist front. It was indicative that neither the Social Democrats nor the Left-Social-

---

[18] All of the major newspapers in Munich ran daily articles on the Bern meeting; for the most extensive coverage see *MP*, 4-12 Feb. 1919, Nos. 28-35. The text of Eisner's major address at Bern was later published as *Schuld und Sühne* (Berlin, 1919). On the way back from Bern, Eisner stopped over in Basel, made a well-received speech there at the University, and spent the night at the home of Robert Michels. See Michels' impressions of "Kurt Eisner," *Archiv für die Geschichte des Sozialismus und der Arbeiterbewegung*, XIV (1929), 364-391.

[19] "Die nächste Aufgabe," *MNN*, 4 Feb. 1919, No. 60. "Zum Berner Sozialistenkongress," *MP*, 12 Feb. 1919, No. 35. LC Washington, RA, "Sturm gegen Eisner!" *Friede auf Erden*, 15 Feb. 1919, No. 3.

ists were interested in identifying themselves with his efforts to launch a program of socialization. The Bavarian Socialization Commission had convened for the first time at Eisner's invitation on January 22. But as the chairman of the Commission, Professor Lujo Brentano, pointed out in a personal letter to Eisner, the fundamental irrationalities of the Bavarian economy were such that even a strong regime would be unable to cope with them in the foreseeable future. Even if one were convinced that a major revision of the economic structure was desirable, Brentano said, the current financial incapacity of the state and the immediate need to provide jobs for the unemployed made a sweeping program of socialization unfeasible. Brentano therefore began his work as chairman already convinced that any compulsory measures ordered by the administration would make "still more trying the almost insuperable difficulties which are connected with such a basic reorganization of the entire economic system."[20] Within a few days the Commission evolved into a small committee which confined itself mostly to problems of water power and rural electrification. In the weeks thereafter it heard report after report from "experts" on the massive obstacles to be encountered in governmental regulation of industry. "The impression which I gained," Brentano later wrote, "was the same as that which a study of the reports of the Berlin Socialization Commission had left with me: an absolute superiority of private enterprise over those owned by the state and managed by bureaucrats."[21] Socialization, like the united front, went no further than wishful thinking and political oratory.

The week which Eisner spent in Bern marked his political decease. By the time he returned he was no more able to pre-

[20] Brentano, *Mein Leben*, 357-359.
[21] *Ibid.*, 360-361. *Bayerische Sozialisierungs-Kommissions-Sitzungsberichte* (2 Jan.–13 Mar. 1919). The Commission held sixteen meetings in all: this volume contains a record of all but the three in early March.

vent political action than he could hope to initiate it. Even had he been decisive, he was no longer in a position to make decisions. What happened thereafter was completely beyond his determination. And since he was powerless to contend with the threat of radicalism, there were others who resolved to do so in his stead.

The Ides of February

On February 12 the Bavarian cabinet of ministers met for the first time since the end of January. In Eisner's absence, and in view of his incapacity, the Social Democratic ministers had prepared to secure their claim to leadership. Without obtaining Eisner's approval, Erhard Auer had set the date for the opening of the Landtag nine days later, and Albert Rosshaupter had issued a directive for the formation of a *Volkswehr* to hold in check "the forces . . . which wish to disturb the peace."[22] Now, on the day of his return from Bern, Eisner was confronted with these *faits accomplis*. Whereas the Majority Socialists had been divided at the time of the *Bürgerwehr* crisis, they were united behind Rosshaupter's proposal for a *Volkswehr*. Apart from the first syllable in the title, there was little difference between the two militia plans, since the *Volkswehr* was also to be recruited primarily from reliable trade union members. It was the intensity of the political situation which had changed. As Auer put it, if the radicals had the right openly to threaten a second revolution, then the government was surely justified in strengthening its security precautions. Johannes Hoffmann, who had refused to support Auer at the time of the *Bürgerwehr* incident, stated the case for the *Volkswehr* in still more drastic terms: "Through the penetration of the Spartacists into the workers' and soldiers' councils, the situation has become untenable." He estimated that three-fourths of the

[22] *Schulthess*, 1919/I, 43-44. Munich was immediately placarded with calls for enlistment: "Aufruf zur Bildung einer freiwilligen Volkswehr in Bayern," *Bekanntmachungen*, F. Mon. 3214.

Munich councils had already fallen under Communist domination, and he submitted that the cabinet's lack of decision was largely to blame. "We are merely urging a policy of conciliation, not of provocation," he said, "and nevertheless we stand before a catastrophe." Every one of the Social Democratic ministers concurred with Hoffmann's view that the regime must be prepared either to resist actively the threat of radicalism or to abdicate all authority. Hoffmann spoke for himself and for his colleagues: "I say now not to abdicate, but to resist" (*Ich sage jetzt, nicht abdanken, sondern wehren*). Eisner could disagree—he contended that the announcement of a united Socialist front would be sufficient to assure the loyalty of the councils and to forestall Bolshevism —but he could not dissuade the others from their decision.[23]

There was no more reason to expect that the radicals would accept the *Volkswehr* than the *Bürgerwehr*. But this time it could not be a simple matter of embarrassing a single minister, nor was there any clandestine plot by a reactionary group which might conveniently serve such a purpose. On Saturday morning, February 15, a congress of the combined Bavarian councils of workers, soldiers, and peasants met in the Landtag building in Munich. With exactly one week before the scheduled convocation of the Landtag itself, the more radical council leaders understandably felt that time was running out for the council system unless the Social Democratic Party could be induced to make a firm commitment to preserve the system and to anchor its prerogatives in the Bavarian constitution. The strategy as it was conceived by the leaders of Left-Socialism was simple and direct. The councils would draw up their demands during the meetings on Saturday, demonstrate for them on Sunday, and then remain in session during the succeeding week either until the demands were granted or until an attempt was made to throw the congress bodily out of the Landtag building.

[23] *Ministerratsprotokolle*, 12 Feb. 1919, BGS Munich, GN 2/1-2/2.

The Saturday sessions of the congress were conducted with the accustomed theatricality. In the morning the *Volkswehr* was branded as "the hydra of counter-revolution," and a resolution was debated which demanded Rosshaupter's resignation and the delegation of his authority to the councils. Kurt Eisner was on hand to speak, and he took the opportunity to repeat much of what he had said at Bern, adapting his remarks to suit the new occasion. After stating that the councils had a task to "overcome bureaucracy and militarism," he proceeded epigrammatically:

> We stand today before a decisive turning-point of the Bavarian Republic. . . . The council system is the most fertile soil for all future democracy. . . . We in Bavaria should have the ambition to carry on the revolution. . . . It may be possible that Bavaria will now give the world a sign that Germany has really become new, and that it is finding the way to socialism by new means.

Despite the ambiguity of Eisner's speech, it was clear that he was prepared to support the councils' demand for a public commitment from the Social Democratic ministers. The morning session then closed with the unanimous adoption of a resolution that "the cabinet of ministers should offer an explanation today of its position on the perpetuation of the councils of workers, peasants, and soldiers."[24]

The afternoon session was long and uneventful, as the council congress awaited a reply from the cabinet. Unfortunately no detailed transcript of the cabinet meeting of that day has been preserved—only the notation of "a dispute between Auer and Eisner."[25] At 6:30 P.M. Eisner's personal secretary, Felix Fechenbach, appeared before the council delegates to confirm that the cabinet was still deadlocked. Finally at 8 P.M. Eisner himself returned, accompanied by

---

[24] "Tagung der Landes-Arbeiter-, Soldaten- und Bauernräte," *MP*, 17 Feb. 1919, No. 39.

[25] *Ministerratsprotokolle*, 15 Feb. 1919, BGS Munich, GN 2/1-2/2.

Rosshaupter, to read the cabinet's decision. It dealt exclusively with the question of the *Volkswehr*, and it was a blanket endorsement of the new militia plan. Eisner also stated that it was "ridiculous" to ascribe any counter-revolutionary intentions to Rosshaupter, since the regime was bound to respect and enforce law and order. Then, obviously aware that the cabinet's declaration had failed to mention the other issue at hand, Eisner added a personal word: "The council system is the school of democracy. Germany cannot move forward without the council system."[26]

Faced with the united opposition of the Social Democratic ministers. Eisner had been unable to alter the *Volkswehr* program, nor had he been successful in securing even a statement, not to speak of a commitment, on the council question. He had performed in his role as mediator between Social Democracy and Left-Socialism, but there had been, in fact, no real mediation. The radical leaders were openly displeased and demanded that the councils reconvene in an extraordinary session that night. At 11:30 P.M. the congress was therefore reopened and presented by the State Soldiers' Council with six "conditions" for a vote of confidence in Rosshaupter:

1. immediate annulment of the *Volkswehr*;
2. all military regulations to require the countersignature of the executive committee of the soldiers' councils;
3. removal of certain reactionary officers;
4. dissolution of the cadet corps;
5. election of officers by the soldiers;
6. implementation of other demands already made by the councils to Rosshaupter.

The debate lasted well past midnight and ended with an agreement to support the six conditions. Again a deadline was set: the cabinet was to have until Monday night to an-

---

[26] "Tagung der Landes-Arbeiter-, Soldaten- und Bauernräte," *MP*, 17 Feb. 1919, No. 39.

nounce its compliance. In the meantime the councils would take their case to the people.[27]

It is no simple matter to describe or assess the public demonstration of February 16. The *Neue Zeitung* said that 150,000 people marched through the streets of Munich that day; the *Münchener Post* claimed that only 9000 participated in the parade. The Left-Socialists said that the people had given a mandate to the council system; the Social Democrats claimed that the evidence of a radical spirit (which was not to be denied) was the work of professional agitators. Trade union and SPD leaders had finally encouraged their followers to join in the demonstration, but for precisely opposite reasons from those of radical leaders who had organized it. So while some demonstrators carried signs "Against Bolshevism" and "For the Landtag," others waved banners reading "Long Live the Council System." A demonstration ostensibly against the policies of Eisner's regime turned out to be led by Eisner in an open car. It was, above all, a demonstration of confusion.[28]

One explanation of the demonstration may be stated dialectically: those who sought to maintain public order stood to gain most from the obfuscation of issues, while those who might have profited from public disorder were trying to clarify them. Time was clearly on the side of the Social Democrats, since the national council leaders in Berlin had already recognized the supremacy of the National Assembly.[29]

[27] "Die Regierungskrisis," *Bekanntmachungen*, F. Mon. 3211.

[28] The Social Democrats immediately regretted their decision to join in the demonstration. "Aussprechen, was ist!" and "Nieder mit der Lügenpresse," *MP*, 17-18 Feb. 1919, Nos. 39-40. Eisner allowed himself to be photographed with his wife and Fechenbach in the midst of a group of demonstrators who were holding aloft a placard: "Die Reaktion marschiert! Hoch das Rätesystem!" See Leonhard Lenk, "Illusion und Wirklichkeit der Macht," *Münchener Merkur*, 20 Feb. 1959, No. 44.

[29] *Schulthess*, 1919/I, 29-30. Thereafter it was technically only

If the more radical demands of Bavarian Left-Socialism could be delayed in Munich until the Landtag had convened, the assumption was that the authority of the parliament would be secure. It was reasonable to suppose that the Landtag would be overwhelmingly conservative on the council issue, and that the vast majority of council members outside of Munich would resist any attempt of radical leaders within the capital to challenge the Landtag's decisions after February 21. Once established, the parliamentary principle would be irreversible. Until then, however, the position of the Social Democratic leadership was a delicate one. Above all, they wished to avoid giving any concrete reason for radical agitation or violence. And they were obliged to respect the divided feelings of many workers who were both council and party members. The SPD therefore wished to avoid a public statement of the council question in its most extreme formulation: council system or not. It was instead to the advantage of the Majority Party to propose the issue more complexly, in terms of the degree of authority which should be allotted to the councils by the Landtag.

Erhard Auer and his colleagues had been consistent in denying that the councils would have any executive or legislative power—Auer had openly said as recently as February 10 that the councils were "not necessary" in that sense—but they had never defined just what authority would reside in the council system.[30] This was the crux of the next personal dispute between Auer and Eisner, at a meeting of the cabinet on February 17. Auer refused to have the cabinet

---

a matter of exacting compliance in those scattered localities in Germany where radicals had gained control of the council system. This was the designated duty of the Free Corps troops. See Robert G. L. Waite, *Vanguard of Nazism: The Free Corps Movement in Postwar Germany 1918-1923* (Cambridge, Mass., 1952), 66-68, 79-93.

[30] "Sitzung des Vollzugsausschusses der Arbeiterräte Bayerns," 10 Feb. 1919, BGS Munich, MA 1943, I.V. 378.

reply to the ultimatum presented by the State Soldiers' Council in the six conditions. When he suggested instead that the council congress should be disbanded, Eisner countered acidly that "the basic assemblies of the revolution cannot be unceremoniously eliminated." But Auer was not to be intimidated, and announced that it would be necessary to call together a conference of his party on February 19 to consult on the matter. When Eisner reported this decision to the council delegates, the congress had little choice but to wait.[31]

Each of these successive resolutions, maneuvers, and counter-maneuvers had shown the anomaly of Kurt Eisner's position as Prime Minister. Technically he was the chief executive officer of the Bavarian government and the chairman of the entire system of councils. Actually he was neither. A conference of the Social Democratic Party was now to dictate the policies of the former, while the leaders of Left-Socialism were able to dominate the deliberations of the latter. In both cases Eisner could advocate and admonish, but he could not determine a coherent course of political action. His premiership rested on the indulgence of the Social Democratic leadership, the uncertainty of the political situation, and the questionable legality of the Basic Law. The convocation of the Landtag was likely to mean an end to all three. In dealing with the question of the *Volkswehr*, Eisner had served as a messenger rather than as a Prime Minister. And even in this role he had been ineffectual. While the Social Democrats proceeded to organize a militia, the Left-Socialists prepared to disrupt it: an order to place command of the *Volkswehr* in the hands of local soldiers' councils was released with the forged signature of Albert Rosshaupter and the spurious notification that "further regulations will be issued by the congress of councils." Reporting this incident to the cabinet on

[31] *Ministerratsprotokolle*, 17 Feb. 1919, BGS Munich, GN 2/1-2/2. "Tagung der A.-, B.- und S.-Räte," *MP*, 18 Feb. 1919, No. 40. "Die Klärung der Lage verschoben," *Bekanntmachungen*, F. Mon. 3207.

February 18, Rosshaupter asked a question which was more than just rhetorical: "Who is really in charge?"[32]

Certainly it was not Eisner. That he was still the Prime Minister more than a month after his electoral defeat was due only to his own intransigence and the caution of the Social Democratic leadership. Rather than force Eisner from office, and perhaps provoke a violent reaction by doing so, Erhard Auer had chosen to wait for the Landtag and to tolerate Eisner. It was a gentlemen's agreement, but one about which Auer wanted no equivocation. On February 18, therefore, the Social Democratic Party gave notice that it intended to claim its due at the first occasion. Reprinting the conclusion of Eisner's speech to the councils on the previous Saturday, in which he had expressed the hope that Bavaria would find its way to socialism "by new means," the *Münchener Post* commented:

> If words have a sense, this speech means *the formal announcement of a new revolution*. . . . The basis of this democratic socialism is to be the *council system* and not parliamentary democracy. . . . The sovereignty of the Landtag is to be restricted in essential particulars. Eisner's whole attitude stands in contradiction to the wishes and demands which the Bavarian people expressed in the election of January 12. . . . Through his attitude in these critical days Eisner has completely isolated himself from the Bavarian people. He is as minister—that is, as servant of the people—simply impossible. *Eisner's resignation is therefore a political necessity.*[33]

Neglecting for a moment the question of whether, or in what sense, the charge that Eisner intended a "new revolution" was justified, one must observe that this editorial administered a political *coup de grâce*. Having abandoned caution,

[32] *"Wer regiert eigentlich?" Ministerratsprotokolle*, 18 Feb. 1919, BGS Munich, GN 2/1-2/2.
[33]"Tatsachen und Folgerungen," *MP*, 18 Feb. 1919, No. 40.

there remained for Auer only the tactical problem of how to overcome Eisner's intransigence.[34]

If Bavaria was a house divided, the Landtag building on February 19 was a perfect representation of the division. In one wing the congress of councils was still in session, while in another a conference of the SPD was holding its first meeting. During the morning the two bodies adopted separate and distinctly contradictory resolutions. The Social Democrats refused to annul the *Volkswehr* regulations, denied that decisions of a minister should be controlled by the councils, reiterated that the councils could expect to have "no legislative or executive power," and moved that the congress "be immediately adjourned."[35] Meanwhile, the council delegates were giving unanimous approval to a motion which stated: "The duties of the congress should be considered accomplished only when the regime has given a guarantee that the installation of the councils in the People's State . . . is to be effected, and when the demands to the cabinet of ministers regarding the military questions are fulfilled without exception; only then can the congress be adjourned."[36] There is no record of any attempted negotiation between the conference and the congress, so that in the afternoon each meeting continued with a seeming lack of interest in the deliberations of the other.

When consultation did occur, it was the result of circum-

[34] When asked upon his return from Bern by a correspondent of the *Frankfurter Zeitung* whether he intended to resign, Eisner had replied that he could see no reason to do so for the time being. "In case the Landtag should have another standpoint and demand his, Eisner's, resignation, he would allow the people to decide through a referendum on the basis of the provisional constitution." "Neue Erklärungen Eisners," *MP*, 13 Feb. 1919, No. 36.

[35] "Beschlüsse der sozialdemokratischen Landeskonferenz Bayerns," *MP*, 20 Feb. 1919, No. 42. "Weitere Beschlüsse der sozialdemokratischen Landeskonferenz," *MP*, 21 Feb. 1919, No. 43.

[36] "Tagung der A.-, B.- und S.-Räte," *MP*, 20 Feb. 1919, No. 42.

stances which had nothing to do with conciliation. While the afternoon sessions were in progress, shots and the explosion of grenades were heard outside the Landtag building. A band of armed sailors quickly forced their way inside and posted sentries at the exits. The meetings dissolved into confusion, excited delegates milled in the hallways, and representatives rushed back and forth between conference and congress. Radical council leaders charged that the commander of the sailors, a man named Lotter, was "a confidence man for Minister Auer and . . . an agent of the Bavarian People's Party." It was learned that Lotter's move was, in fact, directed against the councils and that he and his men had constituted themselves "the Committee for Protection of the Landtag." They had already arrested and deposed Commandant Dürr and Chief of Police Staimer, and had taken possession of the main railway terminal and the central telegraph office. It seemed to be November 7 in reverse. But the Social Democratic ministers denied knowledge of any such committee and insisted that Lotter order his men to retire. Within an hour the sailors had complied: they declared that it had all been "an error," and disappeared.[37]

The so-called "Sailors' Putsch" of February 19 cannot be passed over without comment, even though its importance was only symptomatic. It alleviated neither the impasse within the parliament building nor the tension without. Nor did it alter the basic components of political development: the imminence of the Landtag's convocation and the necessity of Kurt Eisner's resignation. If anything, it showed only the

[37] The official governmental version of the putsch attempt was published as "Amtliche Bekanntmachung," *Bekanntmachungen*, F. Mon. 3206. The scene in the Landtag building is best described in "Ein Putsch in München" and "Tagung der A.-, B.- und S.-Räte," *MP*, 20 Feb. 1919, No. 42. Staimer later testified that Lotter had received 10,000 marks of Krupp money. See Albert Winter, *Der Fall Auer* (Munich, n.d.), 6-7. See also the information given by Lotter in a personal interview with Raatjes, *The Role of Communism*, 95-97.

susceptibility of all these factors to the purposeful use of armed force. But the point was that the incident served no discernible purpose. The password among the sailors was "Auer," and yet it would have been a nonsensical miscalculation on Auer's part to have ordered such a putsch two days before the convocation of the Landtag. The subsequent attempts to defame the Social Democratic leader for having hired the sailors for this purpose are deficient both in logic and in points of fact.[38] It is demonstrable that the Social Democratic ministers had taken steps to protect the Landtag once it had met—and it is even probable that the sailors were in Munich for that purpose—but the putsch attempt itself was no more than a nervous reflex and a disconcerting omen.[39]

On the following day, February 20, Kurt Eisner made his last public speech. The occasion, as it turned out appropriately enough, was the final session of the council congress. The agenda of the day required a choice between the motion of a Social Democratic delegate which was tantamount to outright adjournment, and the countermotion of a Communist delegate that would have bound the congress to remain in session during and in spite of the Landtag. After some debate, the delegates finally adopted neither motion, and supported instead a third formulated by Gustav Landauer: the congress would adjourn temporarily, to meet again "soon," and would in the meantime organize a series of public demonstrations in

[38] Beyer asserts flatly that "the organizer of this putsch was no other than Erhard Auer." Not only is the accompanying argument unconvincing and undocumented, but it is confused by the incorrect dating of the decision of the congress to adjourn. *Von der November-revolution*, 38-39.

[39] One week before, in commenting on the unrest in the Munich barracks, Rosshaupter told the other ministers: "I have therefore already requested for outside troops." Three days thereafter Jaffé reported that 600 sailors were arriving from Wilhelmshaven to help keep order in Munich. Presumably these were the troops of which Rosshaupter had spoken. *Ministerratsprotokolle*, 12 and 15 Feb. 1919, BGS Munich, GN 2/1-2/2.

favor of "the integration of the council system in the constitution." In a sense, each faction got what it wanted. The Left-Socialists obtained a kind of legitimation for public agitation, and the Social Democrats could claim at least an implicit recognition of the Landtag's authority. But in fact no one could pretend to know what would now become of the council system.[40]

After the adoption of the Landauer motion, Kurt Eisner was accorded the last word. He gave an honest speech, and it is worth recording as a summation of his premiership and as a reflection of the attitude with which he faced the final day of his regime. The Sailors' Putsch, he said, had again showed that the revolution was constantly endangered by militarism and by compromise with the bourgeoisie. The latter, in the form of the Landtag, was an immediate prospect, and the former might well ensue. The councils must consequently continue to press for the goals of Socialism and the aims of the revolution. But, he added:

> The second revolution will not be plundering and street-fighting. The new revolution is the assembling of the masses in city and countryside to carry out what the first revolution has started. . . . The bourgeois majority is now to implement bourgeois policies. We will see whether they are capable of ruling. In the meantime the councils should do their job: to build the new democracy. Then perhaps the new spirit will also arrive in Bavaria. . . .

Even as he spoke, Eisner must have been aware that members of his cabinet were devising the means by which he would be forced from office. Yet he concluded in a flourish of rhetoric with his characteristic mixture of optimism and idealism:

> I long for the time when the Socialists, without distinction of party, will finally cease to rule and will again become

[40] "Tagung der A.-, B.- und S.-Räte," *MP*, 21 Feb. 1919, No. 43.

the opposition. As I speak here, the decision is perhaps already made. Tomorrow the Landtag begins—tomorrow the activity of the councils should also begin anew, and then we will see where are to be found the force and vitality of a society consecrated by death.[41]

Notwithstanding the obscurity of the final phrase, Eisner's message was straightforward. He could not hope to forestall the convocation of the Landtag or to elude the eventuality of his own resignation, but he would maintain his faith in the "redemptive" power of the council idea. The religious imagery leads one to recall Eisner's conception of himself as a "Guldar," a suffering servant, and a prophet. It is not too much to infer that he looked forward to his deposition on the following day as a time of crucifixion.

Although the public record is clear, most of what can be written about the private negotiations in the last days of the Eisner regime must be surmise. No cabinet records, personal memoirs, or memoranda remain to describe in detail what transpired within the inner circle of the government. But if the evidence is largely circumstantial, it is nevertheless conclusive. It is certain that the cabinet met at length on February 20 and that Eisner was left no alternative to resignation. To establish this certainty it is sufficient to compare the "New Provisional Basic Law," released by the cabinet on that day, with the original Basic Law of January 4. It may be recalled that Article 17 of the latter document had stipulated that "until the final settlement of the constitutional draft . . . the revolutionary regime exercises the legislative and executive power." This passage was deleted and replaced by the following provision:

The supreme executive power will be exercised by the cabinet of ministers. The chairman will be elected by the Landtag by a simple majority of the total number of its members. The other ministers will be appointed by him.

[41] *Ibid.*

The ministers require for the execution of their office the confidence of the Landtag. They are responsible to the Landtag for the execution of their affairs.[42]

The authority of the Landtag was thereby established beyond question. The "revolutionary regime" was no longer untouchable. That evening Erhard Auer confided privately that Eisner had been persuaded to resign.[43]

Early on the morning of February 21, Eisner was in his office at the Foreign Ministry, preparing the statement which was to be read at the opening session of the Landtag that day. One can imagine that he felt no less emotion than when writing out the first revolutionary proclamations more than three months before. But it was an emotion vastly different in nature and quality, as must be apparent to anyone who reflects (as he might have himself) on the period of Eisner's premiership in Bavaria. Whatever his feelings, they could not mitigate the starkness of the announcement which it would soon be his duty to make: "In the name of the cabinet I declare that all the ministers will resign from their offices and place them at the disposal of the Landtag. The entire administration is furthermore prepared to carry on their duties until a new regime is formed."[44] Eisner's message was one of submission: although he was not prepared to abandon the idea of the council system, he was willing to forego a tone of defiance which could have provoked or served a "second revolution" in any violent sense of the term.

A few minutes before ten o'clock, Eisner placed the prepared text in his briefcase and left the office. Accompanied

---

[42] *Schulthess*, 1919/I, 79-80. The original Basic Law is discussed above in Chapter VI.

[43] Wahl, "Rätezeit in München," *op.cit.*, 16. Müller-Meiningen, *Aus Bayerns schwersten Tagen*, 120. See the statement released by Frauendorfer and Jaffé, confirming Eisner's promise to Auer. *Politische Zeitfragen*, 1919, XIV-XVI, 217.

[44] The text was later published in installments as "Kurt Eisners nicht gehaltene Rede," beginning with *NZ*, 10 Mar. 1919, No. 65.

by his two secretaries and a pair of armed guards, he intended to proceed on foot to the Landtag building a block away. As he rounded the corner into the Promenadestrasse, a young man in a trench coat stepped forward and fired two shots into his head. Kurt Eisner rolled dead onto the sidewalk. His assailant, Count Anton Arco-Valley, was immediately struck down by bullets from one of Eisner's guards.[45] Sixty minutes later a member of the Revolutionary Workers' Council entered the central chamber of the Landtag building and shot Erhard Auer point-blank.[46] It was the end of the first and the beginning of the second revolution.

[45] Arco was taken to a hospital where his life was saved. In 1920 he was tried and condemned to death, but had his sentence commuted to life imprisonment. After serving four years he was released. He died in an auto accident in 1945. His motive for the murder of Eisner is impossible to ascertain beyond doubt. The hypothesis advanced by Sebottendorff, *Bevor Hitler kam*, 82—that Arco was psychologically driven because of partially Jewish parentage to demonstrate his Germanic fidelity—is plausible but not provable. For the circumstances of the assassination see the testimony of the two guards and of one secretary, Dr. Benno Merkle, in Hans Freiherr von Pranckh (ed.), *Der Prozess gegen den Grafen Anton Arco-Valley* (Munich, 1920), 31-33. The other secretary was Felix Fechenbach, *Der Revolutionär*, 62. A brief account has been written by Albert Montgelas, "In der Tasche des Ermordeten fand man die Rücktrittserklärung," *Münchener Merkur*, 22 Feb. 1954, No. 45.

[46] Severely but not mortally wounded, Auer did not return to public life until several years later. Two others present (Osel and Jahreiss) were struck by stray shots and killed. *Verhandlungen des Bayerischen Landtages. Ordentliche und ausserordentliche Tagung 1919. Stenographische Berichte Nr. 1 bis 27* (21 Feb.–24 Oct. 1919), No. 1, 1-2. See the eyewitness accounts of Müller-Meiningen, *Aus Bayerns schwersten Tagen*, 122-127, and Niekisch, *Gewagtes Leben*, 50-51.

CHAPTER IX

The Second Revolution

EBRUARY 21 might well have marked the conclusion of the
revolution in Bavaria except for the political stupidity
and criminal action of Kurt Eisner's assassin. Had Eisner
been permitted to carry out his intention to resign on February 21, a legally elected and constituted parliamentary government would have been inaugurated that day. There is little
doubt that this government would have been at first dominated by a Majority Socialist and Democratic coalition which,
once established, could have been dislodged only under the
most extreme circumstances. Even a subsequent attempt on
the life of Erhard Auer would not have challenged the legal
propriety of the Landtag or the legitimacy of the new regime.
Whether "most extreme circumstances" would have developed had not the consolidation of governmental authority
been delayed, one cannot say. In any case, if a new regime
had been properly invested on February 21, it would have
been in a much stronger legal and political position to cope
with radical agitation than either of the makeshift admin-
istrations which attempted to do so in the month that followed. As one lawless act led directly to another, Bavaria
was suddenly and literally returned to a state of lawlessness,
and every question which might have been settled was at
once reopened.

Considering Eisner's political impotence at the time of his
death, the assassination was gratuitous as well as foolish.
Even in terms of its own motive Count Arco's deed was a
failure. Instead of averting a second revolution, he initiated
it. Since the perverted logic of the murderer sought to assure
the Landtag's authority, public revulsion at his act made a
parliamentary restoration all the more difficult. For many
who thought in terms of personalities, moreover, the disappearance of Eisner and Auer created a temporary confusion

of party loyalty and resulted in a loss of political bearings. Part of this emotional reflex was a frenetic revival of council activity in the provinces. The bureaucratic correspondence was soon filled with reports of new "encroachments" throughout the state. In numerous cases the pattern of the November revolution was repeated, as council representatives marched into municipal offices and disturbed or deposed local officials. For the radicals this amounted to a miraculous reprieve, and they quickly determined to make the best possible use of it. But what were now the actual possibilities?

In any consideration of the confused events which followed Eisner's assassination one must keep in mind the total context of the German revolution. By focusing exclusively on Bavaria it might seem that circumstances were beginning to develop toward a climax. The reality was far different. The decisive moment of the revolution in Germany had in fact already occurred during the second week of January 1919 when the Spartacist insurrection in Berlin was crushed beyond redemption. Within a fortnight orders were issued by *Reichswehrminister* Gustav Noske to eliminate the soviet republic in Bremen (in existence since January 10). Despite offers of negotiation from soviet leaders there, including the Communists, Noske's instructions were executed by General von Lüttwitz with enough alacrity and ruthlessness to indicate that the authority of Berlin would ultimately prevail everywhere in Germany. In the weeks thereafter the repressive activity of the Free Corps throughout the North and the Ruhr was a sufficient confirmation of that fact. Meanwhile, up to the time of Eisner's death, Bavaria remained untouched by "outside" interference and could indeed be considered a paradigm of peaceful transition to a republican parliamentary form. Now the entire matter was placed in doubt in Munich— but not in Berlin, where a flurry of rioting in March was again subdued by force. Even so, there was open talk of a Bavarian soviet republic among men who seriously aspired to power. For some it was a goal; for others, a last resort.

For all of them it was a delusion. So long as the Berlin government survived and had the Free Corps at its command, the sovietization of Bavaria was a mirage. In this respect the situations of Bremen and Munich were similar, except that the time lag made the possibility of a durable soviet republic in Bavaria still more improbable. In the confusion this was too readily ignored by men who were aware of the facts and should have acted accordingly. Their attempt to take advantage of the administrative muddle in Munich was perhaps idealistic; it was certainly irresponsible. The events which seemed climactic to many Bavarians were therefore only an ugly aftereffect of the German revolution.

The Interregnum

During the last weeks of his life Kurt Eisner had suffered one indignity after another. He had been humiliated at the polls, ridiculed in the press, badgered in cabinet meetings, and vilified as a Jew and a foreigner. Now it seemed suddenly that he was the noblest Bavarian of them all. Everyone claimed him as their own: the radicals, as martyr of the revolution, liberator of the proletariat, and champion of the council system; the others, as the man who had been on his way to the Landtag to acknowledge the restoration of parliamentary authority. The name of the man who had been so little known before the beginning of his premiership, and so little respected during it, was momentarily elevated to the status of a Bavarian folk-hero. At the site of the assassination a sort of pagan altar was erected, adorned by Eisner's picture and the wreaths of mourning women. As his body rested in state, thousands filed by beneath a sign: "Proletarians, remove your hat before the blood of the martyr."[1] The funeral

---

[1] "Ein Märtyrer der Revolution," *Nachrichtenblatt des Zentral-Rats*, 22 Feb. 1919, No. 1. See Hofmiller, *Revolutionstagebuch*, 164-167. The expense of Eisner's funeral (9500 marks) was paid by the Bavarian state. "Zusammenstellung der Kosten des Begräbnisses des Ministerpräsidenten Kurt Eisner," 4 June 1919, BGS Munich, MA 1943, I.V. 467.

procession on February 26 was a pageant formerly accorded only to royalty, dignified by the solemn roll of drums and the waving plumes of peasants marching in file in their native dress. The Munich *Rathaus* was draped in black, state and city officials followed in closed ranks behind the hearse, and the bells of Catholic churches were rung by priests (sometimes at gunpoint) to announce the observance of a formal day of rest. At Eisner's grave his friend Gustav Landauer pronounced the final eulogy: "He was one like Jesus, like Huss—oh *sancta simplicitas*—who were executed by stupidity and greed."[2]

It was fitting that those who honored Eisner should also vow to fulfill his legacy. This pledge was repeated often during the final week of February, most conspicuously by armed council members packed in trucks who drove through the streets of Munich shouting "Revenge for Eisner!" But no one seemed to be quite certain as to just what that legacy was. With its press muzzled by censorship, the BVP was confined to reassuring the faithful that "our future lies in God's hands." The SPD called Eisner's murder "a monstrous crime" and demanded the immediate prosecution both of Count Arco and Alois Lindner, the man whose pistol shots had left Erhard Auer critically wounded in a Munich hospital. The press of Eisner's own party promised "to act in the spirit of this man . . .: all power to the working masses, united and decisive in the revolutionary organization of the councils." If this last statement was really no less ambiguous than the others (what, in the view of the USP, was to become of the Landtag?), it did at least point to the most significant political conse-

2 "Gedächtnisrede bei der Beisetzung Kurt Eisners am 26. Februar 1919 in der Halle des Ostfriedhofes," *Politische Zeitfragen*, 1919, XIV-XVI, 231-235. See the contemporary tribute written by Heinrich Mann, "Kurt Eisner," *Essays* ([East] Berlin, 1960), 386-391. The tolling of cathedral bells in honor of Eisner was officially opposed by the hierarchy of the Church. See Karl Forster, "Vom Wirken Michael Kardinal Faulhabers in München," *Der Mönch im Wappen*, 504.

quence of Eisner's assassination: the reopening of the council question.[3]

Ever since the Munich Putsch Bavarian politics had wavered between confusion and compromise. Whenever one mood seemed to become established, the other was somehow reasserted. The condition immediately after February 21 was, of course, confusion. It was not clear what the legal form of the Bavarian state now was, apart from the uncertainty as to who should or could actually govern it. Eisner's cabinet had issued the first Basic Law of its own accord on January 4 and approved another on February 19, but the Landtag had not been in session long enough to ratify the revision. Both the cabinet members and the parliamentary delegates had fled in terror from the Landtag building on the day of the shootings. Many council leaders argued, without feigning disinterest, that the electoral mandate of the Landtag had been thereby abandoned and the revolutionary function of the council system reestablished. However specious as a political theory, this was the political reality for the time being. The first council body to act on February 21 was the executive committee of the workers' councils which called a general meeting of the Munich councils, declared martial law, and warned the city's populace by placard that anyone caught robbing or stealing would be promptly shot. A three-day general strike, conveniently stopping work only over the weekend, and a seven o'clock curfew were put into immediate effect.[4] Other orders came from other sources. One placard, signed simply "Wenz," announced a council assembly for the morning of February 22 and concluded: "Long live Eisner's legacy! Long live the second revolution! Long live the Soviet Republic!"[5]

[3] "Die zweite Revolution," *BK*, 27 Feb. 1919, Nos. 52-58. "Ein ungeheuerliches Verbrechen!" *MP*, 21 Feb. 1919, No. 45. "Ein Märtyrer der Revolution," *NZ*, 22 Feb. 1919, No. 52.

[4] See the series of *Bekanntmachungen*, 21-22 Feb. 1919, F. Mon. 3288-3298.

[5] LC Washington, RA, "Flugblätter der Revolutions- und Rätezeit 1918-1919." I.

Within twenty-four hours of Eisner's death an entirely new council body was organized which governed in Munich and which claimed to rule in all of Bavaria. For opposite reasons, neither of the two bodies which had previously presumed to head the council hierarchy could hope to assert itself under the existing circumstances. The group of the original November revolutionaries, constituted and expanded as the RAR, had been repeatedly refused recognition by the provincial council delegates and was now further discredited by the crime of its charter member Lindner.[6] On the other hand, the executive committee of the council congress, while supported by most provincial delegates, was unacceptable to radical leaders in Munich because of its record of acquiescence toward the authority of the Landtag prior to February 21. By the creation of a new *Zentralrat* of the Bavarian councils—whose first proclamations could be countersigned by the respective chairmen of the state councils of workers, soldiers, and peasants—the opposition of city and countryside was momentarily obscured. The list of the original eleven members was a collage of familiar and unfamiliar names: Niekisch, Kröpelin, and Eisenhut (workers' councils); Sauber, Simon, and Goldschmidt (soldiers' councils); Gandorfer, Hofmann, and Utzenhofer (peasants' councils); Hagemeister and Levien (RAR). When the *Zentralrat* then voted on February 22 to have its number "strengthened" by one delegate each from the SPD and the Free Trade Unions, Levien and Hagemeister threatened but did not submit their resignations.[7]

---

[6] See *Die Attentate im Bayerischen Landtag. Der Prozess gegen Alois Lindner und Genossen vor dem Volksgericht München* (Munich, 1919), and Franz August Schmitt, "Der Lindner-Prozess," *Politische Zeitfragen*, 1920, IV, 49-64. Lindner claimed that his attempt on Auer was undertaken in a fit of nervous excitement in retaliation for Eisner's murder, not as part of a premeditated plot. Although there was no evidence to contradict his testimony, he nonetheless received a sentence of fourteen years in prison.

[7] "An die Arbeiter!" *Bekanntmachungen*, F. Mon. 3236. "Die Einheitsfront des Sozialismus," *MP*, 24 Feb. 1919, No. 45.

The chairman of the *Zentralrat*, and therefore in some sense the provisional chief executive of the Bavarian state, was Ernst Niekisch. It was Niekisch who had earlier led the minority faction of the SPD which supported Eisner's program for a united Socialist front at the time of the parliamentary elections in January. Since then he had become an increasingly important figure in the council system. A schoolteacher by profession, a burly man of twenty-eight years, Niekisch had used his position as chairman of the Augsburg councils to organize and manage the Swabian Provincial Council Committee (*Kreisausschuss*), and then to gain election as the chairman of the executive committee of the combined Bavarian workers' councils. By commanding such an impressive array of titles within the council structure at every level, and at the same time being a card-carrying member of the SPD, Niekisch was suited if anyone was to restore compromise in place of confusion. He could hardly be classified with Auer as a foe of the council system, nor was he as a Majority Socialist so suspect as Eisner as an enemy of parliamentarianism. He had the additional advantage of being closely identified with neither the capital nor the countryside. Whether Niekisch and the *Zentralrat* could actually reconcile these indistinct and sometimes overlapping interests was another matter.[8]

The objective of the *Zentralrat's* first formal action, on the afternoon of February 22, was just such a reconciliation. Three of its members (Niekisch, Fritz Sauber, and Karl Gandorfer) met with lone delegates from the Munich chapters of the SPD and USP and with a representative of the Free Trade Unions. In accordance with the old political principle that the more obvious the *ad hoc* character of an assembly the more pompous its title, this group constituted itself as the "Commission for the Restitution of Unity between the Social Democratic Parties." The six men then drafted a statement

---

[8] Niekisch, *Gewagtes Leben*, 43-45, 51-52.

of agreement as the basis for negotiation between the interests represented. The preamble condemned political murder "from whatever side it is committed" and dedicated a program of Socialist unity "to securing the successes of the revolution and to avoiding fraternal and civil war." Five brief articles followed (here, all but one, in paraphrase):

1. The councils are to be secured in the constitution; council members are to enjoy official immunity; council representatives are to be in each ministry in an "advisory" capacity.
2. The remaining ministers are to retain their positions, to be joined by other Socialists, and also by a member of the BBB in a new Ministry of Agriculture.
3. "The Landtag legally elected on January 12 will be recalled as soon as conditions permit."
4. The standing army is to be disbanded and replaced by the Republican Security Troops, augmented with members from the Free Trade Unions and certified peasant organizations.
5. Freedom of the press is to be restored under certain temporary restrictions.[9]

The crucial article was obviously the third, since the importance of the others would depend on who had the final word in interpreting them—and this was apparently to be the Landtag. Predictably, the leadership of the SPD and the Free Trade Unions gave their immediate endorsement; but there was "strong opposition" within the Munich councils, and a meeting of the USP called to consider the program broke up in a riot.[10] If the *Zentralrat* was prepared to recognize the Landtag, it was doubtful that the councils would recognize the *Zentralrat*. In spite of the settlement the basic question remained the same: what conditions would, in fact, permit the Landtag to be recalled?

[9] "Einheitsfront des Sozialismus," *Flugblätter*, F. Mon. 2595.
[10] "Die Einheitsfront des Sozialismus," *MP*, 24 Feb. 1919, No. 45.

The *Zentralrat* could nevertheless claim that the united front had at last been realized. And there was a good bit of pious talk about securing the "prerogatives" of the council system while still conceding the ultimate authority of the Landtag. It all seemed plausible so long as politicians spoke vaguely of "preserving the achievements of the revolution" (a phrase used frequently by Eisner himself, and one which rivaled "Eisner's legacy" in sheer ambiguity), but the enforcement of specific measures of security in the city of Munich soon showed the impossibility of pleasing all of the people even some of the time. Two of the initial and immediately controversial actions of the *Zentralrat* had been the arrest of fifty hostages and the seizure of the "bourgeois" press. Under pressure from his own party, which in turn was subjected to vigorous protests from officials of the DDP and BVP, Niekisch was forced to back down on both counts. The hostages were released on condition that they remain in Munich, and the banned newspapers were allowed to resume publication under an indulgent censorship.[11] The *Zentralrat's* efforts to organize military security were of no more consequence. Extensive regulations for the "arming of the proletariat" stipulated that only workers over twenty years of age would receive arms, and that they must already be duly registered members of trade unions or of "all Socialist parties."[12] This phrase was clearly a euphemism, since it avoided the word "Communist" even though the KPD was included. Yet no issue was made of that, since the regulations proved to be impossible to enforce. The registration and distribution of arms for an *"Arbeiterwehr"* were to be completed by the end of the month, but on February 26 Chief of Police Staimer conceded that this was "a technical impossibility" and sug-

---

[11] "Festnahme von Geiseln," *NZ*, 24 Feb. 1919, No. 54. "Erklärung," *MNN*, 25 Feb. 1919, No. 92. The censorship was not ended until March 15.

[12] "Bewaffnung des Proletariats," *Bekanntmachungen*, F. Mon. 3239.

gested a new deadline in early March.[13] As it turned out, the registration of weapons was never completed, a trustworthy militia force was never organized, and the only result of the *Zentralrat's* "security precautions" was to put several hundred more rifles into circulation in Munich.

The focus of the revolution in Bavaria was now, more than ever, the capital city. "It is necessary that we consolidate," said one council leader in announcing the reorganization of the executive committee of the soldiers' councils. "Consolidate" was another euphemism: it meant that the process of radicalization in the Munich councils which had begun in January under the aegis of Left-Socialism was being intensified. In some council bodies the process had not much further to go. An open meeting of the Munich councils which jammed the Deutsches Theater on the Saturday after Eisner's assassination acclaimed and adopted a motion which included the demand for the proclamation of a *Räterepublik*.[14] The use of the word "council" in this form had a distinct connotation, and it was known to everyone in the assembly that they were thereby advocating the abandonment of traditional parliamentary government.

This was the state of things on February 25 when the congress of Bavarian councils, which had adjourned less than a week before under vastly different circumstances, was called back into session by the chairman Ernst Niekisch. A huge portrait of Kurt Eisner draped in red and black dominated the speaker's rostrum. Niekisch asked the assembly to rise as he paid an appropriately enigmatic tribute to "this man, our

[13] "Bekanntmachung!" and "Ergänzung zu der Vorschrift über Ablieferung von Waffen," *Bekanntmachungen*, F. Mon. 3328, 3363.

[14] "Münchener Arbeiter- u. Soldatenrat," *MP*, 24 Feb. 1919, No. 45. For a precise analysis of the usage of this term see Kolb, *Die Arbeiterräte in der deutschen Innenpolitik*, 325-328. He is fully justified in correcting the misleading impression created by referring to the Eisner regime as a "rationelle Räterepublik," as does Arthur Rosenberg, *Geschichte der Deutschen Republik* (Karlsbad, 1935), 80.

Eisner. . . . I do not believe it necessary to state explicitly what Comrade Eisner has meant for the proletariat. . . . Now it is our duty to realize our responsibilities and . . . to help our people through these difficult hours. We can best do that when we set as our task the fulfilment of the legacy of the precious deceased."[15]

The congress opened on a Tuesday and was finished with its important work by that Saturday, March 1, after five days of unrelieved tension. The debates were punctuated by rifle shots in the distance, the noise of mobs outside the Landtag building, and by sudden intrusions and interruptions. The delegates showed the strain of past events and of the urgency for an immediate decision. Under the circumstances, the deliberations of the congress were amazingly coherent, and the major issue—the survival of parliamentary government—was never out of sight, despite the fact that Niekisch was embarrassingly ineffectual as a chairman. When he ordered that the balcony be kept closed to the crowds outside, for example, he was overruled and could only request lamely that visitors as well as delegates check their weapons in the cloakroom. It was more like Oklahoma than Bavaria.[16]

Yet the debates (and the editorial comment on them in the newspaper press) did pose the alternatives with unmistakable clarity. A spokesman for the SPD, Walter Löwenfeld, stated that his party was not unalterably opposed to retaining the councils in some form, but that it would not support a dictatorship of the proletariat. "We have a terrible example of this," he said, "in Russian Bolshevism." Löwenfeld warned of confusing ends and means, of allowing a tiny minority of intellectuals to impose their will and to pass it off as the rule of the Bavarian workers and peasants. The

[15] *Stenographischer Bericht über die Verhandlungen der Arbeiter-, Bauern- und Soldatenräte vom 25. Februar bis 8. März 1919*, No. 1, 1.
[16] *Ibid.*, No. 2, 26-27.

form of the Bavarian government was not a matter at the discretion of a few political leaders in Munich, he contended.

> It depends on the whole state (stormy approval). Social revolutions cannot be made by the same means as political revolutions. Even Eisner stressed that. If we declare a dictatorship of the councils, our food supplies can no longer be guaranteed. We would make great speeches, but starve. . . . If we should succeed, however, in combining the councils with true democracy in the sense of Karl Marx, then we would give the whole world an example (vigorous applause from the Social Democrats).[17]

Although the SPD insisted on the restoration of the Landtag, it was now evidently willing to make certain (unspecified) concessions to the council system. The principal rebuttal was by Max Levien. "The second revolution might be delayed," he said, "but not subdued forever." He defended Russian Bolshevism, though admitting that it could not be mechanically imitated in Bavaria. He proposed that the council system be organized to replace the old parliamentary and bureaucratic structure and argued that, while he did not expect every Bavarian to become a Communist, the council system must be given a chance to rescue the state from its present economic and political crisis. In the long run, concluded Levien, there could be no compromise with the old regime.[18]

Munich was meanwhile a more agitated city than it had been in the final week of the war, and the attempts to influence the congress by force from without were in disturbing counterpoint to the debates within. Two of the city's large beer-halls were confiscated each day for meetings of soldiers,

---

[17] *Ibid.*, 32-36. In supporting the immediate restoration of the Landtag, a lead editorial in the SPD journal stated that "the proclamation of a soviet republic in Bavaria would mean a social war with the oppressed majority of the state." "Eine notwendige Entscheidung," *MP*, 25 Feb. 1919, No. 46.

[18] *Stenographischer Bericht . . . vom 25. Februar bis 8. März 1919*, No. 2, 36-43.

workers, and the unemployed. On Tuesday a delegation from the Wagnerbräu, claiming to represent an assembly of five thousand, presented its demands to the congress: permanent dissolution of the Landtag, proclamation of a soviet republic, assumption of diplomatic relations with Soviet Russia, arming of the entire proletariat, and the formation of a Red Army in Bavaria.[19] On Thursday there was a demonstration for the Wagnerbräu resolutions in front of the Landtag building. That evening a gathering in the Mathäserbräu broke out into the city and swept by the military barracks in an unsuccessful attempt to bring out the soldiers. On Friday morning, as the congress prepared to bring the council question to a vote, soldiers with drawn bayonets tried to break up another meeting in the Wagnerbräu, only to send several thousand angry people back onto the streets. At the same moment, a group of armed guards was entering the Landtag building, where they forced the entire congress to stand with hands up as they roughly escorted Max Levien out of the chamber. It was the third attempt by security officers Dürr and Staimer to arrest the Communist leader since November and, like their two previous efforts, it failed ingloriously. Levien soon returned to the congress, received another "stormy greeting," and was able to obtain one more embarrassed public apology from his inept antagonists.[20]

On Friday afternoon, the last day of February, the council congress nevertheless reached a formal verdict. Erich Müh-

[19] *Ibid.*, No. 1, 17. Representing the Wagnerbräu assembly was Rudolf Egelhofer. For his subsequent role as commander of the Red Army, see below, Chapter X.

[20] *Ibid.*, No. 3, 70-73. "Die Ereignisse am Freitag," *MNN*, 1 Mar. 1919, No. 98. Dürr's version of the incident was printed in the same issue as "Die Vorgänge in München am Freitag." His resignation was demanded by the radicals, but he was supported by a delegation from the Munich soliders' councils, an evidence of the division in the military. "Hände hoch! Politik der 'Demokraten,'" *NZ*, 1 Mar. 1919, No. 58. "Resolution der Vertreter der Münchener Kasernen am 1. März 1919," *Flugblätter*, F. Mon. 2598.

sam's motion that "Bavaria be declared a socialistic soviet republic" was defeated by a ballot of 234-70. The congress then approved an alternate motion (with only thirteen dissenting votes) which stipulated an immediate recall of the Landtag. Levien and August Hagemeister at once resigned from the *Zentralrat.* That evening placards pasted on buildings and kiosks ominously announced a protest gathering on the Theresienwiese for the next morning. If the issue had been decided in the congress, it was not yet settled on the streets.[21]

The events of November 7 were not repeated on March 1. While the council delegates were being called to order for the final session of the week in the Landtag building, a crowd of several thousand was congregating before the statue of Bavaria on the Theresienwiese. Shortly after ten o'clock fifty armed security guards appeared, there was a stir in the crowd, shots were fired, and the people scattered in panic. By ten-thirty the meadow was empty and quiet. Three were dead. The news was received in the congress with a mixture of relief and disgust. For the radicals it meant the complete bankruptcy of Social Democracy. Gustav Landauer spoke for them: "In the whole of natural history I know of no more revolting creature than the Social Democratic Party." For many others the incident was regrettable, but it did mean that the decision of the congress would stand. Most of the delegates consequently sat on through a tiresome day of haggling over personnel to fill various committees, and adjourned only after nominating a new provisional cabinet of Socialist ministers to replace the Eisner regime. The only step remaining was to secure the permission of the political parties involved to allow their members to serve as ministers.[22]

[21] *Stenographischer Bericht* . . . *vom 25. Februar bis 8. März 1919,* No. 3, 74-75.

[22] *Ibid.,* No. 4, 77-101. The resulting calm in Munich contrasted with the heavy rioting in Berlin during the first week of March. *Schulthess,* 1919/I, 109-110.

The focus now shifted briefly away from Munich, to the provinces. Just as party officials had retreated from the capital to reorganize after November 7, they withdrew to the countryside to regroup after February 21. They tended to gather in some of the major provincial towns on or above the Danube: Regensburg, Bamberg, Nuremberg, and Fürth. During the week of the council congress, leaders of the major parliamentary groups had conferred and negotiated (so far as the population of Munich was concerned) in silence. Now, as attention turned northward on the first day of March, representatives of the SPD, USP, BBB, and DDP met informally in Nuremberg and agreed to support the five-point program drafted previously by the "Commission for the Restitution of Unity."[23] Two days later a *Landeskonferenz* of the SPD convened in Fürth to decide whether any of its members should participate in the cabinet nominated by the council congress in Munich. The decision of this meeting was that the proposed slate of ministers was "unacceptable," since "a cabinet qualified to rule could only be nominated by the parliament." All of those Social Democrats nominated for cabinet posts, with the exception of Ernst Niekisch (to whom the party also denied permission to serve), thereupon refused to accept the positions assigned by the congress.[24]

For another week Bavaria remained without a political consensus, as delegations traveled back and forth across the Danube with proposals and counterproposals. On March 4 the SPD, USP, and BBB reached an accord in Nuremberg which advocated: "Immediate convocation of the Landtag at a brief session, formation of a Socialist cabinet by the two [!] Socialist parties, recognition of this cabinet by the elected Landtag, creation of a provisional constitution." The Nurem-

[23] "Die Regierungsgewalt in Bayern," *MNN*, 1 Mar. 1919, No. 97. Müller-Meiningen, *Aus Bayerns schwersten Tagen*, 146.

[24] "Die Mehrheitssozialisten und das neue provisorische Ministerium," *MNN*, 4 Mar. 1919, No. 101.

berg Accord also required that the councils be newly elected, and specified that the congress, its executive committee, and the *Zentralrat* "possess no legislative jurisdiction or executive authority."[25] On March 5 the congress, in turn, rejected the Accord and offered to send a delegation to negotiate further. By Saturday, March 8, the Accord was slightly revised (so as to emphasize the right of the councils to demand a referendum on any action of the Landtag) and resubmitted to the congress in Munich.[26]

Despite this elaborate ritual, there was no doubt that the members of the congress would at last accept the Nuremberg Accord, and there was no real question that the vast majority of Bavarians wished them to do so. Although they had not been consulted in the final round of negotiations, the BVP and DDP could be counted upon to support any measure which would restore the authority of the Landtag. The SPD was the principal force behind the Accord (as well as in the congress), and had only the numerically insignificant faction around Ernst Niekisch to contend with in its own ranks. The virtually undivided allegiance of the BBB had been secured through the revised version of the Accord which assured one of its leaders a cabinet post as the "Minister of Agriculture and Forestry."[27] Of the parties which had participated in the

[25] The text of the *Vereinbarung* was published in "Die Regierungskrise in Bayern," *MNN*, 5 Mar. 1919, No. 103.

[26] *Stenographischer Bericht . . . vom 25. Februar bis 8. März 1919*, Nos. 4-8, 97-194. The text of the final version was recorded as the "Vereinbarung nach den gemeinsamen Beschlüssen der sozial-demokratischen Landeskonferenz Bayerns, der Abordnung des Rätekongresses und den Vertretern des Bayerischen Bauernbundes am 7. März 1919," BHS Munich, ASR 1.

[27] The new cabinet proposed by the parties and then accepted by the congress was as follows: Prime Minister, Foreign Affairs, Culture: Hoffmann (SPD); Transportation: Frauendorfer (no party); Social Welfare: Unterleitner (USP); Justice: Endres (SPD); Interior: Segitz (SPD); Commerce and Industry: Simon (USP); Agriculture and Forestry: Steiner (BBB); Military Affairs: Schneppenhorst

January elections, only the USP was badly divided. Those who had been Eisner's closest associates—men like Unterleitner, Jaffé, and Fechenbach—felt that there was no alternative to acceptance and urged their party to act responsibly. But the radicals were in no mood to accept a "reality" prepared for them by others. Erich Mühsam warned openly that if the Accord were accepted "it will lead to a third revolution." In spite of his threat, a show of hands among the congress delegates indicated a clear majority in favor of the Accord.[28] When faced at last with a concrete decision, following the precedent set much earlier in Berlin, the Bavarian council delegates chose to recognize the political and legal preeminence of parliamentary government.

After the sound and fury of the past weeks, the verdict of the congress could signify nothing to the Communists and their supporters but a betrayal of the true interests of the working class. The congress had labored, said Max Levien, and "brought forth a mouse." Within a few minutes of his malediction, however, the congress was adjourned for the last time.[29] Ten days later the Landtag met without incident in Munich, ceremonially adopted a formal Enabling Act which granted full legal authority to a cabinet under Majority Socialist Johannes Hoffmann, and allowed itself to be prorogued. In assuming his office, the new chief executive attempted to summarize the conclusion of the negotiations in one sentence: "The political act which Prime Minister Eisner wanted to undertake on February 21 is now accomplished."[30]

(SPD); Finance: Merkel (no party). Although favored by the congress as Minister of Finance, Edgar Jaffé was unacceptable to the party caucus; Staatsrat von Merkel was then approved by both as a pro tempore appointment. *Schulthess, 1919/I,* 125.

[28] *Stenographischer Bericht . . . vom 25. Februar bis 8. März 1919,* No. 8, 193-197. Since the transcript does not specify the exact count, an individual ballot was evidently not required for a decision.

[29] *Ibid.,* 198-200.

[30] *Verhandlungen des Bayerischen Landtages. Ordentliche und*

The Hoffmann Administration

"The New Bavaria and its Socialist Regime." Thus the placards announced the theme for open meetings at five of Munich's great beer-halls on the evening of March 19, following the Landtag's adjournment the day before. At each of these assemblies the new cabinet of ministers was introduced and the program and policies of the new regime explained. The new leadership projected a sense of confidence, the warm mutual feeling of a team getting off on the right foot, as if an early score were only the first of many to come. The Prime Minister himself was the featured speaker. He certainly cut a more imposing, a more reassuring figure than Kurt Eisner. Johannes Hoffmann was a tall, erect, dark-haired man in his early fifties. He spoke forcefully and clearly, with only a trace of Rhenish dialect to betray his origins in the Palatinate. He had the useful reputation of inclining slightly to the more radical wing of Majority Socialism, a reputation based primarily on his term as Minister of Education and Culture under Eisner when he had supported the curtailment of ecclesiastical supervision in the Bavarian schools. Now he was determined to continue giving no unnecessary quarter to the Catholics, but none to the Communists either. "Every revolution has two enemies," he told his audience: "one stands to the right, the other to the left." He promised to lead his people securely between them, and to get Bavaria moving again on the road to Social Democracy. He took exception to those who could see things in only black or red: "the problem of the present is not parliament or council regime, but rather parliament and, at the same time, a legally regulated cooperation of the councils." In this spirit a new effort would be made to begin a broad program of socialization, Hoffmann announced,

---

ausserordentliche Tagung 1919, No. 2, 16-18. "Gesetz, die Ermächtigung der Regierung zu gesetzgeberischen Massnahmen betreffend ('Ermächtigungsgesetz')," reprinted by Doeberl, *Sozialismus*, 156.

for which the essential condition would be a suspension of all strikes and factional strife.[31]

The new regime was asking, then, for a sort of *Burgfrieden*, a chance to govern quietly through its administrative committees without the public demonstrations which had harassed Bavarian politics since the Munich Putsch. The Enabling Act approved by the Landtag on March 18 had provided Hoffmann with the necessary legal sanctions. It was stipulated that "the Landtag gives to the cabinet appointed by it the authority to proclaim laws and regulations." Such measures as were taken by the cabinet would then be subject to review by the parliament "at its next convocation." The duration of this arrangement remained conspicuously unspecified. Eleven standing committees had been thereupon appointed: for finance, constitutional matters, socialization, the councils, elections, etc., and these staffed by party and bureaucratic officials working in cooperation under the cabinet's general supervision. With the question of legality solved, the success of government-by-committee would now depend equally on the restoration of public confidence and the extent (or appearance, at least) of economic recovery.[32]

When March began the Bavarian economy was, as Hoffmann had openly confessed, "wretched." The outlook for the state as a whole did improve in the course of the month, but the improvement was not at all apparent in Munich. The prospects for agriculture seemed especially promising: there was plenty of farm labor available as a result of demobilization, while the sunny and unseasonably warm weather of the first two weeks of March raised hopes of an early spring and a consequently long growing season. But on March 16 it began to snow again, and a week later a severe cold front spread across the countryside. In Munich the cold touched the city

[31] "Das neue Bayern und seine sozialistische Regierung," *MNN*, 19 Mar. 1919, No. 131.

[32] *Verhandlungen des Bayerischen Landtages. Ordentliche und ausserordentliche Tagung 1919*, No. 2, 18-26.

at its most vulnerable spot. The coal stocks were all but exhausted, and the city magistracy, after hearing a report on the "cheerless circumstances," felt that it had no choice but to cancel all outstanding fuel rations from the months of January and February "even if an injustice is done."[33] Munich's financial condition was equally alarming. Since December 1 of the previous year the municipality had contracted debts amounting to more than 85 million marks, still a lot of money in 1919. The official unemployment figures were holding steady just above 30,000 in Munich alone, although the Central Labor Bureau estimated the real figure to be closer to 45,000. The black market was the liveliest enterprise in Bavaria; the metal, paper, textile, and leather industries were reported to be "unfavorable," the printing and restaurant businesses in Munich were described as "bad as ever," and commerce in general was appraised to be even worse than in February. It was symptomatic that the state bureaucratic and postal officials in Munich had begun refusing to accept the municipality's own emergency currency.[34]

There was certainly no lack of economic planning. Appointed to the newly created "Ministry of Commerce, Trade, and Industry" was Independent Socialist Josef Simon, the only member of the *Zentralrat* to have cabinet rank. Even before the official inauguration of the cabinet, the *Zentralrat* had staked out the question of socialization as its special preserve and as the key issue for keeping alive the activity and ambition of the councils. On March 14 the following announcement had been released through the Bavarian wire service: "The full socialization of Bavaria in accordance with comprehensive plans is on the march. The *Zentralrat* therefore wants to see the establishment of a socialistic

[33] "Plenarsitzung des Magistrats vom 25. März 1919," *MGZ:S*, 29 Mar. 1919, No. 25.

[34] "Sitzung des Gemeindebevollmächtigtenkollegiums vom 27. März 1919," *MGZ:S*, 2 Apr. 1919, No. 26. "Die Lage des Arbeitsmarktes in Bayern im Monat März 1919," BGS Munich, PA, VII, 92.

Central Bureau of Economics (*Zentralwirtschaftsamt*) . . . with far-reaching prerogatives. . . ."[35] A week later, in one of his first official acts as a minister, Simon called Dr. Otto Neurath to Munich from neighboring Saxony. It was not Neurath's first visit to the Bavarian capital: he had consulted with Kurt Eisner and Edgar Jaffé about socialization plans in January, but had returned to Saxony when the chairmanship of the Bavarian Socialization Commission was awarded to Professor Lujo Brentano. When it became clear that the Commission was headed nowhere in planning, not to speak of action, Brentano lost interest and was not even present at its final session (the sixteenth) on March 13. This had cleared the field for the *Zentralrat's* announcement, Simon's action, and Neurath's reappearance.[36]

On March 25 the Committee on Socialization (one of the government's eleven administrative committees) met and heard Neurath deliver a lecture lasting a full two hours on the theme of "full socialization." He presented a detailed outline of his scheme and expressed the hope for an eventual economic union of agricultural Bavaria with industrial Saxony. "We do not believe that we can today operate the factories in a communist fashion; for the time being we must work on within the framework of capitalism and create socialistic foundations. We will then automatically grow into a socialist economy." To direct this program Neurath urged the immediate creation of a Central Bureau of Economics as advocated by the *Zentralrat*. After hearing Neurath's proposal, the Committee unanimously adopted a resolution to that effect and charged the Bureau with responsibility for a study of the housing, clothing, and provisioning of the Bavarian population. The next day Neurath was named director of the project and

[35] "Der Zentralrat und die Sozialisierung," *MNN*, 14 Mar. 1919, No. 120.

[36] See Neurath, *Bayerische Sozialisierungserfahrungen*, 10-17, and Niekisch, *Gewagtes Leben*, 52-57.

Ernst Niekisch boasted that "the Neurath matter may be regarded as a success of the *Zentralrat*."[37]

The boast was premature. Johannes Hoffmann made no secret of his antipathy for Neurath's appointment and threatened to resign should Neurath step beyond (what Hoffmann regarded as) the narrow bounds of his competence. Hoffmann also made it quite clear that "any socialization law submitted by the Ministry of Commerce must first have the approval of the regime and, of course, the Landtag before it can be put into effect." For this policy he obtained support from members of every political party (except the KPD, which was not consulted) and extracted a public pledge of compliance from Josef Simon.[38] If Hoffmann thereby prevailed for the moment over the *Zentralrat*, it would have been equally premature for him to speak of success. In the first place, all the energy spent on the question of socialization did not benefit the staggering Bavarian economy in the least. The deadlock on long-range planning only worsened the frustrations and indecisions of a situation which obviously required more than the creation of another administrative organ. Secondly, such an open test of prestige between the cabinet and the *Zentralrat* was detrimental to Hoffmann's policy of reconciliation. The faintest suspicion of high-handed action by the Prime Minister was bound to aggravate those radicals who had taken badly the "suicide" of the council congress on March 1. This was apparent when Dr. Neurath addressed a gathering of Munich council members in the Hofbräuhaus a few days after Hoffmann's threat of resignation. In reporting the heated discussion

---

[37] "Das Zentralwirtschaftsamt," *Flugblätter*, F. Mon. 2603. "Bayerischer Landtag: Sozialisierungsausschuss," *MNN*, 26 Mar. 1919, No. 139. "Protokoll der Aktions-Ausschuss-Sitzung v. 26.3.19," BHS Munich, ASR 4.

[38] "Ministerpräsident Hoffmann und die Pläne des Zentralwirtschaftsamts," *MNN*, 2 Apr. 1919, No. 151. "Bayerischer Landtag: Sozialisierungsausschuss," *MNN*, 3 Apr. 1919, No. 153. "Die Sozialisierung in Bayern," *MNN*, 4 Apr. 1919, No. 155.

that evening, a newspaper correspondent noted (as if they were scarcely to be taken seriously) that "several speakers prophesied, incidentally, the approach of a new, the third revolution."[39]

In Bavaria's relationship to the German Reich a different sort of revolution was approaching which would undermine the stability of the Hoffmann regime. Ever since Dr. Hugo Preuss had released his draft of a constitution for the new German Republic on January 20, Bavarian representatives had fought stubbornly in Berlin and Weimar to preserve as much as possible of the state's rights and special privileges. In this effort Kurt Eisner had found close but grudging support among the leadership of the BVP, who suspected his motives and methods even while sharing his contention that Germany should retain a decentralized federal system. Some of the other German states—Baden, Württemberg, and to a lesser extent Hesse and Saxony—had likewise shared Eisner's fear of Prussian predominance in any highly centralized form of government, but they too were suspicious of Eisner's eccentric diplomacy. As a consequence, the opponents of centralization had been unable to mount any united resistance to Preuss and his formula (as it was later canonized in the Weimar constitution): *Reichsrecht bricht Landrecht.*[40] After a month of hectic negotiation in committees, a slightly modified form of the Preuss draft was brought to the floor of the German National Assembly in Weimar on the day after Eisner's assassination. "The decisive battle for the provisions of the constitution," Preuss observed, "is just now beginning."[41]

By the time Hoffmann had finally received his discretionary

---

[39] "Die Frage der Betriebsräte," *MNN*, 4 Apr. 1919, No. 156.

[40] Article 13: "The law of the Reich supersedes state law." F. Giese (ed.), *Die Verfassung des Deutschen Reiches vom 11. August 1919* (Berlin, 1920), 97. On Eisner's opposition to Preuss, see above, Chapter VIII.

[41] *Schulthess*, 1919/I, 83-84, 86-91.

powers from the Bavarian Landtag, the battle was nearly over. On March 24, the administrative committee in charge of "foreign affairs" met for the first time, in the presence of the Prime Minister, in a wing of the Landtag building. They heard a bleak report from Bavaria's diplomatic agent in Berlin, Dr. von Preger, on the progress of the constitutional deliberations in Weimar since February 21. He ticked off the losses which Bavaria had already sustained—its own military command, diplomatic corps, post and telegraph, transportation system, and administration of direct taxation—and he warned that the end was not yet in sight: the retention of Bavaria's beer and brandy taxes, indispensable for her financial independence, was already being challenged. In short, Preger told the committee, Bavaria was no longer a sovereign state, "but rather a member state (*Gliedstaat*) subordinate to the Reich."[42] There ensued a debate lasting through two long days at the conference table, mainly between representatives of the BVP and the DDP. If the situation was as Preger described it, said a spokesman for the Bavarian People's Party, "then we would rather not enter the Reich." His Democratic opponent found this view "highly questionable," and was sustained (thereby demonstrating the solidarity of the dominant political coalition in Bavaria) by Prime Minister Hoffmann and other members of the SPD. In observing that it would be his policy to render unto Berlin that which was Berlin's, Hoffmann expressed himself in a phrase stilted but forceful: Bavaria outside of the German Reich, he said, "is a thing of impossibility." The resolution adopted by the committee on March 25 and sent to the Bavarian delegation at Weimar therefore registered the "deep concern" of the Bavarian government with the course of negotiations in the National Assembly, but stated unequivocally that "Bavaria stands true to the Reich."[43]

Hoffmann thereby scored another of his Pyrrhic victories.

[42] "Bayern und das Reich," *MNN*, 25-26 Mar. 1919, Nos. 137-139.
[43] *Ibid.*

He had gained his point, but he lost the support and reliable cooperation of the strongest political party in Bavaria. At best the political attitude of Bavarian Catholicism toward Social Democracy in any form was one of bare toleration; at worst, as things now stood, it verged on malevolence. As the BVP and the Catholic hierarchy saw it, Hoffmann was cheerfully handing out what was not his to give. In the name of national unity he was surrendering without a struggle the sacred rights of a venerable tradition to the Protestant and Prussian North. Such was the oratory recorded in the Catholic press and heard at the meetings organized by the BVP to protest against "Weimar." What practical action their party could realistically have hoped to take, other than actual secession from the Reich, the leaders did not say. They did know that they were opposed to a policy which had brought (as one editorial put it) "Bavaria's deepest degradation."[44] Georg Heim could even recall the Eisner regime with a certain nostalgia: Eisner, at least, had been dead set "against the rape of the individual states." A comparison with the Hoffmann administration, therefore, was all in Eisner's favor.[45] Although the BVP had publicly accepted the republican form of government and though its support of the Landtag was never really at issue, the leaders of Bavarian Catholicism could no longer be counted on to throw their considerable weight behind Hoffmann in the event of a sudden and serious crisis.

Bavaria was by no means the only state threatened by crisis in March of 1919. With the Paris Peace Conference meeting in the West and the Third International in the East, the whole of Central Europe was being pressed in a vise of uncertainty. The crucial issue of European politics, not for the first time nor the last, was the future of Germany. This issue involved

[44] "Die Erwürgung Bayerns," *BK*, 26 Mar. 1919, No. 85. "Bayerns tiefste Erniedrigung," *BV*, 1 Apr. 1919, No. 73. This obviously recalled the famous essay for which the Nuremberg bookseller Palm was hanged at the order of the French in 1806.
[45] "Eisner und Hoffmann," *BK*, 3 Apr. 1919, No. 93.

the inextricable questions of the extent of the Reich and the form of its government. On March 12 a constituent assembly sitting in Vienna had voted that German Austria, detached from other former Habsburg territories, should become an integral part of the Reich. The Social Democratic premier of Austria, Dr. Karl Renner, promised to bring negotiations with Berlin "as rapidly as possible to a conclusion."[46] The situation of Austria was not dissimilar to that of Bavaria. It was now a tiny country of under seven million inhabitants with an economy that seemed barely viable. There were acute food shortages and a soaring rate of unemployment. Austria likewise had one huge metropolis, politically controlled by Social Democracy, surrounded by a potentially hostile countryside which was mostly conservative and clerical. Together Bavaria and Austria might constitute that counterweight to Prussia which had long been the dream of many south German statesmen. Bavarians of nearly every political conviction were prepared to support the *Anschluss* of Austria, all things remaining equal. Of course, they did not.

On March 22 the cold wave arrived in Munich simultaneously with the news of the abdication of Hungarian Count Michael Károlyi. In Budapest a popular front of Socialists and Communists had taken over the government in the name of the councils of workers, soldiers, and peasants. The Hungarian Soviet Republic was proclaimed, formal recognition and warm greetings were sent by Lenin from Moscow in the name of the Third International, and Europe first heard the name of Béla Kun.[47] Now there was a rival for the hand of Austria. The Austrian Socialists saw to it that the new Hungarian regime received "a large quantity" of industrial products from Austria. In the absence of strictly enforced controls, private individuals freely smuggled arms and am-

---

[46] *Schulthess*, 1919/I, 517-518, 520-522. On the response in Weimar, *ibid.*, 133.

[47] *Ibid.*, 572-575. "Neue Umwälzungen in Ungarn," *MNN*, 22-23 Mar. 1919, No. 134.

munition across the border to aid the Hungarians, first against the Czechs, later the Rumanians. But Béla Kun wanted more: the Austrian Socialists should follow the Hungarian example, form a popular front, and rule through the councils. When the Austrians refused, money began passing from Budapest to the headquarters of the Austrian Communist Party in Vienna for purposes of "propaganda." In explaining the obviously self-contradictory policy of his party, Socialist foreign minister Otto Bauer was either naïve or disingenuous: "We could support the Hungarian Soviet Republic, but we were obliged to prevent the proclamation of the Soviet Republic in Austria."[48]

These events had an important, if indefinable, impact on Bavaria. At the beginning of 1919 the threat of Bolshevism had come from the North. The rhetoric of Bavarian separatism had been directed against the machinations of the Berlin radicals, the Liebknechts and the Luxemburgs. There had been much talk and some writing about Bavaria's breaking away from the Reich to join with German Austria and possibly other southern German republics in a new autonomous state. But in March the situation was reversed. Liebknecht and Luxemburg were dead and Berlin was securely in the hands of men who were anything but radicals. The threat of Bolshevism was now from the southeast and the vision of a new autonomous state had an entirely different aspect. Hungary was Europe's second soviet republic; the third might be Austria—or Bavaria.

On the first day of April, incredibly, Munich lay under nearly twenty inches of snow. The snowfall of the last two days in March had been the heaviest recorded in years, and the condition of the city was listed as "catastrophic." For those who obtained a newspaper that day the headlines were no better than the weather: martial law in Stuttgart, riots in Frankfurt,

---

[48] Otto Bauer, *The Austrian Revolution* (London, 1925), 102-103.

a major strike in the Ruhr. In Vienna the restaurants were closed for lack of food to serve, the Council of Workers and Soldiers was in constant session, and armed men roamed the streets.[49] But for the snow it might have been the same— or worse—in Munich. For, while the city was cold and externally quiet that week, the kindling of another revolution was being stacked in place.

Some of Munich's most combustible materials, the unemployed, were gathering nightly to register protests against one or another aspect of governmental policy. Like everyone else, it seemed, they too had a duly elected executive committee, a favorite beer-hall (the Kindlkeller), and demands to make of Hoffmann. This week they were objecting in particular to the increase in cost of utilities and street-car fares which went into effect on April 1. Such complaints were neither unusual nor unexpected. What was alarming—and this was true of more than one protest meeting—was the undisguised and increasingly earnest tone of threat. Should their conditions not be met, the assembly notified the regime and the press, "the unemployed of Munich will be forced to help themselves." In the Löwenbräu another gathering of "more than three thousand revolutionary soldiers" (according to the resolution adopted there) demanded a "thorough cleansing" of the soldiers' councils, the establishment of Communist control in the council system, and the immediate formation of a Red Army. The sound was familiar in Munich, but the pitch was higher; and it was evident that in any crisis the unemployed might be joined by the unreconciled.[50]

The impetus for a third revolution, however, did not originate in Munich. Just as parliamentary leaders had withdrawn to the countryside after November 7 and February 21 to reorganize their parties, several radical council members had left the capital after March 18 to enlist support for the council system. As the base of their operations they had chosen Augs-

[49] *MNN*, 2 Apr. 1919, No. 151.
[50] "Forderungen der Erwerbslosen," *MNN*, 4 Apr. 1919, No. 155.

burg, capital of the province of Swabia and center of Bavaria's struggling textile industry. It was an obvious choice, being the only other major city south of the Danube, just two hours by rail from Munich, and the seat of the most active and influential of the provincial council bodies. On April 3 an extraordinary session of council members was called to order for the ostensible purpose of hearing a speech by Ernst Niekisch on the theme of "The Second Revolution." Although he enjoyed something of the status of a "favorite son" in Augsburg, and although he had as much reason as anyone to feel slighted by Hoffmann's transparent disregard of the *Zentralrat*, Niekisch was not one of those who had left Munich to encourage a revival of radicalism. The councils were on the march throughout Germany, he told his audience, and in socialization Bavaria would soon show the way; but the day for complete control by the council system had not yet come, and "the formation of a Socialist regime" should be recognized for the time being as "the only viable way." To his surprise Niekisch found that he had, in his willingness to compromise with parliamentarianism, very little vocal support. Before the afternoon was over the Augsburg council assembly had adopted by a large majority a resolution in favor of a Bavarian Soviet Republic, an alliance with the soviet governments of Russia and Hungary, and a program of full socialization. The assembly also ordered a general strike for the next day and appointed a delegation to present its resolution to the regime in Munich. As he was their leader, Niekisch consented to join them.[51]

That same day, in Munich, Prime Minister Hoffmann had already informed his cabinet that he intended to call the Landtag back into session on the following Tuesday, April 8.

[51] "Generalstreik in Augsburg," *MNN*, 4 Apr. 1919, No. 156. Niekisch, *Gewagtes Leben*, 63-65. An excellent account of this period is to be found in the unpublished manuscript of Dr. Freiherr von Guttenberg, "Die Räteherrschaft in Bayern und ihr Ende" (1926), located in BHS Munich, Abt. IV.

Even without knowledge of the Augsburg resolution, he had apparently sensed that dissatisfaction with his regime of administrative committees was mounting to a point of danger. What he did not sense was the imminence of a full-blown crisis. After dictating an executive order for the Landtag's convocation (not published until the next day), he took the evening train to Berlin. When the delegation from Augsburg arrived in Munich on the morning of April 4, Hoffmann was gone. The cabinet and the *Zentralrat* conferred. Without their leader, the Social Democrats present would accept no obligations and strike no bargains; the Independents were too divided and too obviously in the minority; the Communists (having resigned from the *Zentralrat*) were not present. Any decision to act, then, could not be made on a party basis. Meeting apart, the *Zentralrat* therefore made its own decision: "According to newspaper reports the Landtag is supposed to convene on Tuesday, April 8. The *Zentralrat* is immediately taking energetic steps to have the summons of the Landtag withdrawn. The convocation will therefore not take place."[52] No stand was taken on the Augsburg resolution. Undeniably, the *Zentralrat* had acted in defiance of Hoffmann's regime, but it left the question of a soviet republic open. Bavaria was in effect back to anarchy, even though most Bavarians probably had no notion and very little direct interest in what the *Zentralrat* did or did not decide.

Munich was once again a city of public meetings, protests, plots, resolutions—and confusion. The Landtag building was fortified by machine guns, but it was uncertain at whose order. The most important single public pronouncement that day came from a disheveled assembly of soldiers: "The Munich garrison declares that, in case of the outbreak of a general strike in Munich, its sympathies will lie on the side of the workers. The garrison will remain neutral. . . . The assembly

[52] "Vor neuen Ereignissen?" *MNN*, 5 Apr. 1919, No. 157. "Neue Ereignisse in Bayern," *BK*, 5-6 Apr. 1919, Nos. 95-96.

of barrack councils in Munich has decided . . . to place no units on alert nor to take any security precautions."[53]

After reading that notification, it would have required a heroic Landtag representative indeed to put in an appearance on Tuesday morning. In the early evening of April 4 a mass meeting in Munich's Löwenbräu Cellar was presented with an amplification of the Augsburg resolution: "Elimination of the parties, union of the entire proletariat, proclamation of a soviet republic, and brotherhood with the Russian and Hungarian proletariat. And then no power on earth will be able to prevent the immediate execution of full socialization." Some stood and cheered; others left the hall.[54]

The three weeks of the Hoffmann administration had proved to be no more conclusive than the interim regime of the *Zentralrat* before it. Both represented attempts to reach some sort of arrangement which would placate radical council leaders while recognizing the legal authority of the Landtag. If successful, this would have meant the culmination of the political course set by "this man, our Eisner." But Eisner's legacy was in reality one of failure, and that failure was only repeated after his death. Hoffmann had deferred, not settled, the problems created by the revolution in Bavaria. He was no better able than Eisner to arrest or resolve the political polarization, and his government was therefore to collapse immediately after its first move to end the deadlock between the parliamentary and council systems.

[53] "Beschlüsse der Münchener Kasernenräte," *MNN*, 5 Apr. 1919, No. 157.
[54] "Ankündigung der Räte-Republik," *MNN*, 5 Apr. 1919, No. 157.

CHAPTER X

The Soviet Republic

SHORT of complete anarchy, only two possibilities remained by the end of the first week in April: either the Landtag would finally assume its designated functions as the sovereign authority of the Bavarian state, or political power would pass by default to a soviet republic. That the alternatives were so starkly posed was equally the responsibility of the SPD and the KPD. In the five months since the Munich Putsch, they had unwittingly conspired to create the symbols and slogans of the revolution. For most Bavarians the Landtag was synonymous with the exclusion of the councils from any significant role in the new order, whereas the term *Räterepublik* automatically conjured the image of a council dictatorship and the complete elimination of a parliamentary form of government. These notions had been the central theme of Communist agitation as well as the burden of Majority Socialist policy at least since January. Both parties were now the victims of their own logic. The talk of compromise was hampered by the lack of an appropriate vocabulary. A genuine reconciliation was conceivable only if one could also conceive of a new meaning for words which had already become inflexibly defined.

There was nothing inevitable about the final episode of the revolution in Bavaria, except the ultimate military verdict once the opposing forces were engaged. To ask why a regime granted extraordinary powers by the Bavarian Landtag and formally endorsed by a congress of Bavarian councils did not survive is, at the same time, to pose the last and most difficult question of this history: how was a soviet republic possible at all? While it is hopeless to untangle even a fraction of the contingencies, one can locate at least a few of the more important factors in the collapse of the Hoffmann administration: a paralysis of the economy, the inadequacy of

304

security preparations, a lack of firm support from the largest single political party in the state, the unsettling effect of developments outside of Bavaria, the concerted agitation of a purposeful minority, the divided ambitions and ineptitude of political leadership. Such factors, in a variety of combinations, have brought a hundred revolutions to victory—or defeat—since 1789. They are, of course, impossible to measure precisely in their relative importance for the final outcome. In this instance, at best, one can attempt to approximate what actually happened in Bavaria during April of 1919, and to suggest why the conclusion in the first days of May was a senseless and brutal tragedy.

The "Pseudo" Soviet Republic

In the early morning hours of April 5 the immediate future of the Bavarian state was determined by a group of some one hundred men gathered, for once without public fanfare, in the Ministry for Military Affairs. By the nature of the meeting and agreement of the participants, no minutes were recorded. Motives were as various as the factions and personalities represented: the Socialists and the Communists, the anarchists and the army, the *Zentralrat* and the police, the RAR, USP, and BBB—all seated in the disorder of one chamber. Many of the names and faces were well known in Munich: Niekisch (the perennial chairman), Gandorfer, Unterleitner, Simon, Mühsam, Landauer, Neurath, Dürr, Staimer, along with other party functionaries and elected officials. But the two most important figures in the room were personally unknown to most of those present: Ernst Schneppenhorst and Eugen Leviné. By the time the meeting broke up shortly before dawn and the men went out into the empty streets, a majority of them had agreed to support the proclamation of a Bavarian Soviet Republic on the following Monday, April 7.[1]

[1] Compare the versions given by Niekisch, *Gewagtes Leben*, 65-66;

In all the political vacillations of the previous five months, at least one factor had remained constant: no decision of any consequence could be taken without the consent of the SPD. The lack of it had deadlocked the conference between party leaders and the *Zentralrat* on the previous day. Now the problem was still the same: the Prime Minister was away and his party lieutenants refused to accept the responsibility for a major political decision. It was this function which Ernst Schneppenhorst performed. His credentials for speaking in behalf of his party were not the best, but they apparently sufficed for men who wanted to hear what he had to tell them. For a dozen years before and during the war Schneppenhorst had been the chief functionary in a lumbermen's union at Nuremberg. In November of 1918 he became attached as a political advisor to the Third Bavarian Army Corps stationed there. From his headquarters he had, during the week after Kurt Eisner's assassination, created a minor sensation in Munich by sending out airplanes to drop thousands of leaflets promising the support of his military unit in the effort "to reject the domination of Dr. Levien and his armed supporters."[2] He was subsequently rewarded for his enterprise by being named Minister for Military Affairs in the Hoffmann cabinet on March 18. He had immediately moved to Munich to take up his office, and it was thus in Schneppenhorst's ministry that the midnight meeting took place. There, to the astonishment of nearly everyone, he now insisted that the Bavarian Soviet Republic should be proclaimed.

There have been several hypotheses advanced to explain why Schneppenhorst attempted to break the political impasse that night by committing his party to a policy it was known

---

Toller, *Eine Jugend in Deutschland*, 144-145; Mühsam, *Von Eisner bis Leviné*, 42-43; Neurath, *Bayerische Sozialisierungserfahrungen*, 21-22; and Rosa Leviné, *Aus der Münchener Rätezeit* (Berlin, 1925), 12-16. See Guttenberg, "Die Räteherrschaft in Bayern," 3-6.

[2] "An alle Arbeiter und Soldaten!" *Flugblätter*, F. Mon. 2597.

to oppose as a matter of principle: that he was an *agent provocateur* who planned to draw the Communists into a soviet republic only in order to combat them by discrediting it; that he now chose to be "true to the united Socialist front" because the SPD would otherwise be excluded altogether from political power; or, that he was just "a Socialist who wanted to hold his job."[3] While a case can be made for each of these views, since they are not mutually exclusive, the truth seems to be that Schneppenhorst himself did not have a clear notion of what he was doing. In common with most parliamentary leaders and with security officers Dürr and Staimer (who now supported his action), he had felt increasingly frustrated by the freedom of the Communists to agitate with impunity. "Levien and his armed followers" could be accused of encouraging violence, but they could not yet be held to account for any specific legal misdemeanor. By drawing the KPD into a coalition regime, Schneppenhorst hoped to commit its leaders to official responsibility for their words and deeds, which could then be—somehow or other—vigorously opposed. He could thereby achieve two objectives at once: keep the SPD in a position of authority and control the Communist threat. It was a dangerous gamble and, as it proved, a mistaken one.

Essential to such a calculation was the assumption that Max Levien would be delighted to transfer "all power to the councils." But Levien was no longer the leader of the Bavarian Communist Party; that was now a man called Niessen. Eugen Leviné, alias Niessen—born in Russia, raised and educated in Germany—had been one of two men designated by Rosa Luxemburg just before her death in January to

[3] These views are endorsed, respectively, by Beyer, *Von der Novemberrevolution*, 68-74; Neubauer, *München und Moskau*, 47-48; and Raatjes, *The Role of Communism*, 130-133. See the analysis by Kolb (who supports Neubauer while evidently assuming that Schneppenhorst was acting as an authorized delegate of his party), *Die Arbeiterräte in der deutschen Innenpolitik*, 332-339.

represent the KPD at the first congress of the Third International in Moscow. Prevented from crossing the border, Leviné returned to Berlin where he was given another assignment by the new chief of German Communism, Paul Levi: to travel to Bavaria and assume command of the Communist Party there. Leviné had therefore arrived in Munich for the first time on March 5. By the end of that month, unknown to all but those on the inside, he had already made "fundamental changes" in the KPD's structure and policy. He assumed the editorship of the party journal, the *Münchener Rote Fahne*, and on March 18 began daily publication. He managed a quiet purge of the party's executive committee, forcing out five of its seven members, retaining only the two original founders, Levien and Hans Kain. He had all of the party's membership cards called in for review by April 1, then reissued less than 3000 of them.[4] At the same time Leviné initiated a program to reorganize solid Communist cells within the council system, especially at large industrial plants (the so-called *Betriebsräte*). Meanwhile, he had supplanted Max Levien as the party strategist. This meant, above all, an end to cooperation with the anarchists and the USP. Though not a doctrinaire Leninist nor, as far as can be established, a Russian agent, Leviné acted with Lenin's instinctive disdain for the undisciplined and the petty bourgeois. He was also acting under instructions from Berlin: "It is to be understood that any occasion for military action by governmental troops must be strictly avoided. In all frankness and with every emphasis the workers must be told that they should forego any kind of armed action, even when a local or momentary success might be possible."[5]

[4] Raatjes, *The Role of Communism*, 112-119.

[5] Message addressed from the KPD Central Committee in Berlin to the Munich chapter, 18 Mar. 1919, BHS Munich, ASR 23. "Leviné had never been a member of the Lenin party nor a pupil of Leninist discipline." Ruth Fischer, *Stalin and German Communism* (Cambridge, Mass., 1948), 105-106.

When confronted by Schneppenhorst's surprising demand for a soviet republic, then, Leviné responded by refusing to allow his party to have anything to do with a putsch "proclaimed from a green table." He gave three reasons why he considered the timing to be "extraordinarily unfavorable" for such a proclamation: that the working masses in the rest of Germany had been temporarily "beaten down" by the mercenary Free Corps of Gustav Noske, that Bavaria was "not an economically sufficient territory which could maintain itself independently for a long time," and that a genuine soviet republic could only emerge as the spontaneous climax "of difficult struggles and of a victory by the proletariat." The Communists were therefore obliged, said Leviné, to reject any compromise or cooperation with Schneppenhorst, "the Nuremberg Noske," and his associates.[6]

The reasons which Leviné offered were valid enough, but in view of his subsequent actions one must conclude that the question of timing was much less important for him than the act of compromise itself. The KPD saw in a *Räterepublik* not so much a form of government as a means of Communist domination—it was therefore acceptable only apart from the "cooperation" of the SPD. Rather than share responsibility, Leviné wanted Schneppenhorst to cede it. But the Communists, as usual, were outnumbered and thereby became unwilling witnesses to the inception of the Bavarian Soviet Republic. And the comedy of perverted intentions was still not complete. At Schneppenhorst's request it was agreed to delay any formal proclamation for another forty-eight hours until the necessary preparations were made. During this time a conference of Majority Socialist leaders was hastily convened in Nuremberg; by a vote of 47-6 they rejected the Soviet Republic and demanded that Schneppenhorst withdrawn his support.[7] By the time he returned from

[6] Rosa Leviné, *Aus der Münchener Rätezeit*, 12-16.
[7] *Schulthess*, 1919/I, 162-166. The entire affair was later aired,

Nuremberg to Munich on the evening of April 6, therefore, both the Majority Socialists and the Communists were officially opposed to an action which he had originally intended them to sponsor jointly. But it proved too late to undo what had been done. A rump session of the *Zentralrat*, the radical Independents, and the RAR convened in the Wittelsbach Palace, drafted the text of a proclamation, and sent it to the printer. On Monday morning crowds gathered on the street-corners to read the fresh placards: "BAVARIA IS A SOVIET REPUBLIC."[8]

The first soviet regime in Bavaria lasted six days. It was a week of raucous and at times ridiculous confusion. Regulations, pronouncements, proclamations, orders and counterorders were drafted, printed, and distributed in hectic tempo. The press would be socialized along with the mines, the banks would be reorganized and so would the bureaucracy, special revolutionary tribunals would replace the courts, living quarters would be registered, foodstuffs would be confiscated, the bourgeoisie would be disarmed and the proletariat armed, the Red Army formed, the Soviet Republic defended, the International greeted, the World Revolution extended. And, as the new regime recognized, the Bavarian population would be bewildered: "Comrades! You do not know what a Soviet Republic means. You will tell it now by its work. The Soviet Republic will bring the new order."[9]

---

inconclusively, in court. "Schneppenhorst *v* die Neue Zeitung," *MNN*, 5-10 July 1919, Nos. 261-268.

[8] "An das Volk in Baiern!" *MNN*, 7 Apr. 1919, No. 159. An appeal for cooperation from the peasantry was sent out in the name of the peasants' councils by Karl Gandorfer: "An die ländliche Bevölkerung," *Flugblätter*, F. Mon. 2576. A public statement on the meeting in the Wittelsbach Palace was issued by Ernst Toller, "Erklärung der Münchener USP," *MNN*, 7 Apr. 1919, No. 159. See Niekisch, *Gewagtes Leben*, 66-71.

[9] "An die Münchener Bevölkerung!" *Bekanntmachungen*, F. Mon. 3337. See the collection of proclamations by Max Gerstl, "Die

In six days, of course, it brought only disorder and appropriately acquired the title of "Pseudo Soviet Republic" (*Scheinräterepublik*). The title was bestowed by the Communist Party; it was appropriate not because the KPD refused to participate in the government, but because there was in reality no government at all. It is useless to examine in detail all the measures signed in the name of the "Revolutionary *Zentralrat*" (as it was now called) between April 7 and April 12, since they existed only on placards. Even those who did the signing had a sense of transience. Gustav Landauer sent a picture postcard (it was his own picture!) to a friend: "I am now the commissar for propaganda, education, science, art, and a few other things. If I am allowed a few weeks time, I hope to accomplish something; but there is a bare possibility that it will be only a couple days, and then it will have been but a dream."[10] He and the other leaders, under the chairmanship of "Comrade" Niekisch (so the transcripts henceforth specified), agreed on April 8 that all titles used to issue administrative regulations should include the word "provisional."[11]

Most of the personnel of the new regime had no more significance than the proclamations they signed, except perhaps insofar as they made the men in Munich a laughingstock in the rest of Bavaria and in Berlin. The most quotable of these was the Foreign Minister, Dr. Franz Lipp, who on April 10 notified Lenin and Checherin in Moscow by wireless that "the proletariat of Upper Bavaria [is] happily united," but that "the fugitive Hoffmann . . . has taken with him the key to my ministry toilet."[12] Several declarations,

---

Münchener Räterepublik," *Politische Zeitfragen*, 1919, XX-XXIV, 311-358.

[10] Landauer to Fritz Manthner, 7 Apr. 1919. Buber (ed.), *Gustav Landauer*, II, 413-414.

[11] "Abschrift. Sitzung [des Zentralrats] vom 8.4.19." BHS Munich, ASR 18.

[12] Gerstl, "Die Münchener Räterepublik," *loc.cit.*, 340. See Volk-

apparently as preposterous as this one, by Lipp and Finance Minister Silvio Gesell have too often been subjected to indiscriminate ridicule. Gesell's schemes for a "free currency" economy, for instance, do not seem so ludicrous when one remembers that he was attempting to be consistent with a policy which both rejected capitalism and renounced the Weimar Republic. Even Lipp's broadcast was probably no more than an insouciant response to a message received from Lenin on the previous day: "Please give us details about the revolution achieved in Bavaria. Apart from a short broadcast of the Bavarian regime we know nothing. Please report to us how events are progressing there and whether the new order is fully and completely in control. . . ." Presumably Lipp felt that Lenin would be amused to know that everything was in order except for the missing key.[13]

Beyond that, the sporadic exchange of messages between Munich and Moscow during April, most of them translated and relayed by the Béla Kun government in Budapest, shows how misleading an unexamined theory of "international conspiracy" can be. The Comintern had almost no useful information, not to mention control, of the soviet regime in Bavaria—no more knowledge than the Bavarian Communists had of actual conditions or Bolshevik tactics in Russia. As late as April it was still a rather distant admiration of "the Russian example" more than any theoretical or practical conformity to Bolshevism which inspired the supporters of soviet rule in Munich.

The character of any soviet regime in Munich obviously depended in the first place on whether the local Communists

---

mann, *Revolution über Deutschland*, 223, and Fischer, *Stalin and German Communism*, 103-104.

[13] "Funksprüche der Sowjetregierung an Béla Kun," *MNN*, 9 Apr. 1919, No. 162. Neubauer, *München und Moskau*, 56-58. For an anecdotal account of "the happy, irresponsible government of the Coffee House Anarchists," see Waite, *Vanguard of Nazism*, 82-84.

could be counted among those supporters. Their position was hard to define and harder to justify after months of agitation for the abolition of parliamentary government. If withholding support of the new regime, for whatever reason, should allow its collapse and the return of the Hoffmann administration, this would represent, at least in their own eyes, a betrayal of the working class. Since they were committed to the continuation of the revolution, their problem was to replace the first soviet regime without destroying it altogether, that is, to create pressure for a "real" soviet regime without provoking an internecine struggle with the "pseudo" soviet leaders. The public oratory was undertaken by Max Levien, the organization for a seizure of power by Eugen Leviné. After two days of closed meetings the KPD announced the creation of a council of ten, in reality a shadow cabinet, which generously offered to participate "in an advisory capacity" in the various administrative commissions established by the Revolutionary *Zentralrat*. At the same time, Levien openly denied the authority of the *Zentralrat* to represent the will of the proletariat and outlined his party's plan to form an entirely new executive organ from the *Betriebsräte*: "Only this really revolutionary council will be capable and qualified to decide *when* the proletarian Soviet Republic should be proclaimed, *when* the struggle should begin. . . ." So while the Communist Party could not recognize the present leadership of the Bavarian Soviet Republic, it would not hesitate in case of an attack "to stand in the vanguard of the defenders."[14] The fine distinction between support (of leadership) and defense (of a regime) was derived from a dual calculation: despite its effort to organize and equip a Red Army, the *Zentralrat* could not hope unaided to hold Munich; and, after gathering forces north of the Danube, Hoffmann would not hesitate to retake it.

[14] "Arbeiter! Folgt nur den Parolen der kommunistischen Partei!" *Flugblätter*, F. Mon. 2699. "Zur Lage," *BSZ*, 13 Apr. 1919, No. 97.

"The regime of the Bavarian Freestate has NOT resigned. It has transferred its seat from Munich. The regime is and will remain the SINGLE possessor of power in Bavaria and is alone qualified to release legal regulations and to issue [administrative] orders. . . ."[15] This manifesto had been signed by Johannes Hoffmann in Nuremberg on April 7, and as he sat in his office at the city hall in Bamberg a few days later, his only problem was to enforce it. Although his government-in-exile had been successful enough in its initial efforts to quarantine soviet rule below the Danube line, to regain the capital was another question. In the cities of northern Bavaria the excitement of the Soviet Republic's proclamation had lasted no more than a day or two: in Würzburg, Fürth, Ingolstadt, Regensburg, and Schweinfurt there had been proclamations, crowds, "encroachments," and then a swift restoration of order. Nuremberg and Bamberg had remained quiet and loyal, while in the countryside the general reaction was either continued indifference or increased hostility to the whims of big city politicians. Only in the triangle bounded by Augsburg, Rosenheim, and Garmisch—an area of less than 2000 square miles in all—could Munich still claim precedence over Bamberg.[16]

If some Bavarians liked to think of their state as large and important in its own right, most Germans—and, above all, the government in Berlin—considered Bavaria an indivisible part of the German Reich. Dr. Hugo Preuss declared that the proclamation of the Bavarian Soviet Republic had been

---

[15] "Volksgenossen!" and "An die Bevölkerung Münchens!" *Flugblätter*, F. Mon. 2632, 2698. These were actually dropped from airplanes over Munich and the surrounding area.

[16] In Bamberg Hoffmann released the list of a new cabinet which excluded the Independents and, of course, all radicals. *Schulthess*, 1919/I, 187. But within Munich the SPD was badly divided: a vote among the approximately 20,000 party members in the capital, of which barely a third participated, showed only a slight plurality against cooperation with the soviet regime. The vote was reported as 3507-3479 in *MP*, 12-13 Apr. 1919, No. 86.

a technical act of secession, and President Friedrich Ebert telegraphed instructions to Prime Minister Hoffmann which left no doubt as to Berlin's intentions. Pointing out that the French government had "offered" to send in troops and had threatened to cut off the supply of foodstuffs entirely unless order was maintained in Germany, Ebert was caustic and blunt:

As we wish to admit Entente troops under no circumstances and [as] the flow of provisions cannot be allowed to stop, I consider it necessary that the restoration of the former condition in Bavaria be accomplished as soon as possible, especially since, according to reports recently received by me from Munich, people are beginning to grow accustomed to the soviet regime there. If the economic measures which you have in prospect do not succeed in short order, a military procedure seems to be the only possible solution. Experience in other places has taught that the quicker and the more thoroughly this is accomplished, the less resistance and bloodshed are to be expected.[17]

For their part, Hoffmann and Ernst Schneppenhorst (still the Minister for Military Affairs in the Bamberg cabinet) wished to deal with Munich without calling in outside help, so as to maintain what was left of Bavaria's autonomy. They had three possible courses of action and, instead of choosing among them, they pursued all three at once. First, they could blockade Munich, stopping all railway traffic and the supplies of food, milk, and coal upon which the city was dependent for survival. But to starve out the soviet regime had the double disadvantage of losing precious time and threatening the existence of thousands of innocent people. Hoffmann consequently vacillated—halting, resuming, finally

---

[17] "Reichspräsident Ebert an Legationssekretär Jordan," 11 Apr. 1919. Reprinted in *Ursachen und Folgen vom deutschen Zusammenbruch 1918 und 1945 bis zur staatlichen Neuordnung Deutschlands in der Gegenwart* (8 vols.; Berlin, 1958-1963), III, 126.

halting again (when he learned that they were being used primarily to provision the Red Army) the shipments of essential foodstuffs to the capital.[18] Secondly, there was the possible course of a military assault. Despite the severe criticism of his part in the initiation of the Munich regime, Schneppenhorst had refused to resign and, supported by Hoffmann, he now sent out urgent appeals through northern Bavaria for armed volunteers. For all his efforts, he was able to gather a force of barely 8000 men by mid-April, whereas the Red Army was rumored (falsely) to have a strength of more than 25,000. It was uncertain, moreover, how reliable his men would prove when actually required to fire upon their fellow Bavarians, whatever the political justification.[19]

The third course was negotiation. Through agents in Munich Hoffmann was able to make contact with a few members of the *Zentralrat* who were known to be receptive and who feared that a Communist coup d'état would make civil war unavoidable. But this course was apparently blocked on April 8 when Ernst Niekisch resigned his chairmanship after announcing that the situation was "untenable."[20] His reluctant successor was Ernst Toller, at the age of twenty-five still unknown as a poet and inexperienced as a politician. Intense and idealistic, Toller had supported the Soviet Republic from the outset and now officially led it, in the genuine (and later regretted) conviction that he did not have the right "to leave the masses in the lurch."[21] Before Toller

---

[18] Leaflets bearing Hoffmann's explanation for the resumption of the blockade were dropped from the air. "An die Münchener Bevölkerung," *Flugblätter*, F. Mon. 2647.

[19] "Bayern! Volksgenossen!" *Flugblätter*, F. Mon. 2676. "Verzeichnis aller der Bayer. Verbände, Freiwilligen Formationen, Volkswehrverbände usw.," BHS Munich, Abt. IV, II Mob. 10, Bd. I. The hard core of the Red Army was officially estimated at a maximum of 10,000. *Darstellungen aus den Nachkriegskämpfen*, IV, 48-52.

[20] Niekisch, *Gewagtes Leben*, 73-76.

[21] Toller, *Eine Jugend in Deutschland*, 145-146. Toller was later to dramatize his experience in *Masse Mensch. Ein Stück aus der*

could be sounded out, the Revolutionary *Zentralrat* was dissolved and the political situation in Munich was drastically changed by Hoffmann's decision to attempt direct military action.

April 13 was Palm Sunday. Before dawn a detachment of the Republican Security Troops broke into the Wittelsbach Palace and arrested several members of the *Zentralrat* quartered there, among them Erich Mühsam and Franz Lipp. It was the kind of putsch-attempt for which Munich was to become famous, in which success would depend on the uncertain threat rather than the immediate presence of great armed strength. In Ingolstadt Ernst Schneppenhorst was standing by with six hundred men, awaiting word that the capital had been taken from within before moving in to secure its "liberation." He and Prime Minister Hoffmann had made this arrangement with Alfred Seyfferitz, who probably had no more than a few hundred reliables among his Security Troops inside of Munich, but who had agreed to make the first move against the soviet regime. By mid-morning a fresh layer of placards pasted on the neighborhood kiosks announced that the *Zentralrat* was deposed and urged the populace to avoid "starvation [and] civil war" by restoring the Hoffmann government.[22] Sunday strollers prudently stayed away from downtown Munich when word was passed for soviet supporters to gather on the Theresienwiese that afternoon. Automobiles with armed soldiers packed inside and on the running boards moved through the streets. At three o'clock there was a fit of wild shooting on the Marienplatz, in front of the *Rathaus*: though several were wounded, the first fatality of the day was a sailor struck while playing billiards on the second floor of a nearby restaurant. An hour later a crowd carrying rifles,

---

sozialen Revolution des 20. Jahrhunderts (Potsdam, 1921). See Walter H. Sokel, *The Writer in Extremis. Expressionism in Twentieth Century German Literature* (Stanford, 1959), 196-201.

[22] "An das arbeitende Volk!" *Flugblätter*, F. Mon. 248.

grenades, and a red flag began moving from the Theresienwiese toward the center of the city—they were led by uni-
formed soldiers of the First Infantry Regiment, contradict-
ing Seyfferitz's claim that "the entire Munich garrison" was
united against the soviet regime. The Republican Security
Troops had meanwhile taken up positions around the main
railway terminal, behind barricades and windows overlooking
the Bahnhofplatz. They still hoped that reinforcements would
soon arrive from Ingolstadt, not knowing that their courier
had been captured while attempting to cross the lines of the
Red Army north of Munich. Shortly after four o'clock the
battle began and lasted into the evening. By nine o'clock no
help had arrived and the terminal fell to the attackers, as the
Security Troops escaped through the rear by train or scattered
into the city. The total casualties numbered more than twenty
dead and a hundred wounded. The Soviet Republic had survived; it was now a question of who would dominate it.[23]

Communist Rule and Civil War

In another part of the city, where the final shots in the
evening were barely audible, the answer was already being
determined. Hidden from the main avenues in the twisting
streets behind the Munich *Rathaus*, the Hofbräuhaus became
that night for the first time a landmark in Bavarian politics.
A meeting in the main hall downstairs was being conducted
by Eugen Leviné. The men seated before him at the long
wooden tables had voted to constitute themselves the Factory
and Soldiers' Councils of Munich (*Betriebs- und Soldatenräte
Münchens*). Their intention was to be the *de facto* legislature
of the Bavarian Soviet Republic, and to make the Hofbräuhaus the parliament building of the soviet regime. As the
Council of Workers and Soldiers had elected Kurt Eisner its

[23] "Der dritte Stoss der bayerischen Revolution," *BSZ*, 30 Apr.
1919, Nos. 98-111. Siegert, *Aus Münchens schwerster Zeit*, 59-63.
See Gerstl, "Die Eintagsdiktatur der Münchener Garnison am 13.
April 1919," *Politische Zeitfragen*, 1919, XXV-XXIX, 359-363.

chairman in the Mathäserbräu and then acclaimed him the Prime Minister over five months before, this new council assembly now made Leviné the chairman of a four-man *Vollzugsrat* and thereby the chief executive of the Soviet Republic. His leadership was to represent "the genuine rule of the proletariat." For the Communists this was the moment they had prophesied, when the Bavarian proletariat "realized that it must also struggle like its Russian brothers and that this struggle is unavoidable. . . ." As the new regime announced: "Finally today Bavaria has also erected the dictatorship of the proletariat. . . . The sun of world revolution has risen! Long live the world revolution! Long live the Bavarian Soviet Republic! . . . Long live Communism!"[24] This was April 13, 1919, in Munich.

In assuming control of the Soviet Republic in Bavaria, Leviné was clearly defying orders from Communist Party headquarters in Berlin to avoid armed action "even when a local or momentary success might be possible." To be sure the situation had not been of his own making, but it was now of his choosing. An actual military struggle became unavoidable only after Leviné decided that it must be so, a decision based on unwillingness rather than inability to surrender a hopeless position. Defeat, not struggle, was unavoidable. Leviné's success was only local, and it could be—as the Communist leaders themselves recognized from the outset—only momentary. Leviné had already said, in refusing to support the "pseudo" Soviet Republic, that Bavaria could not hope to "maintain itself independently for a long time," and this was all the more true of the territory now isolated below the Danube, which was incapable of feeding or supporting itself

[24] "Proletarier! Soldaten! Kämpfer!" *Flugblätter*, F. Mon. 2643. "An die Arbeiter und Soldaten von München und ganz Bayern," *Mitteilungen des Vollzugsrats der Betriebs- und Soldatenräte*, 15 Apr. 1919, No. 2. The formal procedure in the Hofbräuhaus was the election by the Factory and Soldiers' Councils of an Action Committee which, in turn, then appointed the *Vollzugsrat*.

319

for more than a few weeks at most. If the Munich workers had (as the KPD claimed) somehow gained a new stature and maturity by storming the main railway terminal that day, they had not been able to change the military, economic, and political facts. These are the criteria by which the Communist rule must be judged.[25]

Militarily the Bavarian Soviet Republic would stand or fall on the strength of its own Red Army. Hungary had been invaded by Rumanian troops on April 10, and Russia was still locked in civil war. The Austrian *Volkswehr* was able to rout a Communist uprising in Vienna on April 18, an incident which ended any immediate possibility of a soviet republic there and sobered the leaders of Austrian Social Democracy.[26] Northern Germany was (as Leviné had admitted a week before) securely held by the Free Corps, and the other states of southern Germany were unanimous in their support of the exiled government in Bamberg. When a detachment of the Bavarian Red Army was able to wrest Dachau from an advanced patrol of "White" soldiers on April 16, therefore, it was hardly justified for the *Vollzugsrat* in Munich to claim a "great victory" and to assure the populace that there was "no military danger." Nor did it make good sense, then or subsequently, for Communist leaders to castigate the commander of the Red forces at Dachau, Ernst Toller, for not following up a tactical advantage from a strategically untenable position.[27]

The precise number of armed men enrolled and equipped in the Red Army during the fortnight after April 13 cannot be established, and it is doubtful that the commander-in-

[25] An explanation of the Communist position was printed as "Von der Scheinräte-Republik—zur Diktatur des Proletariats," *Mitteilungen*, 15 Apr. 1919, No. 1.

[26] Bauer, *The Austrian Revolution*, 105-106.

[27] "Sieg der Roten Armee! Dachau genommen!" *Bekanntmachungen*, F. Mon. 3353. "An die Bevölkerung Münchens," *Mitteilungen*, 17 Apr. 1919, No. 4. *Darstellungen aus den Nachkriegskämpfen*, IV, 32-38. See Beyer, *Von der Novemberrevolution*, 120.

chief, a twenty-six year old sailor named Rudolf Egelhofer, ever knew himself. Only eight hundred rifles had been issued under the first soviet regime, but it was not for lack of available arms. Egelhofer promised a rifle to any who would volunteer to carry one, and it has been variously estimated that between ten and twenty thousand weapons were passed out to men who thereby received an advance of ten days' salary. The number of guns ever actually used in the defense of Munich was certainly much less, since the defections were to be numerous, particularly after the hopelessness of the Red cause became common knowledge in the last days of April. Despite Egelhofer's energetic preparations and urgent pleas that all units and their elected leaders be registered at Red Army headquarters and assigned from there, an effective force of resistance was never organized.[28]

The odds were, in any case, to be incontestably in favor of the attacking forces. After the failure of the Palm Sunday Putsch, the Hoffmann regime felt that there was no longer any alternative to a large-scale assault on Munich. On April 14 Hoffmann sent out an appeal for the formation of "a genuine *Volkswehr*" and announced that he had accepted an offer of assistance from the Württemberg Free Corps. His confidence that the entire military operation could be successfully directed from Bamberg was dashed by the humiliating news from Dachau, where a disturbing number of White soldiers declined a serious engagement; he was forced to re-

[28] Egelhofer (sometimes spelled Eglhofer) had come to Munich after taking part in the mutiny at Kiel. It was he who had presented radical demands for the proclamation of a soviet republic to the council congress on February 24 (see above, Chapter IX). After April 13 he was made Commandant of Munich and then the military chief of the Soviet Republic. His first official instructions were issued on April 16 as "Proletarier aller Länder, Vereinigt Euch!" *Bekanntmachungen*, F. Mon. 3350. The pay scale of the Red Army was released in a communiqué, "An das klassenbewusste Proletariat!" *MRF*, 26 Apr. 1919, No. 27. See Beyer, *Von der Novemberrevolution*, 97-100.

nege on his earlier boast that "Bavaria needs no outside help" by notifying Berlin of the need for reinforcements. Gustav Noske promptly authorized 20,000 troops to move into Bavaria, of which 7500 were actually to arrive. The Württemberg contingent numbered 3750, and the *Volkswehr* and Free Corps recruited in northern Bavaria (though not entirely comprised of Bavarians) totaled about 22,000—bringing the strength of the fully-equipped invading forces to nearly 35,000 men.[29] For the service of this army Hoffmann paid a price: the supreme command was placed in the hands of the Prussian General von Oven. In a clipped, correct military style Noske gave explicit instructions on April 23: "The operational objective is Munich. In Munich the power of the legally constituted Bavarian regime is to be restored. . . . As soon as Munich is occupied and the resistance in Munich is extinguished, the Bavarian General von Möhl is to assume command in Munich."[30] With that—granted the determination of the Red Army to resist—a military struggle became indeed unavoidable, and the outcome lay beyond the slightest doubt.

The economic condition of the second Soviet Republic was prescribed by its military position. There were few provisions and no prospect of obtaining more. Hoffmann's blockade, except when temporarily relaxed to allow shipment of milk and perishable goods, was virtually total. Nor were the

[29] "Stärkenachweisung der an den 'Unternehmung gegen die Aufständischen in München' 1919 beteiligten Freiwilligenverbände nach dem Stande der ersten Maitage," BHS Munich, Abt. IV, Karton 8. Beyer, *Von der Novemberrevolution*, 120, sets the total strength of the Red Army at 30,000 and the invading forces at 60,000. Both figures are exaggerated.

[30] "Direktive des Reichswehrministers Noske für die Truppenführung im Kampf um München," *Darstellungen aus den Nachkriegskämpfen*, IV, 213-215. Published by the Kriegsgeschichtliche Forschungsanstalt des Heeres, this is the authoritative volume on the military operations.

Bavarian peasants at all disposed to aid the Munich regime, despite an appeal from the *Vollzugsrat* which conveniently offered them a philosophy of history: "Peace and order exist everywhere, and everyone knows that the historical development necessarily leads to a council system, that this development cannot be arrested, that every reasonable man will accommodate himself to it."[31] The day-to-day regulations issued by the *Vollzugsrat* did not always indicate the same confidence in reason: it was declared an act of "sabotage against the Soviet Republic" to churn milk into butter or cheese. By April 25 it had become necessary to forbid milk to all but those certified by a physician to be in immediate danger of death.[32] Other stocks of food and of fuel were approaching depletion. Every single delivery of coal required the direct authorization of the *Vollzugsrat*, the highest organ of administrative authority in the soviet state. Since the general strike begun on April 14 did not end unil nine days later, such industry as there was in Upper Bavaria remained stalled from the first week in April until the last; there was therefore no actual production for the entire period of the Soviet Republic. Without coal the factories could not have functioned anyway. Plans to rationalize the economy were neither agreed upon nor, of course, executed.[33]

The practical measures taken by the soviet regime were so circumscribed in time and scope as to be inconsequential, except as they provoked a falling-out between the Commu-

[31] "An die Bauernschaft des baierischen Landes," *Mitteilungen*, 17 Apr. 1919, No. 4.

[32] "An die Molkereien und Milchhändler!" and "Milch-Versorgung!" *Bekanntmachungen*, F. Mon. 3352, 3380.

[33] "Kohlenlieferung," *Mitteilungen*, 17 Apr. 1919, No. 4. "Sitzung vom 23.IV.1919 im Wittelsbacher Palais zwischen der alten u. neuen Wirtschaftskommission, der bayerischen Verwertungsstelle für Heeresgut und Kriegswucheramt," BHS Munich, ASR 2. The best study of this subject is the thesis of Ludwig Reiners, *Die wirtschaftlichen Massnahmen der Münchener Räteregierung und ihre Wirkungen* (diss.; Tübingen, 1920).

nist and non-Communist radicals in Munich and achieved for both the hostility of most of the city's population. Because of the blockade, the *Vollzugsrat* found it necessary to order the confiscation of all available foodstuffs in the city. This resulted in the entering and searching of private homes by groups of armed men, and permitted thefts and violations of privacy which the regime (though it tried) was helpless to control. If the confiscations were an understandable and, therefore, not altogether unpopular measure (as when a certain countess was reported to be hoarding a bathtub full of eggs), most of the food obtained was consigned to provision the Red Army and never reached the population at large.[34]

Maintaining the Red Army was also the source of the regime's other most serious economic problem: an acute shortage of negotiable currency. To pay an advance averaging about 150 marks to 10,000 volunteers would have required an immediate outlay of 150,000 marks—and this does not begin to calculate the other military and administrative expenses of the government. To secure the needed money, the *Vollzugsrat* first requested citizens to deposit all cash against credit slips, then ordered all private safes and safety deposit boxes opened, finally threatened to force open the vaults of the Munich banks. The net income from these measures was barely 50,000 marks. The regime thereupon placed an order with a paper firm in Dachau to print several million marks in emergency notes of the Bavarian State Bank which—even though they had technically lapsed on April 1—were declared still to be legal tender in Munich. This might render the Soviet Republic monetarily solvent, but it was an admission of economic bankruptcy.[35]

---

[34] "Verfügung über Beschlagnahmen," *Bekanntmachungen*, F. Mon. 3253. "Sitzung der Wirtschaftskommission vom 19.IV.1919," BHS Munich, ASR 2. "Der dritte Stoss der bayerischen Revolution," *BSZ*, 30 Apr. 1919, Nos. 98-111.

[35] "An alle Schrankfachinhaber (Saves)," "Das Papiergeldhamstern ist ein kapitalistisches Verbrechen," and "Gutscheine der Bayer. Staatsbank," *Bekanntmachungen*, F. Mon. 3354, 3356, 3260. Contrast

By the end of Easter Week, then, it was becoming evident to everyone acquainted with the facts that the Soviet Republic was neither economically viable nor militarily defensible. The result, as inevitable as anything can be, was the political collapse of the Communist regime. Opposition to "the Russians," Leviné and Levien, had been mounting since April 13. Much of it was attributable to the calumny against "foreigners and Jews" which had earlier worried Kurt Eisner, but some it it grew from disagreement on specific military and economic measures. Ernst Toller had already had at least two serious altercations with Leviné; after one of them he was briefly detained under virtual arrest but, being the "liberator of Dachau" and the closest thing to a genuine hero among the soviet leaders, he was released and allowed to continue his military command. For a time Toller persisted in believing that he could not in good conscience desert "the cause of the proletariat." He stated publicly that the differences within the regime were "not at all of a basic nature," and he even claimed that "the battle will be fought victoriously to a conclusion."[36] But he soon had second thoughts as to how the proletariat might best be served, and he openly defied instructions from Egelhofer that the prisoners taken at Dachau be shot. When his troops were then ordered to withdraw to new defensive positions on the outskirts of Munich, he returned to the capital on April 21 to protest the military strategy, and to argue that negotiations with Hoffmann should be attempted in case there was still a possibility of avoiding civil war.[37]

In Munich Toller found that opposition to the Communists

the accounts of Kolb, *Die Arbeiterräte in der deutschen Innenpolitik*, 353-356, and Beyer, *Von der Novemberrevolution*, 98-100, 104-110. Reiners concludes that "the entire strength of the Communist soviet regime was exhausted in the attempt to remedy this shortage of currency." *Die wirtschaftlichen Massnahmen*, 114.

[36] "An das werktätige Volk," *Mitteilungen*, 17 Apr. 1919, No. 4. "An das Proletariat!" *Bekanntmachungen*, F. Mon. 3339.

[37] Toller, *Eine Jugend in Deutschland*, 154-180.

was also developing among the Factory and Soldiers' Councils which had been meeting daily at the Hofbräuhaus. The leader of this defection was Emil Männer, a young bank clerk who had been pressed into service as the Commissioner of Finance. Männer's objections were both personal and political: he heartily disliked the man assigned by Leviné to "consult" in his bureau, a Russian émigré named Towia Axelrod, and he considered the appropriation of bank vaults to be "political theft." Together, Toller and Männer presented their grievances and challenged the Communist leaders at a council session in the Hofbräuhaus on Saturday, April 26. They brought three major charges. The first was that Leviné refused to consider negotiations with Hoffmann at a time when conciliation might still be possible and might save the Munich workers from terrible carnage. The second was that the Communists had purposely and irresponsibly kept the economic as well as military facts from the people. Männer recited the statistics: meats, fats, and staples could last but a few days more; the coal shortage would force a closure of bakeries and breweries within five days, leaving an additional 40,000 unemployed and the entire population underfed; and the Soviet Republic could survive financially (it is not certain whether he was being facetious) only so long as the Red Army could defend the paper mill at Dachau.[38]

The third charge was frankly emotional: that "the present regime was," in Toller's words, "a calamity for the working people of Bavaria." His accusation was that Leviné and Levien had made all too effective use of their Russian passports to gain their way with the radical leaders in Munich. "The great feat of the Russian Revolution lends to these men a magic luster. Experienced German Communists stare at them as if dazzled. Because Lenin is a Russian, they are assumed to have his ability. 'In Russia we did it differently'— this phrase upset every decision."

[38] "Aus der Betriebsräte-Versammlung," *BSZ*, 30 Apr. 1919, Nos. 98-111.

Within a few hours the substance of Toller's allegation, in still more explicit language, was set to print: "With each action it is not questioned whether it suits the situation of our special circumstances, the views of the great mass of our working people, the cares for our present and future; but only whether it conforms to the teachings of Russian Bolshevism, whether Lenin and Trotsky in a similar instance would react thus or thus. . . . *We Bavarians are not Russians. . . .*"[39] Despite vigorous denials and counter-accusations of cowardice by Levien and Leviné, the Hofbräuhaus "parliament" met again on Sunday and returned a vote of no-confidence to the *Vollzugsrat*. The two Communist leaders and thirty-five members of their regime thereupon resigned. On April 27, after just two weeks in power, the "real" Soviet Republic was apparently at an end.[40]

If politics were only a matter of votes and sweet reason, civil war conceivably might yet have been averted. In the Hofbräuhaus a new leadership was elected and a new effort was undertaken to open negotiations with Bamberg. But it was hopeless. Hoffmann was in no position to offer terms even if he had wished to: acting under instructions from Berlin, he notified Munich that there was no alternative to "unconditional surrender" and demanded that all soviet leaders surrender themselves for immediate arrest.[41] Nor could Ernst Toller comply: below the Danube he controlled neither the populace, the Communists, nor the Red Army. In the final days of April the decisive voice was that of Rudolf Egelhofer:

[39] "Die Lage," *NZ*, 30 Apr. 1919, No. 100. "Einigkeit des Proletariats," *Mitteilungen*, 29 Apr. 1919, No. 15. Toller, *Eine Jugend in Deutschland*, 183-184.
[40] "Vom Tage," *MRF*, 29 Apr. 1919, No. 29. See the interpretation critical of Toller and Männer by Beyer, *Von der Novemberrevolution*, 121-127.
[41] *Schulthess*, 1919/I, 200-202. Toller, *Eine Jugend in Deutschland*, 186-187.

The Red Army was not founded as an instrument of politics but as an organ for the defense of the dictatorship of the proletariat and of the Soviet Republic against the counter-revolution of the White Guard. In accordance with this assignment, the General Command declares that it will defend the revolutionary proletariat—whatever the cost may be—against the White Guard, and will not allow itself to be forced into a betrayal of the social revolution by any faction, not even by the Factory Councils.[42]

The streets were blockaded, the barracks and public buildings were fortified, and the Red Army ruled in Munich.

So far as the Communist leaders were concerned—and they unquestionably influenced if they did not in fact dictate Egelhofer's decision—there could be no peaceful resolution. For them negotiation was surrender, and surrender would be a betrayal of what they regarded as a "sacred duty." "Between heaven and hell there is no compromise, between communism and capitalism no negotiation." Misled by the visionaries of April 7, they argued, the proletariat had once more displayed its immaturity, but struggle would bring new life, new vigor, a new nobility to the working class. The battle was not lost; it could not be lost—indeed, "victory is near."[43]

To make such a statement while an overwhelmingly superior military force was already moving forward to encircle the city of Munich required a conception of the historical process which was the product of a dedicated and doctrinaire Marxism, a notion that "the wheel of history" can roll in only one direction and that it must, therefore, ultimately crush all who oppose it. For one who holds such a conception, "victory" *is* certain, whatever the outcome at a given historical moment.

---

[42] Egelhofer's statement was printed and approved by the KPD in an article denouncing the decision in the Hofbräuhaus. "Zwischen Schwäche und Verrat," *MRF*, 29 Apr. 1919, No. 29.

[43] "Arbeiter! Parteigenossen! Proletarier von ganz Deutschland!" *MRF*, 26 Apr. 1919, No. 27. "Verhandeln?" *MRF*, 28 Apr. 1919, No. 28.

"Now and then the workers are victorious, but only for a time. The real fruit of their battles lies not in the immediate result, but in the ever expanding union of the workers."[44] This was the experience of 1848; this was the lesson of the Paris Commune; this was to be—for the Communist Party in 1919—the reason for urging hundreds of Bavarians "into battle and death for communism." The Communist leaders were fully conscious of what they were doing and why. "Hard days are to come," Eugen Leviné told his wife. "One must at least have the feeling that they were unavoidable."[45] To anyone who does not share that feeling and who cannot accept the Marxist historical conception, Leviné's action must seem foolish and unjustifiably criminal.

On the first of May Lenin spoke to an immense gathering at the Red Square in Moscow: "In all nations the workers have set foot on the path of struggle with imperialism. The liberated working class is celebrating its anniversary freely and openly not only in Soviet Russia, but also in Soviet Hungary and Soviet Bavaria."[46] That same day the troops of General von Oven closed a tight ring around Munich and prepared for the final assault. There was a celebration in the city—an organized march of school children—yet for most of the day it was strangely quiet downtown, the streets almost deserted. The plan of the invaders was to wait until noon of May 2 before advancing farther, presumably so as to provide no martyrs for future May Day observances. But at that moment it was learned that ten hostages had been murdered inside Munich at the *Luitpoldgymnasium*. This was not only a wicked and futile act—it turned the civil war into a virtual slaughter.[47]

[44] Karl Marx and Friedrich Engels, *The Communist Manifesto* (New York, 1948), 18.

[45] "Weltfeiertag! Weltkampftag!" *MRF*, 30 Apr. 1919, No. 30. Rosa Leviné, *Aus der Münchener Rätezeit*, 57-58.

[46] Cited by Neubauer, *München und Moskau*, 92.

[47] A reliable account of the *"Geiselmord,"* including the names of

Some of the aroused invaders broke formation in the early evening of May 1 and began moving into the city with the avowed intention of giving it "a thorough cleansing."[48] Resistance was quickly and ruthlessly broken. Men found carrying or hiding weapons were shot without trial and often without question. On the evening of May 2 only the main railway terminal and a cluster of military barracks remained to be taken. By the next afternoon the city was quiet again and the dead numbered over six hundred.[49] The irresponsible brutality of the Free Corps continued sporadically during the next few days as political prisoners were taken and sometimes beaten or executed. Munich was finally sobered into silence on May 7 by the news that twenty-one innocent victims had

the victims, is to be found in *Schulthess*, 1919/I, 197-199. Hostages had been taken at the order of Egelhofer, who probably also ordered their execution. "Die reaktionären Plünderer und Diebe in Haft!" *Bekanntmachungen*, F. Mon. 3266. His action was opposed by Toller and publicly disavowed by the Factory and Soldiers Councils. *Eine Jugend in Deutschland*, 189-193. "Erklärung," *Bekanntmachungen*, F. Mon. 3278. See Josef Karl, *Die Schreckensherrschaft in München und Spartakus im bayr. Oberland* (Munich, 1919), 77-96.

[48] Ernst Röhm, *Die Geschichte eines Hochverräters* (Munich, 1934), 100-101. Of the several memoirs left by participants in the invasion, the most disgusting is that of Manfred von Killinger, *Ernstes und Heiteres aus dem Putschleben* (Munich, 1934), 11-28. See Waite, *Vanguard of Nazism*, 85-93. For a full account of the military operations, consult *Darstellungen aus den Nachkriegskämpfen*, IV, 101-170.

[49] "Aufruf an die Münchener Bevölkerung! Eure Stadt ist im Besitz der Regierungstruppen!" *Bekanntmachungen*, F. Mon. 3277. The number of dead is estimated at 1000 to 1200 by Friedrich Wilhelm von Oertzen, *Die deutschen Freikorps 1918–1923* (5th ed.; Munich, 1939), 346. This figure is called (without the citation of any conclusive evidence) "conservative" by Waite, *Vanguard of Nazism*, 90. But see *Darstellungen aus den Nachkriegskämpfen*, IV, 209-212; Zittel, "Rätemodell München," *op. cit.*, 42-43; and Harold J. Gordon, *The Reichswehr and the German Republic 1919–1926* (Princeton, 1957), 48-49.

been murdered when mistaken for Red soldiers.[50] What had begun on November 7 as a demonstration for international peace ended exactly six months later in the tragedy of civil war.

[50] "Meldung des Wolffschen Telegraphen-Büros über Terrorakte in München," *Ursachen und Folgen*, III, 130. More than 5000 separate legal cases were prosecuted as a result of the Soviet Republic. See Emil Julius Gumbel, *Vier Jahre politischer Mord* (Berlin-Fichtenau, 1922), 96 and passim. Of the important soviet leaders only Max Levien escaped altogether. Rudolf Egelhofer and Gustav Landauer were brutally killed without trial. Some others were more fortunate: Niekisch received a sentence of two years; Toller, five years; Hagemeister, ten years; Sauber, twelve years; Mühsam, fifteen years. In the *Geiselmord* case six men were condemned to death; seven were given fifteen years in prison. The most controversial trial was that of Eugen Leviné, who became the public symbol of the soviet regime; despite his eloquent self-defense, he was convicted of treason and executed on June 5, 1919.

CONCLUSION

THE course of revolutionary events in Bavaria, one of the more moderate and peaceful developments in Germany while Kurt Eisner was alive, became the most radical and the most violent after his death. And the conservative reaction to the revolution, initiated with the military conquest of the Soviet Republic by Free Corps troops in May of 1919, was in no German state so drastic as in Bavaria. Undoubtedly the circumstances of the Bavarian revolution provided the setting and, in part, the motivation for the emergence of National Socialism. It is doubtful, however, that a direct causal sequence can therefore be assumed: because of Eisner, the Soviet Republic; because of the Soviet Republic, a conservative reaction; because of reaction, the appearance of Nazism. In each instance the contingencies outweigh the certainties. The strongest link in the causal chain is the second; the weakest is the first. It is unfortunate that Eisner's name has generally been connected with the experience of the Soviet Republic rather than with the occurrences of his own lifetime. Not only is such a judgment unfair, it obscures what was characteristic of the hundred days of his premiership: the bloodless end of the Wittelsbach dynasty and the unsuccessful attempt to achieve a "new democracy." The sequel of the Eisner regime has too often been mistaken for the conclusions which may be drawn from a study of it.

To evaluate the history of the revolution in Bavaria it is useful to consider the principal alternatives which were presented by the success of the Munich Putsch on November 7, 1918. The Communist ambition to transfer full political and military authority to the councils of workers, soldiers, and peasants was the most extreme institutional change which the revolution might have effected. That this would in reality have been a masquerade for the domination of the Communist Party is apparent enough from the precedents set in Russia and Hungary, as well as from the brief practice of soviet government in Munich. The durability of a sovereign council system in Bavaria, however, was entirely dependent on the progress of the revolution elsewhere in Central Europe. From beginning to end the possibilities in Bavaria were circumscribed by the fact that the state was an integral part of the German nation. Given the moderate—not to say repressive—influence of Berlin, it was only a matter of time and military power before any attempt to establish soviet rule in Bavaria would be crushed. An actual act of secession (least of all under a Communist regime) had little or no support even among those "federalists" who most bitterly resented the curtailment of Bavarian autonomy at the National Assembly in Weimar. Within the state, moreover, the program of "all power to the councils" failed to gain ratification from the peasantry. The latent hostility of the countryside for the politics of the city was accentuated by the revolution, and the final withdrawal of the Red Army to a position on the perimeter of Munich was symbolic as well as strategic. As for the Communist leaders inside the capital, they were not the efficient and hard-bitten party bosses of the mid-twentieth century so much as the idealists and idealogues of the nineteenth. Leviné, Levien, and Egelhofer were men embarked on a hopeless crusade without the preparation or the prospect for a lasting success.

A second possibility was to attain some stable compromise between the council and parliamentary systems. This was the position which Eisner represented from the outset and which he abandoned only grudgingly as circumstance dictated he must. But the idea of a second legislative chamber, a *Nebenparlament* elected directly through the machinery of the councils, still remained the notion which most closely corresponded to Eisner's conception of the revolution. Tradition and innovation, management and labor, material wealth and manual power would face one another on terms of parity; and Eisner would become the arbiter, the orator, the moral conscience of the "new humanity." It was a grand design—

333

but hardly anyone favored it. Eisner's scheme demanded too much: the voluntary cooperation of radicals and conservatives, the unflagging support of the Social Democrats, an extended period of political and economic stability, and commanding leadership on the part of Eisner himself. These were all illusions, and he should have realized it even before his electoral humiliation. By doing so and by retiring immediately from office he might have averted the most violent consequences of the political polarization and economic distress. But his early resignation in itself would not have meant a resolution of the basic conflict between the interests of revolution and reaction. As it happened, the polarization was completed, Bavaria became divided into two armed camps, such attempts as were made at negotiation failed, and the result was civil war. To what extent this necessarily followed from Eisner's self-delusions one cannot say. The logic of hindsight is not *a fortiori* the logic of occurrence. Beginning with the day of Eisner's murder, February 21, any number of plausible conclusions might have been written in a work of fiction. But the happy end of a *Nebenparlament*, in any case, was surely among the least likely of them. It deserves to be counted in the venerable tradition of Utopian Socialism, but not as a missed opportunity of the 1918 revolution. Both in a noble and a pejorative sense Eisner was a naïve man, and this ought to remain as his historical epitaph.

Perhaps the most feasible institutionalization of the revolutionary impulse would have been the addition of the councils to the government as bureaucratic agencies. This was the solution publicly supported by Erhard Auer and to which Eisner was finally willing to agree. It had the double advantage, from the Majority Socialist point of view, of indulging as well as controlling the genuine enthusiasm for the council idea among the workers and soldiers and some of the peasantry. There were, however, several obvious difficulties inherent in such a policy. Like the proposal for a *Nebenparlament*, it pleased neither political extreme and invited

334

further agitation from both. If grafted to the existing bureaucracy, the council bodies would have represented an increased and possibly intolerable expense; yet if substituted for a part of the bureaucracy, they would have incurred the resistance of the functionaries replaced and created friction with those who remained—problems not insuperable but still serious in a state with an established bureaucratic tradition. In addition, it was never clear just which essential administrative functions the councils were qualified to perform, or in what sense they might exercise "control" in governmental affairs. Most council members had no training and very little experience to recommend them as civil servants. Any meaningful accommodation with the council system was therefore bound to require a considerable sacrifice of finances or of efficiency. Had the Social Democratic Party been thoroughly revolutionary in spirit, of course, the price would not have been too much to ask. Such was not the case, and the reluctance of Auer and his colleagues to press for the solution which they themselves had proposed figured importantly in its failure. As everyone knew or soon learned, the leadership of the SPD gave first priority to parliamentary procedure and consequently held the councils suspect as a threat to the authority of the party and of the trade unions to speak for the working population. If there was a lost opportunity in 1918, this was the reason for it.

The final alternative was to adopt a unicameral parliamentary system. This abolished the revolutionary councils for all practical purposes while, at the same time, preventing the restoration of the Upper House and the monarchy (which had become anomalous anyway with the inauguration of the Weimar Republic). The eventual result of the revolution, in other words, was to fulfill the major demands of the reform movement prior to 1918 and to realize its republican implications. The Bavarian constitution which was adopted on August 2, 1919, was remarkably similar in letter and spirit to the Auer-Süssheim Bill of 1917. It is tempting to accept this fact as evidence for Arthur Rosenberg's general thesis that Germany lived through an unnecessary revolution in 1918-1919, since the actual result was not significantly different from what might have been accomplished even without a political upheaval. Since 1933 it has been argued, indeed, that Germany was far the worse for its revolutionary experience, and that the most important consequence of the revolution was to create a climate of bitterness and instability which served the enemies of parliamentary democracy. Certainly it cannot be denied that the 1918 revolution was a disappointment. Yet one must add that if the revolution could not provide the German nation with a fresh start, it did afford another chance. The failure to take proper advantage of that chance belongs to the subsequent history of the Weimar Republic. The dissolution of the Republic was not predestined by the outcome of the revolution.

The Communist View of the Bavarian Revolution

IN THE part of Germany east of the Elbe interest in the events of 1918 has been particularly intense since 1945, and the publications on that subject by historians of the German Democratic Republic (DDR) may now be counted by the dozens. It has been a project impressive in its scale and organization: a small army of historians and archivists has cooperated in the classification and publication of documents, the definition of the historical issues (e.g., the influence of the Russian revolutions on events in Germany), and the writing of articles and monographs. For the special case of the revolution in Bavaria this work has been carried out by Hans Beyer, a professor of modern history at the University of Leipzig. Professor Beyer's first article, "Die bayerische Räterepublik 1919," appeared in the *Zeitschrift für Geschichtswissenschaft*, 1954, No. 2, 175-215. This was followed by a pamphlet entitled *München 1919: Der Kampf der Roten Armee in Bayern* (Berlin, 1956) and a year later by a full-scale history, *Von der Novemberrevolution zur Räterepublik in München* (Berlin, 1957). This book was acclaimed in a long review article by Helmut Kolbe (*Zeitschrift für Geschichtswissenschaft*, 1957, No. 5, 1109-1117) as "the first comprehensive Marxist work" on the Bavarian revolution. Kolbe criticizes Professor Beyer for his lack of precision in classification (was the revolution "bourgeois-democratic" or "proletarian-socialistic"?) and for his failure adequately to relate the events in Bavaria to those in the rest of Germany. The first criticism could only concern another Marxist, and the second is not entirely justified for a monograph of 142 pages. But Kolbe nowhere takes exception to Professor Beyer's interpretation of specific events, so that one may presumably regard his account as the current representative view of Communist historiography.

My purpose here, then, is to indicate the nature of my own disagreement with Professor Beyer's discussion of the revolution in Bavaria. I want to examine the treatment of particular events in his book, not to argue the validity of the historical dialectic. So far as I am aware, my own interpretation of the revolution is not "capitalistic," nor even consciously anti-Marxist, although Professor Beyer may find evidence of both. I have not, for example, praised Erhard Auer for wishing to limit the authority of the council system; I have only attempted to establish that he did so, and to evaluate what difference his attitude made in the course of the political development.

During my research I was permitted to make use of the official governmental archives in Munich. This privilege was denied to Professor Beyer, presumably for political reasons. It would therefore be gratuitous for me to insist that his work is superficial—I personally believe that all pre-1945 archives in both parts of Germany should be opened to the unrestricted examination of all scholars—but it would also be unjust and incorrect for Professor Beyer to assume that my work has been done at the behest or under the censorship of the present Bavarian government, or of any other political regime. My remarks are therefore those of one historian (admittedly not a Communist) concerning the work of another (avowedly a Communist); and my criticisms will be restricted to the use Professor Beyer has made of the sources available to him.

The coup d'état of November 7

According to Professor Beyer, the opposition of the Bavarian SPD to the strike attempt in January of 1918 had the effect that "large segments of the working class moved away from the SPD and approached the USPD." As a result the influence of the USP was "mightily strengthened." By the beginning of November, therefore, "the *Volksmassen* wanted the revolution and were determined to act. . . . The masses were determined to end the war and to overthrow the old regime" (pp. 4-8). It is erroneous in Professor Beyer's judgment for "bourgeois historians" to assert that the Wittelsbach dynasty was subverted by a small clique of men under the leadership of Kurt Eisner.

It is not clear why one must be a bourgeois historian to make such an assertion. Professor Beyer cites no evidence—and, so far as I know, none exists—which indicates that a sizable part of the working population shifted its political allegiance from the SPD to the USP after January of 1918. By concluding that the USP was "mightily strengthened" by November, Professor Beyer can portray the events following the demonstration on the Theresienwiese as if Eisner merely joined a huge crowd already bent on revolution. This thesis is sustained by omitting any mention of the march to the Guldein School and the army barracks, led by Eisner, Gandorfer, and Fechenbach. The evidence seems conclusive to me that the coup was consciously planned, in its initial stages at least, by Eisner and his close friends, and that it was not simply a spontaneous outburst of revolutionary enthusiasm by the "mass."

The peculiar use of this term is a characteristic feature of Professor Beyer's book. It is an act of personification: the masses are granted an identity and a will. We are told that they desired revolution, and that they had decided to take action. Since the bourgeoisie is presumably excluded from this category, the term "mass" must include peasants and soldiers of lower rank as well as workers. If we could, without perverting Professor Beyer's meaning, accept these elements of the Bavarian population as the "mass," we would still be far removed from a satisfactory basis for the generalizations which he makes. How has Professor Beyer been able to sample the opinion of the mass, and what evidence is there that "it" was monolithic in its reaction to events? Can it be argued that a majority of Catholic peasants wished to end the Wittelsbach dynasty? And can it be denied that most of the workers who gathered on the Theresienwiese on November 7, 1918, followed Erhard Auer and the trade union leaders in their uneventful march to the *Friedensengel*? The known facts, in my opinion, do not warrant Professor Beyer's conclusions.

The Landtag elections of January 12

The gist of Professor Beyer's explanation of the parliamentary elections is contained in this sentence: "Great masses of workers who had stood behind the USPD at the time of the [January 1918] strike and at the beginning of the November revolution were disappointed, had no more confidence [in Eisner], and shifted away from the USPD mostly to Social Democracy" (p. 22). This argument clearly continues the previous one, and furthermore rests on three judgments which Professor Beyer makes concerning the character of the Eisner regime.

A. The mass became increasingly disenchanted with Eisner's personal leadership and consequently refused to vote for the Independent Party. In Professor Beyer's view, Eisner never ceased to be a revisionist; he compromised with the bourgeoisie, so that "the type of state (*Staatstyp*) remained capitalistic. What was changed was only the form of state (*Staatsform*)" (p. 16). Eisner thereby ignored the "extraordinarily important precept" of Karl Marx that it is the duty of a revolutionary regime to break completely the power of the old military and bureaucratic system. This doctrine, Professor Beyer adds, is still valid: he notes in evidence recent statements by N. S. Khrushchev and A. J. Mikoyan. Eisner's unwillingness to take the necessary action resulted in the disunity of the working population and the defection of many voters from the USP.

After allowance is made for the difference in vocabulary, Professor Beyer's estimation of Eisner's "failure" is not unlike my own. There are at least two basic distinctions. In the first place, I do not believe that Eisner actually had much of a choice. It was not alone a matter of volition: he was never powerful enough personally nor did he ever have broad enough support politically to carry out radical reforms of the bureaucracy and the economy, even if he had passionately wished to do so. In the second place, I can see no reason for believing that there was ever a great defection of the working population from Eisner's party, because at no time did the USP command wide public support in Bavaria. Having placed the mass squarely behind (or, rather, in front of) Eisner before November 7, Professor Beyer is forced to move them away again by January 12 in order to explain how Eisner could have received only 2 per cent of the popular vote. I believe that no such shift of opinion took place, and that the USP remained throughout a small dissident faction of the SPD.

B. The mass, according to Professor Beyer, was confused and betrayed by the SPD. "In their agitation the Social Democratic leaders made use of the foulest lies and slanders" (p. 23). "The bourgeoisie relied especially on such criminal elements which—like Erhard Auer—had sunk down to the level of paid agents of the bourgeoisie, and now the entire corruption and depravity of opportunism was revealed by these traitors to the cause of the working class" (p. 38).

In the notes of my book I have occasionally referred to Professor Beyer's attacks, both personal and political, on Auer and his colleagues. I can only repeat my conclusion that the SPD was consistent in its opposition to the council system as a sovereign form of governmental authority, and that the majority of Bavarian workers and peasants (judging from the statements of their leaders in council meetings and from their own votes in the elections) were in essential agreement. I can therefore find no basis for Professor Beyer's unqualified and undocumented assertion that "the bourgeoisie and the SPD leaders well knew that the Landtag elections were in no way an expression of the real feeling of the masses" (pp. 29-30).

C. Professor Beyer contends, moreover, that the electoral returns must be evaluated while keeping in mind the absence of a "militant Marxist-Leninist party." By January 12 the Spartacist League had been reconstituted as the KPD and had won "many workers," but it had not yet gained the allegiance of the *"Hauptmasse"* (p. 23). Thus, "the only party which really represented the interests of the working class and of all industrious classes, the KPD, did not participate in the election because of an incorrect decision at the party's founding congress" [in Berlin on the last day of December 1918] (p. 29). Unable to vote in good conscience for the USP, and not yet recognizing the KPD as its "true" representative, the mass was left with the unhappy choice between the SPD and the bourgeois parties.

The validity of Professor Beyer's interpretation apparently depends on the assumption that, had the KPD entered the election, the "mass" would have voted for it. Otherwise he is only asserting a tautology: if the people had supported the KPD, they would have indicated their support, given the chance. Either proposition fails to explain adequately why 98 per cent of the voters cast their ballots for parties openly opposed in principle to the Communist program of "all power to the councils." If there had been an unusually large percentage of abstentions in the voting, Professor Beyer's point might merit some consideration. Instead, he must fall back on the classical Marxist argument that the masses were duped and unable to see their "real" interests. Nor is there *prima-facie* evidence for accepting the notion that the real interests of the working population in Bavaria were those prescribed at that time by the KPD. Professor Beyer's interpretation of the Landtag elections may be comprehensible when seen as part of the entire Marxist scheme of historical development, but it does not rest on evidence drawn from the actual historical situation in Bavaria at the beginning of 1919.

POSTSCRIPT

Eisner's death and the second revolution

Although the SPD and the bourgeois parties contended that the elections had been an expression of the popular will, says Professor Beyer, the events which followed showed that "this could not have been the case." With the simultaneous (February 12) announcement of the *Volkswehr* and the date for the convocation of the Landtag, the SPD hoped to force the situation, but "the Munich working class saw through this maneuver . . ." (pp. 29-30). When Kurt Eisner was murdered, therefore, the true situation at last became apparent: "the masses in Munich were against the Landtag. . . . The murder of Eisner had given the impulse for large segments of the working class to go within a few hours from the SPD toward the left to the USPD and the KPD" (p. 44). The measures taken thereafter by the *Zentralrat* were "quite correct," but "they were falsely executed." The period of the second revolution was consequently a confused one, according to Professor Beyer, since the political leadership in Munich was divided, even though the workers were essentially united: "in Bavaria the council idea was at this time extremely popular among the masses. . . . Large segments of the German working class had . . . drawn the correct lesson from the example of the Russian proletariat, that the councils represented the new and most important organizational form of the proletariat in the struggle for power." The issues were thus clarified in the minds of the people, and the KPD began to gain a significant popular following. "The simplest, clearest, and only correct demand was advanced by the KPD: 'All power to the councils!' " (pp. 47-49). It was only through the threat of civil war that the congress of councils in Munich was forced to accept the Hoffmann regime on the basis of the accord reached in Nuremberg by the party leaders.

This is, I believe, an accurate summary of Professor Beyer's account. It strikes me that he is quite consistent, and his consistency requires me to repeat several of my previous questions:

A. Why should the events after February 21 be offered as evidence that the parliamentary elections of January 12 "could not have been" a genuine expression of popular opinion?

B. What evidence is there for asserting that the masses "saw through" the intentions of the SPD? Is this not again a personification? And what evidence is there for supposing that the Landtag, which had been endorsed by at least 98 per cent of the electorate in January, was opposed by the "masses" when it met in February?

C. What is the basis for concluding that there was "another" massive shift of public opinion after Eisner's death? Even if one agrees that "large segments" of the working population were shocked by the news of Eisner's assassination, what evidence is there to show that they thereupon threw their support to the USP and the KPD?

D. What is the criterion for stating that the measures of the *Zentralrat* were "correct," and what measurement has been taken to prove that the council idea was "extraordinarily popular" with the Bavarian people?

E. Even if the policy of the KPD can be said to have been simple and clear, what is the historical criterion for claiming that it was the "only correct" policy?

All of these questions refer to the same point: that Professor Beyer manipulates "the mass" without bothering to document the generalizations which he makes about it. By doing so, he is able to make it appear that the council representatives accepted the Nuremberg Accord for the sole reason that refusal would have meant civil war. Professor Beyer never considers the possibility that a majority of council members had no desire to transfer "all power to the councils," but that they preferred instead a return to parliamentary procedure. Professor Beyer's interpretation seems to follow the old principle: it *must* have been so, therefore it *was* so.

The Soviet Republic and its defeat

Professor Beyer devotes more than half of his book to events after April 7; the same period is presented by my study in a single chapter. Whereas Professor Beyer treats the Eisner regime as an unfortunate prelude to the Soviet Republic, I find that the Soviet Republic was an unfortunate postlude to the Eisner regime. And while he deals with the political maneuvers, administrative measures, and military operations of the Soviet Republic in some detail, I feel that these were all of a desperate emergency character, and that they added nothing to the theory and only a black mark to the practice of International Communism.

In Professor Beyer's view "the masses wanted and demanded the Soviet Republic" (p. 68), but as the first announcement of the Soviet Republic on April 7 was only an attempt by the SPD to discredit the idea of rule through the councils, the KPD was "correct" in refusing to join this "pseudo" Soviet Republic. The failure of the counter-revolutionary putsch on April 13 was greeted by overwhelming mass enthusiasm in Munich, however, and the KPD was impelled to join in the organization of the genuine Soviet Republic. Although the peasants did not cooperate with the new regime, in Munich "the trust of the masses for the Communist Party grew steadily" (p. 113). The policies of the KPD were unfortunately obstructed by the leaders of the USP. For example, "in the interest of historical truth and of the political practice of our present generation we can draw no positive portrait of the political and military activity of Ernst Toller in the Soviet Republic" (p. 124). The same is said by Professor Beyer of other Independents who became leaders in the Red Army: one of them (Klingelhöfer) in fact betrayed the Soviet cause by ordering a retreat, "although the situation on the front was not unfavorable . . ." (p. 128). Thereafter the Red Army was unable to withstand the superior numbers of the invading Free Corps troops: "the days of the battle from the first to the third of May are a heroic example for the audacity, the courage, and the sacrifice of the working class in the struggle against its mortal enemies, the capitalistic exploiters and their lackeys" (p. 132).

Most of what I could say in one paragraph about Professor Beyer's conclusions is already apparent, and can be illustrated by raising a single point. To make much of one Red Army officer's orders to his men to retreat is to obfuscate what was essential about the history of the Bavarian Soviet Republic: that its economic and military situation was entirely hopeless. To say that the position of the Red Army at any particular time was "not unfavorable" is simply a distortion. If it is fitting to speak of heroic sacrifice, it is also necessary to say that the sacrifice was useless. The Communist leaders, by refusing to permit capitulation, in effect sacrificed the lives of several hundred men to a conception of the historical process which demands that the working classes everywhere join against "the capitalistic exploiters and their lackeys." To me these terms seem singularly inappropriate as a description of the revolution in Bavaria. I must regard them as the expression of a belief which I do not share and for which I cannot find sufficient historical evidence in the documentation of this period.

BIBLIOGRAPHY

IT IS my purpose in this essay to review briefly the critical literature directly germane to a study of the 1918 revolution in Bavaria. There is no sense in attempting to draft a complete list of all the scholarly work devoted to the entire revolutionary period in Germany, nor would it be useful to repeat here the titles which can easily be found grouped in the notes. The general studies of Bavarian history are cited in Chapter I; a complete list of Kurt Eisner's writings accompanies Chapter II; and most of the pertinent memoirs are introduced in Chapter III. Should the specialist need an alphabetized listing of all the titles (other than those added here) used in the preparation of this book, he should consult my doctoral dissertation, "Kurt Eisner and the Question of Soviet Government in Bavaria, 1918-1919" (Harvard University, 1961). What follows, then, is a discussion of the state of research on my subject up to the time of this writing.

The fact that it is now necessary to specify the date of the "German Revolution," as it was called in the early years of the Weimar Republic, is a commentary on the failure of that event, until very recently, to sustain the curiosity of a significant number of qualified historians. No adequate synthesis of the revolutionary period has yet been conceived. Part of the explanation has obviously been the subsequent political development in Germany. Not only was the ledger closed after 1933, but the towering importance of the National Socialist era and the Second World War has tended to make the end of the *Kaiserreich* seem insignificant by comparison. And it is undoubtedly true that 1918 proved to be a much less decisive historical moment in Germany than 1789 was in France. The result is that the former has not been and may never be the subject of a life's work by a Tocqueville, an Aulard, a Mathiez, or a Lefebvre. The best general account is still to be found in the two books of Arthur Rosenberg, *Die Entstehung der Deutschen Republik* (Berlin, 1930) and *Geschichte der Deutschen Republik* (Karlsbad, 1935). These have been reprinted in a single volume as *Entstehung und Geschichte der Weimarer Republik* (Frankfurt a. M., 1955). Even Rosenberg's work suffers somewhat from the tendency, still more pronounced in later attempts at synthesis, to interpret the revolutionary movement exclusively from the standpoint of political events in Berlin. This is true both of Rudolf Coper, *Failure of a Revolution. Germany in 1918-1919* (Cambridge, 1955) and of Eric Waldman, *The Spartakist Uprising of 1919* (Milwaukee, 1958). As an episode in the international development of Socialism, the revolution in Germany has been ably set in context by Carl Landauer, *European Socialism* (2 vols.; Berkeley, 1959).

Concentrating on the most striking aspect of the revolution and basing his well-drawn conclusions on extensive documentary research (among others, in the Bavarian archives), Eberhard Kolb, *Die Arbeiterräte in der deutschen Innenpolitik 1918-1919* (Düsseldorf, 1962) has made the most significant contribution to the study of the revolution since Rosenberg. Kolb's findings, which contradict the simplistic notion of a concrete alternative in Germany between a parliamentary system and a "soviet dictatorship," have been confirmed by Peter von Oertzen, *Betriebsräte in der Novemberrevolution* (Düsseldorf, 1963). Otherwise excellent, this book is unfortunately without detailed reference to Bavaria. Such recent research now takes precedence over the essay of Walter Tormin, *Zwischen Rätediktatur und Sozialer Demokratie. Die Geschichte der Rätebewegung in der deutschen Revolution 1918/19* (Düsseldorf, 1954), which is centered on Berlin and restricted for the most part to published sources. The revolutionary councils in Bavaria have been treated in detail only by Wilhelm Mattes, *Die bayerischen Bauernräte* (Stuttgart and Berlin, 1921), a monograph begun at the suggestion and under the direction of Max Weber. Unfortunately there is no comparable study of the Bavarian councils of workers and soldiers, although the importance of that subject has been signaled by Bernhard Zittel, "Rätemodell München 1918/19," *Stimmen der Zeit*, CLXV (1959), 25-43. The research of Helmut Neubauer, *München und Moskau 1918/1919. Zur Geschichte der Rätebewegung in Bayern* (Munich, 1958), convincingly demonstrates the superficiality of direct contact between Bavaria and Leninist Russia, but the author does not pretend to supply a thorough survey of the council system. Apart from Kolb, the best narrative of council activity during the Bavarian Soviet Republic is still the unpublished manuscript of the Freiherr von Guttenberg, "Die Räteherrschaft in Bayern und ihr Ende" (1926), on file in BHS Munich, Abteilung IV. This may be supplemented by the capable dissertation of Ludwig Reiners, "Die wirtschaftlichen Massnahmen der Münchener Räteregierung" (University of Tübingen, 1920). An economic history of Bavaria which evaluates in depth the importance of the war and the revolution is yet to be written. Alois Schlögl, *Bayerische Agrargeschichte* (Munich, 1954), is competent, but the works of Otmar Emminger, *Die bayerische Industrie* (Munich, 1947) and Wolfgang Zorn, *Kleine Wirtschafts- und Sozialgeschichte Bayerns 1806-1933* (Munich, 1962) are only a minimum.

Historians of the German Democratic Republic (DDR) have displayed special interest in evaluating the impact of the Russian revolutions on Germany. Two recent and representative examples are Albert Schreiner (ed.), *Revolutionäre Ereignisse und Probleme in Deutschland während der Periode der grossen sozialistischen Oktoberrevolution 1917/1918* (Berlin, 1957) and Leo Stern (ed.), *Die Auswirkungen der grossen sozialistischen Oktoberrevolution auf Deutschland* (Berlin, 1959). An earlier account of the revolution in Bavaria by a Communist participant, Paul Werner (Paul Frölich), *Die bayerische Räterepublik. Tatsachen und Kritik* (Petrograd, 1920), has now been superseded by Hans Beyer,

Von der Novemberrevolution zur Räterepublik in München (Berlin, 1957). Professor Beyer's history is dealt with at length in the Postscript of the present study.

The literature on the political parties in Bavaria is, on the whole, not distinguished. Although infelicitously written, the best documented account of the Bavarian KPD is the doctoral dissertation of an American student, John Raatjes, "The Role of Communism during the Munich Revolutionary Period, November, 1918–May, 1919" (University of Illinois, 1958). Also intensively researched, but much too brief (less than eighty pages of text) to do justice to either term in its title, is the published thesis of Franz Schade, *Kurt Eisner und die bayerische Sozialdemokratie* (Hannover, 1961). The story of the Bavarian SPD up to 1918 is better told through the life of the party's leader by Reinhard Jansen, *Georg von Vollmar. Eine politische Biographie* (Düsseldorf, 1958). The political organization of Bavarian Catholicism has been the subject of two books and a dissertation, of which the oldest is still the most useful: Anton Pfeiffer, *Gedankenwelt und Tätigkeit der Bayerischen Volkspartei* (Munich, 1922); Friedrich Hilpert, *Die Grundlagen der bayerischen Zentrumspolitik 1918-1921* (Berlin, 1941); and Herbert Speckner, "Die Ordnungszelle Bayern. Studien zur Politik des bayerischen Bürgertums, insbesondere der Bayerischen Volkspartei" (University of Erlangen, 1955). The only attempt to treat the entire party spectrum in Bavaria is the unsatisfactory dissertation of Theo Eberle, "Die grossen politischen Parteien und die Revolution 1918/19 in München" (University of Tübingen, 1951).

Special note should be made here of the need for a reconsideration of the history of German Social Democracy during and following the revolutionary period. The background of the schism in the SPD has been expertly depicted by Carl E. Schorske, *German Social Democracy 1905-1917* (Cambridge, Mass., 1955). But the continuation of this story still depends on three dated studies, each of which ought to be replaced: A. Joseph Berlau, *The German Social Democratic Party, 1914-1921* (New York, 1949); Eugen Prager, *Die Geschichte der USPD* (Berlin, 1921); and Ossip K. Flechtheim, *Die Kommunistische Partei Deutschlands in der Weimarer Republik* (Offenbach a. M., 1948). One step in this direction has been taken by Werner T. Angress, *Stillborn Revolution. The Communist Bid for Power in Germany, 1921-1923* (Princeton, 1963). The book by Richard N. Hunt, *German Social Democracy, 1918-1933* (New Haven, 1964), unfortunately fails to meet the high standard set by Schorske and is, in any case, too thin to fill the existing gap.

Apart from Jansen's study of Vollmar and the sketch of Eisner by Schade, there is little of importance in the recent biographical literature. One may mention the family affair of Josef Held, *Heinrich Held. Ein Leben für Bayern* (Regensburg, 1958) and the two biographies dedicated to a lost cause: Joe J. Heydecker, *Kronprinz Rupprecht von Bayern. Ein Lebensbild* (Munich, 1953) and Kurt Sendtner, *Rupprecht von Wittelsbach, Kronprinz von Bayern* (Munich, 1954). One American undergraduate thesis, otherwise worthless, is valuable for the interviews which its author (a student of Flechtheim) held with several of the revolutionaries after their emigration to the United States: Harold J. Hurwitz, "The Bavarian Revolution and its Significance for the Sociology of Revolution and of National Development" (Bates College, 1946). A study of the personnel of the bureaucracy, which might be profitably extended through and beyond the revolutionary period, is by Walter Schärl, *Die Zusammensetzung der bayerischen Beamtenschaft von 1806 bis 1918* (Munich, 1955). A more elusive biographical theme is suggested by a few pertinent essays in the volume of Hans Lamm (ed.), *Von Juden in München* (Munich, 1958).

The military history of the time is adequately provided for by the publication of the Kriegsgeschichtliche Forschungsanstalt des Heeres, *Darstellungen aus den Nachkriegskämpfen deutscher Truppen und Freikorps*, IV: *Die Niederwerfung*

351

der Räteherrschaft in Bayern (Berlin, 1939). Two American scholars have added their commentary during the past decade: Robert G. L. Waite, *Vanguard of Nazism: The Free Corps Movement in Postwar Germany 1918-1923* (Cambridge, Mass., 1952) and Harold J. Gordon, *The Reichswehr and the German Republic 1919-1926* (Princeton, 1957). A detailed investigation of one of the forces which assisted in capturing Munich from the Red Army is available in the dissertation of Hans Jürgen Kuron, "Freikorps und Bund Oberland" (University of Erlangen, 1960).

Even though the question of Bavaria's relationship to the German Reich was obviously re-opened by the revolution, that subject is far from exhausted, as is indicated by the recent anthology of Otto Schlottenloher (ed.), *Bayern: Staat und Kirche, Land und Reich* (Munich, n.d.). The theme of the dissertation by Jenny Feil, "Bayerischer Separatismus der Eisner-Zeit" (University of Munich, 1939), is intriguing, but the work needs to be done again. Several earlier analyses of the constitutional problems raised by the revolution have been summarized and augmented by Werner Gabriel Zimmermann, *Bayern und das Reich 1918-1923* (Munich, 1953). Zimmermann admits that he was unable, because of the wealth of material available, to carry his work on to 1933 as he had intended. Written from a Catholic and mildly particularist bias, which leads the author to stress the role of the Bavarian People's Party, the only general treatment to date of Bavaria's place in German affairs during the entire Weimar period is that of Karl Schwend, *Bayern zwischen Monarchie und Diktatur* (Munich, 1954).

The title of Schwend's book suggests one final problem which is just beginning to attract the detailed scholarly research it requires: the consequences of the revolutionary period in Bavaria for the development of National Socialism. A general statement on the subject was made some time ago by Alan Bullock, *Hitler: A Study in Tyranny* (London, 1952; rev. ed., New York, 1964). The latest attempt to amplify this, however, has misfired: the study of Georg Franz-Willing, *Die Hitlerbewegung: Der Ursprung 1919-1922* (Hamburg, 1962), is wrongheaded and occasionally erroneous. The documentary basis for an investigation of this subject is certainly not lacking: witness the volume published by Ernst Deuerlein (ed.), *Der Hitler-Putsch. Bayerische Dokumente zum 8./9. November 1923* (Stuttgart, 1962). But at present one must still turn to the professional journals: Carl Landauer, "The Bavarian Problem in the Weimar Republic, 1918-1923," *Journal of Modern History*, XVI (1944), 93-115, 205-223; Heinz Gollwitzer, "Bayern 1918-1933," *Vierteljahrshefte für Zeitgeschichte*, III (1955), 363-387; Georg Franz, "Munich: Birthplace and Center of the National Socialist German Workers' Party," *Journal of Modern History*, XXIV (1957), 319-334; Ernst Deuerlein, "Hitlers Eintritt in die Politik und die Reichswehr," *Vierteljahrshefte für Zeitgeschichte*, VII (1959), 179-185; and Reginald H. Phelps, "Hitler and the *Deutsche Arbeiterpartei*," *American Historical Review*, LXVIII (1963), 974-986.

LIST OF DOCUMENTS AND OFFICIAL
PAPERS CITED

UNPUBLISHED SOURCES

I. BAYERISCHES GEHEIMES STAATSARCHIV, MUNICH

A. *Politisches Archiv VII. Reihe* (cited as PA VII)

71. Gründung der Republik, 1918 (Nov.-Dez.)
72. Grenzverkehr, Passwesen, Zuzug, 1918 (Dez.)–1919 (März)
73—78. Korrespondenz Eisners und seines Privatsekretärs Fechenbach, 1918 (Nov.)–1919 (März)
79. Presse, besonders Eisners Beziehung hiezu, 1918 (Nov.)– 1919 (Feb.)
80. Unterricht und Kultus, 1918 (Nov.)–1919 (März)
81. Warenversorgung Deutschlands und Nahrungsmittelfrage, 1918 (Dez.)–1919 (Apr.)
82. Wissenschaft und Kunst, 1918 (Dez.)–1919 (Feb.)
83. Zollwesen, 1918, 12.XI
84. Provisorisches Parlament, Nationalversammlung, 1918 (Dez.)–1919 (Jan.)
85. Reichsverfassung, 1918 (Dez.)
86. Justizwesen, 1918 (Nov.)–1919 (Feb.)
87. Polizeiwesen, Polizeistunde, Schutzbriefe, 1918 (Nov.)– 1919 (Jan.)
88. Bank- und Kreditwesen, 1919 (Jan.)
89. Finanz- und Rechnungswesen, 1919 (Jan.-Feb.)
90. Kriegswesen, Waffenstillstand, Demobilmachung, Friedens-schluss, 1918 (Nov.)–1919 (Jan.)
91. Landwirtschaft, 1919
92. Gewerbewesen, Industrie, 1918-1919
93. Armenwesen und Wohltätigkeit, 1918-1919
94. Beamtenfrage, Beamtenpolitik, 1918-1919
95. Eisner bzw. Fechenbach, deren Entwürfe amtlicher Schreiben, 1918-1919
96. Drucksachen und Aufrufe von 7 deutschen Hochschulen über das Selbstbestimmungsrecht von Elsass-Lothringen, 1918 (Nov.)

97. *Korrespondenz* des Min. Rates von Stockhammern mit Dr. Merkle, 1919

98. Amtliche Korrespondenz des bayer. Gesandten bei der tschechoslowakischen Republik, Prof. Dr. Weiss, in Prag, 1918

99. Korrespondenz auch in Regierungsangelegenheiten von Dr. Merkle, 1919

100. Politische Berichte bayer. Gesandtschaft in Berlin, 1918-1919

101. Räterepublik (Dr. Lipp), Telegramme, 1919 (Apr.)

102. Telegramme verschiedenen Inhalts vom 9.11.1918-27.2.1919

103. Dienstliche Papiere aus der Regierungstätigkeit Eisners

104. Ministerratsangelegenheiten u.a., 1918 (Nov.)-1919 (Feb.)

104a. Ministerratsprotokolle, 9.11.1918-18.1.1919

105. Verhältnis zwischen Bayern und Reich, 1918 (Nov.)-1919 (Jan.)

106. Beziehungen zum Ausland, 1918 (Nov.)-1919 (Feb.)

107. Berichte der bayer. Gesandtschaft in Wien an den bayer. Ministerpräsidenten, 1918 (Nov.)-1919 (Feb.)

108. Bern, bayer. Gesandtschaft, 1918 (Nov.)-1919 (Feb.)

109. Die bei Fechenbach aufgefundenen und vom Gericht an das bayer. Staatsministerium d. Aeuss. übermittelten Akten, welche Eisner aus dem bayer. Min. d. Aeussern entnommen hatte

110. Privatklage Fechenbach, Felix, Kaufmann in Halle gegen Dr. Paul Nikolaus Crossmann, Professor in München und Genossen wegen Beleidigung (Fälschung eines Gesandtschaftberichtes Juli 1914), 1922

111. Fechenbach, Entwendung politischer Aktenstücke durch denselben, 1920-1935

112. Kriegsschuldfrage, 1919

113. Varia, 1915-1928

114. Briefschaften des ehem. russischen Gesandten von Isvolsky (1914, in dessen Villa in Egern a. Teg. beschlagnahmt)

115. Nachlass Eisner (3 Akten) [See p. 154, n. 15]

B. *Grassmann Nachlass* (cited as GN)

1. Protokolle der Ministerratssitzungen vom 14.11.18 bis 25.2.1919. Kurzschriftliche Aufzeichnungen Grassmanns. 118 Blätter

BIBLIOGRAPHY

2/1—2/2. Protokolle der Ministerratssitzungen vom 14.11.18 bis 25.2.1919. Uebertragungen der kurzschriftlichen Aufzeichnungen Grassmanns. 741 Seiten.

3. Protokolle der Ministerratssitzungen vom 9.11.18 bis 18.2.1919. Ausgearbeitete Texte, handschriftl. Entwürfe Grassmanns u. Reinschriften. Gelegentl. Beilagen.

4. Darstellung der Zeitereignisse vom 2.XI.1918 bis 16.XI. 1918. Kurzschriftl. Aufzeichnungen Grassmanns.

5. Zur Geschichte der Revolution. Zeitungsausschnitte, Nov. 1918–Nov. 1922. Einige sonstige Drucksachen.

6. Provisorischer Nationalrat 12.XII.1918–10.II.1919. Drucksachen, haupts. "Stenographische Berichte" u. "Beilagen."

7. Aufsatz Grassmanns über Kurt Eisner für *Deutsches Biographisches Jahrbuch*:

   A. Handschriften Grassmanns, 1927
   B. Kurzschriftliche Aufzeichnungen Grassmanns zur Sache
   C. Würdigung Eisners durch den Schweinfurter Bürgermeister Dr. Merkle, 21.V.1927
   D. Würdigung Eisners durch den Chefredakteur der Münchener Post E. Auer, 4.VI.1927

8. Die von Eisner eingesetzte Kommission zum Entwurf einer bayer. u. einer Reichsverfassung, 1918-1919

9. Vorläufiges Staatsgrundsetz des Freistaates Bayern, 1919

10. Entwürfe zur Verfassungsurkunde, 1918-1919

11. Verfassungsurkunde, Einzelbestimmungen, 1919

12. Verfassungsausschuss, 1918-1919

13. Unterlagen zur Verfassungs-Urkunde, 1919

14. Vollzug der Verfassung, 1919-1922

15. Verfassung des Deutschen Reiches, 1918-1919

C. M.A. 1943. Innere Verhältnisse, 1918-1933 (cited as MA 1943, I.V.)

10. Staatsverfassung

17. Die Räteregierung

62. Ministerium für soziale Fürsorge

135. Wochenberichte der Regierungspräsidenten, 1919

377. Korrespondenz des Ministerpräsidenten Kurt Eisner, Band I, 1918

356

BIBLIOGRAPHY

378. Korrespondenz des Ministerpräsidenten Kurt Eisner, Band II, 1919

467. Ministerpräsident Kurt Eisner u. dessen Personal

II. BAYERISCHES HAUPTSTAATSARCHIV, MUNICH

A. *Akten des Staatsministerium des Innern* (cited as M. Inn.)

54190. Die Arbeiter-, Bauern- u. Soldatenräte: Allgemeines, 1919-1921

54191. Die Arbeiter-, Bauern- u. Soldatenräte: Allgemeines, 1919-1921

54192. Wahlen der Arbeiterräte, 1919-1920

54193. Landessoldatenrat, 1919-1921

54194. Kreisarbeiterräte, 1919-1920

54195. Zentralrat geistiger Arbeiter, 1918-1920

54196. Umbildung des Bayer. Staates; hier: die Bauernräte, 1919-1926

54197. Kosten der Arbeiter-, Bauern- u. Soldatenräte, 1919-1923

54198. Räterepublik: Entwurf eines Rätegesetzes

54199. Umbildung des Bayer. Staates; hier: Arbeiter-, Soldaten- u. Bauernräte, 1918 (2.XI–31.XII)

54200. Umbildung des Bayer. Staates; hier: Arbeiter-, Soldaten- u. Bauernräte, 1919 (1.I–3.III)

54201. Umbildung des Bayer. Staates; hier: Arbeiter-, Soldaten- u. Bauernräte, Pressestimmen, 1918

54202. Die Arbeiter-, Soldaten- u. Bauernräte im Regierungsbezirke Oberbayern, 1919-1921

54203. ———— Niederbayern, 1919-1920

54204. ———— Oberpfalz u. Regensburg, 1918

54205. ———— Oberfranken, 1919-1920

54206. ———— Mittelfranken, 1919-1920

54207. ———— Unterfranken u. Aschaffenburg, 1919-1920

54208. ———— Schwaben u. Neuburg, 1919-1920

B. *Akten betref. Arbeiter- und Soldatenräte* (cited as ASR)

1. Räterepublik Bayern. Allgemeines, 1918-1919

2. Zentralrat und Vollzugsausschuss. Aemterorganisation, 1918-1919

3. Zentralrat und Vollzugsrat. Sitzungsberichte, Satzungen, 1918-1919

4. Aktionsausschuss. Sitzungsberichte, 1918-1919
5. Tagung der Arbeiter- und Soldatenräte am 13.2.19
6. Delegiertenwahlen zum Rätekongress, 16.3.19
7. Wahl der Arbeiter- und Bauernräte in den Bezirksämtern Oberbayerns, 1918-1919
8. ——— Oberbayerns, 1918-1919
9. ——— Niederbayerns, 1918-1919
10. ——— Niederbayerns, 1918-1919
11. ——— Oberfrankens, 1918-1919
12. ——— Mittelfrankens, 1918-1919
13. ——— Unterfrankens, 1918-1919
14. ——— Schwabens, 1918-1919
15. Ermordung Kurt Eisners
16. Landessoldatenrat, Militärgerichtsbarkeit, 1918-1919
17. Schulkommission, Lehrerrat, 1918-1919
18. Lebensmittelbewirtschaftung, Schleichhandel, 1918-1919
19. Verkehrsmittel, 1918-1919
20. Wirtschaftliche Demobilmachung, 1918-1919
21. Schutzhaft, Geiseln, 1918-1919
22. Gesandtschaften, Schutzbriefe, 1918-1919
23. Pressebüro des Arbeiter-, Bauern- und Soldatenrates; Kommission für Politisches; Propaganda-Kommission; Zensur, 1918-1919
24. Arbeitslose, Arbeitslosenfürsorge, 1918-1919
25. Sozialistische Arbeitsgemeinschaft, Sitzungsberichte, 1919
26. Schriftleitung der "Neuen Zeitung," München, 1919
27. Bayerischer Bauernbund, 1919
28. Kulturelle Veranstaltungen, 1918-1919
29. Beziehungen zu auswärtigen Räterepubliken; Rätekongress in Berlin, 1918-1919
30. Schriftwechsel mit den Arbeiter-, Bauern- und Soldatenräten Oberbayerns, 1918-1919
31. ——— Oberbayerns, 1918-1919
32. ——— Oberbayerns, 1918-1919
33. ——— Niederbayerns, 1918-1919
34. ——— der Oberpfalz, 1918-1919
35. ——— der Oberpfalz, 1918-1919
36. ——— Frankens, 1918-1919

BIBLIOGRAPHY

37. ———— Schwabens, 1918-1919
38. ———— der Pfalz, 1918-1919

C. *Abteilung IV* (*Kriegsarchiv*) (cited as Abt. IV)
II Mob 10, Bd. I. Volkswehr, Eiserne Schar, Republikan-
          ische Schutztruppen
X C 25q, Bd. I. Kosten anlässlich Umsturz und Räteregier-
          ung, 1918-1919
Karton 8. Verschiedenes: Revolution, Räteherrschaft

III. INTERNATIONAAL INSTITUUT VOOR SOCIALE GESCHIEDENIS,
AMSTERDAM

Kautsky-Archiv (cited as KA)
  "Briefe an Kautsky," D/X, Nos. 139-172

IV. LIBRARY OF CONGRESS, WASHINGTON, D.C.
Rehse-Archiv (cited as RA)
  "Flugblätter der Revolutions- und Rätezeit 1918-1919"

V. MÜNCHENER STADTBIBLIOTHEK, MONACENSIA-ABTEILUNG,
MUNICH

Bekanntmachungen (cited with code F. Mon.)
Flugblätter (cited with code F. Mon.)

VI. NATIONAL ARCHIVES, WASHINGTON, D.C.

Aktenzeichen Bayern 40–Bayern 65
  Annotated in the publication of the American Historical
  Association, Committee for the Study of War Documents,
  *A Catalogue of Files and Microfilms of the German Foreign
  Ministry Archives 1867-1920* (Oxford, 1959), 175-182

PUBLISHED SOURCES

(Note: for daily newspapers, see the List of Abbreviations)
*Allgemeiner Kongress der Arbeiter- und Soldatenräte Deutsch-
lands vom 16. bis 21. Dezember 1918 im Abgeordnetenhause
zu Berlin: Stenographische Berichte*
*Bayerische Dokumente zum Kriegsausbruch und zum Versailler
Schuldspruch* (Munich and Berlin, 1922), Pius Dirr, ed.

Dokumente und Materialien zur Geschichte der deutschen Arbeiterbewegung (vols. II-III; [East] Berlin, 1957)

Hof- und Staatshandbuch des Königreichs Bayern für das Jahr 1913

Die Kriegsschuldlüge vor Gericht. Bericht über den Prozess um die Eisnerschen Dokumentenfälschungen am Amtsgericht München I, 27. April bis 11. Mai 1922

Mitteilungen des Vollzugsrats der Betriebs- und Soldatenräte Nachrichtenblatt des Zentral-Rats

Papers relating to the Foreign Relations of the United States, 1918, Supplement 1 (2 vols.; Washington, D.C., 1933)

Papers relating to the Foreign Relations of the United States, The Paris Peace Conference (vols. I-II, Washington, D.C., 1942)

Die Pfalz unter Französischer Besatzung. Kalendarische Darstellung der Ereignisse vom Einmarsch 1918 bis November 1924 (Munich, 1925), L. Wappes, ed.

Politische Zeitfragen, 1919, Anton Pfeiffer, ed.
1. "Parteiprogramme," I-II, 3-40
2. Joseph Würsdörfer, "Die Wahlen zum Bayer. Landtag am 12. Januar 1919 und ihr Ergebnis," III-IV, 41-76
3. Franz August Schmitt, "Die neue Zeit in Bayern," Part 1, V-VII, 77-123
4. ———, "Die neue Zeit in Bayern," Part 2, VIII-IX, 125-140
5. "Die Gemeinde-, Bezirks- und Kreiswahlen in Bayern," X-XIII, 145-208
6. Schmitt, "Die Zeit der zweiten Revolution in Bayern," Part 1, XIV-XVI, 209-254
7. ———, "Die Zeit der zweiten Revolution in Bayern," Part 2, XVII, 255-278
8. Oskar Doebing, "Die Wasserkräfte Bayerns," XVIII-XIX, 279-310
9. Max Gerstl, "Die Münchener Räterepublik," XX-XXXI, 311-440
10. "Ergänzungsheft zu den Dokumentensammlungen," XXXII, 443-456

Protokoll über die Verhandlungen des 14. Parteitages der Sozial-

demokratischen Partei Bayerns am 12. und 13. Oktober 1918 in München

Schulthess' Europäischer Geschichtskalender, 1918-1919

Statistisches Jahrbuch für den Freistaat Bayern, 1919

Stenographischer Bericht über die Verhandlungen des Kongresses der Arbeiter-, Bauern- und Soldatenräte vom 25. Februar bis 8. März 1919

Die Ursachen des deutschen Zusammenbruchs im Jahre 1918: Das Werk des Untersuchungsausschusses, 4. Reihe (11 vols.; Leipzig, 1928)

Ursachen und Folgen vom deutschen Zusammenbruch 1918 und 1945 bis zur staatlichen Neuordnung Deutschlands in der Gegenwart (8 vols.; Berlin, 1958-1963)

Verhandlungen der Kammer der Abgeordneten des bayerischen Landtages: Stenographische Berichte, XX, Nos. 488-495 (16 Oct.–7 Nov. 1918)

Verhandlungen der Kammer der Reichsräte des bayerischen Landtages: Stenographische Berichte, V, Nos. 57-72 (28 Sept.– 2 Aug. 1918)

Verhandlungen des bayerischen Landtages. Ordentliche und ausserordentliche Tagung 1919: Stenographische Berichte, I, Nos. 1-27 (21 Feb.–24 Oct. 1919)

Verhandlungen des provisorischen Nationalrates des Volksstaates Bayern im Jahre 1918–1919: Stenographische Berichte Nr. 1 bis 10

INDEX